RETHINKING
the HISTORY
of RHETORIC

Polemics Series

Series Editors
Michael McGee and Barbara Biesecker,
University of Iowa

Rethinking the History of Rhetoric:
Multidisciplinary Essays on the Rhetorical Tradition,
edited by Takis Poulakos

FORTHCOMING

Rhetoric and Marxism, James Arnt Aune

Confronting Male Power: Andrea Dworkin's Rhetoric,
Cindy Jenefsky

RETHINKING the HISTORY of RHETORIC

Multidisciplinary Essays on the Rhetorical Tradition

EDITED BY
Takis Poulakos

Westview Press
BOULDER • SAN FRANCISCO • OXFORD

Polemics Series

Published in 1993 in the United States of America by Westview Press, Inc., 5500 Central Avenue, Boulder, Colorado 80301-2877, and in the United Kingdom by Westview Press, 36 Lonsdale Road, Summertown, Oxford OX2 7EW

Library of Congress Cataloging-in-Publication Data
Rethinking the history of rhetoric : multidisciplinary essays on the
    rhetorical tradition / [edited by] Takis Poulakos.
      p.   cm. — (Polemics series)
    Includes bibliographical references and index.
    Contents: Introduction : alternative approaches to the rhetorical
tradition / Takis Poulakos — Rhetoric and the crisis of legitimacy
in Cicero's Catilinarian orations / David Konstan — The price of
art in Isocrates / Andrew Ford — Terms for sophistical rhetoric /
John Poulakos — The marginalization of sophistical rhetoric and the
loss of history / Jane Sutton — Instituting the art of rhetoric :
theory, practice, and productive knowledge in interpretations of
Aristotle's *Rhetoric* / Janet M. Atwill — Violence, apathy, and the
rhetoric of philosophy / Page duBois — Revisionary history / James
A. Berlin — Coming to terms with recent attempts to write women
into the history of rhetoric / Barbara Biesecker — The duality of
rhetoric / Christine Oravec and Michael Salvador — Some rudiments
of histories of rhetorics and rhetorics of histories / Victor J.
Vitanza — Afterword : reading rhetorical redescriptions / Hans
Kellner.
    ISBN 0-8133-1800-9 (hc.)   ISBN 0-8133-1801-7 (pbk.)
    1. Rhetoric—Historiography.   I. Poulakos, Takis.   II. Series.
  P301.R357   1993
  808'.009—dc20   93-8535
                                                                          CIP

Printed and bound in the United States of America

10   9   8   7   6   5   4   3   2   1

75116

To Tom Goodnight

*whose vision of the public sphere
this volume has tried to articulate*

Contents

Acknowledgments

This project began as a set of panels on the history of rhetoric at the Eastern Communication Association Conference (Baltimore). I am grateful to Gerald Hauser, Michael Leff, Nancy Streuver, Beth Bennett, Dilip Gaonkar, Trevor Melia, David Williams, Helen Warren, Ted McGuire, Nancy Harper, and Richard Thames for their contributions and encouragement; and I am especially grateful to Carole Blair, Phil Wander, Ray McKerrow, Donovan Ochs, and Tom Kane.

Research assistance for this collection was made possible by a grant from the University of Pittsburgh (Dean Peter Koehler) and by the generous research allocations from Dennis Moore and Fred Antczak at the University of Iowa; moreover I am indebted to Gerald Mast, Lee Artz, and Janice Norton for their endless checking and rechecking of documentation. And I am most indebted to the staff at the Rhetoric Department (Bonnie Bender, Deb Loss, and Cindi Stevens) for their continuous and timely help with retyping some of the manuscripts. Finally, a special note of appreciation and gratitude goes out to Doug Trank.

Takis Poulakos

Introduction:
Alternative Approaches
to the Rhetorical Tradition

TAKIS POULAKOS

In this volume, the contributors make a concerted effort to dramatize some of the issues involved in the task of writing the history of rhetoric today. They write from a perspective that takes into account rhetoric's current interdisciplinary status.

As long as the discipline of rhetoric was thought to revolve around a distinct subject matter and a stable set of concepts, the writing of its history proved to be fairly uncomplicated. All a historian had to do was link together one concept of rhetorical theory with another and one rhetorician with the next, in such a manner that the historian's finished account would constitute a narrative of rhetoric's movement across time, complete with continuities and discontinuities. George Kennedy's account of rhetoric's history in the classical period continues to function as a paradigmatic expression of this type of history writing; paradigmatic not only because it gives us a thorough sense of rhetoric's history in the classical period but also because it makes evident the end toward which this type of history writing orients itself: the perfect coincidence between the history of rhetorical theory and the tradition of rhetoric.

In retrospect, it now seems certain that this type of history writing may have served a historically necessary function as well. Indeed, at a time when rhetoric's legitimacy as a field of scholarly inquiry was contested, a narrative account of rhetoric's stable subject matter across time proved to be an effective response to charges of illegitimacy. It also proved to be a successful way of resisting pressures exerted by a widespread scientific impulse that, not too long ago, had sought to turn the study of rhetoric into a positivistic investigation of communication and to approach all instantiations of human speech as communicative phenomena with discernible and measurable effects.

But times have changed since then, and drastically so. For one, the study of rhetoric has for some time now enjoyed the status of a bona fide discipline in the humanities. Housed under the "Speech" side of Speech Communication departments for over three-quarters of a century, rhetoric was able to preserve its identity by means of a strong and lasting departmental affiliation. For another, rhetoric's place in the academy is becoming increasingly more secure as more and more disciplines are beginning to establish formal links with the study of rhetoric. Whether these links have resulted in the formation of a distinct area of study within a traditional department (as is the case with several English departments today) or in the formation of a program or a center meant to provide a common area of study among several departments (as with the POROI [Project on Rhetoric of Inquiry] Program at the University of Iowa), the study of rhetoric continues to move into a broader interdisciplinary setting.

Today, at a time when Richard McKeon's pioneering conception of rhetoric as an architectonic art is being realized beyond anyone's expectations, several of us rhetorical critics and theorists find ourselves swept up by the contradictory sentiments of jubilation and worry. Are we to celebrate rhetoric's expansion outside the disciplinary tracks marked by a history of rhetoric's affiliation with speech and receive its newest devotees from other disciplines as our allies? Or are we to take issue with the current uses rhetoric is being put to in other disciplines and consolidate our efforts to prevent rhetoric's growth in any direction that falls outside the purview of our own disciplinary perspective? Are we to take rhetoric's multidirectional growth as a sign of an oncoming triumph or as an indication of a pending disaster? Is our disciplinary identity positioning rhetoric on its way to becoming the Queen of All Arts or is our identity being divided up into too many fronts and headed toward some final and irreversible dissolution? And how are we to regard Hayden White, Paul de Man, Thomas Kuhn, or Paul Ricoeur? With gratitude, for having given rhetoric the kind of visibility we would not have been able to give it ourselves, or with resentment, for having taken rhetoric to paths we would not have taken it ourselves?

While these newest developments are generating conflicting reactions and contrary responses among us, they also manage to bind us together around a shared purpose: to address rhetoric's new role in this recently established interdisciplinary setting within the academy. They make clear to us all, in other words, that the time has come to take a good look at the wherefrom and whereto of our discipline, reconsider its tradition, and rethink its history. It is with an eye to providing a timely response to this need that the present volume was designed. When the chapters were written, the diversity in perspective, scope, and method that emerged made it evident to me that the contribution of this volume is to be found not so much in the character of the responses it provides as in the urgency of the need to respond it underscores. The gift of this volume, then, lies in the space it opens up for subsequent responses and further formulations.

*   *   *

As the chapters in this volume make clear, the recent interdisciplinary turn of rhetoric opens the way to new explorations about alternative approaches to the rhetorical tradition rather than efforts to supplant its subject matter. The question is not whether to incorporate into the rhetorical tradition a Marx or a Derrida and make their texts a permanent part of its history; rather it is a matter of considering alternative perspectives, entertaining novel ways of thinking about our tradition, and examining new methods of reading its texts. Hence, the inquiry initiated by the contributors to this volume is an inquiry into perspectives opened up by conceptions of rhetoric operative in several disciplines. The viability of rhetoric's interdisciplinary links is embodied in the alternative readings authors give of traditional figures (the Sophists, Isocrates, Aristotle, or Cicero) as well as in the alternative narrative accounts they construct of rhetoric's history.

In this sense, even the scope of this volume is significant. Readers used to associating historical accounts of the tradition with lengthy narratives extending over the span of several centuries at a time may be surprised to encounter chapters that take up a single rhetorician or even a single work and may doubt that such limited efforts can have any bearing on our conceptions of the rhetorical tradition. Yet the narrow scope of the individual contributions is itself indicative of a growing impulse across disciplines to conceive history in terms of brief, multidirectional strands and complex, interdependent networks, rather than unidirectional, extensive, and comprehensive narratives. There is the influence of Nietzsche here—his call for a historiography that would question the way the chain of history has been linked and would consider alternative ways of relinking the chain by taking a few links at a time. As there is also the indelible imprint of Foucault and his call for a historiography that would attend to the microscopic and the local and would place in the foreground the simultaneous, uneven, and interdependent development of multiple relations. Of course, attention to the local makes an impact on the global in precisely the same way that the rearrangement of a few links makes a great difference in the way the entire chain turns out.

The precise source of influence aside, the overall effect of rhetoric's interdisciplinary turn can be seen all too clearly in the authors' self-understanding of their role as producers of accounts of the history of rhetoric, accounts in which neither "history" nor "rhetoric" are proper names or signifiers of some homogeneous terrain. Indeed each historical account offered here presents itself as only one of several possible histories, and as only one of several equally vital conceptions of rhetoric. Along that direction, chapters by Konstan, Ford, and J. Poulakos explore rhetoric's relation to culture by taking up selected aspects of rhetoric and narrow perspectives and by promoting a version of history that would be constructed on the basis of distinct historical strands. Konstan in Chapter 1 takes a close look at Cicero, focusing exclusively on Cicero's attempts to restore authority at a time of crisis and to legitimate valuations that were rendered questionable by Catiline's insurrection. In this detailed look at an orator's use of language for political ends, in this carefully laid out process of rhetoric's intervention in the struggle for legitimation, one cannot miss the makings of a sophisticated perspective that provides not only a valuable way of reading the Catilinarian Orations but also a method of exploring rhetoric's role in stabilizing power and validating authority. Drawing on Derrida to supplement Habermas, Konstan situates rhetoric's potential to resolve legitimation crises in a process of persuasion that mobilizes valuations so as to strengthen the link between authority and morality, and that manipulates the spatial boundaries of identity and difference so as to fortify the hold that power relations have on human desire. The Catilinarian Orations are a decisive step in the direction of a historical account of rhetoric that would explore rhetoric's relation to power along the lines of the orator's capacity to negotiate identity and difference.

Ford (Chapter 2) moves artistic considerations of Isocrates' rhetoric outside the traditional realm of aesthetics and repositions them in the public domain, a sphere of practical activity within which rhetoric can be explored in terms of a craft and within which rhetoric's development can intersect with social and economic factors. In this highly focused take on Isocrates' rhetoric, Ford makes visible the first signs of a narrative strand—the story of rhetoric as a craft nurtured by a community of craftsmen and shaped by the socioeconomic conditions of their trade as well as their own socioeconomic aspirations—and the initial guideposts of a historical account whose telling would extend from Democritus and Gorgias, through Plato and Isocrates, to Aristotle and beyond. Along similar lines, John Poulakos in Chapter 3 takes a few key terms from extant sophistic fragments (the timely, the playful, and the possible) and grafts on them a theory of rhetoric that accounts for sophistic practices and their relation to aspects of the Hellenic culture. The view that sophistic rhetoric is born out of cultural practices and driven by an ongoing desire to position these practices at the intersection of timeliness, playfulness, and possibility is a way of reading sophistic texts but also a manner of narrating rhetoric's history. A perspective that charges rhetoric with the mission to take up the culturally given, submit it to the play of language, and turn it into the culturally possible is a perspective that can be used productively to investigate the reciprocal relationship between rhetoric and culture across time.

*   *   *

Perhaps the strongest tie that binds the essays in this volume together is the self-consciousness that contributors exhibit about the rhetorical character of their own historical accounts. "Rhetorical" is understood in two ways, both in the sense of figuration and in the sense of persuasion. To begin with, there is the self-consciousness that a historical account is a rhetorical construction, a figure, a trope. The authors are fully aware that their accounts of the past are narrative accounts, stories constructed in the present and made intelligible by their own art of narration. There is no illusion entertained here that the past can be disclosed in full view and made to speak for itself, unmediated by the agency of the historian. Nor is there a supposition that the distant past can be recovered, that actions and events can be reconstructed, or that attitudes and purposes can be recuperated in an account that would claim to represent the real as it once was. Sensitive to the fact that history comes to us through previous texts and that textuality is of a different order than reality, contributors are in agreement with Hayden White's view of history and aware that their historical accounts are narratives based on idiosyncratic criteria of selection and arrangement.

Because criteria for selecting and arranging textual "facts" guide choices among options of narrativizing the past, and because authors make these criteria and these choices explicit, the narrative accounts in this collection are rhetorical in yet another way—"rhetoric" now being understood as persuasion. Far from being disinterested figurations, stories about the past are purposeful constructions, outcomes of the historian's desire to shape readers' understanding of the past and indirectly influence readers' self-understanding and attitude. Thucydides tells us that he recounted the events of the Peloponnesian Wars, not to educate the Athenians about their history, but to influence their decisions in the future. In the same spirit, authors in this volume narrate the history of rhetoric, aware of their persuasive appeal and conscious of their advocacy concerning some pre-ferred vision of being and acting in the future. Though they position themselves differently at present—seeing themselves first and foremost as members of this culture, or this society, or this academic setting—all of the authors unite behind the notion of history as persuasion, as narrativity shaped by a set of commitments regarding the future direction of cultural, societal, or academic practices.

Sutton, Atwill, and duBois give historical accounts of rhetoric that fore-ground professional attachments and institutional commitments. Sutton (Chapter 4) tells the story of rhetoric as a discipline whose own anxiety for legitimacy has made its practitioners susceptible to understanding its his-torical development solely along the trajectory of philosophy, a trajectory already anticipated in and validated by Aristotle's *Art of Rhetoric*. Sutton's historical account reveals Aristotle's spell on our own disciplinary self-un-derstanding by shedding light, not on the direction we have taken follow-ing Aristotle, but on the historical accounts we customarily give of pre-Ar-istotelian rhetorical practices. In this backward-moving history, Sutton shows our tendency to make out of our "originator" a way of deciphering all aspects of our history, even those occurring before him.

Like Sutton, Atwill (Chapter 5) also views disciplinarity as debilitating and seeks to rescue a strand of our tradition that has been covered over by disciplinary blinds. For Atwill, though, the blind spot in question concerns a dimension of rhetoric within Aristotle's *Rhetoric* itself, and the debilitat-ing effects of disciplinarity are to be detected not in our tendency to make too much of our origins but in our failure to appreciate them enough. Atwill's chapter examines a line of Aristotle's reception that delivers rheto-ric over to us as a formal discipline, complete with its rules and guidelines, its applicability and pertinence to human behavior. Pointing to Aristotle's view of rhetoric as a productive art, an art concerned with "making" rather than with predicting and with situated production rather than generalized application, Atwill brings our attention to the transformations rhetoric was subjected to before it could be turned into a formal discipline. Show-ing that Aristotle's reception in modern times reflects the aftermath of a desire to shape rhetoric into a modern discipline, Atwill helps us see at what cost the disciplinization of rhetoric was attained.

In the meantime, what Sutton and, to a lesser extent, Atwill lament as a loss finds new energy and vitality in the history of another discipline. In duBois's account of philosophy, rhetoric is shown to have sustained its demystificatory function and to have preserved its capacity to expose claims to objectivity, disclose judgments masked by the language of disciplinary expertise, and place in the foreground convictions papered over by the ostensive neutrality of professional talk. Interrupting the discourse of philosophy, duBois uses rhetoric to short-circuit the nonreferential movement of philosophical language and break open the self-enclosed space of its conversation. When rhetoric intervenes to recode discourse among experts as speech by and about humans or to rewrite conversation among professionals as language shaped by and seeking to shape human valuations, then, we can say with duBois, rhetoric is the last means available to us to turn all historical accounts into accounts about human beings.

*   *   *

As a whole, then, this collection repeats the old debate between rhetoric as figuration and rhetoric as persuasion but shifts the site of the debate from the rhetorician to the historian of rhetoric. The traditional inquiry into the rhetorician's purposeful and effective use of figurative choices is now turned toward the historian, whose deployment of figuration and narrativity always entails some advocacy in the present. This is not the place to take issue with those who still understand history as an objective enterprise; who regard as biased, subjective, or distorting any impulse to represent past events other than objectively; or who are still trying to revive the hermeneutic principle of validity of interpretation in order to prove that validity is on their side. For lack of self-consciousness does not prove absence of purposefulness; claims to objectivity do not automatically bypass the mediation of rhetoric; and ignorance of rhetoric is not a convincing way of defending truth. As James Berlin points out in Chapter 7, the time has come for historians of rhetoric to acknowledge openly their own subjective choices rather than conceal them behind veils of objectivity, and to admit candidly their own ideological commitments rather than disguise them as disinterested representations.

In Chapters 7 and 8, which concern rhetoric's relation to otherness, the debate between figuration and persuasion is recast in terms of recent theories of historiography, as a debate between poststructuralist and Marxist versions of history. In these chapters, the question of the viability of orchestrating figuration and advocacy pivots on the historian's manner of negotiating the tension between re-presentations of otherness in the past (as in philosophical re-presentation) and representations of otherness in the present (as in political representation). Does the historian's constitution of the other in the past amount to an advocacy of the other's interests in the present? Is the historian, in other words, to be understood as Marxists would have it, as the other's political representative? Or is otherness something indecipherable, its identity non-re-presentable, its difference always under erasure? Is the historian to be understood, as poststructuralists would have it, as the agent of the other's difference and nonrepresentability? The authors address this dilemma and suggest alternative solutions.

Berlin opts for a political representation of the other in the present that would be as tentative and provisional as the historian's re-presentation of the other in the past. According to Berlin, the historian's account of rhetoric in the past is inevitably shaped by the historian's political commitments in the present, commitments that depend on a dialectical relation between the historian and the political context within which his or her account is produced. And since this relation is contextual, contingent, and subject to change, the historian's constitution of otherness in the past remains, according to Berlin, a provisional enterprise, always changing, forever renewable.

Like Berlin, Biesecker (Chapter 8) opts for a history of rhetoric that would be informed by Marxist and poststructuralist historiographical principles and that, in addition, would be gender-specific. According to Biesecker, a gender-sensitive notion of the rhetorical tradition would have to do more than insert a few women orators into the canon: It would have to challenge the ideology of individualism and the binary logic of activity/ passivity out of which the canon emerges. Mobilizing the insights of Derrida and Foucault, Biesecker proposes an alternative understanding of *techne*, a name for a "making do" that is necessitated but not thoroughly determined by the constraints of everyday existence. It is Biesecker's suggestion that, when taken together, these *technai*, or plurality of practices, which are performed in the interstices between intention and subjection, choice and necessity, activity and passivity, and which together constitute the everyday must be rethought as a key site of social transformation and the stuff out of which public rhetorics emerge.

*   *   *

It should be clear by now that this volume shifts the site of the history of rhetoric from people, events, and dates to issues of interpretation concerning rhetoric's relation to politics, society, and culture, the status of rhetoric as an academic discipline, and the interpreter's own ideological or institutional commitments. Although these issues overlap from chapter to chapter, each author takes up one overriding issue and makes a case for its pertinence to the history of our tradition. To the extent that authors have argued their cases convincingly, we can no longer think of the history of rhetoric as our predecessors did, in terms of a single narrative that can be fully recounted.

Only Oravec and Salvador and Vitanza still adhere to the dream of producing all-inclusive accounts of rhetoric, complete with classifications, categories, and subcategories. Yet the panoramic view sustained by their chapters purports to be neither comprehensive nor unidirectional. In Oravec and Salvador's case, in Chapter 9, the account of recent work done in the history of rhetoric is sustained by the desire not so much to survey what is already available as to make visible the institutional assumptions and goals that have thus far guided the discussion and given it purpose and direction. Oravec and Salvador survey in order to uncover possibilities already inherent in discussions of rhetoric; they classify in order to identify alternative institutional goals that may provide new direction and purpose; and they recount in order to open up new spaces for linking rhetoric to culture.

The dream of accounting for all recent work done in the history of rhetoric comes very close to being realized in Vitanza's extensive Chapter 10, where the impulse to be all-inclusive acquires the proportions of an epic gesture. Yet the chapter entertains neither the illusion necessary to the logic of a dream nor the totalizing view necessary to the coherence of an epic. For the desire to categorize is accompanied by the opposite desire to question, critique, and subvert all categorizing. The net result is that what is erected, unified, and made to cohere by the one is immediately flattened, scattered, and laughed at by the other. In this manner, the account of rhetoric issues from the dialogical exchange of two simultaneous and antithetical voices—one replicating the stable taxonomy of a Northrop Frye and another reproducing the destabilizing critique of a Nietzsche, one carrying out the Marxist historian's desire for collectivity and another inhabiting the poststructuralist historian's desire toward extreme forms of individuality, one displaying rhetoric's drive toward signification and another performing rhetoric's affinity with playfulness.

The volume closes with Vitanza, then, to make a point: that the enterprise of writing the history of our tradition must always remain open, at all costs, even if the only voice left to prevent its closure is the voice of ridi-cule, the weaker argument, or the misplaced laughter. For when we begin to agree with one another that we have weighed all options and have made the best case, or when we concur that we have told the whole story of our discipline, we will have all lost sight of the richness and diversity that make up the body of our tradition and the texture of our history.

1 Rhetoric and the Crisis of Legitimacy in Cicero's Catilinarian Orations

DAVID KONSTAN

Nothing appears more surprizing to those who consider human affairs with a philosophical eye than the easiness with which the many are governed by the few; and the implicit submission with which men resign their own sentiments and passions to those of their rulers. When we inquire by what means this wonder is effected, we shall find that, as FORCE is always on the side of the governed, the governors have nothing to support them but opinion. It is, therefore, on opinion only that government is founded; and this maxim extends to the most despotic and most military governments as well as to the most free and most popular.

—David Hume, *Of the First Principles of Government*

If rhetoric is an art rather than a science, that is because rhetoric, or at least political rhetoric, even as it appeals to first principles, inevitably performs a kind of bootstrap operation. Language is deployed in such a way as to make those principles implicit in the position of the speaker appear self-evident and natural; it invests a specific set of signs and images with the qualities of myth, so that they serve to validate values and distinctions to which they seem merely to refer.[1] Under normal circumstances, when the ruling strata maintain a certain minimum solidarity, there may be sufficient public consensus on the vocabulary and syntax of civic values to mask the arbitrary and interested character of the discourse. But in potentially revolutionary situations, when contending interests generate a genuine crisis of legitimacy, the myths of public discourse become more transparent, and rhetoric must be pressed ever harder to sustain authority as contrary interests begin successfully to mobilize support and threaten to take command of the resources of the state.

Between November 8 and December 5 of the year 63 B.C., Cicero delivered four addresses exposing and denouncing a revolutionary conspiracy led by the senator and patrician Catiline. The speeches were published by

Cicero, with some revisions, in the year 60 or 59.[2] I propose to examine these orations as a group in order to exhibit what we may call their strategies of ideological stabilization, that is, the ways in which Cicero in a time of crisis contrives to represent himself and his party as squarely on the side of virtue, while Catiline and his followers are depicted as irredeemably evil. The rhetorical instruments for such descriptions were well known, and Cicero avails himself of what were apparently conventional tropes in the discourse of the optimates (aristocrats) to secure assent to his distinctions.[3] But the distinctions he puts into operation are not fixed and unambiguous, and the categories to which he appeals as self-evident and secure are not uncontested; they must be established by the argument. To make his distinctions seem natural is precisely the task of persuasion, but in the general crisis of authority, where both sides lay plausible and possible claim to power and legitimacy, a posture of transcendent moral superiority is not only difficult but also rings hollow. The status of the antagonist must be acknowledged, if only obliquely, in order to justify the magnitude of the struggle and the measures required to win it, and this places a strain on the discourse that is manifested symptomatically as lapses and inversions, weak points in the logic and imagery of the text. I propose, then, to call attention to such signs of stress in the Catilinarian Orations.

I

Catiline was present in the audience for Cicero's First Catilinarian Oration, delivered before the Senate, which was meeting, exceptionally, in the temple of Jupiter (on the choice of meeting place, see Bonnefond 1983). Cicero, who had inside information about the conspiracy, taunts Catiline concerning the exposure of his secret plans: "Do you not realize that your counsels lie open; do you not see that your conspiracy is clenched in knowledge of every one of these men? What you did last night and the night before, where you were, whom you invited, what plan you adopted—is there anyone of us who you imagine does not know it?" (1.1.1; all translations are my own). Note the interlacing or interpenetration of the two sides: Just as Catiline and his supporters are present in the Senate during its deliberations, so Cicero and his party have access to the most hidden deliberations of Catiline. In the Latin, the mirroring of the two positions is vivid: Catiline's plot or plan is called a *consilium*, and the verb "adopt" ("what plan you adopted") is *capio;* the public session or deliberation of the Senate is also labeled *consilium*, and Catiline is described as *particeps*, "participant," from the same stem as *capio*. Perhaps that is coincidence. I suspect that Cicero's emphasis is on the word "public," which marks the contrast with Catiline's private counsels. Cicero at once reveals, of course, that Catiline's deliberations are in fact also public, known to the same body of senators. Each is party to the other's plans. Instead of difference there is likeness or participation. The sharp line that Cicero means to draw between virtuous men and loyal senators (*boni*) and Catiline's circle fades. Catiline is among the *boni*.

This exegesis may seem oversubtle, but the ambiguities it exposes are in the nature of the case, as Cicero himself reveals. Armed with the ultimate decree of the Senate, which empowered the consul to take any necessary measures in defense of the Republic, Cicero proclaims that he can execute and ought already to have executed Catiline—to have directed at him the infection, as he puts it, which Catiline was contriving against the rest (1.1.2)—but has refrained from doing so out of one consideration: "Then shall you be eliminated," he threatens, "when there can be found no one so wicked, so abandoned, so like yourself, who would not confess it done with justice" (1.2.5). The point is that Catiline has supporters and—for these are the ones that count—in the Senate. Whether they are not persuaded of his guilt or connive at his designs, Catiline is not so isolated as Cicero pretends. His isolation is the intention, not the basis, of Cicero's address.

Cicero's aspiration to win over the wicked and abandoned down to the last individual is a pleader's license. If everyone save Catiline were of one opinion, Catiline himself could hardly constitute a serious threat and his life might as well be spared. Catiline's forces are perhaps formidable—but just how formidable Cicero, at the moment of this oration, does not really know. It will depend in large measure upon the behavior of the Senate. Who counts among the good people, the *boni*, is what Cicero must decide—and decide in both senses of the word, for he must judge the situation and size it up and also bring about the majority he desires. In other words, he must decide the outcome by his rhetoric. The confusion in the Senate is real, and who stands with the good people is still to be determined.

Persuasion differs from demonstration, where essential terms are agreed upon in advance and the purpose of proof is to assign objects their proper position in the universe of discourse. Persuasion contends over the very structure of the fundamental categories, and as a result, all classifications depend upon its effects. There is no ultimate or transcendent logic that informs the art of persuasion; to this extent, Plato was right in the *Gorgias*. But the orator is obliged to make it seem as though his argument rests upon a secure set of values. It is in the very nature of rhetoric for Cicero to assume the absolute alienation of Catiline from all right-thinking human beings at the very moment when it is precisely this alienation that he is working to achieve.

In Cicero's representation of Catiline at the beginning of the first oration, two images predominate: that of intrusion, as though of a foreign element, and that of concealment. Cicero portrays Catiline as having penetrated into the heart of Rome from without. "His camp is in Italy, stationed in the passes of Etruria against the Roman people. ... The general of this camp and the leader of the enemy we see within the city walls and even in the Senate working destruction daily in the bowels of the Republic" (1.2.5). This image of penetration will run throughout the four discourses. It is enabled by secrecy and deception, and Cicero presents himself as driving out the corruption by bringing it to light. "What more can you hope for, Catiline, if the night cannot veil in darkness your sacrilegious undertakings and a private house cannot contain within its walls the voices of your conspiracy, if everything is illuminated and bursts forth? ... You are contained everywhere, all your plans are clearer than light to us" (1.3.6). Naming names and places, Cicero shows Catiline thwarted at every turn, and he warns, "You do nothing, you work nothing, you think nothing that I do not hear about and actually see and plainly perceive" (1.3.8).

Cicero then exposes a secret meeting that occurred on the previous night. He can see the conspirators themselves seated now in the Senate house, and he must, he says, call upon their votes and repress even a harsh word against men who deserve slaughter by the sword. The contamination of the Senate is now explicitly acknowledged. At the same time, Cicero denounces a scheme of Catiline's to murder him in his bed the previous night, just before the light of dawn. Cicero, alerted, had placed guards around his house and turned away the conspirators who had come on pretense of a morning salutation. We shall leave aside the question of the truth of these charges. Let us observe rather how, in a moment of crisis, Cicero's images seem to have reversed themselves. Catiline's men occupy the Senate; Cicero is surrounded in his house. There are still eminent men, *summi viri* (1.4.10), in whom Cicero can confide, but his security is very imperfect. Only the association of night with the plot of the conspirators, dawn with Cicero's safety, can preserve a semblance of order among his own symbolic values. As part of the plan for insurrection, however,

Catiline had, according to Cicero, indicated his intention to leave Rome as soon as Cicero had been dispatched, and Cicero now makes this his text: "In that case, Catiline, push on where you started to, leave the city at last. The gates are open. Set forth!" (1.5.10).

One translator of Cicero remarks of the First Catilinarian Oration that "the speech as we have it still ends with something of an anticlimax because after the recital of Catilina's allegedly horrible record and intentions Cicero concludes with a rather tame suggestion that he should relieve Rome of his presence" (Grant 1973, 75). Grant conjectures that the anticlimax was deliberate. The Senate was supposed, he says, to call for Catiline's immediate arrest, and when it did not, Cicero turned the situation to his own account by driving the man openly into the arms of his fellow insurrectionists. Others have agreed with Cicero that once the leading conspirators were outside of Rome and in arms, the state could use its full resources to crush them. In any case, Cicero has cast the argument so as to make Catiline's departure look like a confession of guilt.

A biographer of Cicero reminds us that at the time of the first oration, Cicero still lacked real proof of Catiline's crimes. He speculates that "Catiline's appearance in the Senate may have disconcerted Cicero and thrown him off balance. ... For all his braggadocio he knew that to have Catiline executed would be an act of madness" (the ultimate decree of the Senate that Cicero had exacted did not confer on the consul the right to impose capital punishment upon citizens without a trial). "Catiline must go," this writer continues, "he must assume the command of the forces of insurrection; only then would all the world know that Cicero was telling the truth" (Stockton 1971, 118). Whatever Cicero may have known of Catiline's intentions, the force of the argument depended also on the effect of what we may call Cicero's moral geography, by which inside and outside, at Rome and abroad, were to be read as loci of good and evil.[4]

The line that Cicero wishes to draw between the good men, the *boni*, and the bad, the *improbi*, is the wall of the city of Rome. "Lead out all your men with you, or as many as possible; purge the city. You will free me of all my fear as soon as there is a wall between you and me" (1.5.10). Cicero rehearses a series of attempts against his life before he was elected consul, attempts that he resisted with his own private resources, though he perceived that even then his fate was bound up with that of the Republic. "Now you are openly attacking the entire Republic, the temples of the immortal gods, city buildings, the life of every citizen, all of Italy you are beckoning to ruin and destruction" (1.5.12). The circles ripple outward:

Cicero at the center, whose own death, as he says, would mean "disaster for the commonwealth"; then the city; finally, all Italy. Cicero wants the filthy sewage drained from the city. "The consul," he says, "orders a public enemy to leave the city" (1.5.13). To Catiline's interruption here, Cicero replies that he does not order him into exile. This the consul had no power to command; Catiline is a citizen who has not stood trial. "But if you ask my opinion," Cicero adds, "I urge it." There is a drama here being played out as a struggle for the control of symbols. Cicero has cast himself and the Senate and Rome as concentric. His aim in forcing Catiline beyond the perimeter is to ratify this image by Catiline's own action.[5]

According to Cicero, Catiline's presence in the Senate proved him a pariah. An empty space opened around him as his neighbors withdrew. Hatred and fear were in the eyes of all. No one greeted him. No one condemned him. "Do you expect spoken insults, when you have been crushed by the heaviest of verdicts, silence?" (1.7.16). It is a theme to which Cicero will return, and of necessity, for he has still not secured Catiline's condemnation in the Senate. The Republic of Rome itself, to which Cicero lends his voice, speaks, he says, silently (*tacita*), as it were (1.7.18). The *boni* remain strangely, even ominously, inarticulate. Cicero's is the only voice. He listens for the word that refuses to be uttered, that will decide who is alone, Cicero or Catiline. Once again Cicero identifies himself with the commonwealth, and in that persona, begs Catiline to depart.

To still suspicion, Catiline had offered to give himself into the custody of certain leading citizens. When a certain Manius Lepidus refused him, according to Cicero, Catiline had the gall to approach Cicero himself. Cicero is in no mood to see the humor in this. "There is no way I can be safe inside the same four walls with you, when I am in grave danger to be contained by the same city wall" (1.8.19). Catiline has again threatened to insinuate himself into Cicero's private sanctum; again, Cicero expresses his anxiety to have the boundary of the city between himself and Catiline.

For a second time, Catiline interrupts: "Refer it to the Senate!" or, as Stockton translates the phrase, "Put it to a vote!" (1.8.20; Stockton 1971, 118–119). Stockton comments, "Cicero prudently declined the offer." It has been suggested that he did so because the Senate had no authority to impose a sentence, but Cicero was none too certain of his support. Instead, he presumes to convey the opinion of the house: "Leave the city, Catiline, free the commonwealth from fear, into exile, if that's the term you are waiting for—go! What is it, Catiline? Are you listening for something, do you notice their silence? They suffer and keep still. Why do you look for their spoken authority, when you perceive their silent will?" (Quid expectas auctoritatem loquentium, quorum voluntatem tacitorum perspicis? 1.8.20). Cicero rises to a flourish of oxymorons: "Quiet, they judge; impassive, they vote; silent, they cry out." This is fine rhetoric in its fashion, but it conceals a qualm: If things may be their opposites, who is to judge what the silence means? What happens to the opposition between public and private, openness and secrecy? The valences that have served to distinguish Cicero from Catiline, public good from individual will, threaten to collapse.

This is not, I think, an idle paradox. For within a few sentences, Cicero betrays the anxiety that his fate is linked with Catiline's. "If in terror of my voice you take the decision to go into exile, I see," he says, "what a storm of hostility looms over me, if not at once, when the memory of your crimes is still fresh, then in the future" (1.9.22). A commentator observes that these words are prophetic, as Cicero was later accused of exceeding his consular authority, above all, in the execution of some of the conspirators, and was himself driven into exile for a year. It is possible that Cicero's prescience was retroactive, having found its way into the text at the time when it was being revised for publication. But a recent trial might have inspired his fears. At the instigation of Marcus Crassus and Julius Caesar, an old man called Caius Rabirius was charged with treason for a murder committed thirty-six years earlier and under circumstances not altogether unlike those in which Cicero was preparing to mete out punishment. The nub of the case was whether the ultimate decree of the Senate justified summary violence in the alleged interest of the state. Cicero pleaded for the defense (see Tyrrell 1978 for the background to this speech).

II

A few weeks after the first speech against Catiline, Cicero acquired sealed letters testifying to the conspirators' efforts to involve a Gallic tribe in the insurrection. In the Third Catilinarian Oration, delivered before the people in the late afternoon of December 3, Cicero describes how at last he had been able to lay everything before the Senate, "brought to light, exposed, and discovered" (3.1.3). What was incredible to the ears would now be visible to the eyes, and "the entire affair may be palpably grasped not only by me," says Cicero, "but by the Senate and by you as well" (3.2.4). Confessions had been extracted from the conspirators, with the additional information that Catiline was preparing to enroll slaves among his forces. Confronted with written evidence and the testimony of the Gauls, the accused lost their capacity to refute. Either they fell silent, like Cethegus, "enervated and cast down by what he knows" (the word here is *conscientia*, denoting something between guilt, or conscience; and knowledge, or self-consciousness), or else they blurted out their guilt openly, "mad with their crime, and demonstrating what the power of knowing is" (3.5.10–11).

Cicero conjures up a notion of a kind of absolute moral force, in the face of which, when it is supported by documentary evidence, even arrogance and viciousness fail. "To me, fellow citizens," he affirms, "while the tablets and the seals and the handwriting and finally the individual confessions seemed positive proof and evidence of their crime, even more positive were their complexions, their eyes, their expressions, their silence" (3.5.13). Writing is a mere outward sign, and the inner truth is revealed not by language but by mute tokens, silently. The guilty betray themselves because they regard themselves as guilty. Now only Catiline is left, and he was to be feared only so long as he was contained within the city walls (3.7.16). "If I had not driven this man (I say what I think, citizens) from treachery at home into his bandit camp, a man so fierce, so bold, so ready, so shrewd, so alert in crime, so careful about destruction, I could not easily have lifted so great a weight of evil from your shoulders" (3.7.7). Cicero's point is that Catiline would never have been so careless as the deputies he left behind. Only his departure from the city could produce the final evidence of his complicity. Within the walls, Cicero and Catiline would have faced each other as single champions. Although Cicero might meet and forestall each of his devices, the decisive battle would have remained to be fought between them (*dimicandum nobis cumillo fuisset*, 3.7.17). Catiline, as Cicero presents him, cannot be trapped by his conscience, any more than Cicero can falter from the just cause. Between these two, the rest of the Romans are drawn this way or that, compelled by the power of persuasion.

At this point, Cicero discovers divine endorsement of his position in a miraculous coincidence. The very day on which the documentary proof of the conspiracy was at last manifested, there occurred the long-postponed inauguration of a statue of Jupiter, which had been dedicated to avert omens of ruin and civil dissension. The word Cicero employs for "statue" is *signum*, the term applied as well to the seal of a letter and which also means proof or token, a sign.

As he enters upon his peroration, Cicero begs of his audience only one reward for his services: consciousness of them. "Nothing can please me that is mute, nothing silent. ... My deeds will be nourished by your memories, citizens, will grow great in your conversations, will be established and confirmed in literary memorials" (3.11.26). From the mind to the tongue to the pen: The need is to make the meaning manifest, to give it substance in signs. Cicero then appeals to the public to keep him safe. He has confidence in the good party (*boni*), the Republic will silently (*tacita*) defend him, and the power of knowledge, of *conscientia*, will accuse the wicked (3.12.27). But the citizens themselves will have to look to Cicero's security, if one day the onslaught of the enemy, deflected from themselves, should turn upon Cicero alone (3.1.28). Despite the evidence, despite the signs, the danger remains.

Two days later, as he spoke before the Senate, Cicero's anxieties again came to the surface. "I see," he begins, "all eyes, all looks, O conscript fathers, turned toward me, I see you worried not only about your own danger and that of the Republic, but also, if that should be repelled, about my own" (4.1.1.). Again and again he sounds the theme, that having preserved the commonwealth from ruin, he alone now lies exposed to fortune (4.1.2). He prides himself on being prepared to face death bravely, though he grieves for the sorrow of his near relations (4.2.3). Clearly Cicero is fearful, but of whom? Catiline has departed Rome to join his army, his henchmen in Rome have been captured, the plot exposed.

The answer, of course, is that isolating the conspirators is not at all so neat and surgical an operation as Cicero has been intimating. Cicero attempts with skill and wit to concentrate the evil in the person of Catiline: "We have prisoners who remained in Rome to burn the city, to slaughter you all, to welcome Catiline"—the rhetorical figure is the crescendo. "We have letters, seals, handwriting, individual confessions; they arouse the Gauls, stir up the slaves, invite"—again the triple crescendo—"Catiline" (4.2.4). The evil has, he says, spilled over into Italy, beyond the Alps, throughout the provinces (4.3.6). But all necessary measures, Cicero insists, have been taken against this threat. "Men of every class, every type, every age are with us" (4.7.14). The equestrian order has at last become wholly reconciled with the senators; so too the tribunes and the clerks. All free-born citizens, even the humblest, are at hand. The freedmen think more of their adopted country than do men of the highest station, who have deemed their fatherland an enemy city. The slaves—provided they have been well treated—stand with the commonwealth. Even among the shops and taverns the population is loyal. "Since this is the case, conscript fathers, the support of the Roman people is not lacking; you must make sure that you do not appear to fail the Roman people" (4.9.18). The infirmity is at the center, in the Senate itself: precisely the place from which Cicero had tried to banish it by driving Catiline out of the city.

Cicero's suspicions are not mysterious. Crassus and Caesar, the two most influential men then in Rome, had been closely associated with Catiline and might well be suspected of complicity in his conspiracy. Sallust relates that just before Cicero's speech, one Lucius Tarquinius had burst into the Senate, alleging that Crassus—who was not present at the meeting—had commissioned him to summon Catiline to Rome. Stockton reports the episode: "The Senate exploded in uproar. Some refused to believe such a story. Others found it credible enough, but judged it wisest to avoid provoking Crassus into a violent reaction. Many were personally in his debt. All joined in demanding that Tarquinius be kept in fetters and given no opportunity to say anything further unless it were to reveal the author of the lie. It is a very odd business," he concludes (Stockton 1971, 131–132). Caesar, for his part, was not only in attendance at the session but also spoke forcefully against applying the death penalty to those of the conspirators who had been apprehended and accused, invoking the law according to which citizens were guaranteed the right of appeal in capital cases (4.5.10). To be sure, he proposed instead permanent arrest in rural quarters, but that was the mildest option under the circumstances. Cicero's rejoinder is evasive but revealing: "Anyone who is an enemy of the Republic cannot be a citizen." The question that lurks behind the entire debate is here in the open: What is the Republic? or rather: Whose?

We may recognize here a crisis of legitimacy, with characteristics specific to a state dominated by an aristocracy but having also certain traditions and institutions of popular authority.[6] Stockton pauses in his solid biography to reflect philosophically on the issue. "In every country," he observes, "a situation may arise in which the fabric of society and the rule of law are threatened by movements which draw their strength from illegality, violence, and terrorism. Confronted by such challenges, or by their imminent threat, governments may find that the normal processes of law-enforcement are inadequate—too slow, too cumbrous, too hedged about with safeguards and caveats." And so: "In an emergency it may become necessary to suspend the customary rules of law" (Stockton 1971, 93).

Stockton is aware of a problem here, inasmuch as the government, if it suspends the law, will have difficulty sustaining the charge of illegality against its enemies. Stockton (1971, 93) points to a solution: "Sometimes a state specifically provides by law for emergency action in such a crisis. In

Great Britain we have the so-called Riot Act, which can in certain circumstances ... authorize action to control or suppress a civil commotion by the use of methods that would normally be illegal." This law that sanctions illegality is a muddy business, and the fact that, as Stockton (94) remarks, "Rome had no Riot Act, nor anything like it" may say something for the rigor of the Roman legal mind. Even with the Riot Act, questions remain, as Stockton says, such as whether its application is justified. Stockton is not terribly patient with quibbles on this score. "It is ... ridiculous to demand of the civil authorities that in such a situation every action taken shall be flawless. The only question worth asking is whether their conduct was such that a reasonable man can accept that it was by and large justified and untainted by partisanship, vindictiveness, or unnecessary brutality" (94).

In a genuine crisis, this only puts the question back one step: Who is a reasonable man or woman? (Stockton's faith in reason at such a pass is touching.) Hugh Last, whose cogitations Stockton is following here, puts the issue more baldly: "About the action taken by the agents of society during such an interruption it is futile to ask whether it was legal; for legality means conformity to law, and when law has ceased to run there is no law to which to conform" (Last 1943, 94; cited in [cit.] Stockton 1971, 94). The difficulty that remains in this crisp formulation is, of course, Who are "the agents of society"?

I do not cite Last and Stockton because of the profundity of their thoughts on repression on the part of the state, but rather because the confusion into which they fall strikes me as exactly that of Cicero himself, though it is expressed in a different register. Where Stockton speaks of reasonable men, Cicero says good men, *boni*. I myself would substitute "people in power," but that puts the matter in a new light. If the crisis represented by Catiline's insurrection was a real one, and there is reason to suppose that it was, then the task of Cicero's rhetoric is to define a point of view as reasonable, as constitutive of society, at the very moment when the appeal to such a view and to society so conceived is precisely what is at stake. One may draw boundaries, but the regions so defined are liable to reverse their values: Catiline in the Senate turns Cicero's topology inside out, and his supporters may succeed, as in fact they will, in driving out Cicero from the center. The claim that the whole population is united in its feeling about the Republic leads naturally to Cicero's anxiety about his own isolation. His sense that he and Catiline are engaged in a personal struggle for control of the Republic, that each is the opposite and obstacle of the other, reduces the whole question of morality and society to the mind and character of a single pair, while the Senate and people of Rome simply incline toward the stronger in persuasion.

In the events leading up to the Catilinarian conspiracy, perhaps nothing is more surprising, at this distance, than Cicero's idea of defending Catiline in court two years earlier and of having him as his running mate for the consulship in the fateful year 63 (Stockton 1971, 75; Cicero *Letters to Atticus*, July 65 [Shackleton Bailey 1965, 422]). Michael Crawford remarks: "The career of L. Sergius Catilina was up to a point normal: he had reached the praetorship already in 68, two years before Cicero, but he failed repeatedly to reach the consulship and late in 63 ... he turned to serious advocacy of a programme of redistribution of land and cancellation of debts. The underlying threat to the established order," Crawford continues, "was, in my view, real and was not overestimated by Cicero. Already in 64 the government had felt it necessary to suppress the *collegia*, trade guilds, which were used as a way of organizing popular discontent; earlier in 63 Cicero had ensured the defeat of a Lex Servilia proposing agrarian settlement, *inter alia* by using his oratorical gifts to secure the support of the urban population" (Crawford 1978, 164; cf. Wood 1988, 50–51; on the class character of the conflicts in the late Republic, see Wood 1988, 28–41; Carter 1972). Catiline himself had said, according to Cicero, that "there were two bodies politic, one weak and with a poor head on its shoulders, the other strong and with no head; but, as long as he was alive, he would be its head" (Cicero *Pro Murena* 51, trans. Crawford 1978, 162–164).

G.E.M. de Ste. Croix remarks quite justly that the motives of the leaders of popular reform in the late Republic "are comparatively unimportant, and they can rarely be reconstructed with any confidence. What makes these men figures of real historical significance is the fact that they provided the essential leadership without which the struggles of the lower classes could hardly have emerged at all at the political level" (Ste. Croix 1981, 351–352). Ste. Croix makes a partial exception of Catiline himself, noting that "only once in the Late Republic ... do we hear of those in weakness and poverty being warned that they ought not to put their trust in the promises of rich and prosperous men, and that only a man who was poor himself would be a faithful defender of their interests" (352; Cicero *Pro Murena* 50–51). With more credulity, I think, than is his custom, Ste. Croix goes on to mention "a moving letter" in which "Catiline asserted that it had been his habitual practice to uphold the interests of the poor in public life" (cit. Sallust *Catiline* 35.3). Crawford quotes the same passage (he is suspicious of its authenticity) more fully:

> Provoked by injuries and insults, since I had been robbed of the results of my toil and energy and had not achieved a position of *dignitas*, I openly took up the cause of the dispossessed, following my natural inclination. ... It is for this reason that I have turned to plans for preserving what is left of my *dignitas*, plans which are entirely honourable for someone in my position. (trans. Crawford 1978, 164)

As Crawford observes, the letter, even if forged, is remarkable evidence for "what the upper orders of the period regarded as plausible motivation for armed revolt." Julius Caesar, in his *Civil War*, similarly expressed his motive in marching on Rome as an affront to his *dignitas*, which we may render as "prestige" or "standing," or, in a sense more political than ethical, "honor" (on Cicero's moral vocabulary, see Wood 1988, 193–199).

Traditions of absolute competitive autonomy among the aristocracy, which they called *libertas*, "freedom," combined with radical class divisions that were available to be exploited by dissident patricians: This was the society that Cicero attempted to embrace in an ideal harmony of all the orders—above all, the upper classes of senators and equestrians—in support of the Republic and Rome itself, in which Cicero posits goodness, piety, and human feeling. Catiline and the conspirators are the poison in this mix. Cicero conjures up a gruesome image of Rome in flames, Catiline's men dancing on the exposed corpses of citizens, the groans of the women, flight of the children, rape of the vestal virgins, to show why execution of the conspirators is not cruel or inhumane but merciful and kind ("for who is gentler," he asks, "than I?" [4.6.11]). Hence the oxymoron: "If we are violent toward these men, we shall be deemed merciful; but if we desire to be too easy, we shall suffer a reputation for utter cruelty with the destruction of our country and its citizens" (4.6.12). He adds the rule, which to the modern mind sounds candidly amoral but in antiquity was proverbial wisdom: "In my view a man is ruthless and iron-hearted who does not soothe his own pain and anguish with the pain and anguish of the malefactor."

If Catiline had sympathizers in the audience, just this sentiment might put Cicero in danger. At the moment of his triumph, his thoughts turn to death and to eternal war against men who are not, as he says, foreign enemies, but citizens turned enemy, and implacable (4.10.22). For all that he has done to save the Republic, he again asks only the solidarity of the upper orders and the memory of his consulship. "So long as that remains fixed in your minds, I shall regard myself surrounded by the very safest wall" (4.11.23).

III

We may now return to the passage in the first oration that was the occasion for this long detour. Cicero will accept, he says, the opprobrium that forcing Catiline into exile will bring upon him, provided that it is his own private disaster and dissociated from danger to the Republic (1.9.22). There is perhaps an unconscious echo here of an earlier phrase, in which Cicero asserted that his own destruction was bound up with disaster to the Republic (1.5.11). The reversal points to the ambiguity of Cicero's position, for why should the Republic, that association of good men, *boni*, abandon Cicero to his private fate when their common enemies have attacked him? The question is, of course, precisely the degree to which Cicero's personal enemies, his *inimici*, are perceived as public enemies, *hostes*, that is, as the enemies of those who are in a position to speak with the voice of the Republic. We have heard Cicero assume that voice in his reproach to Catiline. He will make the Republic speak once again, toward the end of the first oration, as he gathers his energies for the final effort to divide Catiline from Rome, whether as exile, if, as Cicero says, Catiline wishes to bring Cicero into disfavor, or as consul, if he prefers to serve Cicero's glory (1.9.23), at all events, outside of Rome. For the fruit of Cicero's victory over Catiline in the consular election is that Catiline must wage his campaign as exile rather than as consul, *exsul potius quam consul*, a campaign that, by that very circumstance, will bear the name of bandit raid rather than war, *latrocinium potius quam bellum* (1.10.27). As consul, then, Cicero speaks for the Republic; Catiline, he insinuates, is already out of the way.

The Republic, with Cicero as ventriloquist, demands the death of Catiline rather than his departure, which looks less like expulsion from the city than admission into it (1.11.27). "What stops you?" asks the Republic. "Tradition? … The laws that were advanced concerning the punishment of Roman citizens? But those who have defected from the Republic have never had the rights of citizens in this city" (1.11.28). There is, one supposes, no arguing with the Republic itself over who fits that description. Nor must Cicero fear ill-will or ill-repute, *invidia*, in such an action, which in any case Cicero would chalk up to renown. Cicero's answer to the Republic is that not everyone sees the case the way they, the Republic and Cicero, do. There are some who, out of ignorance or malice, have sustained Catiline, and the charge of tyranny might find a wide hearing if he ordered Catiline's execution. Only if Catiline leaves will everyone, fool or villain, recognize the plot (1.12.29–30).

Besides this, if Catiline alone is eliminated, the conspiracy will continue to fester within Rome. "So let the wicked withdraw, let them separate themselves off from the good, let them assemble in one place, let them be separated off from us, as I have said again and again, by a wall" (1.13.32). Whatever else may have inspired Cicero to force Catiline from the city, his need for a kind of moral cordon is surely uppermost among his motives. "Let there be inscribed on the brow of each and everyone what he feels about the Republic!" (1.13.32). Conscience is, after all, not enough; Cicero demands an outward sign.

Sallust tells us that after Cicero took his seat, Catiline in a modest and humble manner implored the Senate not to imagine that he, a patrician, and distinguished like his ancestors for service to Rome, had need of destroying the Republic, whereas Cicero, a "naturalized immigrant" in the city of Rome, to borrow Stockton's felicitous translation, was the man to save it (*Catiline* 31). Stockton (1971, 119) comments: "Five centuries of gentle birth was claiming its due from its equals against a jumped-up nobody from a small Volscian country town, Roman only by Rome's granting, and at that for barely a hundred years. It was a wicked, wounding phrase, and twisted in the wound by Cicero's knowledge that even those nobles who were on his side would savour and repeat it." Perhaps. But we may also note that Catiline has turned Cicero's own imagery against him. Cicero is the outsider who has moved into Rome—the *inquilinus civis urbis Romae*—while Catiline is the native of the city, who may properly identify himself with the heritage of the Republic. Each is struggling to occupy the position at the moral center of Rome.

In the Third Catilinarian Oration, Cicero remarks that whereas citizens in the past have fought to rule the Republic, Catiline is bent on destroying it (3.10.24). The reference is to an alleged plan of the conspirators to set fire to the city so that Catiline's forces may more easily penetrate it in the confusion. By reducing revolution to incendiarism, Cicero can invoke in his cause the sacred places and traditions of the city of Rome, as well as appealing to the practical fears of the people. Religion draws the final boundary.

IV

I have suggested that it is in the nature of persuasion to assume what is to be proved. More precisely, persuasion is effective to the degree that it projects the prior validity of the categories whose relevance and meaning are what is to be demonstrated.[7] There is, accordingly, a kind of gap or distance within rhetorical discourse. It implicitly refers to a frame of reference, a set of signifieds, that are valorized by the discourse itself, that is, by the signifiers. It seeks, of course, to mask this bootstrap action by exempting certain meanings from challenge. Cicero identifies his cause with the security of temples and holy images; Catiline appeals to the solidarity of the patricians. At a deeper level, by adjuring his audiences to remember, to keep alive, against a time of personal insecurity, the record of these events in talk and literary memorials (advice that Cicero himself scrupulously followed), Cicero is, in the very process of persuasion, projecting the events of the moment—that is, his construction of those events, for which he is just then arguing—as the touchstone or ultimate point of reference for future judgment. The present harmony of orders, the closing of ranks among all good men—which is what Cicero's rhetoric must effect—is to be the ideal moment, the discourse against which to evaluate all displays of meaning, all interpretations of events. By making a case in progress the standard for all cases, Cicero is appealing to the present as, so to speak, its own past.[8] It becomes self-authorizing, pending, to be sure, the verdict. The trial of Catiline is to stand as the ground of all signs, whether those future testimonies that Cicero encourages or the political sentiments that Cicero would have inscribed on every man's brow. Knowledge, *conscientia*, may be silent, but the truth must be compelled to betray itself in signs.

It would not, perhaps, be amiss to advert to the ambiguity in the Latin word *signum*, which means both sign and seal—the thing that shuts in meaning—and discover there the kind of essential ambiguity that Derrida found in Plato's use of *pharmakon*, which means both remedy and poison. Derrida's text was the *Phaedrus*, which goes to the heart of the issues of writing and memory as tokens of absence, and the authorizing function, the paternity, in Plato's metaphor, of the living voice (Derrida 1981b). We may note that Cicero was intellectually heir to the Platonic Academy. The academy had, in the generations since its founder, altered its angle of vision. The Platonic forms were not denied but had retreated beyond the knowable, as an ideal irrecoverable in practice. The academy thus became host both to skepticism and pragmatism of a sort.[9] The authority for judgment was no longer direct knowledge of the real, but the best that men had done and said: in effect, other discourses. Cicero casts his philosophical essays as dialogues among Rome's remembered statesmen. Authority becomes, in the Roman manner, invested in tradition, the ways of the ancestors. The struggle thus becomes to control the interpretation of the tradition; Plato's ultimate reality or, in Derrida's phrase, the transcendent signified, is thereby historicized at the same time that Cicero would try to locate it beyond history.

We may recognize another version of this issue in Cicero's deepest meditation on rhetoric, the dialogue entitled "On the Orator," where Cicero addresses the question of whether the good orator must also be a good man. At stake is the authority of persuasion, whether the stronger argument must be in the juster cause. We have observed Cicero's custom of referring to his supporters as the party of *boni*, the good men. A school commentary remarks on "the political sense of the word, including all persons in the speakers' party, and excluding all others" (Johnston and Kingery 1910, 75–76, ad *Catiline* 1.1.1). More narrowly, the term was appropriated by the conservative aristocracy. Sallust observes that "whoever was richest and the stronger in doing harm, because he supported the existing state of affairs, was held to be a good man" (*Histories* Fr. 1.12M; cit. Ste. Croix 1981, 355, in a slightly different translation). But this does not mean that the moral significance of the term may simply be ignored; it means rather that it is problematized, as is always the case in politics. To imagine Cicero and his peers as self-consciously motivated by nothing but interest and ambition is "the *naiveté* of cynicism" (the phrase is that of Shackleton Bailey 1965, 28; the latter [10] appears to have forgotten his own insight for a moment in his description of Cicero's rise to the consulship). No one claims to represent the party of the wicked. But Cicero could not guarantee the moral superiority of his cause ostensively, by pointing at an absolute and unambiguous pattern of values. This is in the nature of a crisis of legitimacy, where appropriation of the symbols of authority is the work of the discourse itself.

After the confrontation in the Senate, Catiline left Rome. "He has gone, departed, escaped, broken out," says Cicero in an address before the people (2.1.1) delivered the following day. "No longer will that ill-omened monster contrive the ruin of our walls within the walls. ... No longer will that knife be turned in our side, nor shall we grow fearful in the voting ground, in the forum, in the Senate house, within the very walls of our houses. He was dislodged from his position (*loco motus est*) when he was driven from the city."

I have argued that in the Catilinarian Orations the real power of the opposition, of a party by which Cicero himself might be isolated as a tyrant (cf. 2.7.14), presses up against his discourse, so to speak, and limits his control of symbols. There are moments when the walls seem not to hold, when inside and outside are troublesomely confounded. The contingency of opposites becomes manifest; differences cease to appear rooted in nature but are perceived to be introduced and maintained in order to justify advantages. In these circumstances, the contestants seem symmetrically alike, and Cicero's case seems to hang upon a move by Catiline. Our own age is one in which the factitiousness of social discriminations, their constructedness, is a theme for criticism. Although I shall not pursue the issue here, I believe that classical rhetoric was to a large extent informed by an understanding that persuasion does not so much appeal to values as it appropriates them. That is why argument in rhetoric is less proof than the appearance of proof, the enthymeme.

The tense balance between Cicero and Catiline surfaces in the dramatic version of their story staged by Ben Jonson, who, in his *Catiline*, fancied himself Cicero, just as he had earlier identified with Horace in his *Poetaster*. Gabriele Bernhard Jackson notes the symmetries:

> Catiline fights for nobility as a standard of virtue, Cicero for virtue as a standard of nobility. ... They compete for the consulship, for the loyalty of Antonius, for the sympathy of the Allobroges, and for the life of Rome. Each has one prime supporter more zealous than he is himself against the opposition (Cato and Cethegus), each employs one of the two self-enamored courtesans in the play, and each has in his party one important man who is actually in sympathy with the other (Caesar and Curius). (Jackson 1968, 153; cf. Leggatt 1981, 150–151; Scanlon 1986)

In this "mirror-like 'opposition' ... between hero and villain," the differentiating principle is language, according to Jackson (1968, 152).

> The more the conspirators attempt, in their verbal linkings, to impose a false pattern on events and circumstances and values, the more sharply they set off the true pattern that relentlessly emerges beneath and around the language in which they think they have confined it. And, of course, the presence of Cicero, easily putting to its right use each device that the conspirators stumble over, picking up their mis-

used words and returning them to their proper contexts, completes the verbal interaction of this most language-conscious of dramas. (157)

Style is the sign of virtue. Politics is control of discourse. Cicero's achievement was to silence Catiline, converting his departure from Rome, which perhaps he had intended before the fateful hearing in the Senate, into a sign of his abandonment of the moral center. Only then does Cicero gain the power to define which are the right and wrong uses of words, which contexts are proper or not. And, as we have seen, his victory was at best temporary. In Jonson's drama, a subtler figure than Catiline lurks, whom Cicero dares not question openly (4.535–536; cf. Leggatt 1981, 154). It is, of course, the man who will, in the end, successfully breach the walls of Rome, and for motives, like those of Catiline, of personal *dignitas:* Julius Caesar.

Notes

1. Barthes 1972, 125, speaking of a photograph on the cover of an issue of *Paris Match* depicting a black soldier saluting the tricolor, observes that the salute "freezes into an eternal reference meant to *establish* French imperiality."

2. The best general introduction to this phase of Cicero's career is Mitchell 1979.

3. See the exhaustive inventory of such tropes in Achard 1981, esp. 22–53, 110–119, 348–349. Cf. also Favory 1975, esp. 113–116, 163–175, 211–215; Vasaly 1985; and, for points of style, Wooten 1983, esp. the summary chapter, pp. 169–175. Wooten concludes: "The tools that they [i.e., Demosthenes, Cicero, Churchill and their kind] forged, quite apart from the political goals that they pursued, are their unquestionable contribution to Western civilization, for they are eloquent expressions of basic human values, always focused most clearly in times of crisis and upheaval, when traditional attitudes are questioned and rejected, values that represent the 'unchanging essence of human identity'" (p. 175; the quotation is from Osborn 1967, 120). Wooten's remarks may be taken as an eloquent statement of the view diametrically opposite to my own.

4. The significance of the city walls in marking off Romans from strangers was a pervasive trope; for another example, see Konstan 1986.

5. At this point, Cicero laces into the personal depravity of Catiline. The details need not detain us. Their purpose is to place Catiline and his band beyond civilization by suggestions of unnatural lust and violence against the family, a device that is to be expected wherever hostilities are intense but the cause is far from unambiguous.

6. Cf. Habermas 1975, 20: "In traditional societies the type of crisis that arises proceeds from internal contradictions. The contradiction exists between validity claims of systems of norms and justifications that cannot explicitly permit exploitation, and a class structure in which privileged appropriation of socially produced wealth is the rule. ... Class struggles finally threaten social integration and can lead to an overthrow of the political system and to

new foundations of legitimation—that is, to a new group identity." Leff 1973 plays down the seriousness of the conspiracy, and sees in Cicero's description extreme hyperbole (158–159, 168) resulting from the need to externalize his own sense of guilt (161); Cicero is obliged to exaggerate the viciousness of his opponents precisely because "Catiline's conspiracy is an act of civil violence from within the state and from within the ranks of the nobility" (171).

7. Cf. Enos 1988, 57: "Advocates like Cicero became the very premises for their arguments, for they 'symbolized' themselves as spokesmen for values lauded by their audience."

8. In attempting to project into the future his own interpretation of Roman social relations as authoritative, Cicero seeks to forestall a crisis of identity and thus of legitimacy; cf. Habermas 1975, 4: "In historiography, a rupture in tradition, through which the interpretive systems that guarantee identity lose their social integrative power, serves as an indicator of the collapse of social systems. From this perspective, a social system has lost its identity as soon as later generations no longer recognize themselves within the once-constitutive tradition."

9. On Cicero's philosophical commitments, see Wood 1988, 58–60; for a detailed reconstruction of the development of academic skepticism, see Ioppolo 1986.

2 The Price of Art in Isocrates: Formalism and the Escape from Politics

ANDREW FORD

My purpose in this chapter is to explore the early history of a metaphor that lurks in the last two letters of "rhetoric" and orients it as a field of study. For the most profound contribution of the Greeks to our study of rhetoric may well be the very idea that there can be an "art" of speaking—a *technê rhêtorikê*—at all. We teach and study rhetoric as heirs to those Greeks who began to think of eloquence no longer as a gift of the gods or an inborn talent but as something that could be learned and systematically taught. Though the Greeks had long admired the ability to use language to persuade, excite, and even deceive (one has only to think of Homer's Nestor and Odysseus), it was only in the second half of the fifth century that professional teachers of speaking in Greece promulgated and defended the idea that the uses of language could be studied as an art. And it seems that it was only in the fourth century that the new substantive, "rhetoric," was found to name this new art of language.[1]

The history of the idea of an "art" of speaking may raise basic theoretical issues for any of us who teach writing or speaking when we try to name what it is exactly that we know and can teach. Few, I think, would elevate the knowledge we impart to the status most highly prized in our society and claim to have a "science" of speech; there are too many imponderables and unpredictables at play in effective speaking to try to reduce it all to demonstrable and universal principles. We may speak instead of the "art" of speaking or writing well, using that word in its modern sense (a sense to which it was driven by the rise of the prestige of sciences) to imply that it is both a skill and a special sensibility that can be acquired through training. If "art" sounds a shade too elitist or mystified, an alternative, not far off in sense, is to speak of what we practice as a "craft." This has attractive democratic overtones—anyone can acquire a craft through honest application—and suggests old world social relations: something imparted in an apprentice-like relationship and not the sterile transmission (or sale!) of doctrines. However we may respond, if we use such terms as "craft" or "art" or if we find them intelligible, we are the heirs to the Greeks and so remain open to the debates they themselves began about the status of this art.

For the rise of rhetoric to become the basis of higher education in Greece was accompanied by debates about the status of this new art and indeed about its very nature as an art. In the long-running dispute between Plato and Isocrates one can see how open the question was, as each in his own way sought to define rhetorical education and its relation to something each called philosophy. Plato's side of the story, as reflected in works such as the *Gorgias* and the *Phaedrus*, is well known, as indeed he and Aristotle may be said to have succeeded in their different ways in subordinating rhetoric to philosophy or dialectic, "the capstone of the sciences" (*Republic* 534E; Hunt 1962; Lord 1981). But alongside them was Isocrates, who resisted Plato's attempt to replace rhetoric with philosophy and Aristotle's attempt to assimilate it as the "counterpart to dialectic." Although his response too has been much studied (Benoit 1990, 1991), Isocrates' part in the debate is worth looking at once again to make clear what was at stake at that time and also in considering alternatives to some defects of too academic a conception of rhetoric.

I propose to examine some metaphors for the "craft" or "art" of speech in the arena in which they were originated and refined by debate, taking Isocrates as my special focus. In two penetrating articles, Michael Cahn (1987, 1989) has explored the tensions in Isocrates' attacks on *technê* and his presentation of rhetoric as a not quite scientific "discipline." Reading the rhetoric of Isocrates' self-presentation to his students, Cahn shows that "by denigrating the power of the art and making its success a function of the natural ability of the student, Isocrates seriously endangers the status of the art as an independent entity" (Cahn 1989, 141). Cahn's insights into how Isocrates grounded his discipline for his students may be extended to the wider context of how Isocrates presented it to his society as a whole. And a fruitful method for such an inquiry may be a study of certain central metaphors, for Cahn has well shown that "as a result of its para-scientific nature, rhetoric resorts to various models and metaphors to present itself as a discipline" (143).

The metaphor I will consider is that of the speaking "art" (*technê*) itself, figuring rhetoric as a productive and expert activity. Reading Isocrates' metaphors that speak of the oration as a work of art and of the orator as a "model" for his students, I will explore the relation of the rhetorician's knowledge and skill to those of the other artisans of his time. I think Isocrates' complex use of this metaphor and its ambiguous implications were fundamental for the orientation of rhetoric, even providing the space for the figure of Cahn's interest, the *orator perfectus* (the "finished," or "well-made," speaker), to emerge. Such an examination may allow us to raise again basic questions that the Greeks raised: To what extent can the study of speech proceed on rules internal to a rhetorical art, abstracted from the moral purposes of its speakers, its functions in the city, and its relation to a real world?

This analysis of the position that Isocrates staked out will bring into relief an issue that proved to be of enduring significance in subsequent debates on rhetoric, which I call formalism. By this I mean the set of preconceptions and implications surrounding the tenet that the "form" of an utterance may be abstracted from its "content." From this point of view, the task of the rhetorician could appear as manipulating the "style" of a given message, and his "art" could be seen as analogous to the skills of a craftsman working and shaping raw materials into form. Such a perspective may encourage the hope that successful speech can be mastered, that analyzing language methodically as an empirical given will uncover the elements and procedures that best ensure success. In addition, the use of artisanal metaphors for the professional rhetorician's trade has evident attractions in presenting that art to the public: Emphasizing the aspect of formal skill and tangible results may support the rhetorician's claim to the status of artist, purveying a valuable product.

At the same time, neither rhetorician nor philosopher would wish to reduce rhetoric entirely to formal artistry, for a purely formal skill is too strikingly amoral. One may allow that to an extent the artisan's skill and knowledge are focused on properties inherent in his materials, but one may then demand that this must be complemented by his turning an eye to the original in the "real" world. Hence, as Tzvetan Todorov shows, the Platonic and Aristotelian view on the "art" severely discounted its formalistic aspects as subsidiary means to its primarily social end: "Rhetoric grasps language not as form—it is not concerned with utterances as such—but as action. ... Rhetoric deals with the functions of speech, not its structure" (Todorov 1982, 61). But Todorov also observes that this position led to a series of recurrent crises in rhetoric: When rhetoricians who despaired of a real pragmatic power in eloquence fell back upon their purely formal expertise in language, they exposed their art to charges of being immoral, merely beautiful, or finally useless.[2] If pure formalism is rarely allowed a dominant role among the components of rhetorical knowledge, the purely artistic aspects of a rhetorician's knowledge have remained an invariable part of Western rhetoric, and the ways in which this knowledge is connected to other requirements of the perfect orator is one key index of how the project as a whole is justified.

Though the formalist approach to studying language did not originate with Isocrates, and though he indeed opposed such a reduction of the true rhetorician's skills, it played a key role in his evolving views of his work. Developing a materialist view of language, which can also be seen in Gorgias, Isocrates saw at least a part of the rhetorician's task as "working" (*ergazesthai*) on language in the way that an artist works on raw materials; for him there were certain "basic forms" that language could take, and these were to be mixed, shaped, fitted together, in the same way that a painter mixes colors or a sculptor smooths a joint. Though constantly insisting on the philosophical or civic aspects of the orator's training, Isocrates, like his teacher, was willing for some purposes to reduce speech to an objective thing with concrete properties and to describe the rhetorician's "work" as giving structure and shape to that thing.

This formalism and the relatively new objectification of speech it entails are what sustain a metaphor repeated several times in Isocrates' works, where he speaks of his speech as a wrought "icon"—a crafted material likeness (*eikôn*)—that can preserve his thought in fixed, finished form. A study of these metaphors in Isocrates' defense of his career as teacher of rhetoric shows that for him the project of establishing a putatively philosophic art of speech was closely attached to the need for professors of this new art to create for themselves a respectable and remunerative position in the political and economic life of Athens. At the same time, I hope to show how the attempt to objectify the rhetorician's work on language as a parallel to the artisan's fashioning plastic artifacts was not the inevitable result of the rationalization of the art of speaking, but part of a conflicted attempt to secure a professional standing that could be viewed as rationally based, independent, and a neutral service to the state. Viewing this time-worn *topos* of the verbal "work of art" in its historical context will show that in Isocrates, far from being a banal "commonplace" (Rummel 1979, 33 n. 48), the *topos* marks a new step in the definition of rhetoric and a new attempt to reconcile the intrinsic properties of speech with the referential functions of language; in Isocrates craft supports a special sense of rhetoric as a "living" art, a quasi-scientific technique whose "productions" were moral literature and a moral speaker.

To plumb these metaphors I will first consider teaching rhetoric as an economic project and situate the claims for or against its technical status in that context. At that point, a reading of Isocrates' metaphors for the "work" of the rhetorician will show how he managed the relation between the attractions of this formalism and the need to establish himself as a "philosopher," someone above mercantile hucksterism or mere banausic labor. But of course, as the history of rhetoric may well show, the very attempt to formulate an objective, apolitical analysis of language may be read as part of the social and economic situation it aims to rise above. My analysis will thus show that when the notion of art itself migrated from the crafts to characterize a special knowledge of language, it clarified some of the rhetorician's particular contributions, but it also brought with it problems of how to define the artist in society. Among Isocrates and his contemporaries, viewing speech as an art opened up fruitful perspectives and successful methodologies, but its concomitant social ambiguities also prefigured difficulties in any theoretical attempt to isolate and control the purely technical components of rhetoric.

Professing Rhetoric

Isocrates' influential humanist defense of teaching rhetoric was not simply a matter of debating educational philosophy with intellectuals like Plato and rival rhetoricians like Alcidamas. It also aimed to justify his choice of profession to the city as a whole, for what Isocrates said and wrote about rhetoric came from a man at times crucially involved in quite tangible and powerful economic forces beyond the academy. This is not the place to treat once again Isocrates' long and eventful life (Jebb 1893, 2:1–260; Kennedy 1963, 70–74, 174–202), but I would like to stress the economic and social context of two episodes that bracket his long career—his entry into the profession of rhetoric, as announced in the early program/advertisement, *Against the Sophists* (hereafter, *Sophists*), and his defense of himself and his profession in the *Antidosis*, written when he was eighty-two. A sketch of the circumstances surrounding these incidents will highlight the interesting and tenuous place of the professional rhetorician in the city. We might surmise from what we know of Athenian attitudes at that time that precisely defining his social position was a somewhat difficult matter, and certainly it is an issue that he himself takes up repeatedly in his writings. In these speeches his task was not simply to theorize abstractly about education and the role of rhetoric within it but also to justify his profession within the economic and political life of Athens. What we can piece together from his own revelations and from the ancient biographies of him by Dionysius of Halicarnassus (hereafter, D.H.) and Pseudo-Plutarch (hereafter, [Plut.]) shows us a man quite concerned not only (and quite understandably) with concrete success but also with projecting an image of how he wanted his success to be understood.[3]

Isocrates maintained that he was born into the "middle" class of citizens, but his father, who owned a factory for manufacturing flutes, "must have been one of the 400 richest men in Athens in the 430's and 420's" (Davies 1971, 246). His father was able, as Isocrates himself tells us, to give him as fine and finished an education as one could get in his day, including, according to tradition, lessons with Gorgias of Leontini (*Antidosis* §159ff.; D.H. 1; [Plut.] 836E–F; Blass [1892] 1962, 2:14). But during the Peloponnesian War his father's enterprise was destroyed, and the talented, wellborn, and well-educated Isocrates, who was already in his thirties, was left to find a new role for himself in the city (*Antidosis* §161; [Plut.] 837A). Ruling out an active political life because, he says, he had neither the voice nor the temperament for public speaking (*Panathenaicus* §9–10; *Philip* §81–82), Isocrates turned for a while in the 390s to being a *logographos*, a professional writer of court speeches for wealthy and anxious litigants.

In his writings Isocrates never mentions the part of his career when he was a *logographos* and speaks of forensic speech writing as a thing quite different from his own work. Kennedy 1963 (176–177) judges that Isocrates suppressed these early speeches because they were "essentially mundane," but the reason for the omission must be that such an activity could be regarded as slightly disreputable. Aristotle is reflecting more than his own attitudes when he says that early rhetoricians devoted themselves to forensic oratory although deliberative rhetoric is "nobler and of more civic value than disputes among individuals" (*Rhetoric* 1.1.10), and Isocrates' self-presentation is very much as the civic philosopher and writer. In fact he goes as far as to disparage his former trade along the same lines as Aristotle: "We cannot dismiss without blame those rhetoricians before our time who dared to write the so-called 'arts' and who promised to teach people 'to go to law,' to use that most insulting word that those who despise this art would have used" (*Sophists* §19).

It seems that around 390 Isocrates was able to abandon this not altogether reputable profession and to open up his own school to teach "speaking well" (*eu legein*) under the title "philosophy" (this a few years before Plato started the academy). For nearly half a century Isocrates was the most famous, influential, and successful teacher of politically ambitious young men in Greece (*Antidosis* §224–226; D.H. 1; [Plut.] 837C, 838; cf. Jebb 1893, 2.431). He also became one of the wealthiest teachers of his day. The fee for his course was 1,000 drachmas, at a time when a day laborer was paid about 1 drachma a day (*Antidosis* §87; R. Johnson 1957, 297–300). In addition, Isocrates was among the first Greeks to make money from writing. Though we can hardly speak of publishers' royalties at this time, a great many of Isocrates' pamphlets, orations, and letters were circulated outside his school. Some of these were written in support or celebration of powerful figures at home and abroad, like Evagoras the king of Cyprus, or Timotheos the Athenian general; they, in the Greek way, would sometimes reciprocate his "gifts" in prose with countergifts of their own of a more monetary nature. According to the Plutarchan life (838A), Nicocles paid Isocrates 20 talents (about 120,000 drachmas) for a eulogy of his deceased father, and his Athenian student Timotheus gave Isocrates the "gift" of 1 talent ([Plut.] 837C).

But higher education in rhetoric was a relatively recent invention of the Sophists, and the high fees they charged for it had yet to be assimilated by the public at large. Hence, even if his stint as a *logographos* were glossed over, the role of professional teacher that Isocrates assumed had an ambiguous status: Clearly he offered his students something more than the essentials of grammar, traditionally taught by slaves; yet a well-born Athenian citizen might well not wish to be assimilated to that gaggle of teachers, often foreigners, who taught disputation and political success at remarkable prices. The sophistic "finishing" schools were widely regarded (as the mirror of comedy shows) as a public nuisance and worse.

David Blank has collected the evidence on attitudes toward teaching for payment at this time and notes that over and above the general popular feeling that the Sophists were overpaid parasites, there was an aristocratic feeling that it was not a proper occupation for an Athenian gentlemen; for it was felt that the professional teacher offered his services on the basis of who could pay and therefore would not base his associations on higher considerations such as character or personal loyalty (Blank 1988). Something of this may be reflected in an anecdote about Isocrates when he took up teaching for a living: He is said to have seen what high fees he was being paid and broken out in tears and cried, "I see now that I have been sold to my students" ([Plut.] 837B). Thus even the self-proclaimed teacher of "philosophy" was in danger of appearing like a huckster selling his wares to all comers: Socrates in *Protagoras* 313C says that the sophist seems to be definable as "some sort of merchant or hawker of merchandise on which the soul is fed" (cf. *Sophist* §223C–224E, §231D).

Isocrates wanted to be thought of finally not as a teacher of orators but as the teacher of the nation, as a serious and weighty commentator on the affairs of Greece (*Panathenaicus* §11). One of his most devoted readers, Werner Jaeger (1970, 3:62), persuasively claims that Isocrates tried to carve out a place for himself in the state as the successor to the poets, assuming their prestige and educational function. But poets did not teach for money, and two ancient biographies agree that Isocrates made the most money from the academic life (D.H. 1; [Plut.] 836E). A crisis in Isocrates' attempt to find a respectable place in the city was precipitated in the 350s when he was brought to court on a charge of *antidosis* and lost the suit. The *antidosis*, or "exchange of property," was a peculiar Attic law that allowed its wealthy citizens an avenue of appeal from the regular burden imposed on them of funding major public enterprises. If such a citizen thought that a wealthier candidate might more easily bear the expense, he could turn around and initiate a suit of *antidosis* against him. If the suit was successful, the defendant would have either to take over the funding or exchange his property with the plaintiff. Isocrates lost this suit and was compelled to undertake the furnishing of a warship for the state. Losing impressed on Isocrates that he was not as widely popular and respected as he thought he ought to be, so in 353 he composed the long *Antidosis*, a fictional defense speech of his own life and work. By taking an action of *antidosis* as the point of departure for this *apologia pro vita sua* (the *Antidosis* is deeply indebted to Plato's *Apology*), Isocrates already lets us know that the major themes of his life and thought on education are linked to his economic place in the city. The problem with defining the status of his work can be focalized by considering those passages where he comes to speak of the art of rhetoric as like the plastic arts.

Rhetoric and the Arts in the *Antidosis*

An alternative for the rhetorician to the charge of hucksterism was to represent himself as an artisan, one who was not a seller or middleman but a skilled producer. The economic parallel between great speech sellers and artists was a matter of remark and even concern at the time. "The science [of rhetoric], qualifying as a sort of exchange-good, ends up being aligned with the other remunerative artisanal arts. But its generous recompense could not fail to cause perplexity among conservative aristocratic circles, especially in the Socratic circle" (Bernadini and Veneri 1981, 154). So Socrates speaks pregnantly when he says in *Meno* 91D, "I know that Protagoras got more money from this skill than Pheidias, who wrought such beautiful objects of art, and ten other statue makers," or when he illustrates the wealth of Gorgias and other Sophists by saying that they "have made more money than any craftsman (*dêmiourgos*) in any other art" (*Hippias Major* 282D).

Though we will see that Isocrates rejected in theory the idea that rhetoric could ever be reduced to an art, at times he embraced comparisons between rhetor and plastic artist, especially in passages where he compares his speeches to beautiful artifacts and his work to crafting. The prologue of the *Antidosis* takes time to alert its audience to the fact that it is a new kind of speech, that Isocrates has tried to write not a forensic or epideictic oration but a speech "like an icon (*eikôn*) of my thought and life, whereby I hoped that what I was would be known and, in the same way, I would leave behind a memorial of myself far fairer than bronze statues" (*Antidosis* §7). With important qualifications, Isocrates claims for this special verbal production the durability and beauty of sculpture. And a little later he describes his procedures of composition with metaphors relevant to the arts of the painter or sculptor:

> I have written in this speech some things that are fitting (*preponta*) to be said in court and other things that do not harmonize with disputation of that sort ... but are profitable for young men to hear ... also mixed into the present speech are some of my earlier writings, not without reason nor without a sense of the moment (*kairos*), but fitting together with the matters being spoken of. ... It is no small task to take in under a single glance a speech of such length and to harmonize (*sunharmosai*) and bring together so many disparate ideas, adapting (*oikeiôsai*) what is said to what has been said so as to make them all agree with each other. (*Antidosis* §9–11)

Though there is an appeal to the educative benefits of this speech on its intended audience, its virtues are also aesthetic ones: It is a well-fitted, smoothly crafted artifact; Isocrates is not only a teacher but also an artisan putting his materials in orderly form.[4]

But at the same time, a striking passage in the speech expresses a discomfort with too complete an equivalence of the two activities:

> I am aware that some sophists [i.e. professional teachers of rhetoric] speak outra-
> geously against my occupation, claiming that it is essentially speech-writing for
> courts, and carry on generally as if one should dare to call Pheidias, the one who
> wrought our statue of enthroned Athena, a doll maker, or should say that Zeuxis
> and Parrhasius practice the same art as those who paint those little votive tablets for
> sale in the market place. (*Antidosis* §2)[5]

Once again attempting to separate himself from the law court writers, Isocrates gropes to establish a separate category for his art, a new category that in some ways suggests the modern notion of fine art. This attempt to draw a distinction between mechanical arts and some "higher" arts is novel in Greek thought and indeed seems to go against the grain of the language, which assimilated under "art" (*technê*) all orderly production, whether it was the making of shoes, houses, or speeches (Pollitt 1974, 32). But Isocrates struggles against this view to set up a qualitative reserve at the top of each art, for himself and for other great artisans recognizably worth their wages. Note that no theoretical difference is offered to explain the difference postulated between the art of Pheidias and that of a doll maker: We can only assume that Pheidias must somehow be qualitatively different from other sculptors because he was paid such money—reportedly 48,000 drachmas for eight years of work (Bernadini and Veneri 1981, 152); for similarly vague reasons the celebrated painters Zeuxis and Parrhasius are to be distinguished from those nameless painters in the agora whose goods were available to almost any citizen wishing to leave some offering in a temple.

   Though Isocrates here approaches a novel and striking idea with pro-found implications, I think it would be inadequate to read this passage only as an advance in the history of Greek aesthetics. For its attempt to an-alyze the categories of Greek art has an economic basis and a social mo-tive; its sense of "fine art," a kind of art that is higher than the banausic arts, is tied to an ambivalence about taking refuge in a socially constructed category of *technê*. This ambivalence arises from the difficult position of proclaiming an art that was at once highly respectable and yet also in some sense a form of exchanging art objects for money; his solution is to insist that his speeches are not run-of-the-mill artifacts. It may be that it was with a sense of Isocrates' pretensions to Greece's Chair of Philosophy rather than Verbal Manufacture that a contemporary comic writer brings back his banausic origins, ridiculing him as a "flute-borer."[6] In any case, similarly novel and self-praising assertions about the nature of art can be found in Isocrates' other ingenious variations on the notion of the verbal artifact. But before we can interpret these passages, we must have a general consideration of the place of "art" in Isocrates' education.

Teaching the Non-Art of Rhetoric

Isocrates' ideas on the nature of rhetoric were partly formed in reaction to Plato, who denied that there ever could be an art of speech apart from philosophy. In his *Gorgias*, the title character, Isocrates' teacher, is made to defend the view that a rhetorician is the "craftsman of persuasion" (453A).[7] Rhetoric is thus held to be a neutral skill and expertise in manipulating language; on this formalist view, if a trained speaker uses his powers for evil, he is to be blamed, not his teacher or the art (456D). Socrates objects, asserting that there cannot be any skill or craft without its proper object, as medicine studies health; hence, if the rhetorician would presume to speak on affairs of justice and injustice, he would need to know those things too, a point Gorgias oddly and fatally concedes (Irwin 1979, 125–126). Plato continues the assault in the *Phaedrus* (esp. 270Bff.), saying that the only possible rhetoric would have to be based on a mastery of philosophy.[8] Aristotle's *Rhetoric* vindicated the study of the art, but only as the "counterpart to dialectic" with the limited task of "discovering the available means of persuasion in a given case" (*Rhetoric* 1.1.1; 1.14; cf. Solmsen 1929, 196–229).

According to George Kennedy (1963, 185), Isocrates answered not by argument but in practice, and it is true that Isocrates shied away from abstract theorizing and remained tentative about what exactly he claimed to teach. Such theory of rhetoric as he had must be extracted from his frequent theorizings on education (e.g., *Antidosis* §45–50, §258–269; *Encomium of Helen* 1–14; and *Sophists*). These texts make clear that Isocrates claimed to be a teacher not of rhetoric but of "philosophy," which he used in its normal, pre-Platonic sense for "training the mind" (e.g., Thucydides 2.40.1; Herodotus 1.30.2; cf. *Antidosis* §271–282; Jaeger 1970, 3:49). Isocrates' definition of "philosophy" aimed to keep it quite distinct from eristics, on the one hand, mere captious arguing and hairsplitting (*Sophists* §8; *Antidosis* §262); on the other hand, he resisted sublimating "philosophy" to Platonic mathematics or dialectics, for he disputed the notion that there could ever be an exact science of "justice" (*Sophists* §21, cf. *Antidosis* §271, §274ff.). Nor will the presumed exact sciences, such as astronomy and geometry, help us toward "philosophy" (*Antidosis* §266), because they offer no help in practical life (Masaracchia 1983). According to Isocrates, we are by nature condemned to operate on our *doxa*, "opinion," and "true knowledge" (*epistêmê*) in human affairs will elude us. Hence the best philosophy can do is to strive for an informed opinion of what virtuous conduct is, governed by training and experience (*Sophists* §2–8; *Antidosis* §261, §271–282; *Panathenaicus* §26. Cf. Blass [1892] 1962, 2:28; Kennedy 1963, 177–179).

Hence, although Isocrates saw himself in the business of preparing statesmen, he did not claim to teach any "political art" as Protagoras seems to have (Plato, *Protagoras* 319A). A fortiori there can be no "rhetorical art." Blass has rightly stressed that Isocrates never speaks of rhetoric as the *technê* of language (Blass [1892] 1962, 2:110, n. 1. Pace Jaeger 1970, 3:301, n. 12). Indeed, as Jaeger (1970, 3:304, n. 52) says, he seems to use the word *technê* only in "quotation marks."

Cahn (1989) has located Isocrates' most significant contribution to rhetoric in his refusal to represent rhetoric as a *technê* at all. Yet the rhetorician did have some definite things to teach. Isocrates did believe that there were a finite number of formal patterns from which speeches were composed, and he seems to have called these elements of rhetoric "ideas," again differing from Plato, for whom the ideas were fixed ontological schemata, basic forms (Jaeger 1970, 3:61). For Isocrates, the rhetorical *ideai* seem to be the elements from which all speeches are made, including indiscriminately not only what we would call figures of speech and figures of thought but also the types of speech and their functions (cf. *Panathenaicus* §2 and *Antidosis* §45f.). The essence of Isocrates' "ideas" of speech is that they are fixed entities and limited in number so as to be teachable and learnable (Blass [1892] 1962, 2:107; Lidov 1983).

Nevertheless, what is teachable in rhetoric is only a preliminary knowledge, as knowing the alphabet is the mere first step in knowing how to write. Though one might acquire and communicate an exact knowledge of the *ideai* of speech, it would be foolish to equate this with knowing how to speak well, so those professing to make a science of political discourse are wrongheaded: "They do not attribute the power [to speak well] to natural ability or to practice, but claim that they can teach an exact science (*epistêmê*) of speech, as if they were teaching the letters of the alphabet" (*Sophists* §10). The knowledge of science is one of stable but lifeless forms; the challenge for the true teacher of rhetoric will be to turn the mechanical process of selecting and arranging fixed elements into a human and creative affair:

> I am amazed when I see people presuming to take on students and yet who don't realize that they are applying the model (*paradeigma*) of a fixed and set art to an affair of productive skill (*poiêtikou*). For who doesn't know that the art of using the alphabet is one that stays the same so that we always use the same letters for the same things, but the case of speaking is exactly the opposite? (*Sophists* §12)

Two elements of Isocrates' educational ideal make rhetoric "creative" and keep it from being reduced either to a science or to a purely mechanical activity: It requires a student with a certain nature or "soul," and it is not attainable without practice. Practice is required because even a scientific understanding of the workings of language can be put to use only by observing the *kairos*, or "right moment," in each situation (Kennedy 1963, 66–68). The student's soul cannot be excluded from rhetorical education because it is on the basis of his character that he will make such choices. Thus a certain "art" or technical knowledge of language does exist, but it is only a small part of the ideal training of an orator, as described in *Against the Sophists* (§16–17, a passage later reprised in the *Antidosis* §194):

> To gain a clear knowledge (*epistêmê*) of the elements (*ideai*) which we use in speaking or composing our speeches is easy enough if one entrusts oneself not to people making easy promises but to those who know something about such things. But to choose (*prohelesthai*) from these elements those that should be used for a given subject and to mix (*mixai*) them together and to arrange (*taxai*) them properly, all the while not missing the *kairos*, and to adorn (*katapoikilai*) the whole fittingly (*prepontôs*) with striking thoughts and balanced and musical words, all this needs much practice and is a task for a spirit that is determined and capable of shrewd conjectures.

Only the rightly born, rightly trained orator is the real master of rhetorical technique.

Isocrates' strategy then in responding to charges like those of Plato was not to neglect the technical aspects of rhetoric, but to play down their importance and to link them indissolubly to practical experience and to the character of the student. The threatening immorality of thinking of rhetoric as a purely neutral skill is controlled by inserting the "artistic" aspect of rhetoric into the traditional and influential formulation of education as needing natural talent, practice, and art—the classic triad of *natura*, *exercitatio*, and *ars* (Shorey 1909). In Isocrates' version of this scheme, inborn talent is said to be far more important than *technê* (*Panegyricus* §47–50; cf. *Antidosis* §185–188; *Sophists* §14ff.), which preserves the old aristocratic idea that birth is to be ranked above acquired skill.[9]

It may be that Isocrates is too optimistic if he hopes to reconcile art and nature in this way (Cahn 1987), but his appeal to innate virtues usefully incorporates into teaching the art the need to form the character of the student, which is precisely the direction that Plato pushed Gorgias in his dialogue. Nonetheless, Plato would have found Isocrates' education of his student's soul insufficient to the extent that it did not embrace the ultimate truths of his own "philosophy." Hence in the *Gorgias*, he parodies Isocrates' description of the ideal student's soul: Arguing against the status of rhetoric as "art" (454Bff.), Socrates pronounces, "It seems to me then, Gorgias, that this is not a technical pursuit, but one for a spirit good at guessing and determined, and naturally very clever in dealing with men" (*Gorgias* 463A; Shorey 1909, 195, n. 1; pace Guthrie 1975, 308).

Given their different conceptions of what philosophy is, Isocrates would seem to have successfully isolated the amoral aspects of rhetoric in its purely technical, teachable elements and to have controlled these within his comprehensive view of education. But even as he tries to limit the purely artistic component of rhetoric, he manages to suggest quite vividly how much the rhetorician and artisan have in common. In his preliminary process of focusing on pure art in order then to rein it in, Isocrates isolates a potent ingredient in rhetorical theory that was not always easy to contain. For the attractions of laying claim to a purely technical skill in language remained strong for him (and no Greek writer ever lavished more care in finishing and polishing his speeches). The idea of finely fashioning and finishing language as a good in itself is never dropped altogether by Isocrates and returns in various disguises to trouble his later, less theoretical speeches.

Verbal and Plastic Artifacts

When Plato attributes the definition of rhetoric as the "craftsman of persuasion" to Isocrates' teacher, he seems to have been, if not historically accurate, at least not unfair, for from the little we have of Gorgias, it is clear that he took a proudly scientific view of his skills. A dominant theme of his

Encomium of Helen is that speech is magic, and Gorgias' aim is to be a "theoretician of the magic spell of words" (de Romilly 1973, 1975; Segal 1962). But it must be remembered that ancient magic works through physical means and so does rhetoric. For Gorgias, speech is a material thing; it has "a minuscule, nearly invisible body" and yet can "accomplish great things" (*Helen* §8). The *Helen* contains an encomium of the power of speech to "work" effects on its hearers (the Greek *ergazesthai* is cognate with our "work," "wreak," and "wrought"); and Gorgias draws analogies with the "workings" of other arts. He adduces the many cases in which people persuade others of all sorts of things by "fabricating" (in the sense of "fashioning") false speeches (*plassein*, §11). His art of rhetoric is very much an art of giving language a particular form so that it will do a particular work. Speeches "written with art rather than spoken with truth" are said to act physically on the soul, "stamping" it (*tupoô*, §13). The power of this craft to "machine" language for its effects is like the skill of painters and sculptors to "stamp" the souls of their spectators and "work" a pleasure "in" them (*en-ergazesthai*, §15).

The theoretical consequences of associating speech with artisanal production are evidently great, but again such a view should not be regarded simply as a "discovery" of theory. It is also part of the economic scene in which aristocrats came to serve as the patrons of rhetoricians as they had for poets and sculptors. As economic agents, encomiastic orators had predecessors in fifth-century poets like Simonides and Pindar, both highly paid professionals who sold epinician odes to aristocratic families. These families would also commemorate and publicize their great public victories by hiring sculptors to make statues of them, which they might leave in a shrine as an international sign of their status and success. Gorgias himself had brought his rhetoric into connection with statues in a very concrete way when he was invited to give an oration to the festival crowds at Delphi: His Pythian Oration was such a success that he was allowed to dedicate at the shrine a gold statue of himself (Philostratus *Lives of the Sophists* 1.9.4; Cicero *De Oratore* 3.32.129; Pliny *Hist. Nat.* 33.83; Pausanias 10.18.7).

Such extravagant display occasioned comment: According to an anecdote in Athenaeus (11.505D), when Gorgias appeared in Athens after this incident, Plato teased him, saying, "Here comes our fair and golden Gorgias." Another statue of Gorgias, one dedicated at Olympia by his great-nephew, seems to be responding to such attitudes in the note of self-justification detectable in the inscription: "Eumolpus dedicated this for two reasons: teaching and friendship. No mortal ever discovered a finer art to exercise (*askêsai*) the soul for contests of excellence; his likeness (*eikôn*) stands in the soil of Apollo, a model not of wealth, but of pious ways" (Diels and Kranz 1952, Fr. 82 A 7; for the text of the inscription see Fr. 82 A 8). We may note here the stress on voluntary association ("friendship") rather than salesmanship, and the definition of the art as a "practice" for the soul, only the preparation for a life aiming at public virtue; finally, we are urged to look on the artifact as a sign not of wealth but of active virtue.

Public perception of the Sophists' wealth and status had to be managed, and the message that rhetors wanted to send to their wealthy students and patrons was likely to be close to the dictum of Gorgias: "Cimon got money so that he could use it, and he used it so that he could be honored" (Plutarch *Cimon* 10; Gorgias Fr. 82 B20 DK). Still, there remained very visible displays of wealth to be assimilated, for in a sense real statues were a by-product of the rhetorician's art: In the *Phaedrus* (235B–E), Phaedrus tries to tempt Socrates into offering a speech by vowing to set up for him a statue of wrought gold at Olympia. Socrates declines, saying that Phaedrus is very sweet and "truly golden" to think so highly of his powers, but it is interesting that the bait for the speech is a statue. Isocrates himself produced some real as well as verbal icons: His model pupil Timotheus (cf. *Antidosis* §101ff.) erected a bronze statue to Isocrates in Eleusis that cited his "friendship and sagacity" ([Plut.] 838D). Piety is the keynote too of the inscription on the statue of Isocrates erected by his son, "revering the gods and the excellence of his ancestors" ([Plut.] 839B).[10] One might say that the alchemy of the Sophist is to transform his economic relations into relations of friendship or some more noble purpose.

In his own writings on the *logos*, Isocrates played down its magical but masterable powers, which Gorgias had emphasized, and preferred to see language as a natural attribute of the human species, one that leads to progress and civility by clarifying and expressing thought (*To Nicocles* §5–9; *Antidosis* §253–257; de Romilly 1975, 52ff.). But if language is a natural human endowment, what then is the function of the speech teacher? It can only be that the teacher somehow improves this natural endowment and so the ideology of craft as putting raw nature into more serviceable or beautiful form imposes itself again as a solution. Hence there may be some truth in Quintilian's tentative ascription to Isocrates of the definition of the rhetor as "craftsman of persuasion" (as in *Gorgias* 453A): "Though [Isocrates] is far from those who would defame the office of the orator, he somewhat boldly defined the art as the artificer of persuasion" (*persuadendi opificem, id est peithous dêmiourgon: Institutio Oratoria* 2.15.4).[11] Isocrates does not use this expression in what we have of his writings, but a slightly elevated version of the same idea may underlie his speaking of the polished orator as a "poet," that is "maker," of speeches (*poiêtês logôn, Sophists* §15). Yet more common are those passages in which Isocrates reflects on the relationship between speeches and statues as enduring artifacts that may memorialize a subject's fame. Here again there is a simultaneous desire to assume some of the prestige of artisans and to distance himself from them; and here again the context is economic.

In dealing with the Cyprian dynasty of Evagoras and his son Nicocles, Isocrates more than once brings up the issue of how the great should reward those who offer encomiastic writings compared with those who offer more solid tributes such as statues. Again, this was a real as well as theoretical issue: Evagoras had allied himself with the Athenians in 394, in return for which the Athenians made him a citizen and set up a statue of him in the Ceramicus. There is thus an economic as well as paideutic element in the advice Isocrates gives to Evagoras' son: "Prefer to leave artistic images (*eikonas*) of your excellence rather than of your body as your memorial" (*To Nicocles* §36). At the same time, he is far from presenting himself as a huckster: "Those who are accustomed, Nicocles, to bring to you who are kings fine garments or bronze or wrought gold or such things as are very rare for them but quite plentiful with you, seem to me very plainly to be making not a gift but a sale, and they are far more artful in selling these things than those who are admittedly salesmen" (§1).

In another speech to Nicocles, Isocrates expands upon the differences between speeches and artifacts. He opens his *Evagoras*, an encomium of the prince's father (*obiit* 374), by describing Nicocles honoring Evagoras' tomb with both material offerings and festivals. Isocrates imagines that Evagoras might prefer to these artifacts and festivities a written account of his life that would ensure his enduring fame: "Spending money can work (*ex-ergazontai*) nothing of this kind, but is only a *sign of wealth*; those involved in music and the other competitive arts, make only themselves the more honored as they make a show of their strength or skill. But speech, if it shall fairly go through his actions, would make Evagoras' excellence always remembered among all men" (§4, emphasis added). One commentator labels the passage "some solemn platitudes extolling the literary tribute over other methods of paying honor to the dead" (Stuart 1928, 91), but dismissing the passage in this way misses two interesting points: In the first place, the idea of writing down elaborate prose encomia to the recently deceased does seem to be a new form of Greek literature at that time; secondly, the comparison has more than a platitudinous connection to eco-nomic life: We should remember the epigram on Gorgias' statue claiming that it had been erected as a sign not of wealth but of a pious character.

Later Isocrates takes up the topic of physical monuments again: "I con-sider icons of a body to be a fine memorial but far more worthy are those likenesses of a man's actions and thoughts which one can see only in speeches that are made with art" (*Evagoras* §73–74). He offers three rea-sons for the superiority of his verbal memorial to any costly marker: "These (speeches) I prefer to statues firstly because serious men would rather be honored for their deeds and intelligence than admired for the beauty of their bodies"; secondly, borrowing a motif from Pindar (*Nemean* 5.1–5; *Isthmian* 2.44–46), he sets prose art above the plastic arts because "the stamped images (*tupous*) of a man" stay in one place, whereas his speeches can pass through Greece. He adds a third advantage, that writing is more efficacious moral instruction: One can imitate the manners and virtues as revealed in speeches but cannot press the body to be like admira-bly "fashioned" (*peplasmenois*) statues or paintings. The devaluation of the plastic artifact here is a way for Isocrates to settle the tensions that Takis Poulakos (1987) has read in the *Evagoras* between its status as artificial construct and as "true" moral exemplar. Figuring the speech as a statue that is not a lifeless mass but a mirror of the soul reconciles the contradic-tory claims to have made something that is artistic but also true and useful.

Such passages support a new conception in Isocrates of the text as a spe-cial kind of artifact, "embodying" the inner aspects of its subject in the way that painters depicted their models (*To Demonicus* §5). This sense of the text as image of life, as plastic yet dynamic creation, leads him to be able to envision his own writings as "models" (*paradeigmata*) used by students (*Busiris* §48; *Panathenaicus* §16). But Isocrates always keeps the saving dif-ference of a kind of motion or vitality reserved to the verbal work of art; he constantly insists that the dynamic qualities of virtue could be made mani-fest and memorable by speech alone: Only the written model captures the deeds of, for example, a good king's life as "model" to his citizens, or the conduct of a state as "model" to others (*Nicocles* §37; *Evagoras* §12). Isocrates' ideal of "good speaking" may produce beautiful texts or ora-tions, but these are not ends in themselves; rather, they are the external manifestation, the "image" (*eidolon*), of a noble and trustworthy soul (*Nicocles* §8).

Hence, a kind of artisanal power is granted to the productions of the noble rhetor; but with his insistent attention to the action both before and after speech, Isocrates emphasizes the dynamic powers of the rhetorician's monument and minimizes the "stamping" powers of the mere artisan on his inert materials. Yet it is notable that despite these attempts to circumscribe the realm of art, the artisanal model returns and comes to embrace the entire life of the teacher, for Isocrates describes himself a "model" that students may imitate and be stamped by (*Sophist* §18). In this figure the process of teaching the non-art of rhetoric to students is granted metaphorically the artistic powers of a craftsman shaping his raw materials. This is the art that produces the *orator perfectus* and carries to living completion the plastic effects of mere mechanical instruction: "Instruction makes people endowed with natural talent more skillful (*technikôteros*) and more resourceful ... but those who lack such native ability it will not fashion (*apoteleesein*) into successful competitors or good 'poets' of prose, though it might make them more thoughtful" (*Sophists* §15).

Isocrates' novel but now familiar ideas about the verbal "work of art" are in part a function of the new status of written prose in this time. In the fourth century, ceremonious prose becomes more widely circulated and usurps some of the traditional functions of poetry such as eulogizing the living and producing memoirs of the deceased (T. Poulakos 1987). The special powers of writing to produce prose that deserves to endure and circulate throughout Greece are becoming apparent, and it has been noted that with Isocrates rhetoric begins its process of *letteraturizzazione* (Kennedy 1980, 109–119; Lentz 1989, 136–144). Accordingly, he was able to conceive of his works as products and properties, as objects to be exchanged and handed down through time. The *Evagoras* is explicitly composed, "thinking that it would be useful for you, your children and other descendents of Evagoras if someone should gather together his virtues, ornament them in language and hand them over to you to contemplate and study" (§76). Formulating this novel status as a writer of universally interesting and enduringly valuable prose was one of Isocrates' major new ideas, as Jaeger says: "In the Antidosis speech ... Isocrates presents himself to the world of literature as the perfect classic, and his own works as models to be imitated. This, it is to be noted, is the root from which all classicism sprang" (Jaeger 1970, 3.134). These judgments are true, but we may note that such idealizations were also a part of an attempt to locate the art of speaking and writing among the other well-rewarded crafts.

It is usually said of Isocrates that he had little significance as a theorist. Grube assigns his place in the history of criticism typically: "Except for his own peculiar style, Isocrates did not contribute much directly to literary theory or criticism, but his indirect influence can hardly be exaggerated because it was his kind of education which triumphed over all others and dominated the Graeco-Roman world" (Grube 1965, 38; cf. Jebb 1893, 2:431). His great admirer Jaeger depicts his position as essentially a pragmatic one: "The essential was to find a mean, as it were, between the moral indifference which had previously characterized rhetorical education, and the Platonic resolution of all politics into morality, which from a practical point of view was certain to lead away from all politics" (Jaeger 1970, 3:53). But this very resistance to theory is significant—it was more than just shyness on Isocrates' part. It was a deliberated and principled attempt to distance himself from the dialecticians and the idealists, from empty speech, and from overly regulated speech. It is quite possible to see Isocrates' mild skepticism as an important humanist voice, a persistence of that liberal, nondogmatic strain of sophistry that conceived of study as being directed "not at art but at education" (Plato, *Protagoras* 312B). Indeed Isocrates was just such a figure for Cicero and through him for Petrarch and the Renaissance (Snell 1953, 246–263). *Panathenaicus* §28 implies that teachers who do not go beyond the ordinary topics in education are in many respects less educated than their students, indeed than their slaves, and the ancient tradition preserves the germ of this view in the story that to a father who proposed to educate his son in the usual way by hiring a slave grammarian, Isocrates is reported to have said, "Go ahead, but you will then have two slaves" ([Plut.] 838A–B). But the difference between the slave and the philosophical teacher is as much economic as philosophical, and the defense of rhetorical education is not unconnected with what Jaeger calls Isocrates' "practical bourgeois" pride in his wealth (Jaeger 1970, 3:142). Though there is an attractive lack of dogmatism in the position Isocrates finally takes, his sense of a valuable but theoretically limited power in the art of language was not without political and social consequences. Indeed, it seems that it was arrived at not without political and social motives.

Throughout his life, the nontechnician Isocrates flirted with a formalist view of language, an equation of the art of speech with the arts and crafts. In this chapter I hope to have illustrated how his in many ways admirable and prophetic attempt to put rhetoric on a modest but tenable objective basis was itself ideological to a great degree in context and that it arose from two opposed tensions. On the one hand, the idea of the rhetorician as verbal artist offered Isocrates a refuge from the philosophic absolutism of Plato, but it could also put him uncomfortably close to banausic artisans; this was not only uncongenial to him as an aristocrat but also implicated the art in a popular opposition to "hucksters." On the other hand, Isocrates' need to distinguish himself from banausic artisans (as in

Antidosis §2) opened up briefly a new way of thinking about verbal art but could only be grounded in appeals to traditional aristocratic values like "inborn talent" and the "liberal arts" as those practiced in indifference to economic pressures.

Of course any claim of an apolitical, scientific, or objective knowledge is inescapably a political choice. I have hounded Isocrates' metaphors because I find them seductively "natural" in our time and because I find his mildly skeptical position one with many attractions. And because in the humanities today the scientific model of knowledge very often involves a kind of formalism, a search for repeatable regularities and stable elements in human conduct. Formalisms of any sort are reductive; in the case of rhetoric, the extremely complex and ever-varied phenomenon of verbal communication are reduced in the first place to a presumably objective and autonomous thing called language, and this in turn is reduced to its essential "building blocks," speech and thought "stamped" into "figures," which are "shaped" and "assembled" according to certain rules and procedures. This was a fair enough procedure and remains a fruitful one for composition as well as criticism. But we should realize that these methods, along with their concomitant approbatory metaphors for the orators' art, were not initially purely aesthetic discoveries; they were arrived at in part through a need to find a justified economic position for the speech seller in the city. It would probably be vain and not even desirable to hope to evade all formalistic reductions; a great deal of heuristic and practical power can derive from descriptions that are, admittedly or not, reductive and partial. Perhaps it is enough to say that no formalism can be objective and that the purchase it gives on power in the world has its price, its place in the economy in which it operates.

Notes

I thank Takis Poulakos for bibliographic and other suggestions.

1. Two scholars have recently concluded (independently) that *rhêtorikê* was coined by Plato: Schiappa 1990a, 457–470; and Cole 1991, 2, 98–99, 121.

2. Todorov 1982, 60–83. I would amend Todorov's survey chiefly to note that the "first crisis" in rhetoric was not in the Roman Empire, with its limited opportunities for effective eloquence (essentially Tacitus' view); rather, the view I put forward here suggests that these and later episodes were but the realizations of tensions inherent in the actual "first crisis" of rhetoric—the foundational struggle to establish the classical art of rhetoric itself. See further, note 4 below.

3. The extant works of Isocrates have been translated in the Loeb Classical Library by George Norlin (vols. 1 and 2) and LaRue Van Hook (vol. 3). My translations are from the Teubner text of Benseler-Blass (Leipzig 1879).

4. Among the terms employed in this passage, the most notable may be *kairos*, which Todorov (1982, 62) underscores as the classical principle that most strongly connects the art of speaking to the real occasions and actors of political life. Yet here I think *kairos* may describe a more formalist quality, "appropriateness to the other elements in an assemblage." Vallozza 1985, 119–123, has drawn attention to the fact that on occasion Isocrates adapts the meaning of *kairos* to give it the sense, "adequacy of expression to subject matter, novelty of expression." Hence, pace Todorov, already with Isocrates we may see the *kairos* being drawn away from the arena of action into the self-contained harmonies of form.

5. This may be the source of the tradition of comparing the styles of orators with those of sculptors. D.H. §3: "It is fair to compare Isocrates to Polycleitos and Pheidias for his grandeur, high art and great seriousness." There are similar comparisons in Cicero *Brutus* 70–71; *Orator* 3.26; Quintilian 12.10.1–9.

6. So [Plut.] 836E–F and Athenaeus 592D (Stratis Fr. 3 Kock). Though the word likely had a sexual double entendre (see Kock's notes, vol. 1, p. 213), it seems that the poet will not let Isocrates forget his origins; Aristophanes also mocked Isocrates for his flutes (Fr. 700 Kock; 722 Kassel-Austin).

7. Dodds 1959, 203, discredits a late scholiast's attempt to trace the phrase to the "Sicilian" school; he says the phrase is "typically Platonic or Socratic," comparing such expressions as "craftsman of health" for a physician (*Charmides* 174E) and "craftsman of friendship between gods and men" for the seer's art (*Symposium* 188D). If the phrase is not Gorgias', it nevertheless neatly encapsulates the tendencies of Gorgianic rhetoric to understand the "workings" of the linguistic and plastic arts (cf. his frequent use in the *Helen* of *ergazesthai* and *ergasia* discussed in this chapter).

8. I am inclined to read the *Phaedrus* as does Guthrie 1975, 413: He says that though some have taken the *Phaedrus* as a revision or even recantation of the strictures on rhetoric in the *Gorgias*, what really happens is that Plato "by pretending to take [rhetoric] seriously only discovers that 'true' rhetoric is philosophy."

9. Plato may be twitting Isocrates' aristocratic pretensions in *Phaedrus* 279A, Socrates' famous left-handed compliment to Isocrates saying in effect that his young contemporary might grow up to do real philosophy. (Isocrates was well into his sixties at the time the dialogue was written!) The basis for Socrates' optimistic hopes is that Isocrates is "naturally" better at speeches than Lysias and has a more "noble character" (*êthei gennikôterôi*); birth and breeding thus elevate Isocrates above Lysias—the son of a wealthy Syracusan armorer, who settled in Athens as a resident alien under Pericles and moved in the best intellectual circles.

10. Philostratus's *Lives of the Sophists* 506 (214K) vainly tried to deny that Stratis' "fluteborer" (see note 6 above) referred to Isocrates, on interesting grounds: "It was his father that the Athenians used to call the 'flute-maker,' but he himself had nothing to do with flutes or any other banausic art. For he would not have got a statue of himself in Olympia if he worked at such a sordid occupation."

11. Fr. 18 in Radermacher 1951; cf. Fr. 19 (Sextus Empiricus, *Against the Mathematikoi* 2.62): "Isocrates says that rhetoricians pursue nothing other than the 'science' (*epistêmê*) of persuasion." Cicero praises that "finished orator" whose house "lay open to all Greece as a kind of school or workshop of speech" (*officina dicendi, Brutus* 8.32).

3 Terms for Sophistical Rhetoric

JOHN POULAKOS

The fragmentariness and disparity of the Sophists' surviving discourses make any discussion of their rhetoric difficult.[1] How can these materials be read profitably? What is a reader to do with hundreds of pieces of discourse and several more or less complete rhetorical compositions (speeches) attributed to an unspecified number of authors, some of them unknown? On the one hand, reading each fragment or speech individually, in itself, may produce as many isolated understandings as there are fragments and speeches but cannot provide common threads that would weave them into an intelligible whole. On the other hand, reading all of the pieces as a totality may yield a sensible gestalt, but it will be a gestalt inevitably marked by gaps, breaks, inconsistencies, and contradictions. How, then, can readers resist the temptation of fidelity to the pieces of the reconstructed textual evidence and at the same time produce a telling story out of them? Conversely, how can they guard against the tendency to force into a tightly woven discursive pattern textual pieces that do not fit, and at the same time avoid risking an unintelligible rhetoric?

Addressing the issue of reading the Sophists' materials, Havelock (1957, 157) argues that "the task of piecing them together to make a coherent picture requires philological discipline, a good deal of finesse, and also an exercise of overall judgment which must be content to leave some things unsettled." For Havelock, these requirements might produce interesting results but only if the commentator is aware that the Sophists were men of "intellectual status and prestige" and decides to treat what they are said to have said "seriously or not at all" (160). Finally, the crucial importance of the reader's perspective cannot be ignored: What a reader looks for determines in large measure what he or she will or will not find (167).

Addressing the same issue with greater specificity, R. F. Holland (1953, 215) rejects the notion of some classical philologists that "a fragment ... is like a code message which it is the task of the scholar to decipher." The goal for him is not decipherment but understanding; and understanding can be accomplished neither by considering "the history and etymology of the words" of a particular fragment nor by assigning exact meanings to each of them (215–216), but by entertaining various "uses to which the statement may be put" or by ascertaining the functions it was meant to serve according to its author (217–218). Holland insists that a fragment from antiquity cannot be treated as a cryptogram whose decoding requires the discovery of "the" correct linguistic key. This is so because what a fragment says depends less on the "verbal" clarification of each of its terms and more on the circumstances of its utterance. Therefore, readers can only reconstruct those circumstances the best way they can, search for the fragment's "context of argument" (218), and make reference to the kinds of discussions in which it could have been included (219).

Havelock's and Holland's methodological insights are well taken. Even so, Holland is helpful only where a single fragment is concerned. His minimalist approach offers no guidance on how to move from fragment to fragment or from fragment to speech, how to arrange them intelligibly, what goes with what. Havelock does not specify what constitutes "finesse" or, for that matter, how or when one knows that one has "a good deal" of it. Nor does he caution about the limitations and pitfalls of the strict uses of "philological discipline." Despite his warning that any story about the Sophists will necessarily be incomplete, he does not instruct us, save by way of his own example, how to read the available textual pieces. Clearly, Havelock's and Holland's suggestions offer two problematic ways of reading the Sophists' materials. Havelock would have us piece them together without expecting to achieve closure. Holland, for his part, would have us situate each piece of discourse into a reconstructed historico-linguistic context without venturing beyond a single piece and without inquiring into the relationship of any two or more pieces. But if we grant that the wish to make sense of sophistical rhetoric can be fulfilled neither by a hopelessly incomplete narrative (Havelock) nor by a myriad of isolated understandings (Holland), we are faced with a methodological dilemma. How can we, on the one hand, avoid a scattered rhetoric, a rhetoric without a general view of the whole and, on the other hand, escape a totalized rhetoric, one that ignores the peculiarities of the parts of our fragmentary record?

One way out of this dilemma is to read the Sophists' materials in the light of a set of singular terms derived from their rhetorical fragments, compositions, and reported practices. Addressing the efficacy of this approach, Weaver (1953, 211) points out that "a single term is an incipient proposition, awaiting only the necessary coupling with another term." Defining a term as "a name capable of entering into a proposition," he argues that single names are provocative not in themselves but because they "set up expectancies of propositional embodiment." Although Weaver was searching for terms offering "a descriptive account" (212) of the prevailing rhetoric of his culture, the same procedure can be followed when trying to interpret a corpus of texts from another culture or another time (Williams 1976). Proceeding synecdochically, this approach attempts to illuminate the whole (sophistical rhetoric) with the light of some of its parts (singular terms). As applied to the texts of the Sophists, this procedure does not privilege the conceptual parameters of any one fragment or speech as it happens to have been copied, recopied, canonized, and handed down; nor does it favor the construction of a perfectly self-enclosed narrative that would incorporate onto itself and account for all the fragments and speeches. Rather, it focuses on a set of three terms out of thousands and argues that most sophistical discourses can be said to issue from and point to these terms. In so doing, it advances plausible narratives that despite their incompleteness and partiality can, if considered together, help us make some sense out of the Sophists' textual remains. Of course, much of the understanding gained by the execution of this procedure depends on the terms one chooses to emphasize and on their relevance to contemporary rhetorical thought.

A set of terms-in-themselves, however, rarely furnishes understandings free from the risks of nominalism. Strictly speaking, terms inherited from classical antiquity are found in and taken from specific texts, and it is to those texts that they must be returned for their meaning, illustration, and justification. By extension, texts containing those terms were produced within a cultural horizon of discourses, and it is in the light of that horizon (as presently reconstructed) that they must be seen. Accordingly, the following discussion of sophistical rhetoric features three terms by situating them culturally and illustrating them textually.

However, no set of terms, no set of illustrative texts, and no reconstructed cultural horizon can exhaust the Sophists' preserved discourses. Their rhetoric is not an object to be uncovered and brought to the light of its own truth, nor is it a project to be finished once and for all. Rather, it is an enterprise in which to be engaged again and again. To follow Dodds (1973, 92), historical judgment can never be finalized; rather, it must be "for ever in the making because the present is for ever in the making and we cannot see the past except by the light of the present." As long as there are readers of sophistical rhetoric, their attempts to make sense out of it will always be guided and influenced by their own circumstances, on the one hand, and by its relevance to their sensibilities, on the other. In short, sophistical rhetoric constitutes an open-ended proposition, a proposition demanding to be rearticulated, rewritten, and rethought every now and then according to the preoccupations of its readers and commentators.

The three terms I am using in this essay are *kairos* (opportune moment, right time, opportunity), *paignion* (game, play, playfulness), and *to dynaton* (that which can be done, the possible, possibility). Each term appears in some form of propositional embodiment somewhere in the fragments. Precisely where or how many times are not very interesting questions;[2] and as suggested earlier, the same holds true when it comes to the etymology, the exact meaning, or the verbal clarification of each term. Although the beneficiary of much philological research, this is not, strictly speaking, a philological study. As such, the terms it highlights are significant not because the Sophists used them, or because they appear in their texts more frequently than other terms, or because they hold some privileged meaning; rather, they are significant because, as I will show, they can help explain common features or tendencies of the available sophistical texts and because they can render the rhetorical practices of the Sophists meaningful.

The Cultural Setting

When the Sophists appeared on the horizon of the Hellenic city-states, they found themselves in the midst of an enormous cultural change: from aristocracy to democracy. Its causes and sociopolitical ramifications aside, this change created the need for a new kind of education, an education consistent with the new politics of limited democracy. The Sophists rose to the occasion, defined the new education as rhetoric and disputation, and professed to be able to teach it for a fee. Before their emergence as a class of professional educators, youths were either educated at home or trained in athletics, music, poetry, and ethical conduct under the supervision of an elder. Much of that traditional education was drawn from Homer, whose epic poetry constituted the Greeks' "basic educational text-book" (Marrou 1956, 9). For the most part, "higher" education in presophistic times was pursued within closed circles and reserved for the members of the aristocracy.

But with the advent of the Sophists, which coincided with the rise of the middle class, the picture changed drastically. Family name, class origin, or property size no longer mattered, at least not as much as they had in the past. Education could now be sought and acquired by anyone aspiring to become a major political player or a prominent voice in his community, provided he could afford the Sophists' fees. Beyond its wider availability, sophistical education also pointed to new goals, as it concerned itself neither with intellectual culture for its own sake nor with ethical culture for the sake of perpetuating societal norms; instead, it concerned itself with rhetorical empowerment for specific, especially political and legal, purposes. In this way, the Sophists capitalized on the *opportunity* that the need for new education presented. At the same time, they created, in and through their rhetoric, new opportunities for those intent on thriving under or simply surviving the new political changes. Judging from their notoriety and financial success, their response to their circumstances was opportune, timely. But if we rely on the conservative reactions it drew from the likes of Aristophanes (*The Clouds*), the Sophists' response clashed with the forces of tradition, which declared it improper. In addition to the aforementioned change, the Sophists were surrounded by two cultural features: the ethic of competition and the aesthetic of exhibition. The Hellenic culture encouraged competition in nearly all fields of human endeavor and celebrated its victors lavishly. Promoting a competitive ethic, it was bent on creating for itself the conditions for producing as well as challenging the best it could in each department of life. The way to the highest point of human excellence was filled with contests, struggles, and battles. But the arrival at the pinnacle signaled neither the elimination of all opposition nor the recognition of one's achievement for all time. Once at the top, a victor could expect to be confronted by a challenger. Whether in war, athletics, education, political debates, or art, what drove individuals and institutions was competition. Competition was so pervasive that it could be found in the numerous binary oppositions of the Greek language or even within a single sentence (Garner 1987, 60–77).

Before the emergence of the Sophists, poets like Pindar had stood at the sidelines of athletic contests exalting the sons of aristocrats and praising heroic deeds and ideals (Jaeger 1970, 303–310; Marrou 1956, 10–47). By contrast, the Sophists, like other athletes, musicians, poets, and dramatists in their era, thought of themselves as contestants and participated in competitions, seeking to achieve victories by overcoming other contestants, dislodging opponents, and overpowering adversaries (Plato *Protagoras*,

335a; *Hippias Minor*, 363c–364a). With this change from observation to participation in place, to be an orator meant both to accept and to issue symbolic challenges of various kinds (Sprague 1972 [82 A 1a]). It also meant to engage in the production and critique of rhetoric, the sort of linguistic combat in which no point of view remained unopposed and no argument stayed unassailed for long. Last, it meant to acknowledge that a prevalent argument was prevalent not by virtue of its historical status or its compelling logic but because it had been tested by and had withstood the attacks of the opposing side(s). But if this is so, the well-known portrayal of the Sophists as instructors teaching their pupils how to make the weaker argument stronger seems perfectly justified. Judging from the tone and arguments of Gorgias' discourses on Helen, Palamedes, and nonbeing, it seems that sophistical rhetoric included several instances of *playfulness*. Now playing the game of language by stretching its rules, now changing the game by playing with its rules, the rhetoric of the Sophists was apparently successful in effecting many weaker-stronger reversals. But if we rely on the critical responses it elicited from the likes of Plato and Xenophon, that rhetoric put the Sophists at odds with the intellectuals of the fourth century, who pronounced it *weaker* (than philosophy).

The second cultural feature surrounding the Sophists was the aesthetic of exhibition. The Hellenes of the second half of the fifth century B.C. loved spectacles. That this is so is apparent in their frequent sponsorship of theatrical events, gymnastic games, state festivals, and public debates. In that culture, rhetorical performances often amounted to public exhibitions of linguistic compositions designed to function as diversion for the masses. In this regard, the tradition aptly depicts the Sophists as virtuosos of extravagant displays of language who amazed their audiences with their brilliant styles and impressed them with their colorful appearances and flamboyant personalities (Sprague 1972 [82 A 1(2)–(4)]). Even Aristotle (*Rhetoric* 1.3.2), who would have sacrificed an eloquent oration for a soundly constructed enthymeme, acknowledged the performative dimension of rhetoric by positing that the epideictic kind of discourse depends on an audience of spectators (*theoroi*). But to the extent that diversion can offer both an escape from and a critique of the routine of sociopolitical life, one has to link the rhetorical spectacles of the Sophists to the dual attempt to fix the attention of audiences away from the burdens of the present (*actuality*) and onto the delights of a brighter future (*possibility*). This, for example, was one of the functions of funeral orations, which relied on the power of public eloquence both to alleviate communal sorrow for the recently dead and to create collective hopes for a more desirable polis (Loraux 1986, 15–76).

The Textual Illustrations

In the above discussion, I attempted to show that the three terms I chose to highlight in this essay on sophistical rhetoric (opportunity, playfulness, possibility) correspond to, indeed issue from, the Sophists' circumstances and practices. As it should be apparent, *opportunity* corresponds to the Sophists' responses to the need for a new education, *playfulness* to the ethic of competition, and *possibility* to the aesthetic of exhibition. At the same time, I have also sought to suggest that each term makes sense not in itself but as an alternative to a specific binary opposition: *opportunity* to the opposition between the proper and the improper (*to prepon* and *to aprepon*); *playfulness* to the opposition between the stronger and the weaker (*to kreitton* and *to hetton*); and *possibility* to the opposition between the actual and the ideal (*to energon* and *to idanikon*). Diagrammatically, what I have shown thus far looks as follows:

Culture	*Oppositions*	*Sophistical Rhetoric*
circumstances	proper-improper	opportunity
competition	stronger-weaker	playfulness
exhibition	actuality-ideality	possibility

In what follows, I discuss each opposition by reference to a particular text attributed to a particular Sophist.

Before discussing each of the above oppositions separately, I should note that all three are informed by Protagoras' notion of *dissoi logoi*, the notion that there are two arguments on every issue opposing each other (Sprague 1972 [80 A 1(51)]). Asserting that human language manifests itself in at least two opposite ways at any given time, Protagoras' insight suggests a twofold symbolic world consisting of contrary discourses and counsels against attempts to fuse them into one unified entity. In a Protagorean world, universal agreement on any one matter is not possible. Everything that gets said can only be understood in terms of something other, not only different but also opposite. Even the notion of *dissoi logoi* itself can be said to make sense only as opposing and opposed by the notion of *heis logos* (one argument, one view, one position). Likewise, the other

well-known Protagorean dictum, of all things man is the measure, is meaningful only insofar as it counters and is countered by the Platonic view that
of all things god is the measure (Plato, *Laws* 716c).

In a univocal world, every single utterance would have its place unques-
tionably, and there would be no need for debate and persuasion—everyone would be listening to and speaking the same *logos*. But in the polyvocal
world we inhabit, the status of all things is questionable; and that is why
people often find themselves at odds with one another, disagreeing, and
seeking to resolve their conflicts symbolically. This state of affairs accounts for the pervasive presence of rhetorical persuasion in human communities. Because every issue admits of at least two contrary *logoi*, and because the imperative to action generally permits only one of the two to
prevail in a given instance, rhetoric affords people a means through which
they can persuade one another to favor at a given moment one *logos* over all
others.

Clearly, Protagoras' notion of *dissoi logoi* provides a worldview with
rhetoric at its center. Stressing a particular kind of difference (opposition)
rather than identity, this worldview demands of the human subject a multiple awareness, an awareness at once cognizant of its own position and of
those positions opposing it. In fact, it goes as far as to posit that one's very
position cannot even be articulated except against the background of an
opposition. This means that any one discourse is oppositional and, as such,
always directed against other discourse(s). Moreover, it means that in order to understand an issue, one must be prepared to listen to at least two
contrary sides; and in order to decide how to act, one must espouse one of
the two sides or come up with a third.

Since we have no Protagorean discourse that illustrates the notion of
dissoi logoi, I turn to Prodicus' story of *Heracles at the Crossroads* [84 B 2],
which does.[3] Unlike the heroes of epic tales, whose fate is often determined by the Olympian gods and whose actions are prescribed by a well-
defined and rigid system of rules and roles, Prodicus' hero, Heracles, finds
himself torn between two equipotent tendencies, one toward vice and the
other toward virtue. Uncertain of which of the two to follow, he goes to
ponder the matter in seclusion. There, he is met by two women, Vice and
Virtue, both of whom are aware of his ambivalence. Vice approaches him
first and urges him to take her path to happiness, a path promising to her
followers carefree living, sensuous pleasures, enjoyment of the fruits of
others' labor, and full satisfaction of their appetites. Then Heracles is approached by Virtue, who promotes her path, a path whose rewards (divine

favors, human love, community honors, national admiration, material gains, and bodily vigor) require service to the gods, to one's friends, to community and country, hard work, and the subjection of the body to the mind. There ensues before Heracles a heated exchange between Vice and Virtue during which each argues for the superiority of her own way to happiness as well as the inferiority of the way of her competitor. The story ends with no sign of decision on the part of Heracles.

This story has been read variously, sometimes as a "masterpiece of stylistic elegance" (Xenophon *Memorabilia*, 2.1.[34]), sometimes as an ethical treatise attesting to the Sophists' interest in ethics (Smith 1920; Duprell 1948; Picard 1951, 1953). One of the more interesting readings is S. Biesecker's (1991, 159–169). Contrasting the epical to the rhetorical consciousness, she argues that Prodicus' story articulates a "subject position" according to which an individual is inhabited by opposing tendencies from which he is, from time to time, expected to choose one. For Biesecker, when the difference between at least two alternatives is great, choice is relatively easy. But when the alternatives are equivalent, choice is often difficult, if not impossible.

Indeed, a perfectly rational assessment of such alternatives always leads to a point of balance, a dilemma, which entails a standstill, immobility, no movement. But since the imperative to action demands that an impasse be overcome and that a choice be made, the human subject must in some way disturb the balance of perfectly opposed alternatives. This means that in the final analysis one must prefer one option over all others. Such preference can be brought about through rhetorical persuasion, which consists of comparing available options and finally giving more weight, however slight, to one over all the rest. In specific terms, Heracles, whom Prodicus portrays as "ἀποροῦντα ποτέραν τῶν ὁδῶν τράπηται" (pondering which of the paths to follow) (Xenophon *Memorabilia* 2.1.[21]), will have to break out of his aporetic state and choose the way of Vice or Virtue on account of the persuasive force of one appeal over the other. Put differently, Heracles will sooner or later have to choose, if he is to act, and follow the path of what he considers to be the more persuasive advocate. The fact that he does not choose in the preserved version of the story need not concern us here. For the purposes of this discussion, the point is that Heracles has been addressed not by a single *logos* but by *dissoi logoi*.

With Protagoras' notion of *dissoi logoi* in mind, let us turn to the discussion of the three oppositions that inform sophistical rhetoric and to the three corresponding alternatives it offers. First, the *to prepon–to aprepon* pair. Springing from one's sense of placing a particular thing in a particular place and one's will to repeat, *to prepon* alludes to the realization that speech exists in space and is uttered both as a learned response to and a habitual linguistic imposition on a situation reminiscent of the past. According to this realization, occasions for speech are finite in number (i.e., funerals, festivals, trials) and have a way of reappearing from time to time. Thus any one encounter in and with the world constitutes a variation of a previously experienced situation and calls for a more or less predictable restatement of what has already been said. In this regard, *to prepon* represents a conventional principle according to which the production of meanings in language is historically determined; at the same time, it posits that in most respects the present resembles and, therefore, must be understood in terms provided by the past.

To prepon is the result of general agreements on how to address recurring topics and occasions suitably. As one grows within a set of parameters of rhetorical practice, one learns that on certain occasions and before certain audiences only certain utterances are proper, appropriate. In this regard, one also learns that speaking in public is highly regulated according to established norms of propriety, appropriateness, norms that one is more or less expected to observe. Over time, these norms tend to harden to the point of becoming highly specific types of rhetoric (i.e., the apology, the eulogy, the encomium). When this happens, most orators tend to address typical situations in typical ways. In other words, they tend to speak following predictable rhetorical forms and searching for predictable responses from their audiences.

The rhetor who operates mainly from the sense afforded by *to prepon* relies on normative standards of speech and speaks in terms of familiar *topoi* (categories, commonplaces), which address a situation in its typicality, its resemblance to prior and similar situations. In so doing, the rhetor serves as a reminder of previous utterances, as a voice endorsing the way things have traditionally been addressed. At the same time, he suggests, by virtue of his practice, that the unfamiliar should be understood in terms of the familiar.

To prepon opposes and is opposed by *to aprepon*. Like the proper, the improper is largely the outcome of a set of discursive practices that derive their weight and justification from past agreements. In other words, the improper, too, is a category learned historically and sustained by the force of certain accepted prohibitions against specific utterances. What is improper is so by virtue of its deviation from or disregard of standard rhetorical practices within a community of orators and listeners (Isocrates *Helen* 14–15). Insofar as the *to prepon–to aprepon* opposition concerns itself with already settled discursive territories, it disregards the uniqueness of a given situation and, in so doing, leaves out of account unsettled linguistic regions. These regions can begin to be settled when one creates and capitalizes on opportune rhetorical moments (*kairoi*).

Springing from one's sense of timing and one's will to invent, *kairos* alludes to the realization that speech exists in time and is uttered both as a spontaneous formulation of and a barely constituted response to a new situation unfolding in the immediate present. According to this realization, time is understood as "a succession of discontinuous occasions rather than as duration or historical continuity" whereas the present is conceived not as "continuous with a causally related sequence of events" but as "unprecedented, as a moment of decision, a moment of crisis." In this regard, *kairos* represents "a radical principle of occasionality" that sees "the production of meaning in language as a process of continuous adjustment to and creation of the present occasion" (E. White 1987, 14).

The rhetor who operates mainly with the awareness of *kairos* responds spontaneously to the fleeting situation at hand, speaks on the spur of the moment, and addresses each occasion in its particularity, its singularity, its uniqueness. In this sense, he is both a hunter and a maker of unique opportunities, always ready to address improvisationally and confer meaning on new and emerging situations.

Because what gets said kairotically is unprecedented, without precedent, it has no ready-made audience. As such, it can startle or perplex its listeners; and once the moment of its utterance has passed, it can well be forgotten or remembered for its impropriety. But if what gets said on the spur of the moment happens to fall on receptive ears and make unexpected sense, it will eventually find its place in the audience's standard linguistic currency and thus become part of their storehouse of appropriate responses, ready to be recalled at some future occasion. In other words, what is spoken in and through the awareness of *kairos* can, in time, turn into one of the categories of *to prepon*. The reverse does not obtain. Because what gets said from the vantage of *to prepon* is decided historically, it seeks to perpetuate or strengthen the density it has acquired over time. As such, a proper utterance recommends itself as a criterion of the traditionally acceptable and resists innovation except insofar as innovation constitutes a "natural" extension of the tradition. Because it reinforces what listeners already know and because it reassures them of the continuing value of their discursive sensibilities, an appropriate expression can usually count on an already well-disposed audience.

By contrast, what gets said kairotically strives to expand the frontiers of acceptable language and invite an audience to settle them. In so doing, it ignores the proper-improper opposition and underscores the crucial role occasionality and temporality play in the practices of rhetoric. In effect, *kairos* demands the awareness that one's sense of appropriate and inappropriate speech is not especially useful at the precise moment of a given utterance. Further, it insists on the view that something is not appropriate or inappropriate at all times and in all situations. What is said at any one time and in any one situation can be construed as appropriate or inappropriate regardless of prior construals; but how it will be construed depends not only on one's reading of the occasion of its utterance but also on its persuasiveness (Sprague 1972 [90 II 19–20]).

That *kairos* can overturn the tradition-bound categories of *to prepon* or *to aprepon* and reverse their status does not mean that "anything goes"— before anything can go, a great deal must be in place. Rather, it means that what is generally regarded as appropriate or the reverse has no necessary bearing on a discourse uttered in a new temporal, occasional, and situational context. What is believed to be appropriate or inappropriate is based only on past agreements about the proper boundaries of discourse. However, by virtue of their nonnecessity, these agreements are vulnerable to the force of new linguistic creations produced at the point where an utterance disturbs silence or precedent. Thus whether certain versions of propriety or impropriety will be acknowledged and invoked at any given time is indeterminate; and whether they will remain unchanged in the future is an open question. In the domain of rhetoric, every agreement is subject to review and dissolution whenever spontaneity manages to outweigh memory and habit. Second, the capacity of *kairos* to challenge a particular form of *to prepon* means that what is considered appropriate today has not always been so; there was a time when that form, too, was introduced for the first time, either in addition to or at the expense of other notions of propriety. The authority or presence of *to prepon* at any given moment signifies only that it continues to be useful or that the opportune moment that would reverse or displace it has yet to arrive.

To illustrate the *to prepon–to aprepon* opposition and its dissolution by *kairos*, I turn to Alcidamas' discourse *Peri ton Sophiston* (Blass 1892).[4] Composed at a time when written rhetorical compositions had begun gaining popularity in a predominately oral culture, this speech argues for the superiority of the spoken over the written word. Although Alcidamas shows himself to be cognizant of the paradox he is engaging in by *writing* about extemporaneous speaking (*Peri ton Sophiston* 29–33), he nevertheless argues that it is only in and through this kind of speaking that orators can meet the situational demands of public, forensic, and private discourse. Likewise, he proposes that it is only during a rhetorical performance that orators can speak on the spur of the moment and address efficaciously unexpected crises that may arise. By contrast, written discourses are removed from the immediate circumstances of the present and are thus unable to capitalize on or make evident an opportune moment (9). In other words, written compositions are always too late to save the day and tend to fail at the critical moment (10). Attention to *kairos* demands the orator's full presence and his readiness to speak on whatever arises during a rhetorical event.

Likening speeches to live human bodies, Alcidamas hints at the difference between the fluidity of spoken utterances and the rigidity of their written copies: "And, just as the living human body has far less comeliness than a beautiful statue, yet manifold practical service, so also the speech which comes directly from the mind, on the spur of the moment, is full of life and action, and keeps pace with the events like the real person, while the written discourse, a mere semblance of the living speech, is devoid of all efficacy" (*Peri ton Sophiston* 28). But even as he declares his preference for the oral over the written mode of rhetoric, Alcidamas gets caught in the nonkairotic character of his own discourse. Arguing for the primacy of the occasionality and situationality of all oral discourse, he nevertheless finds himself outside the very practice he advocates. In other words, he comes very near to saying that the appropriate thing for an orator to do is speak, not write, his orations with an ear to their creation of and response to specific opportunities. But in saying so, Alcidamas seems to be attempting the impossible: to make *kairos* a subset of *to prepon*.

Addressing the dilemma that Alcidamas or anyone who seeks to formalize *kairos* faces, Eric White writes: "No treatise on the occasional nature of utterance could be itself exempt from occasionality, or the inevitability of its own supersession. If every occasion presents a unique challenge to the situational, context-oriented consciousness of the sophist, then the sophist's interpretive ingenuity will nowhere find itself resumed in a definitive statement" (White 1987, 20). To White's observation we can add that "knowledge of *kairos*" is a contradiction of terms, now asking us to attend to the opportune moment, now to knowledge about it.

The second opposition that informs sophistical rhetoric is that between *to hetton* and *to kreitton*. *To hetton* denotes that which is weaker, inferior, lesser than something else. In rhetoric, it refers to that argument or position that is marginal because the majority shuns it or is not persuaded by it. By contrast, *to kreitton* denotes that which is stronger, superior, greater than something else. In rhetoric, it refers to that argument or position that is dominant because the majority has found it more persuasive than other alternatives. When advocating something *hetton*, the rhetor relies on the resources of language and its surrounding circumstances to move what is regarded as weaker to a position of superior strength. At the same time and in a similar manner, he attempts to show how *to kreitton*, despite its dominance, is defective, ineffective, or harmful, that is, weaker than generally thought. To be successful in this endeavor means to reverse in some measure the established hierarchy of things. By contrast, the rhetor who speaks about a *kreitton* argument depends on the audience's familiarity with discourse that has won their approval and seeks to have them reendorse that of which they are already persuaded. At the same time, he attempts to point out that *to hetton* belongs precisely where it is: under the rule of *to kreitton*. To be successful here means to reaffirm established structures of symbolic strength and weakness and thus to secure the perpetuation of some aspect(s) of the present state of affairs.

An argument or position is not *hetton* or *kreitton* in itself but in relation to another argument and as a result of one or more rhetorical contests. Put differently, *to hetton* and *to kreitton* allude to a past verdict that pronounced a winner and a loser at the conclusion of a competitive event (*agon*). According to this agonistic view of rhetoric, an argument acquires or loses power in use, and no argument is victorious or vanquished once and for all. Because the circumstances calling for arguments change, any one argument can lose its strength or overcome its weakness at some future contest. This is another way of saying that the status or position of an argument is always bound by time and situation. Therefore, today's loser may be tomorrow's winner and vice versa. Because people often seek to resolve their differences symbolically, and because differences can be settled only temporarily, the *to hetton–to kreitton* opposition turns rhetoric into symbolic combat carried on by willing players/contestants seeking the laurels of victory. By extension, it turns the rhetor into a contestant who competes against others to win. Finally, it turns words into instruments or maneuvers used to defeat an opponent.

A contest requires at least two contestants. Usually, many contestants enter a round of discursive competition; but in the end there are generally many losers and only one winner. Of the many discourses competing for victory in a given contest, one pattern of discourse finally emerges victorious. Once a particular contest is over, *to kreitton* concerns itself with how to avoid losing future contests while *to hetton* becomes preoccupied with how to win in the days ahead. An argument that has lost a contest may never reappear to fight another round of symbolic competition; or it may reappear reworded and reformulated, ready to challenge the winner(s) of the past. By contrast, an argument that has won a contest may in time have to defend itself in future contests. In rhetoric, competition between arguments never ceases.

To enter arenas of symbolic competition means to be willing to play, win or lose. Whether one enters as challenger or challenged, by virtue of entering, one helps perpetuate competition as a practice. In doing so, one not only agrees to play a particular game but also endorses the tacit understandings that have made "the game" possible. By extension, one plays not only for a victory but also for the pleasure inherent in playing. In rhetoric, one plays both specific games, as in the case of a legal battle or a political race, and the infinite game of language. In the former instance, one generally seeks to win, which means to bring the game to a particular end. In the latter, one seeks pleasure, which requires that one prolong the game as long as possible. Within a specific rhetorical game, one wins not by having the stronger argument but by playing the game more skillfully than one's opponent(s); conversely, one loses not by having the weaker argument but by playing the game less skillfully than one's opponent(s). In other words, it is skill in language that determines rhetorical strength or weakness in a specific game. But within the infinite game of language, there are no winners or losers—only players; therefore, it matters not whether one's argument is judged stronger or weaker (Carse 1986).

To illustrate the weaker-stronger opposition and playfulness as a third alternative, let us turn to Gorgias' *Encomium of Helen* (Sprague 1972 [82 B 11]). This oration apparently seeks to refute Helen's detractors, that is, those who believe that she was responsible for the Trojan War and all the ills that befell the Hellenes as a result. It also seemingly attempts to restore Helen's reputation by removing all the blame attached to her name. Toying with language as well as with his readers throughout the speech, Gorgias offers a splendid demonstration of the way in which a widely held opinion (*kreitton*) can be shown to be groundless (*hetton*). Working against the generally accepted argument of the mythopoetic tradition (Helen is blameworthy for eloping with Paris) Gorgias exposes its logical weaknesses and suggests an alternative argument (Helen is innocent of the charges against her).

His approach is as simple as it is ingenious. Helen did what she did because the gods so decided, or she was physically overpowered by her abductor, or she was persuaded by words, or she fell in love. In all four cases, she cannot be blamed because the gods, a man, persuasion, and love are much stronger than a woman. The details of each argument aside, Gorgias' case is held together by the notion that "it is the nature of things, not for the strong to be hindered by the weak, but for the weaker to be ruled and drawn by the stronger, and for the stronger to lead and the weaker to follow" (πεφυκε γὰρ οὐ τὸ κρεῖσσον ὑπὸ τοῦ ἥσσονος κωλύεσθαι, ἀλλὰ τὸ ἧσσον ὑπὸ τοῦ κρείσσονος ἄρχεσθαι, καὶ τὸ μὲν κρεῖσσον ἡγῆσθαι, τὸ δὲ ἧσσον ἕπεσθαι) (§6). However, Gorgias undermines this very notion as he takes something weaker (Helen is praiseworthy) and tries to make it stronger. What allows him to do this is a shift from the natural to the social domain as well as the awareness of the power and instability of language. As he explains in the middle part of the speech (8–14), *logos* manifests itself in various ways (poetry, incantations, argument), all of which can affect the human psyche powerfully, the way certain drugs can affect the human body. As evidence of the instability of *logos*, Gorgias points out that if one were to study scientific discussions, public debates, and philosophical disputes, one would easily see that over time one opinion is always displaced by another. No opinion can prevail forever.

For the purposes of our discussion, whether Helen is blameworthy or praiseworthy is beside the point. The point is rather that no argument or position, no matter how entrenched, can dominate the mental world of an audience once and for all. In and through the interplay of language use, any one argument can be overthrown and replaced by another. This is so because, as Gorgias points out, opinion, which most people take "as counselor to their soul ... is slippery and insecure [and] it casts those employing it into slippery and insecure successes" (§11). More specifically, Gorgias suggests, arguments come and go on account of the artistic skills and the swiftness of thought of those who make them (13).

Gorgias concludes his speech by revealing his affinity for playfulness: "I wished to write a speech which would be a praise of Helen and a diversion to myself" (ἐμὸν δε παίγνιον) (§21). In light of the discussion of the stronger-weaker opposition, he seems to suggest that in and through his composition he has opposed the discourses blaming Helen and at the same time diverted himself. But if this is so, the story of Helen has taken yet another turn, a fact that makes it far from over. Judging from the tone of the speech, Gorgias does not seem overly concerned whether his argument will ultimately unseat the arguments of his predecessors. He is content to have diverted himself by playing with language, playing, that is, with a malleable medium of dynastic powers and deceptive qualities (8). Put another way, he is content to have partaken of the game of language, to have demonstrated to his audience that he is a splendid player, and to have tried to bring the audience into the game.

The third opposition that informs sophistical rhetoric is that between actuality and ideality. Actuality refers to the way things are in the world. In rhetoric, actuality is what is believed to be known and understood about reality. Actual things are so by virtue of their presence and most people's conviction that they "know" what is the case about the world around them, how it works, and why. When speaking from the frame of actuality, the rhetor emphasizes the "here," the "now," and the "is." More specifically, he highlights those aspects of the world that exhibit a certain fixity by virtue of which they can be had or mastered cognitively. In so doing, he not only draws the boundaries of the world as generally known but also confines his listeners within those boundaries. The ends of this rhetoric are within reach because they are construed as "natural" extensions or necessary implications of the way things are.

By contrast, ideality refers to the way things should be. In rhetoric, ideality is what is envisioned and known about a world that can never be made actual. Ideal things are so by virtue of their absence and a few visionaries' conception of things in their perfect form. When speaking from the frame of ideality, the rhetor emphasizes the "nowhere," the "never," and the "should be." More specifically, he highlights a world that, no matter how untenable, one should always strive to approach. In so doing, he not only disparages the world as it is known but also prompts his audience to imagine a world that can never be actualized. The ends of this rhetoric are beyond reach but are construed as worthy of endless pursuit.

As a third alternative to the actuality-ideality opposition, possibility refers to things that are not but can be. Possible things are so by virtue of their absence and most people's proclivity to give primacy to what lies near their immediate grasp or beyond their reach. When speaking from the awareness of possibility, the rhetor favors the "there," the "then," and the "can be," thereby underscoring the fluidity, the elusiveness, and the malleability of human experience. In so doing, the rhetor acknowledges the known boundaries of the world but urges his listeners to go beyond them. The ends of this rhetoric can be reached because people are endowed with the capacity to see themselves and the world not only as they are but also as they can become.

In its various forms, the possible confronts the actual-ideal opposition by negating the efficacy of either term, that is, by exposing the unactualizability of the ideal and the imperfections of the actual—it makes no sense to count on what can never become actual; and there is little or no incentive to stay where one is, perfectly content with the way things are. Recasting the ideal as a version of the impossible and the actual as a version of the unacceptable, the possible urges the kind of movement that oversteps the boundaries of the actual and undercuts the appeals of the ideal. Put differently, the possible refuses the actual-ideal antagonism and offers itself as a third alternative. In so doing, it declares that actuality can only furnish the ground for endorsements of the facticity of the world, whereas ideality provides a wide-open field of dreams. At the same time, it posits that the world need not be inhabited only by pedants and dreamers—there is always room for those between the extremities of immanence and transcendence. In effect, the possible cultivates the awareness that knowledge of and attachment to the actual hinders one from aspiring to transcend it; utopian ideals, however, amount to unimpeded fantasy, the kind that refuses to come to terms with the materials of actuality. Finally, the possible advances the view that what is actual now has not always been so but has resulted from a sequence of possibles; by contrast, what is ideal now can always be expected to remain so.

In its proposed forms, the possible often meets with the resistance, objections, or rejection of audiences unable to see the world under a different light. This is so because the possible is a version of the novel; and the novel is often dismissed on the grounds that it is "really" a variation of the old, it demands too many changes, it offers no guarantees of success, and it has yet to be tested for its workability. But if the orator's display succeeds in firing the imagination of his listeners, and if their hopes triumph over their experiences, the possibilities before them can well be on their way to actualization. When such a transformation does occur, new possibilities are in order.

To illustrate a way in which the possible emerges out of the opposition between the actual and the ideal, let us turn to Thrasymachus' *The Constitution* (Sprague 1972 [85 B 1]). This fragmentary speech shows that rhetoric emerges as a response to a crisis. At the same time, it depicts the current state of affairs under a negative light and expresses dissatisfaction with the actual conditions of the present. Whether it suggests a specific course of action that would alleviate the prevailing ills, we cannot tell from what is preserved of the speech. What we can tell is that for Thrasymachus rhetoric constitutes the first step toward any kind of corrective action. This is so because rhetoric can display a more desirable future, a future free from the pain and suffering afflicting the present, a future often analogous to a nostalgically conceived past.

The Constitution points out that there is no need for rhetoric in times of order, calmness, and contentment. During such times, silence will do: "I wish, Athenians, that I had belonged to that ancient time when silence sufficed for young people, since the state of affairs did not force them to make speeches and the older men were managing the city properly." But in times of disorder and discontent, "one really has to speak." In other words, when rhetoric is called into being during times of urgency and upheaval, it makes its objections heard and its alternative visions of possibility known. Throughout the speech, Thrasymachus takes it for granted that his audience agrees with him that the current conditions are miserable: "Instead of peace, we are at war; danger [has brought us] to such a pass that we cling to the day that is ending and dread that which is to come; instead of comradeship, we have fallen into mutual enmity and turbulence." One of the points of contention, however, is whether vocal protest is warranted. The speaker sees no reason why one ought to keep silent in the face of an intolerable situation: "Why should anyone put off speaking [what] is in his mind, if [it has fallen] to him to be injured by the present situation and he thinks that he is on to something that will put an end to such things?" (Sprague 1972 [85 B 1]).

On the other side of the actuality of the present conditions (improper city management, war, danger, and enmity), Thrasymachus imagines the ideals of proper city management, peace, safety, and comradeship. Yet, he surely knows, these ideals are not perfectly attainable in the world of real politics—and that is why politicians mention them as often as they do in their speeches. Accordingly, Thrasymachus offers no prescription for their attainment. All he wants is to have people express their outrage, speak out their dismay. Whether such speaking will arrest the present conditions is uncertain. Returning to the utopia of the good old days is not in the hands of his listeners; but speaking is something they can do. But if this is so, the version of possibility Thrasymachus puts before the eyes of his audience is rhetoric itself.

The Constitution has been read by Dionysius of Halicarnassus as an example of a hybrid rhetorical style, one that fuses the severe and the simple styles (Sprague 1972 [85 B 1]). In more recent times, Guthrie has read it as an argument "for efficiency and principle in government, and for reconciliation between the parties to that end" (Guthrie 1971, 296). For Havelock, the speaker portrays the actuality of rival politicians whose thoughtlessness has created a political crisis and expresses interest "in the possibility of agreement" (Havelock 1957, 238). How agreement is to be reached, the speaker does not say. But even if he had, it must be noted that the question "how" is addressed by the rhetoric of practicality. The rhetoric of possibility is mainly concerned with the creation of desire for a state of affairs that can be brought about.

As one of the chief exponents of the sophistic movement, Thrasymachus must have been sensitive to the notion of *dissoi logoi;* and as a sophistical orator, he must have been familiar with the notion of *kairos* and the *to hetton–to kreitton* opposition. If this is so, he cannot be said to speak about agreement as an abstraction that must be favored once and for all over yet another abstraction (conflict)—there is nothing inherently better about agreement over conflict. What he delineates in *The Constitution* is not a speculative line of thought designed to arrange the world of ideas in a certain way; rather, it is a specific rhetorical response to an alarming political crisis, a response aiming to evoke the indignation of his listeners and to firm up their resolve to voice their dismay. Under different circumstances, the same Thrasymachus could have blasted the actuality of like-minded politicians in perfect cooperation with one another and expressed interest in the possibility of dissent.

Conclusion

In this chapter I have sought to make some sense of the preserved discourses of and about the Sophists. Having relied on their cultural situation, some of their better known compositions, and three terms from those compositions, I have shown how three culturally grounded oppositions play out in three sophistical discourses and how each opposition is exploded by a third alternative term. Inasmuch as the oppositions and texts chosen are representative, and insofar as we can generalize from the above discussion, we are in a position to attempt a preliminary characterization of the rhetoric of the Sophists.

Sophistical rhetoric is a rhetoric of third alternatives. Moving between commonly accepted versions of propriety and impropriety, it relies on clever uses of time to capitalize on and create opportunities for itself and its adherents. In this sense, it is opportunistic. Operating within polarities of discursive strength and weakness, it exploits the paradoxical character of language to invent reversals. In this sense, it is playful. Working in the midst of real actualities and unattainable ideals, it combines elements of both to point to possibilities. In this sense, it is prospective.

Although driven by *kairos, paignion,* and *to dynaton,* the discourse of sophistical rhetoric is destined to move either into the domains of *to aprepon, to hetton,* and *to idanikon* or those of *to prepon, to kreitton,* and *to energon.* In the former case, it resumes its efforts for recognition. But in the event the latter case obtains, sophistical rhetoric does not hasten to galvanize its new status; rather, it undertakes anew its assault on what, in effect, once was its own discourse. This is so because it considers any rhetorical endeavor to reflect both the power and the instability of logos. In view of this awareness, sophistical rhetoric has no unchanging commitment to any one position, including what it itself has uttered—and that is why it has often been condemned for being inconsistent, contradictory, and unpredictable. Sophistical rhetoric, in other words, does not offer once and for all an alternative better than the one(s) already adopted or practiced. It can only offer by way of the example of its own practices several linguistic approaches to human experience, approaches that can only yield provisional and ultimately disposable understandings.

Notes

1. The discourses I am referring to are mainly those collected by Diels and Kranz 1952 and translated in Sprague 1972. Throughout the text I am using Sprague's system of reference. For example, [82 A 1(6)] refers to passage (6) in Philostratus' commentary on Gorgias, and [84 B 2(23)] refers to passage (23) in Xenophon's version of *Heracles at the Crossroads,* attributed to Prodicus.

2. These or any other term in the texts of Greek antiquity can be located almost instanta-
neously thanks to recent computer technology (IBYCUS) and the TLG (*Thesaurus Linguae
Graecae*) compact disk.

3. One could also turn to the discourse referred to as *Dissoi Logoi* [90 (1–9)], but it does not
serve as a good illustration, as it mostly provides a discussion of the notion of contrary arguments and furnishes several examples.

4. The inclusion here of Alcidamas, not generally regarded as a member of the first generation of Sophists, is somewhat of an anomaly. Even so, his reported studies under Gorgias
and his arguments in favor of orality justify such an inclusion.

4 The Marginalization of Sophistical Rhetoric and the Loss of History

JANE SUTTON

In his brief history of classical rhetoric, Forbes Hill gives an account of *Rhetoric:*

> Aristotle's *Rhetoric* follows his usual method [examining a problem involved start-ing with a collection of materials from the Sophists, then refuting propositions he considered unsound until he had arrived at a core of truth]. It shows its origin in Plato's *Gorgias* and *Phaedrus*. However, if these dialogues provided the sperm, ... all that the Sophists had written on rhetoric provided the egg. In general outline, the offspring [*Rhetoric*] exhibits ... the paternal side. (Hill 1972, 19–20)

The work is said to be a development of something prior. It starts with the previous collection of the Sophists and eliminates what is unsound. And yet, the text is said to be first, an original, and something new. There is an offspring called *Rhetoric*. Hill's synopsis exposes a historical contradiction in the relationship between Aristotle's *Rhetoric* and the Sophists: It is both indebted to them and distinct from them; it is both shaped by them and in-dependent of them.

Demonstrating a sensitivity to this historical paradox, Paolo Valesio (1980, 25) describes *Rhetoric* as a text "of laborious and delicate compro-mise," mothered and fathered out of divergent tendencies. Typically, how-ever, interpreters of the *Rhetoric* read it either in juxtaposition to or in in-teraction with earlier rhetorics—its parental gene pool. This means that interpretations, through their neglect of one side of the parental gene pool, until the early twentieth century, have had to deal with two incommensurable dimensions of *Rhetoric* (e.g., Cope 1867, 1877; Cooper 1932, 1935; Ross 1959; Hunt 1962; Corbett 1965; Hill 1972; Grimaldi 1972a, 1980[1]). Thus, the contradiction lies within the *Rhetoric*, and thus Aristotle's contradictory relationship to past rhetorical practices can be determined in the text itself, as a textual contradiction.

In this chapter, I argue that talking about the *Rhetoric* as origin and as development of the art of rhetoric is a contradiction that Aristotle's text tries to resolve. I show that Aristotle resolves this contradiction successfully by imaging or prefiguring *Rhetoric* as the origin of a progression and growth, thereby creating an illusion that the only story to tell about the history of rhetoric is the developmental, evolutionary story. However, something else happened as well. I show that this talk of growth and progression, later interpreted in the language of a Darwinian biology (evolution and survival of the fittest) and/or a Hegelian dialectic (development and teleology), put forth a version so powerful and so far-reaching in its effect that it manages to trap within its grasp the entire tradition of rhetoric, which is taken to be the history of rhetoric. In doing so, this traditional history of rhetoric—sustained by a textual illusion of *Rhetoric*'s independence of past rhetorical practices and of its originality—marginalizes sophistical rhetoric. The rich history of past rhetorical practices, particularly judicial oratory—the attendant circumstance for the proliferation of rhetoric itself—is abandoned. But then again, a text is more than what any writer, be it Aristotle or commentator, intends. Understanding language as excess, I conclude by raising questions about how turning rhetoric into a text did kill its history and, paradoxically, did ensure the rebirth of it.

Disposition (*diathesis*)

Antiphon used the word "disposition" for mind or thought. He also used it for arranging a speech; i.e., for expressing something. In the second book of the Truth the same author uses it for the arrangement of the world.

(87B 95 in Sprague 1972)

Aristotle has a contradictory relationship with past rhetorical practices (e.g., Jebb 1962; Ross 1959, 262). In the beginning of *Rhetoric* (1354a 1–1354a 30),[2] Aristotle complains that predecessors rely on different kinds of character and on an arousal of emotion such as prejudice, compassion, or anger in reaching decisions. Rhetoric, he writes, relies on the enthymeme to be a persuasive art of practical reason. And then, Aristotle incorporates past practices and adds emotion (*pathos*) and character (*ethos*) to the art of persuasion. In other words, he denounces past rhetorical practices because they use emotion and character. Yet, he announces the uses of character and emotion as modes of proof—emotion (*pathos*) and character (*ethos*)—

for future rhetorical practices. Thus, I find Aristotle's contradictory relationship with past practices at the textual level. *Rhetoric* exhibits a return or an indebtedness to past practices only to depart from and be independent of them.

Working within the traditional history of rhetoric, Aristotelian commentators (e.g., Cope 1867, 1877; Cooper 1932, 1935; Ross 1959; Corbett 1965; Hill 1972) discern the value of only one side (independence from the past) of the contradiction. The value of the other side (indebtedness to the past) escapes their notice. Explaining Aristotle's indebtedness to the past, interpreters and commentators of the *Rhetoric* tell us consistently that Aristotle turns to his predecessors *just* to thematize rhetoric as a faculty for the purpose of rational investigation and speculative discussion. Indeed, *Rhetoric* is unified around the post of rationality and the region of political discourse, so much so that when Aristotle addresses an important feature of Sophistical rhetoric—emotion, W. D. Ross (1959, 264) refers to this discussion an "interruption." As such, the *Rhetoric* is not indebted to the Sophists; the text is annoyed by them.

From this perspective of history, the past is ignored, albeit sometimes recognized as a nuisance, not a valuable contribution in Aristotle's production of the art. For instance, Lane Cooper (1935) recognizes the sophistical tradition as an alien collective with suspicious parameters and persons. Being sympathetic to Bishop Copleston's position, Cooper (1935, 18) cites him: "If ever an author labored more than another, in an age of sophistry and dogmatism, to establish the *empire* of common sense and reason, it was Aristotle." Cooper also cites Rhys Roberts, who, in a similar line of thinking, writes: "[*Rhetoric*] stands apart and [is] pre-eminent even where the predecessors and successors are so numerous ... " and "his [Aristotle's] repeated references either to 'the present-day writers on rhetoric' generally, or to specified teachers and theorists, are enough to show that he has faithfully reviewed the rhetorical field of his own and previous days. And in the light of current shortcomings he lays down the true philosophical principles of rhetoric" (in Cooper 1935, 18). To lay down the principles of the art, Aristotle finds it necessary to look to the past and to recount the art's history. Yet as the critical commentary I have been referring to makes clear, the historical foundation established by Aristotle's retrospective look rests on philosophical rather than rhetorical principles. It is equally clear that Aristotle finds the origins for the art in Plato rather than in the Sophists.

The magnitude of Aristotle's indebtedness to his predecessors escapes serious notice because it is not acknowledged by the *Rhetoric*. Indebtedness is, in fact, covered over by the *Rhetoric*'s posture as a self-sufficient text, entirely independent from past practices. It is covered over by the creation of an illusion of the text's autonomy, its utter independence from its historical context. What I mean by *illusion* is the text's capacity to mask the conditions that made it possible and to present itself as self-sufficient, as quite independent of that very past out of which it draws its sustenance and gains life. To use the words of a recent theoretician,

> the literary work or cultural object ... brings into being that very situation to which it is also, at one and the same time, a reaction. It articulates its own situation and textualizes it, thereby encouraging and perpetuating the illusion that the situation itself did not exist before it, that there is nothing but a text, that there never was any extra- or con-textual reality before the text itself. (Jameson 1981, 82)

If I use the insight put forth in the passage above, I may better explain how Aristotle's *Rhetoric* simultaneously appropriates and covers over sophistical rhetorical practices. In addition, I can show how Aristotle can reduce the rhetoric of the Sophists into a mere subtext, a subtext with no historical referent and no other life than that provided by the contours of the "real" text. This move, in turn, is what enables Aristotle's readers to see the *Rhetoric* as the origin of all rhetoric. If we understand Aristotle's *Rhetoric* as a paradoxical event—drawing the Sophists' rhetoric into his theory of rhetoric while, at the same time, denying their contributions to the history of rhetoric—we can disable the textual contradictions. Rhetoric's double relation to the past, though partly covered over through the illusion of self-sufficiency and independence, is not obliterated entirely. It makes its appearance in the way in which Aristotle and his commentators talk about rhetoric as development. To see how *Rhetoric* cannot sustain a total illusion of autonomy from the past, I focus on language that metamorphoses the concept of origin into the concept of origin of development. If I recognize that style—the way commentators talked about Aristotle's relationship with past rhetorical practices—did affect the art's intelligibility as well as its history, I am well on my way into an inquiry that discovers how *Rhetoric*'s disposition (arrangement) could foster an illusion of development and that determines what is lost when the illusion of development is taken as the real history of rhetoric.

In *Rhetoric*, Aristotle dismisses crucial issues of rhetoric's nativity and its relation to an earlier culture in favor of what has been described as "a groping attitude toward the Sophists" (Valesio 1980, 25) that invites the reader to be dissatisfied with their rhetoric because it is parasitic on the misuse of *ethos* and *pathos* in judicial discourse. Having corrected the deficiencies of his predecessors, Aristotle offers the "correct" version of rhetoric and then treats that version as a mode of proof for differentiating an "ethical" theory of public action from an immoral nontheory based on false opinion. With this rhetorical strategy, Aristotle presents the *Rhetoric* as a higher form of the origin of rhetoric and, at the same time, gives license to his audience to use his text as a historical resource for prosecuting sophistical rhetoric further.

The case Aristotle puts forward is so powerful that even present-day histories of rhetoric leave outside their accounts the history Aristotle ignored, even though they acknowledge that history's existence. In these accounts, a history of the "correct version," in all its logical manifestations, becomes tantamount to the entire history of rhetoric told through the language of biology and expressed through analogies with evolution. Here is George Kennedy's account:

> The most satisfactory image would be to think of the rhetorical tradition as a great interwoven vine leading from two main trunks. [One of these trunks,] the practical side, was nurtured by a rich culture and put forth an exceedingly green foliage for a brief time, supported in part by its fellow trunk. Thereafter the other, theoretical trunk alone continued to grow, drawing strength and sap from its dying mate. (Kennedy 1963, 263)

The notion of a dominant, stronger strand responsible for carrying rhetoric through time is reiterated in Donald Stewart's account: "The historian of rhetoric in this period [nineteenth century] has to confront the fact that rhetoric ... splintered into a number of strands, some of which underwent mutations and survived, *others of which simply disappeared*" (Stewart 1983, 135). I do not argue against these accounts. In light of rhetoric's devastating conflict with philosophy, it makes good sense to describe rhetoric's development as an evolving life form. But I do wish to point out that they give us a delimiting scope of rhetoric.[3] Rhetoric's development, articulated through the language of biology, authorizes a preferred reading of the history of rhetoric. This reading relegates the Sophists to a subordinate position and their practices to the path of extinction within the larger evolutionary scheme. But this story has already been foretold by *Rhetoric*. By its own empirical claim to represent the times, the *Rhetoric* reexpresses sophistical rhetoric as something alien or barbaric (not of the *polis*) and inessential, or external, to rhetoric's development. Aristotle alters something already established (rhetorical practices before him), and under the purview of rational interest, he supplements the "small portion of the art" (1354a 13) with what it lacked. His is a text that supplements a rhetoric "dealing mainly with non-essentials" (1354a 15).

By the end of the first half of Aristotle's introduction to *Rhetoric*, he makes it clear that the art is already something fully constituted and fully cultivated. Already, the supplement has become the original, the correction is now the standard, and the text in the history of rhetoric has become the text of the art, the source of history. Nevertheless, this rhetorical strategy does not obtain without some subtle contradictions. Thus, when Aristotle "interrupts"—to recall the words of Ross (1959, 264)—"specific proofs" to discuss the passions, something is amiss: A sophistical contribution is being reflected exiguously in Aristotle's "new" rhetoric rather than being deflected from it.

Thus far I have tried to lay out the paradoxical gestures that inform Aristotle's *Rhetoric*. Drawing sophistical rhetoric into itself *and* denying it, the *Rhetoric* enlarges and enriches the art while dissembling and rejecting the Sophists' contributions to it. What addresses this contradiction most directly is Aristotle's disposition, his decision to give primacy to persuasion through reason and a secondary status to persuasion through arousing the emotions (*pathos*) as well as through the character (*ethos*) of the speaker. In this manner, I note that the sequence from Book 1 to Book 3 rests on a hierarchy of reason over emotion and of political over judicial oratory, two hierarchies that also prescribe the essentially rhetorical distinction from the inessentially rhetorical one. Consolidating rhetoric into an art by classifying its various forms (such as modes of proof or taxonomy of speeches), Aristotle turns sophistical rhetoric into a small portion of his huge inventory. Since it is through these generalizations that Aristotle restricts the art and develops it fully, I will identify those generalizations and address them as structural techniques for disabling the sophistical tradition of rhetoric. And since the very status of rhetoric as art depends on the organization of this inventory, I describe Aristotle's organizing gesture as a strategy of containment. As a "new," "original" art, *Rhetoric* projects the illusion that it is self-sufficient and a self-contained whole (Jameson 1981, 10). With rhetoric so identified and described, I can move toward gaining insight into a problem mentioned earlier, namely, how the hegemonic absorption of sophistical rhetoric belies the development of rhetoric as described through biological language.

This is, then, the illusion of development. The problem is not how to get into the history of rhetoric but how to get out of the *Rhetoric* and the magic of the counterfeiter's ruse of passing an alloy as refinement (H. White 1982). In textual terms, the problem is not how to resolve or close the textual inconsistencies of *Rhetoric*, but how to open them up so as to see the process that dissolves sophistical rhetoric into an impoverished or nongenuine discourse. Since my assessment of the illusion operative in the early history of rhetoric is based on Aristotle's schematism, deconstructing it as a strategy of containment will suggest how the art, at the site of writing, differentiates sophistical rhetoric (always linked to orality) from its other, *Rhetoric* (always associated with writing).

Aristotle offers the most convenient model for addressing the textual contradictions and their resolution in the *Rhetoric*. He says that "the way a thing is said does affect its intelligibility" (1404a 10). So, for example, given Aristotle's encounter with a rhetorical tradition, how is it that Aristotle arranges this consultation with the Sophists in his own text? Given his admission of the effect of that style and disposition, what effect do the style and the disposition of the *Rhetoric* have on the sophistical tradition? What does it mean, furthermore, to call the modes of proof—*ethos/pathos* and *logos*—inessential and essential, respectively, and then to use this arrangement to talk about the Sophists' previous courtroom speeches? It is most appropriate, then, to pay attention to Aristotle's style and arrangement (disposition) of *Rhetoric* and to note how modern commentators make use of both in their historical investigations.

In what follows, I examine how Aristotle's arrangement (*diathesis*) of the relationship between (1) the modes of proof (*pathos, ethos,* and *logos*) and (2) the taxonomy of speeches (judicial, epideictic, and deliberative) formulates the sophistical rhetorical practices into an art that denies its own historicity. The assumption here is that to make a methodological distinction between, on the one hand, *ethos, pathos,* and *logos,* and, on the other hand, deliberative, judicial, and epideictic is to abandon the possibility of allowing rhetoric to be an art that can reach timely, socially pertinent solutions.

The Aristotelian
and Sophistical Traditions

... what has happened in regard to rhetorical speeches ... for those who discovered the beginnings of them advance them all only a little way ... and there-

*fore the teaching they [like Gorgias] gave their pupils was rapid and unsystem-
atic.*

Aristotle 1984b, 183b–185a

That Plato was hostile to the Sophists and their rhetoric is a hackneyed observation but, nevertheless, a necessary point of departure especially since, as C. J. Classen (1981, 11) observes, "Aristotle is not only 'first' to inherit the Platonic disposition, but also 'first' to [agree] with Plato in his contempt for the unscientific nature of the instruction given by other [sophistical] teachers of rhetoric."

To be sure, Aristotle does not condemn the Sophists outright (J. Poulakos 1983a). But his handling of *pathos* and judicial rhetoric is such that the effect is the same. Aristotle finds the Sophists' practice in the law courts deficient. His unfriendly but reflective systematization of rhetoric's modes of proof figures centrally in compensating for this deficiency. The first one concerns the hierarchical opposition of the modes of proof through which his notion of rhetoric is distinguished from and made superior to sophistical rhetoric. To save rhetoric, Aristotle conjoins the art of discourse to philosophy through reason [1354a 11–16]. In making this "correction," *logos* is empowered to the extent that the arousal of emotions (*pathos*) becomes subordinate and foreign to the "essential" nature of rhetoric. Aristotle writes, "The modes of persuasion [those attempts at *logical argument*] are the only true constituents of the art: everything else is merely accessory" [1354a 13]. We can summarize his classification of the modes of proof as shown in Figure 4.1.

Undoubtedly, Aristotle's system of classification preserved rhetoric, but the hierarchy among the proofs created a disparity among the constituents of the art. Aristotle created the possibility that the art be developed along the line of a schism that cuts across itself. Indeed the history of rhetoric has been nothing other than a process of eliminating the "other" rhetoric, the deviant, secondary, one from the "main" rhetoric. If we visualize Rhetoric walking in history, we can imagine it running into a razor-sharp road of antitheses: *logos* versus *pathos*, literal versus figurative, reason versus imagination, concept versus precept, public versus individual, and political versus judicial oratory. The principle operating in this walk is reductive (parts sliced from the whole) rather than synthetic, and in tropological terms, the principle is synecdochical. As the road narrows, with only enough room for one part to pass through, the latter part of each antithesis is pared from

| *logos* | essential | *Rhetoric* |
| primary | | (Aristotle) |
| RHETORIC——————————————————————— |
pathos	inessential	
secondary		Rhetoric
		(Sophistical)

FIGURE 4.1   Modes of proof

the true art.[4] Development is based both on an evolution of those parts that are fit for survival and a rejection (shedding) of those other parts that cannot adapt. The criterion for survival, the factor governing the direction of this evolution, is something already determined by the *Rhetoric*, that is to say, rhetoric's liaison with philosophy.

In addition to partitioning the modes of proof, Aristotle also divided rhetoric by "inventing" three genres (deliberative, judicial, epideictic). He develops new genres because, he says (1354b 25–30), the rhetoric of his predecessors—the Sophists—is strictly judicial.[5] Addressing the historical importance of the division of speeches, George Kennedy (1963, 72) says: "As far as we know Aristotle originated the concept of the three kinds of oratory." Furthermore, Kennedy adds that Aristotle "intended the classification to be a universal one because of the universal terms in which it is originally laid out" (72). To understand this origination as a limitation of rhetoric and the loss of its history, we must show how the rejection of sophistical rhetoric concerns the taxonomy of speeches vis-à-vis the modes of proof.

The significance of the interrelationship between the taxonomy of speeches and the modes of proof has not been observed often enough by commentators even though Aristotle asserted their relationship in his schema. By taking this relationship into account, we can see how *"logos"* casts out "mere" rhetoric (i.e., the Sophists along with their courtroom speeches) and allows for the political genre. Aristotle's text must ultimately exclude judicial rhetoric, for it must demonstrate how political rhetoric— the emerging higher form of the art—differs from the courtroom practices and "model" speeches. At the same time, for his text—the preservation of what philosophy kills—to be taken seriously, it must employ a "system" that would exclude his object of study, a heretofore "system"-less rhetoric.

In this sense, Aristotle makes a deal with rhetoric. *Rhetoric* won. The Art lost.

Prior to his discussion of the three types of speeches, Aristotle claims that although rhetoric encompasses all sorts of public speaking, it is primarily practiced before juries in law courts. More specifically, the Sophists say "nothing about political oratory, but try, one and all, to write treatises on the way to plead in court" (1354b 26). What is implicit in characterizing sophistical rhetoric as strictly a judicial preoccupation is an attack on *ethos* and *pathos*. In his classical studies of the Sophists, Kennedy (1963, 37) states that the aim of judicial oratory is "to produce an impression of character and to direct the judges' emotions." The Sophists' overindulgence in the forensic genre goes hand in hand with their preoccupation with nonessentials (1354a 15). The explanation in the *Rhetoric* is clear: "The reason for this is that in political oratory there is less inducement to talk about non-essentials. Political oratory is less given to unscrupulous practices than forensic, because it treats of wider issues" (1354b 26–30). On this basis, judicial oratory operates in the realm of *pathos* and *ethos* and thus is lowered to their level. Also, the phrase "wider issues" makes it apparent that Aristotle is speaking of a value for rhetoric inimical to self-interest.

To understand this value, we turn to happiness, the object of rational choice, which is a key concept in Aristotle's ethical theory and rhetoric (Hill 1972, 36–38; Johnstone 1980). The ethical treatises provide insight into how Aristotle arrived at his hierarchy of genres in *Rhetoric*. Sophistical judicial rhetoric, as Aristotle tells us, is for the individual, not for the *polis*. As such, it will not achieve the means to happiness, an idea that rhetoric clusters around, particularly when Aristotle discusses the genres (1360b–1362a 15; Valesio 1980, 25–33). When Aristotle (1984a [1094a 10]) speaks of happiness, he says that the "attainment of good for one man alone, to be sure, is a source of satisfaction; yet to secure it for a nation and for states is nobler and more divine." Judicial rhetoric (oratory for the one) is subordinate to deliberative rhetoric (oratory for the many) because it can achieve only personal satisfaction, not the general good. Politics is the master science of the good or happiness. "The master arts are to be preferred to all the subordinate ends; for it is the sake of the former that the latter are pursued" (Aristotle 1984a [1094a 15]). Rhetoric (1362a 23) subscribes to this idea. When Aristotle (1962 [1094b 2–4]) says "that the most honored capacities, such as strategy, household management, and oratory, are contained in politics," he subordinates rhetoric to politics. Thus, *Rhetoric* is arranged through a textual strategy geared toward sustaining this hierarchy.

primary	essential		
	logos (invention, enthymene, topics, commonwealth)		
		POLITICAL	*Rhetoric* (Aristotle)

RHETORIC

secondary	inessential		
	pathos (psychology of author, stylistics, personal thematics)		
		JUDICIAL	Rhetoric (Sophistical)

FIGURE 4.2   Aristotle's classifications of the modes of proof

At 1359a 20–21, the order is deliberative, epideictic, judicial. It is this order he follows in Book 1: deliberative (Chapters 4–8), epideictic (Chapter 9), judicial (Chapters 10–14) (Grimaldi 1980, 86). Because judicial sophistical rhetoric is not "political" (in Aristotle's sense of the term), it is subordinate to deliberative rhetoric. Because it flourished at a time when the art was at its initial (weak) stage of development, it cannot be taken seriously at a time when rhetoric has acquired the status of a real art.

Thus, through his descending order of merit in the classification of the modes of proof, which privileges *logos* (enthymeme, logic of probability), Aristotle also "politically" elevates the deliberative genre over the judicial kind (1354b–1355a), a logic that rationalizes rhetoric's "origin" in the law courts as counterfeit and inessential. Following Aristotle's move of severing *pathos/ethos* from *logos*, Aristotle's outline can be presented in Figure 4.2.

When rhetoric is thus reduced to the pair of alternatives as shown above, a (sophistical/judicial) rhetoric based on *mere* (secondary/inessential) proofs is strategically contained as a deceptive practice, a means without a proper end. Aristotle's analysis of the state of the art reveals an unadvanced, ill-advised rhetoric that has been *passed off as* state of the art. As such, the art demands to be restored. Hence, the illusion of development, as viewed through the strategy of containment, is a way to repress the inversion of origins under the guise of improving the art of rhetoric. This perspective can be summarized in Figure 4.3.[6]

End	Form: *logos*, enthymeme
	Content: political rhetoric
(= primary rhetoric)	
	End: *polis*
Means	Form: *pathos*, figuration
	Content: judicial rhetoric
(= secondary rhetoric)	
	End: individual

FIGURE 4.3   Primary and secondary rhetoric

The new additions to the art unambiguously give its future over to a mode of proof and a kind of speech. In this model, the import of sophistical rhetoric "naturally" dissolves because it is constrained to nothing beyond an individual's mere means to success in courts. If sophistical rhetoric stands out, it does so only to substantiate retroactively the background of Aristotle's supplement: Rhetoric ought to be left alone to develop along the lines of good reasons and appropriate eloquence in the domain of public affairs. In this manner, *Rhetoric* tells the tale of rhetoric rising above its past, emerging triumphantly beyond its initial and embarrassingly naive nonrational origins.

Implications and Conclusions

The barley-drink comes apart if not stirred.

Heraclitus, Fr. 125

The repression of sophistical rhetoric by Aristotle's supplement, which we have located in the relationship between the modes of proof and the taxonomy of speeches, is more than just a denial masked as development. If it were the case of mere denial, it would simply be a matter of pointing out the repression—which, in turn, would change our attitudes and approaches to the history of rhetoric. However, the strategy of containment does something more, projecting, as I have shown, a determinate structure onto sophistical rhetoric. In this manner, sophistical rhetoric becomes marginalized. Annexed entirely to the emotions, associated exclusively with speeches in the courtroom, it is deprived of any political or moral coloration. The ancient drink called barley captures poignantly Aristotle's impact on sophistical rhetorical practices. The drink, made by stirring wine, honey, and barley grains together, can be likened to sophistical rhetoric, an art that, however unself-conscious, did blend together deliberative, epideictic, and judicial components by means of a motion generated by the Sophists' practices. Taking the motion (*rhóe* in rhetoric) of practice away, the *Rhetoric* allows these components to settle into separate theoretical layers, claiming the top layer for itself, the bottom for the Sophists. Such is Aristotle's systematization of rhetoric: The very force that defines the kinds and uses of rhetoric turns its history into separate categories and, in time, kills it by dividing oratory into genres (Wilcox 1943) and proof into essential and inessential modes of speech (Sutton 1986).

When, however, one dares to ignore Aristotle and to position oneself outside the control of Aristotle's universal classification, one is likely to see sophistical rhetoric in a radically different light. Many of the ancients, for instance, who responded to sophistical practices themselves rather than to Aristotle's uses of them, paint a brilliant picture of Protagoras, Lysias, Antiphon, Gorgias, and Thrasymachus as ambassadors and statesmen, as superb stylists of poetic expression and orators of civic discourse, and as practical educators and intimates of political leaders (e.g., Sprague 1972; Thucydides 1960; Wilcox 1942; Freeman 1966; Bonner 1927). The surviving fragments about ancient Greek rhetoric claim a much broader program, one that decidedly fuses the political with the judicial and the epideictic. But only few investigations, made very recently, have sought to disclose the political side of sophistical rhetoric. A few examples will suffice.

Addressing the invention of rhetoric, D.A.G. Hinks (1940) points out that the minor Greek rhetoricians agree that the origin of Corax's rhetoric was political. With his version of rhetoric, Corax was able to exert influence on the new assembly after the death of Hieron and, hence, guide the state to democratic reforms. Also, Wilcox (1943, 2) reexamines the Greek beginnings of rhetoric and confirms the authority of the *Prolegomena*. "Their words [that Corax wished to influence the people of Syracuse] imply that the first teachings were deliberative rather than dicanic [judicial] and contradict Aristotle as preserved in Cicero." Aristotle ignores this tradition and, as represented by Cicero [*Brutus* 46], regards Corax's rhetoric exclusively as a forensic activity.[7] In other recent investigations, classical scholars have indicated that sophistical rhetorical training prepared Athenian students to speak in the assembly and council as well as in the law courts. "It is reasonable to suppose," H. LL. Hudson-Williams (1951, 72) concludes, "that the methods advocated by Gorgias, Protagoras, Alcidamas, and Anaximenes are based on methods of speaking used in public life. The innovation of Alcidamas seems to have been that he wished to extend this method [structure and arrangement of political speeches] to all forms of speaking, i.e. to forensic and epideictic as well as demegoric [political] speeches." Stanley Wilcox (1942, 154) considers "specific evidences of such [deliberative] instruction and the testimonies of ancient authorities" showing that early rhetorical instruction seems to have been aimed primarily at training speakers for the assembly. "The facts about rhetoric remain clear and receive ample indirect confirmation from Aristophanes, Plato, Isocrates, Alcidamas, and Aristotle himself. The teacher promised to and did train speakers for the assembly as their pupils desired" (154).

In the view of these commentators, then, evidence from the ancient past does not negate the judicial role of the Sophists' rhetoric; nor does it suggest an exclusive affinity to the courts. Available evidence suggests that the judicial and deliberative components of sophistical rhetoric cannot be separated and that their teachings did not distinguish persuasion in the assembly from persuasion in court. The distinction between political and judicial rhetoric is a postsophistical one. Its origin is, in effect, coeval with Aristotelian rhetoric. The division of or the distinction of or the separation of rhetoric into categories had not been "invented" when Protagoras, Antiphon, Gorgias, and other Sophists were teaching rhetoric.

In Aristotle's systematization, sophistical rhetoric is reduced both in scope and in function, its meaning lost to a larger and more comprehensive scheme of human knowledge, its history relegated to pedantic explorations as rhetoric becomes the heir of terminologies, functions, and forms and as its development is carried out in a territory marked by philosophy's degradations, narrowings, and transformation of applications (Rorty 1987, 26–66; Foucault 1972, 215–237). What is needed is to shift the grounds and to construct a view of the early functions of rhetoric consistent with the sophistical movement. Toward that end, this chapter has enumerated the controls that have guarded the sophistical tradition and that have emptied it of its dynamism and drama. Noting the effect of the prolonged Platonic condemnation, G. B. Kerferd (1981b, 11) remarks that the "sophists have suffered from being set in conflict with the idealist tradition." Indeed, even though Plato's and Aristotle's philosophical challenge to rhetoric rescued the art from the dangers of neglect, trivialization, or abandonment, at the same time, they contained rhetoric to philosophy.

To tell the history of rhetoric in a way that does justice to sophistical practices, we need to exit the tracks of progression and development and situate ourselves within the more open-ended sequence associated with storytelling. In arguing for the value of narrativity, Hayden White (1981, 5–6) reminds us: "Official wisdom has it that however objective a historian might be in his reporting of events, however judicious in his assessment of the evidence ... his account remains something less than a proper history when he has failed to give reality the form of a story." Clearly, then, to restore the properly dramatic activity of the story of rhetoric, sophistical practices need to be placed *within* a historical mise-en-scène radically different from the one of rhetoric and philosophy in conflict.

The larger aim of this chapter is to stir up the contradictions punctuating the unsettling story of the Sophists and, thus, begin the task of altering our concept of rhetoric as a stale art to an art—to follow the barley-drink metaphor—desirously drinkable. To do that, we need, as Valesio (1980, 25) says, "a serious but, so to speak, irreverent commentary on [*Rhetoric*], one that will set the text free from the mists of archaeology, and will dare to confront it on terms of equality."

Notes

1. Before specific arguments on *Rhetoric*'s contradictions are presented in the chapter, I want to examine this idea in Grimaldi (1972a, 1980). Recognizing that in spite of the fact that Aristotle's attack on emotional rhetoric (e.g., *Rhetoric* [1354a 15–1355a 3]) is a countermotif to his ultimate position on rhetoric, namely, a thematic pronouncement of both reason and emotion, Grimaldi (1972a, 43) claims that Aristotle's attack on the sophistical use of emotion and character is "in no way at odds with his [Aristotle's] later statements on the place of *pathos* and *ethos*." Grimaldi, I argue, is able to make this statement by a substitution in language. First, Grimaldi notes that Aristotle's initial rejection of *ethos* and *pathos* (1544a 1–30) is directed at the misuse of emotion by the Sophists. The emotions, which Aristotle has referred to as "inessential," have been misused in the judicial branch because they can be orchestrated in such a way as to be for or against the litigant without regard to the facts. Since the attack centers on the notion of "misuse," Grimaldi (1972a, 44) interprets that what Aristotle *intended* by the polemical use of "inessential" was really more benign—in the sense of "irrelevancies." And thus Grimaldi maintains "one cannot claim that Aristotle is arguing simply for the logical and rational proof of the case." To reach his conclusion—Aristotle's philosophical system is coherent—Grimaldi alters the standard translation of Aristotle's rendering of *ethos* and *pathos* as "inessential" to "irrelevancies" in order to present these inconsistencies as un-

important. That is, these passages on judicial oratory have the meaning of inconsistent only under the construct of *inessential*. This is a very serious exchange of words. Whereas "non-essential" connotes dispensable, "irrelevant" means "not becoming," but still *present*. Grimaldi's conclusion concerning the inconsistent treatment of *ethos* and *pathos* vis-à-vis the thematic pronouncement of a unified rhetorical theory rests upon the reader's permitting this little word exchange. If *ethos* and *pathos* are "nonessentials," as the standard translations go, then Aristotle's so-called commitment to a unified account of the three modes of persuasion is not a total commitment. If, however, following Grimaldi, *ethos* and *pathos* are "not becoming," like an irrelevant sentence in a paragraph, then they are still present even if at a minimal or undesirable level. But by changing "inessential" to "relevant" has not Grimaldi further diminished the relationship between the modes of persuasion by establishing no relationship at all between *ethos* and *pathos* to reason? At least the notion of "inessential" carries with it a functional relationship, albeit a secondary one. That is, *ethos* and *pathos*, in the "inessential" distinction, have been established, at least in traditional accounts, in a hierarchical relationship to *logos*. But where is the relationship of *ethos* and *pathos* to reason if the former have been stylized as irrelevancies?

2. All references to Aristotle are from the *Rhetoric* (1954) unless indicated otherwise. Passages from it are cited parenthetically in the chapter by line rather than page number.

3. With Ricoeur I lament what has been papered over, even though that may be a weak gene in the history of rhetoric's evolution: "It [was] this deep-seated conflict between reason and violence [undisciplined and idiosyncratic interest] that the history of rhetoric has plunged into oblivion; emptied of its dynamism and drama, rhetoric [was] given over to playing with distinctions and classification" (Ricoeur 1977, 12).

4. See Sutton (1986, 1987). I refer to the translation (1987) because it includes an illustration of Rhetorica's walk, with the Swedish poem "Hercules" as caption: "She, she is heading on a broad and even road, easily gone, but slowly sloping down to disaster, more and more narrow, until then the wanderer will be falling, falling, faster and faster in the abyss."

5. However, Aristotle contradicts this claim. For discussion, see Sutton (1991).

6. This reading is an adaptation of Jameson's (1981) adaptation of Louis Hjelmslev (1961), *Prolegomena to a Theory of Language*, trans. F. J. Whitfield (Madison: University of Wisconsin Press). See Chap. 13 in Jameson 1981.

7. This other tradition is well known: "The art of rhetoric was invented in the second quarter of the fifth century B.C. in Syracuse in Sicily. As a result of the overthrow of the Syracusan tyrants much litigation had arisen, and either Tisias or Corax or both undertook to teach a technique of judicial rhetoric to those unaccustomed to public speaking" (Kennedy 1963, 26). As Wilcox (1942) puts it: "Of course this statement contains an implication of limited activity, but ... such indirection was the characteristic weapon employed in the attack upon rhetoric by comic-poets and philosophers, and we cannot tell how accurately or fully the knowledge of Aristotle's passage has been transmitted to Cicero" (142). See also B. Smith 1921; and Sutton 1991.

5 Instituting the Art of Rhetoric: Theory, Practice, and Productive Knowledge in Interpretations of Aristotle's *Rhetoric*

JANET M. ATWILL

Whenever a canon is critically examined, whether it is a canon of texts, interpretations, or historical representations, one comes up against a contradiction implicit in the very notion of canonicity: A canon embodies a unique set of institutional values, but at the same time it must rise above the particularities of history and circumstance. In other words, to confer the status of canonicity on a particular text is to assert that it both expresses and transcends the values, conventions, and circumstances of a discipline at a particular historical moment.

Much is at stake in this paradox of canonicity: the values affirmed by a canon, the means by which a discipline both demarcates its objects of study and secures its cultural authority, and the very role of the university in the social and political world. Indeed, it is argued by many that the boundary between the university and the world is most illusory at that moment when the university claims its otherness to both history and the interested world of politics and economic exchange. It is at that point that the university *defines* the world by claiming only to *describe* it and secures a set of cultural values by repeatedly "discovering" them in its objects of study. From this perspective the institutional practices of the university—its construction of departments and objects of knowledge, its judgments, theories, and professionalized "practitioners"—are not only the means by which the university reaffirms its own status but also the means by which it institutes a world.

These institutional practices have come to be analyzed by a widening circle of scholars. Critics as diverse as Jacques Derrida, Barbara Herrnstein Smith, Magali Sarfatti Larson, Burton Bledstein, Samuel Weber, Stanley Fish, and Pierre Bourdieu have argued that formal disciplines are constructed by strategies designed to obscure the constitutive forces of time and circumstance.[1] Weber, for example, argues explicitly that the autonomy of an individual discipline is dependent on its ability to secure a field that is "self-contained, subject to its own laws, to principles or rules that are in essence independent of all that surrounds them, of all they are not" (Weber 1987, x). It is the faith that objects of intellectual inquiry are "found" rather than constructed and the conviction that it is the university's role to provide "objective" theories to represent accurately these objects of study that lie at the heart of epistemological foundationalism.

The erasure of social and historical contingencies in discipline formation poses an especially complex problem for rhetoric, for one would be hard-pressed to point to an area of study more dependent on time and circumstance. Indeed, for both the Sophists and Aristotle, rhetoric was in part the art of analyzing and exploiting the indeterminacies of time and circumstance, the very contingencies that traditional disciplinary strategies suppress.[2]

It is my purpose here to focus on the operation of one particular disciplinary strategy, the theory/practice binary, in two interpretations of Aristotle's *Rhetoric:* the work of the nineteenth-century commentator Edward Meredith Cope, and his twentieth-century counterpart, William S.J. Grimaldi. Both scholars wrote introductions to and commentaries on the *Rhetoric,* and both use the theory/practice opposition to define rhetoric's "object" of study and secure its disciplinary identity. Cope, on the one hand, argues that rhetoric is a "practical art," whereas Grimaldi, on the other, contends that rhetoric is theoretical, or philosophical, knowledge. Though each defines the theory/practice opposition differently, their use of the binary illustrates its role in the institutionalization of epistemological foundationalism.

For two decades now, the theory/practice binary has been the subject of antifoundationalist critiques in virtually every academic discipline—by Kuhn and Feyerabend in science, Rorty in philosophy, Fish in literary theory, and Bourdieu in anthropology. Thus far, however, little attention has been paid to its role in interpretations of rhetoric. This neglect is particularly significant because the distinction between the theoretical and the practical is rooted in ancient thought, and it plays a particularly important role in the Aristotelian corpus. One of Aristotle's chief means of confronting the conflicts among ancient science, Platonic dialectic, and sophistic instruction in rhetoric and politics was to demarcate three orders of knowledge, each with its own domain of inquiry and methodology. Theoretical knowledge encompassed the study of philosophy, mathematics, and the natural sciences; and practical knowledge included the study of ethics and politics.[3]

Theoretical and practical knowledge, however, were only two of three epistemological domains in Aristotle's taxonomy. The corpus also clearly marks out a third domain, that of productive knowledge. Productive knowledge subsumed all *technai*, or arts, from medicine and architecture to poetics and rhetoric. What all of these arts had in common, according to Aristotle, were three critical characteristics: their epistemological and axiological indeterminacy, their implication in an "interested" act of social exchange, and their contingency on time and circumstance.

Though productive knowledge is invariably dismissed when the Aristotelian corpus is used to authorize rhetoric as a discipline, both Aristotle's epistemological taxonomy and rhetoric's classification as productive knowledge are generally accepted with little question when rhetoric's disciplinary status is not at issue. For example, Abraham Edel's *Aristotle and His Philosophy*, a textbook treatise within the discipline of philosophy, is largely organized according to the three domains of knowledge; and rhetoric, together with poetics, is clearly classified as productive knowledge. However, when rhetoric's institutional status is at stake, the domain of productive knowledge is generally obscured, and rhetoric is figured as some variant of either theoretical or practical knowledge.[4] Moreover, when the distinction between the theoretical and the practical is used to secure the canonicity of Aristotle's *Rhetoric* and the disciplinary respectability of rhetoric itself, that distinction ceases to refer to two distinct domains of inquiry. Instead, theory and practice are arranged in a conceptual hierarchy whereby theory either governs or reflects rhetorical practice. For both commentators on Aristotle's *Rhetoric*, the theory/practice binary demarcates the "practice" of rhetoric as an object of study. Thus, both Cope and Grimaldi institute rhetoric as a formal discipline only by suppressing the very contingencies of time and circumstance by which rhetoric was once defined.

Theory, Practice,
and Epistemological Foundationalism

Before delving more deeply into these epistemological categories in Aristotle, Cope, and Grimaldi, we should elucidate more specifically the role of the theory/practice binary in modern foundationalism. Simply put, a foundationalist conception of theory consists of two interlocked assertions. First, foundationalist theory claims to provide the general principles that mirror, interpret, or govern an object or activity. Theory in the "strong" sense, as Fish would say, promises to be a general hermeneutic, guided by principles that are invariant because they rise above the particularities of time and circumstance (Fish 1985, 106–108).[5] Using Chomskian linguistics as an example, Fish offers the following characterization of foundationalist principles:

> They have their source not in culture but in nature, and therefore they are *abstract* (without empirical content), *general* (not to be identified with any particular race, location, or historical period but with the species), and *invariant* (do not differ from language to language). As a system of rules, they are "independent of the features of the actual world and thus hold in any possible one." (Fish 1985, 108)

In the discipline of rhetoric, theory is often characterized as mirroring rhetorical practice. However, in order to represent rhetoric by invariable rules, one must depict rhetorical practice as a virtually immutable behavior, more of the character of what we would consider a natural process than a social activity. Put another way, rhetorical practice must have a basis other than culture—in either biological nature or "human" nature.[6] In either case, rhetorical behavior is excised from its social and historical contexts.

The second assertion of foundationalist theory, inextricably linked to this break between nature and culture, is that the very practices of interpreting and theorizing escape the impress of time and circumstance. Not only may objects of interpretation be excised from history and culture, but also "interpreters" themselves. Thus, the foundationalist model of knowledge is characterized by its demarcation of an unsituated, dehistoricized object of study, over which an equally decontextualized observer may exercise interpretive mastery.

Again, Fish offers a succinct explanation of the fallacy in this relationship between unsituated interpreters and interpretations. Foundationalist theory, according to Fish, can never achieve its objective of exhaustive description because "the primary data and formal laws necessary to its success will always be spied or picked out from within the contextual circumstances of which they are supposedly independent" (Fish 1985, 110). Put more simply: "The objective facts and rules of calculation that are to ground interpretation and render it principled are themselves interpretive products: they are, therefore, always and already contaminated by the interested judgments they claim to transcend" (110).

Bourdieu takes the analysis of the interpreter's perspective a step further, arguing that the very perspective of distance on a practice or object of study is a social as well as epistemological stance. One of the primary arguments of *An Outline of a Theory of Practice*, Bourdieu's detailed critique of the theory/practice opposition, is that the position from which an interpreter views practical activity as "an *object of observation and analysis*" betrays a social as well as epistemological break (Bourdieu 1977, 2). The "social conditions of objective apprehension," according to Bourdieu, reflect a set of social relations in which the scientific perspective is privileged by those who control "dominant systems of classification" (178, 169). Bourdieu contends, quite explicitly, that the theoretical perspective is a distinguishing mark of a particular class, a perspective won against "the conditions of existence and the dispositions of agents who cannot afford the luxury of logical speculation" (115).[7] In effect, Bourdieu argues that epistemological orders are indissolubly bound to social orders.

It is precisely the contingencies of context—historical, economic, and social—that foundationalist theory must allege to transcend. Indeed, in the foundationalist paradigm, the very cultural authority of the university depends on its claim to stand outside culture.

Theory, Practice, and Productive Knowledge in the Aristotelian Corpus

When we examine the background of Aristotle's theory/practice/production triad, the relationship we find between theoretical and practical knowledge appears to have more in common with that outlined by Bourdieu than that depicted by either Cope or Grimaldi. John Burnet notes that the theoretical/practical/productive distinctions appear in the Pythagorean "Doctrine of Three Lives," which predates Aristotle's divisions of knowledge by approximately 200 years. Burnet offers the following explanation of the three lives—"the Theoretic, the Practical, and the Apolaustic":

> There are three kinds of men, just as there are three classes of strangers who come to the Olympic Games. The lowest consists of those who come to buy and sell, and

next above them are those who come to compete. Best of all are those who simply
come to look on (*theorein*). Men may be classified accordingly as lovers of wisdom
(*philosophoi*), lovers of honour (*philotimoi*), and lovers of gain (*philokerdeis*). (Burnet 1964, 42)

In the Pythagorean Doctrine, each life denotes a specific social order, and
the apolaustic life (the life associated with "gain") is identified with production. Epistemological orders are, in a very literal sense, social orders.

Historians and classicists who have traced the theory/practice distinction generally agree that the binary as we know it in modern foundationalist theory would have been inconceivable to ancient thinkers.[8] *Theoria* is
never characterized as governing or reflecting practice; nor is it an abstract concept that subsumes a particular example. Nicholas Lobkowicz
explains:

When the Greeks opposed to each other *theoria* and *praxis*, they did not have in
mind abstract doctrines in contrast to their concrete application. ... Rather, what
they had in mind was a distinction between various kinds or walks of life—a distinction which permitted them to tackle the kind of questions which of yore it was
customary to ask at the Delphic oracles: Who is the most pious, the most happy,
the wisest, the best man? (Lobkowicz 1967, 3)

Lobkowicz argues that the ancient Greeks had no conception of applied
science—or of theory applied to practice. Instead, the technological
achievements of classical Greece evoke the ancient sense of *theoria* as the
observation of spectacle. The "inventions" of Greek science were "little
more than toys," according to Lobkowicz: "One only has to think of the
various gadgets invented by Hero of Alexandria, which include curiosities
such as an altar at the side of which figures offer libations when a fire is
raised on it" (Lobkowicz 1967, 41). Lobkowicz also cites an ancient defense of catoptrics, the science of mirrors, as a science deemed "worthy of
study" because it "produces spectacles which excite wonder in the observer, for example, the view of one's own back" (41).

Although there is little basis outside the Aristotelian corpus for a mimetic relationship between theory and practice, there is even less justification for it within the corpus. The most explicit treatments of the theory/
practice/production triad appear in Chapters 3 through 7 of Book 6 of the
Nicomachean Ethics and Chapters 1 through 3 of Book 1 (A) of the *Metaphysics*. In both treatments the three domains demarcate distinct bodies of

knowledge, not conceptual hierarchies. Though the three domains of knowledge refer to specific areas of inquiry, they are also demarcated according to two critical and inextricably tied elements of Aristotle's doctrine of teleology: (1) source of motion (or agency) and (2) first principles and ends. These elements define the extent to which each body of knowledge is subject to the contingencies of time, circumstance, and economic interest; and they determine whether each body of knowledge is either probable or certain, indeterminate or bound by the laws of necessity. For example, knowledge of that which moves for a purpose outside itself is interested, contingent, and probable; whereas knowledge of the very principles of movement is disinterested, universal, and certain.

Aristotle explains in the *Nicomachean Ethics* that theoretical knowledge is concerned with first principles, the highest objects of knowledge (*EN* 1141a15–20).[9] Because these principles include the very laws of motion and causality, they rise above the particularities of time and circumstance. Theoretical knowledge is the "belief about things that are universal and necessary" (*EN* 1140b31). Thus, philosophy, mathematics, and the natural sciences are considered to be certain, as opposed to probable, knowledge. Since theoretical knowledge is concerned with that which is self-moved, it is sharply distinguished from knowledge used for an end outside itself. Theoretical knowledge is consummately "disinterested." Thus, Aristotle insists that it can be pursued only by those who are so socially and economically secure that they will not even be tempted to seek this type of knowledge for material gain.

As with the Pythagorean Doctrine, Aristotelian epistemological order is closely tied to social order. In the *Metaphysics*, Aristotle offers a description of the theoretical life:

> It is owing to their wonder that men both now begin and at first began to philosophize; they wondered originally at the obvious difficulties, then advanced little by little and stated difficulties about the greater matters. ... [T]herefore since they philosophized in order to escape from ignorance, evidently they were pursuing science in order to know, and not for any utilitarian end. And this is confirmed by the facts; for it was when almost all the necessities of life and the things that make for comfort and recreation were present, that such knowledge began to be sought. (*Met.* 982b12–15)[10]

The man of philosophy views theoretical knowledge as an object of wonder; he does not *use* it. And, like Plato's philosopher-king and the members of Aristotle's guardian class, the man of theory is supported by the very circumstances that his knowledge must transcend.[11]

Practical knowledge, identified with ethics and politics, is described in the *Nicomachean Ethics* as "a reasoned and true state of capacity to act with regard to human goods" (*EN* 1040b20). The objective of both ethics and politics, according to Aristotle, is to enable wise deliberation on human behavior—specifically to determine what means will bring about the end of *eudaimonia*, or the good life. Practical knowledge is opposed to certain knowledge because "it is impossible to deliberate about things that are of necessity" (*EN* 1140b1). In contrast to theoretical knowledge, practical knowledge does *not* include principles outside the realm of human interest and behavior. Thus, with regard to the source of motion and the end of knowledge in this epistemological domain, practical knowledge contains its own end, for "good action itself," Aristotle explains, "is its end" (*EN* 1140b6–7). Practical knowledge is not the "application" of theoretical principles to human "practice," nor is it simply "useful," utilitarian knowledge in the modern sense of the word "practical." Finally, "practical" in the Aristotelian corpus does *not* refer simply to human practice or action per se, as both Cope and Grimaldi want to construe the word.

The relationship Aristotle creates between *praxis* as action and practical knowledge as the set of precepts elaborated in such treatises as the *Politics* and the *Nicomachean Ethics* is not an easy one to decipher. The role of *praxis* in Aristotelian teleology in general and in the domain of practical knowledge in particular is a problem over which Aristotle himself puzzled. The *telos* of practical knowledge is clearly *eudaimonia*, variously translated as happiness or the good life. But is *eudaimonia* itself an action (*praxis*), or is it a state (*hexis*)? In the *Nicomachean Ethics*, Aristotle makes the following observation: "It makes ... no small difference whether we place the chief good in possession or in use, in state or in activity. For the state may exist without producing any good result, as in a man who is asleep or in some other way quite inactive" (*EN* 1098b34–1099a).

Aristotle attempts to resolve the dilemma with a number of definitions that try to reconcile *praxis* and *hexis*. At one point he describes the happy man as one who will both "do and contemplate what is excellent" (*EN* 1100b20); and at another point he defines happiness as "an activity of soul in accordance with complete excellence" (*EN* 1102a5). Later in the *Nicomachean Ethics*, he describes happiness as a "continuous" activity of contemplation, explaining that "we can contemplate truth more continuously than we can *do* anything" (*EN* 1177a15–25). In the *Politics, eudai-*

monia will be defined by the following oxymoronic figure: It is the "realization and perfect exercise of excellence" (*Pol.* 1332a9). What is at issue here is the indeterminacy in the corpus itself regarding the status of *praxis* and practical knowledge. At least three characterizations are outlined: practical knowledge as a body of precepts on ethics and politics, *praxis* as an activity, and *praxis* as a state. What the corpus does not offer us with any security is a conception of practice as "objective" human behavior; and in different ways, this is precisely the characterization of *praxis* on which both Cope and Grimaldi will depend in figuring rhetoric according to the theory/practice ratio.

If practical knowledge is identified in some way with "acting," then productive knowledge is concerned with "making." It is a *poesis* distinguished by instrumentality as well as epistemological and ethical indeterminacy. Aristotle explains in the *Nicomachean Ethics:* "All art is concerned with coming into being, i.e. with contriving and considering how something may come into being which is capable of either being or not being" (*EN* 1140a10–12). In contrast to both theoretical and practical knowledge, the end of productive knowledge is always "outside itself," residing not in the "product" but rather in the use made of the artistic construct by a receiver or audience. Just as in evaluating the art of architecture, "the master of the house will actually be a better judge than the builder" (*Pol.* 1282a21–22), so also in rhetoric, "the hearer ... determines the speech's end (*telos*) and object" (*Rhet.* 1358b1).[12] Productive knowledge is concerned with the indeterminate and the possible—that which may or may not come into being—and that which presents us, as Aristotle explains in the *Rhetoric*, with "alternative possibilities" (*Rhet.* 1357a5). In direct contrast to theoretical knowledge, productive knowledge is both consummately instrumental and consummately situated. Rather than rising above the contingencies of time and circumstance, productive knowledge is absolutely dependent on them.

The most common examples of art in the Aristotle corpus are medicine and architecture; and just as there are no lengthy treatises justifying their inclusion as types of productive knowledge, there are no detailed defenses of rhetoric's place in this domain. However, rhetoric is consistently characterized in conformity with the criteria that distinguish productive knowledge. Aristotle is careful to explain that the end of rhetoric is "outside" itself—in the "hearer" (*Rhet.* 1358b1). Moreover, the insistence that rhetoric is "not concerned with any special or definite class of subjects" (*Rhet.* 1355a35) reiterates another key criterion of productive knowledge: its concern with what can be otherwise. In maintaining that the subjects of rhetoric must "present us with alternative possibilities" (*Rhet.* 1357a5), Aristotle exempts rhetoric from the epistemological determinacy of theoretical knowledge and the ethical determinacy of practical knowledge. Rhetoric as productive knowledge is thus defined by the characteristics that modernist foundationalist theory tries to efface in its model of knowledge: (1) its implication in an exchange, the value of which is both social and economic, (2) its resistance to determinate epistemological and axiological ends, (3) and its consummate dependence on time and circumstance.

Thus, the ancient relationship between the theoretical and the practical contrasts sharply with its modern refiguration in the theory/practice binary. For Cope and Grimaldi, the theory/practice binary transforms rhetoric as an exchange embedded in culture into a static object—or stable activity—grounded in nature. Moreover, whether they define rhetoric as "practical art" or philosophy, theory becomes a means of guiding and interpreting the "practice" of rhetoric.

Managing *Empeiria:* Cope's Interpretation of Rhetoric as a Practical Art

E. M. Cope's *An Introduction to Aristotle's Rhetoric* and *Commentary* were composed in the mid-nineteenth century at Trinity College, in the midst of the industrial transformation of England. Cope's treatment of Aristotle's concept of art reflects both the associationist psychology, current in England at the time, and a concern with predicting and improving the efficiency of human behavior. Cope is one of very few scholars even to consider rhetoric's classification as productive knowledge; and though he finally argues that rhetoric does not belong in this epistemological domain, he finds it necessary to mount a detailed defense of his reclassification of rhetoric as a "practical art."

The disciplinary character of rhetoric, which Cope finally affirms, is not an example of strict epistemological foundationalism. Unlike Grimaldi, Cope makes no claim for a mimetic relationship between rhetorical theory and rhetorical practice. What Cope does is to focus attention on Aristotle's descriptions of rhetoric's relationship to politics (*Rhet.* 1354b2; 1356a25), endeavoring to identify rhetoric as a subdiscipline of politics and thus a type of practical knowledge. Rather than reinforcing rhetoric's social and temporal contingencies, however, this identification works more to associate rhetoric with "action" over "production" and finally to constitute rhetoric as a science of human behavior—a subdiscipline of what we might call "political science."

Cope begins his case for rhetoric's classification as a practical art by confronting head-on two epistemological taxonomies that recur throughout the corpus: (1) the distinction between probable and certain knowledge and (2) the theoretical/practical/productive triad. He acknowledges that the "division of philosophy and knowledge into *theoretike, praktike,* and *poietike,* defined severally by their *tele* or objects, truth, practice, and production, 'speculative' 'practical' and 'productive,' is set forth at length in Metaph. E.I. and assumed elsewhere as the only true and natural classification" (Cope 1867, 18 n. 1).[13] Against this taxonomy, Cope sets what he calls a "two-fold division of objects of knowledge," which he purports to draw from the *Nicomachean Ethics* 1.2: "(1) things which are entirely independent of human action and human power, which are the objects of speculative philosophy, and (2) things whose origin does depend upon human will impulse and action, whether they terminate in the action or *energeia* itself or are carried on to an *ergon,* the production of something permanent and concrete, as in art proper" (18 n. 1).

Cope's exposition of the *Nicomachean Ethics* passage elaborates the preceding discussion, which defines rhetoric in terms of the opposition of certain (or "scientific") to probable knowledge. Rhetoric is restricted to "human actions characters and motives," which are, according to Cope, "by their very nature only contingent and probable; nothing can be *predicted* of them with certainty" (Cope 1867, 10).[14] In contrast, certain knowledge can be reduced to "necessary" laws and conclusions. Cope thus summarizes rhetoric's distinguishing features: "Rhetoric with few exceptions excludes the universal and necessary, and deals only with the probable; and this is the *essential* difference between it and the scientific or demonstrative processes" (10). Thus, Cope's distinction between that which submits to and that which resists human intervention is finally reducible to the difference between certainty and probability.

When one turns to the first two chapters of Book 1 of the *Nicomachean Ethics,* what one finds is more a prolegomenon to Aristotle's contention that politics is the "most authoritative art and that which is most truly the master art (*architektonikes*)" than a careful elaboration of the distinction between that which is independent of and that which is contingent on human action. Cope's references to these chapters, however, accomplish several objectives. At the simplest level, the opening passages of the

Nicomachean Ethics allow Cope to affirm rhetoric's identification with politics. Aristotle insists that politics ordains what subjects should be studied in the state, and rhetoric is a part of this important curriculum: "the most highly esteemed of capacities to fall under this, e.g., strategy, economics, rhetoric" (*EN* 1094b2). But this association of rhetoric with politics also allows Cope to identify rhetoric with the domain of action, so that the triadic epistemology is reduced to a binary. Finally, as we shall see, *praxis* becomes identified with *empeiria;* and rhetoric as a "practical art" will be used to manage this positivist conception of "experience."

It should be noted that Cope explicitly acknowledges that the two taxonomies are guided by different principles. In Aristotle's parlance, the tripartite taxonomy is governed by the *telos,* or final cause, of each domain. In contrast, the basis of classification of the two-part taxonomy is "the origin or cause to which the objects upon which the speculation is exercised owe their existence" (Cope 1867, 18 n. 1). Although this description would appear to refer to Aristotle's concept of formal causality, Cope goes on to explain that this "origin or cause" is what "gives rise to a two-fold division of objects of knowledge" (18 n. 1). Thus, it is largely the character of the objects of knowledge—in other words, their "material cause"—that determines their classification as either probable or certain knowledge.[15]

However, the privileging of Aristotle's material cause is bought with the annulment of final causality and, hence, the domain of productive knowledge. This abridgement of productive knowledge, which enables Cope to subordinate the three-part taxonomy to the single distinction between certainty and probability, requires Cope to make two arguments. First, he must argue, as he does above, that the distinction between productive and practical knowledge is peripheral at best. Indeed, referring to the discussion of productive knowledge in Book 4, Chapter 4, of the *Nicomachean Ethics,* Cope goes as far as to suggest that the passage in which Aristotle "*seems* … to confine the term 'art' to rules and practice which end in production" is spurious, attributing it to Eudemus (Cope 1867, 16 n. 2). Cope insists that this definition could apply only to "art in its strictest sense" (16 n. 2); and he goes on to argue that rhetoric cannot be productive knowledge because it "does not result in the production of something permanent and concrete, as in art proper" (18 n. 1). Finally, Cope falls back on Quintilian's resolution of the dilemma in the *Institutio Oratoria,* in which Quintilian argues, rather unsatisfactorily, that in contrast to such arts as painting, rhetoric is "concerned with action" (2.18.2). Consequently, "since it is with action that its practice is chiefly and most frequently concerned, let us call it an active or administrative art" (2.18.5). Cope simplifies Quintilian's classification by calling rhetoric a "practical art" (Cope 1867, 19).

But Cope's reclassification of rhetoric as a "practical art" requires him to make a second argument. In order to explain rhetoric's relationship to *techne*, Cope must identify the "practical" quality of the art not only with "acting" but also with "experience." Cope's conception of experience, however, is constructed through nineteenth-century associationist psychology and its positivist interpretation of *empeiria*. The transformation of rhetoric into a natural behavior seems, on the one hand, paradoxical in light of Cope's desire to affirm rhetoric's status as a "subordinate branch of *politike*" (Cope 1867, 17). On the other hand, when human behavior is viewed as governed by "natural laws," in this case, the laws of association, politics can indeed become a kind of "science"; and all of the social and historical contingencies that seem to be the very fabric of politics become its borders.

In identifying acting with "experience," Cope refers to the opening passages of the *Metaphysics*, where Aristotle describes processes of intellection. Cope's summary of 980a27–981a2 largely agrees with W. D. Ross's translation.[16] Cope explains: "Sensation of some kind is the distinctive mark of *animal* life: from sensation, in *some* animals, arises memory, and in proportion to the strength of this faculty is the force of intellect and the power of acquiring knowledge. In man, memory, by repetition of the same impression, gives rise to experience, *empeiria*, and from it proceed art, and ultimately science" (Cope 1867, 20). Cope's interpretation of both memory and sensation, however, are explicitly interpreted through nineteenth-century psychology, then called "mental philosophy." In his further elaboration of the *Metaphysics* passage, Cope translates 981a5: "When from many mental impressions (*empeirias*) arising from experience a single universal conception is formed about their common properties."

Cope's identification of *empeirias* with "mental impressions" is perfectly in keeping with the associationist psychology of his time. Based on the work of John Locke, nineteenth-century associationist psychology attempted to provide an empirical account of human thought and behavior by placing the source of ideas in sense data. Associationist psychology argued that these ideas, generated by sense data, were then rearranged in the mind according to various laws of association, such as the laws of contiguity and similarity. As William Woods points out, associationist psychology is indebted to Aristotle's theories of perception and memory.[17] However, the strongly empirical cast of Cope's description of sense perception most likely owes far more to Francis Bacon and John Locke than to Aristotle. As

G.E.L. Owen has argued, to interpret Aristotle's theories of sensation in terms of Bacon's conceptions of empirical facts is most likely to make a distinction between *phainomena* (observed facts) and *endoxa* (common conceptions on the subject), which Aristotle does not consistently maintain.[18] Associationist psychology was obviously strongly positivist, and this focus on the facticity of sense experience was to be used explicitly by the utilitarians to describe human behavior according to laws of nature—in other words, to make ethics an exact, even predictive, science.[19]

Cope's argument concerning rhetoric is similarly designed to affirm the discipline's usefulness on the basis of its capacity for predicting and controlling a natural behavior. In order for this art to have a predictive function, it must deal with regular, if not immutable, behaviors, and this regularity is ensured for Cope by the laws of association. In order to secure an empirical base and predictive function for rhetoric, Cope draws on a passage from the *Rhetoric* that defines the field of study as "the faculty of observing in any given case the available means of persuasion" (*Rhet.* 1355b25). In his explication of this passage, Cope suggests that "the available means of persuasion" are empirical constraints that determine rhetorical performance. Cope explains: "*Empeiria* is an *irrational* procedure; manifests itself in a merely mechanical mode of operation, working like a machine, and displaying a skill which results from nothing but habit and association, and is acquired by mere repetition; ... it deals only with individual cases, and never rises to general conceptions or rules" (Cope 1867, 22, emphasis added). Rhetoric is useful, according to Cope, because it both resembles and improves upon the operations of nature: Rhetoric "acts in combining and generalizing and reducing to rule and system, and so making applicable the scattered and desultory observations of phenomena already noted and existing in various departments of nature and human speculation" (26). Cope goes on to insist that Aristotle's notion of "the available means of persuasion" is designed "to withdraw the notion of the art in some degree from the exclusively practical application of it encouraged by the sophistical school, and to fix attention upon theory and method" (33). This formulation of rhetoric, he contends, makes art dependent "in no respect upon the result, but only on the method employed" (33). This, he argues, is a "more scientific treatment of the subject" (34).

Despite Cope's insistence that rhetoric resides in the domain of probability, the theory that "explains" rhetorical behavior has a distinctly scientific cast. The art of rhetoric is thus refigured in Cope as scientific theory—its objective is to be more effective than the "natural" laws of association at predicting and controlling experience. Though at one level

Cope acknowledges that rhetorical theory is instrumental in managing experience, at another level its value lies in its potential to "predict results" (Cope 1867, 23). Consequently, method functions like modern scientific theory: It predicts a behavior because it is a coherent set of laws that closely resembles that behavior.

Cope's attempt to match methodology to reality is at the heart of epistemological foundationalism. Though Cope does not insist that rhetorical method either mirrors or represents these laws of nature, the subtle suggestion remains that the legitimacy of rhetorical method is secured by its resemblance to natural processes that retain a significant degree of stability. Experience, itself, is restricted by the limited set of laws by which sense impressions, or *empeirias*, are combined in memory. Thus, however "situated" a positivist theory of perception may be, the laws that explain perception are still detemporalized. From Cope's perspective, the "problem" of rhetoric—what Kuhn would call rhetoric's disciplinary "puzzle"—is *not* exploring the means by which a social exchange is enabled but rather defining the principles that govern rhetoric as a form of human behavior.[20] The institutional payoff of this perspective is that any explanation of rhetoric will be evaluated by the standards by which we judge "theory" itself, standards such as coherence and economy. The more formal the set of principles, the more stable rhetoric becomes as an object of study.

Representing Truth and Justice: Grimaldi's Interpretation of Rhetoric as Theoretical Knowledge

One hundred years later, Grimaldi's deployment of the theory/practice binary is a far more explicit attempt to transform rhetoric from a social and temporal exchange into a static—and "natural"—object of study. If theory in the "strong" sense, as Fish argues, claims not only to be "abstract ... general ... and invariant" but also to provide a general hermeneutic that both mirrors and determines practice, then Grimaldi's interpretation of Aristotelian rhetoric is a paradigmatic example of epistemological foundationalism.

Whereas Cope appears to have been strongly influenced by nineteenth-century associationist psychology, Grimaldi might be said to be equally influenced by structuralist linguistics. Rhetoric's province extends to both language as an "organic whole" and all behavior concerned with the apprehension and communication of reality (Grimaldi 1972a, 8). In *Studies in the Philosophy of Aristotle's Rhetoric,* Grimaldi makes a rigorous and detailed case for viewing the rhetorical syllogism, or enthymeme, as a kind of "deep structure" that both enables and explains perception, communication, and moral reasoning. Indeed, at points Grimaldi's claims for the enthymeme strongly resemble the objectives Chomsky sets out for both linguistics and experimental psychology: that "of mapping the intrinsic cognitive capacities of an organism and identifying the systems of belief and organization of behavior that it can readily attain" (Chomsky 1965, 56–57).

For Grimaldi, the enthymeme is the substance of rhetorical art, a formal structure that organizes all other disparate appeals and *topoi*. But Grimaldi also argues that the enthymeme is a "general method of reasoning," a "methodology of deductive and inductive inference" (Grimaldi 1972a, 49, 103). The "universality" of the enthymeme as both a model of human communication and a mode of reasoning provides the rationale for Grimaldi's argument that the enthymeme broadens rhetoric's province to include both philosophy and ethics—theoretical *and* practical knowledge; Grimaldi does not even raise the category of productive knowledge.[21] In defining rhetoric's epistemological and axiological function, Grimaldi goes as far as to argue that the enthymeme can represent both the "true" and the "just": "Rhetoric is mimesis and ... it is supposed to represent the real (i.e., truth and justice) in any situation for an auditor" (Grimaldi 1980, 27). Indeed, in the Kuhnian sense, Grimaldi's enthymeme might be the disciplinary exemplar par excellence, for it is explicitly, at once, both an object of study and a theoretical explanation. The arguments Grimaldi must construct in order to make the enthymeme occupy the spaces of both theory and practice are far too detailed to summarize adequately here. As with the discussion of Cope, I shall simply point to the ways in which the theory/practice binary defines rhetoric's disciplinary status and then briefly outline the "strong theory" interpretation of the enthymeme offered by Grimaldi.

As the title of Grimaldi's introduction to the *Rhetoric* suggests, his objective is to identify rhetoric with philosophy, an identification that first broadens rhetoric's province to encompass theoretical knowledge. From the outset, Grimaldi defines the problem of the legitimacy of both rhetoric as a discipline and Aristotle's *Rhetoric* as textual exemplar in terms of the theory/practice opposition:

> In reading the treatise the conflict which arises between the philosophy of rhetoric (*theoria*) and applied methodology (*praxis*) has been sufficient to cause careful stu-

dents of the text to question the unity of the work, the authenticity of the third book, the arrangement of the material in the books, and the consistency of Aristotle's thinking on major themes of his work like the *enthymeme, ethos, pathos.* (Grimaldi 1972a, 15)

Grimaldi resolves this theory/practice question with an answer that pays far more attention to rhetoric's disciplinary character than to its role as a social practice. To understand these problems, he insists, "we must recognize that Aristotle is trying to establish a theory of discourse and to give it a ground in philosophy" (Grimaldi 1972a, 15).

Grimaldi defines rhetoric's relationship to philosophy through a conception of discourse that is strongly indebted to structuralist linguistics. Grimaldi explains that "all significant human discourse is structured language, an organic whole," and rhetoric is occupied with the "analysis of underlying principles of discourse" (Grimaldi 1972a, 8, 17). Because the study of rhetoric is necessarily the study of language as a "structured" whole, rhetoric is also concerned with analyzing the apprehension and communication of reality: "The heart of the problem of rhetorical study as seen in Aristotle is that all significant human discourse is structured language, an organic whole, which communicates effectively man's reflection on and articulation of, reality" (8). Early on, Grimaldi stresses rhetoric's representational function: "Rhetoric is the art which presents man with the structure for language, and, by way of structure, enables language to become an effective medium whereby man apprehends reality" (8). Moreover, Grimaldi is quite candid that these "underlying principles" define rhetoric's disciplinary province. He explains, "In his *Rhetoric* Aristotle developed the work of the Sophists and Isocrates into an analysis of the underlying principles of discourse bringing about the one thing of concern to Plato: a union of rhetoric and philosophy" (17). As we shall see, Grimaldi's conception of language as a "structured whole" detemporalizes rhetorical discourse, just as the laws of association detemporalize rhetoric for Cope. The end result for both scholars is rhetoric—conceived as either human behavior or communication—reconstructed as a stable object of study.

Rhetoric's disciplinary expansion, however, does not end with the annexation of philosophy. Although Grimaldi must acknowledge that rhetoric does not strictly conform to the criteria for theoretical knowledge, he marks rhetoric's distinctiveness from philosophy in large part only to extend the discipline's province to ethics, or practical knowledge. Grimaldi notes that rhetoric, unlike theoretical knowledge, does not depend on *logos* alone but encompasses two other *pisteis, ethos* and *pathos*. Grimaldi explains that the enthymeme, as "the integrating structure of rhetorical discourse," brings together reason and emotion; it "incorporates ... all of the elements demanded by language as the vehicle of discourse with another: *reason, ethos, pathos*" (Grimaldi 1972a, 16–17). Because rhetoric draws on all three modes of proof, Grimaldi insists that rhetoric encompasses both philosophy and ethics. According to Grimaldi, rhetoric—in the tradition of Isocrates, Plato, and Aristotle—was an "art of *logos*" that could bring "together the results of the activity of the speculative intellect and those of the practical intellect" (53–54).

Grimaldi's argument that rhetoric belongs in the domain of practical knowledge resembles Cope's at points. Grimaldi is similarly careful to differentiate certain and probable knowledge. Rhetoric is concerned with "contingent reality," which is "subject to change," rather than with reality that is certain and invariable (Grimaldi 1972a, 24). Also like Cope, Grimaldi identifies practical knowledge with *praxis*, or action, and not with the body of precepts concerning practical wisdom that constitute Aristotle's treatises on ethics and politics. Grimaldi explains that "the speculative intellect moves toward Being, or ultimate reality, in itself whereas the practical intellect moves toward Being, or reality, insofar as this Being is to issue in human action" (25). Grimaldi is quite explicit that these two types of intellection play a role in defining rhetoric's place in Aristotle's epistemological taxonomy: "The moment Aristotle decided that the art of rhetoric directs its major effort upon the world of contingent reality and the area of the probable, and calls into play deliberation and judgement he places it under the domain of what he calls the practical intellect rather than the speculative intellect" (25). The contrast between the certain and the probable and between the speculative and the practical serves two functions for Grimaldi. It both identifies rhetoric with action and reinforces the opposition of theory to practice, thoroughly negating any trace of the domain of productive knowledge.

But if Grimaldi seems to offer, with one hand, a firm distinction between theoretical and practical knowledge, it is a distinction he seems intent on taking away with the other hand. Immediately following his discussion of differences between the speculative and the practical intellect, he initiates an argument designed to illustrate their similarities to the end that speculative intellection appears to depend on practical intellection. Grimaldi offers a very thorough and insightful treatment of Aristotle's discussion in the *Nicomachean Ethics* (1109b30–1115a3) of desire (*orexis*), deliberation (*bouleusis*), and *proairesis*, the type of reasoning that integrates both desire and deliberation (Grimaldi 1972a, 26–27). Though it would seem that desire would be excluded from the static world of the speculative intellect, Grimaldi insists that the "appetitive element in the psyche" is a requisite part of *nous theoretikos*: "There can be no question that in the effort to grasp and comprehend the nature of ontological reality … , the speculative intellect must receive an initial assist from the appetite" (25).

The dependence of the speculative intellect on the appetitive works not only to extend rhetoric's province to certain knowledge but also to bring certain knowledge under the aegis of rhetoric. As Grimaldi states explicitly, the art of the *logos*, embodied in the enthymeme, unites both theoretical and practical knowledge. However, this institutional identity is secured only by suppressing the conception of rhetoric as an instrumental art with a *telos* and by defining rhetoric primarily in terms of formal causality. This contest between rhetoric as a formal object of study and as an instrumental art—a contest in which the formal object is the foregone victor—is finally reducible to the dissonance between theory and practice. As we have seen, Grimaldi attempts to resolve this tension by putting the enthymeme in the paradoxical position of functioning as both a theoretical model of communication and an instrumental art: "As the *instrument of rhetorical argumentation* the enthymeme possesses a … *universality by reason of its form*" (Grimaldi 1972a, 93, emphasis added).[22] Determined as it is by the theory/practice binary, Grimaldi's argument must attempt to hold the enthymeme in the spaces of both theory and practice; and he can only do that by arguing that one mirrors the other. Although this position seems to guarantee rhetoric a respectable disciplinary space alongside philosophy and ethics, it also confers on rhetoric an epistemological and axiological determinacy that the domain of productive knowledge specifically precluded.

Grimaldi's privileging of formal causality thus ensures a representational function for the enthymeme, and it is in his final discussion of the "materials" of the enthymeme—signs, probabilities, and topics—that this representational function of rhetoric is made most explicit. There is no way to do justice to the complexity of Grimaldi's treatment of the sources of enthymemic reasoning. At the most general level, Grimaldi's discussion incorporates two major arguments. He argues first that the enthymematic "materials" of signs and probabilities are sufficiently "grounded in the real order" to confer on rhetoric the function of representing both reality and truth.[23] Grimaldi's second argument is that the "if, then" structure of the enthymeme is a form of inferencing that mirrors the "natural ways in which the mind thinks" (Grimaldi 1972a, 131, 130).[24] These forms of inferencing may be found, according to Grimaldi (130–131), in the twenty-eight *koinoi topoi* in *Rhetoric*, Book 2, Chapter 23.

In his first argument concerning signs and probabilities, Grimaldi uses the *Prior and Posterior Analytics* to distinguish three types of enthymematic materials: (1) *eikota* (probabilities), (2) *semeia anonyma* (nonnecessary signs), and (3) *tekmeria* (necessary signs) (Grimaldi 1972a, 104). In the broad context of Grimaldi's discussion of the enthymeme as the rhetorical syllogism, what is at stake in these distinctions is finally rhetoric's relationship to both philosophy and truth; in the specific context of this analysis of signs, what is at stake is their probative and/or demonstrative force. According to Grimaldi, by the standards of the *Analytics*, both types of signs, necessary and nonnecessary, hold "a stronger demonstrative force than *eikos*" (111). Thus, the ability of *semeia* to resemble the demonstrative logic in the domain of theoretical knowledge is secure enough not to require an extensive argument. What Grimaldi must defend is the notion that probabilities can be sufficiently rooted in objective reality to make "an inference from *eikos* … an eminently reasonable guaranty that the conclusion represents the objective fact" (109).

Grimaldi admits that the demonstrative force of probabilities cannot reside in the relationship of "internal necessity" that characterizes *semeia* and *tekmeria* in the syllogistic demonstration of the *Prior and Posterior Analytics* (Grimaldi 1972a, 111).[25] The demonstrative force of *to eikota* must come from their relationship to what Grimaldi defines variously as the "objective fact" and "the metaphysical … (and) ontological reality of the subject" (109, 133).[26] Though Grimaldi's argument concerning *eikos* is especially detailed, at points he offers quite cogent summaries: "*Eikos* is that which the generality of men think, or may think, and as such it carries persuasive force to the mind. Aristotle's *eikos* and the knowledge which comes from it is rooted in the real order and it is this existential aspect of it which makes it a legitimate source for further knowledge" (110). Elsewhere, Grimaldi simply argues that the *Rhetoric* characterizes *eikos* as "permanent and stable"; thus, "*eikos* expresses a reasonable and stable aspect of the real order" (108, 109).

Once Grimaldi has grounded probabilities and signs in an external reality that is more essentialist than positivist, he turns to the twenty-eight common topics to argue that they are forms of inferencing that reflect "natural" processes of reasoning. *Eikota* and *semeia* provide the "premises of enthymematic reasoning"; and the rhetor may find those materials in both the general and the particular topics.[27] Of course, in arguing that the enthymeme is a form of reasoning, Grimaldi must acknowledge that he is defining two functions for the enthymeme: the enthymeme as a mode of invention and as a mode of proof. Quoting de Pater, Grimaldi asserts that the "general *topos*" must be characterized as both an "acte de l'invention" and as "probatif" (Grimaldi 1972a, 127). However, when Grimaldi describes the role of the *koinoi topoi* in enthymematic reasoning, it is virtually impossible to determine when he is describing the enthymeme as a mode of invention and when he is outlining it as a mode of proof.

Grimaldi contends that the twenty-eight *koinoi topoi* are "general axiomatic propositions," which are themselves "valid forms of inference" (Grimaldi 1972a, 130). In enthymematic reasoning, they are "applied to the subject-matter presented by the *eide*" (130). As modes of inference, Grimaldi insists that the twenty-eight topics fall into three "inferential and logical patterns": antecedent-consequent (also cause-effect), more-less, and a form of relation (131).[28] The logical patterns revealed in the *koinoi topoi* correspond to "natural ways in which the mind thinks" (130). Grimaldi explains that the *koinoi topoi* "are ways in which the mind naturally and readily reasons, and they are independent, in a way, of the subject to which they are applied, and may be said to be imposed as forms upon this material in order to clarify and determine it further" (134).[29] These three modes of inference, found in the mind but reflected in the *koinoi topoi*, function much like Cope's laws of association. They confer a formal structure on both a practice and a body of principles, a formal structure that Grimaldi maintains has its sources in the "nature" of reality rather than in the shifting possibilities of culture.

The enthymeme, however, is not only a means of representing reality. Since the "universal" form of the enthymeme also bridges the gap between rhetoric and ethics, the enthymeme has the capacity to represent both truth and justice. Consequently, the enthymeme functions not only heuristically to determine the most effective proofs but also philosophically and ethically to determine the "best" proofs. Grimaldi makes this argument explicit in his commentary on 1355a21–25, a passage that W. Rhys Roberts translates as follows: "Rhetoric is useful because things that are true and things that are just have a natural tendency to prevail over their opposites, so that if the decisions of judges are not what they ought to be, the defeat must be due to the speakers themselves, and they must be blamed accordingly."[30] Grimaldi's alternative translation clearly raises both the epistemological and axiological valence of rhetoric: "Rhetoric is useful because truth and justice are naturally stronger than their opposites; and so, if judgements are not made as they should be, it follows necessarily that truth and justice are defeated by their opposites [untruth and injustice]. And this merits censure" (Grimaldi 1980, 27).

Grimaldi makes an even stronger claim for the axiological and epistemological determinacy of rhetoric in his explication of 1355a21–25:

> Implicit in this statement, and worthy of note, is that rhetoric prevents us from making wrong judgements, and in doing so it protects truth and justice. To defend the usefulness of rhetoric on this ground, as A. does, is to attribute to rhetoric an important and significant position. For what A. is quite pointedly saying is that rhetoric is mimesis and that it is supposed to re-present the real (i.e., truth and justice) in any situation for an auditor. Rhetoric does this the only way it can: through language. ... If truth and justice are defeated, it is because rhetoric has failed in its function as mimesis. (Grimaldi 1980, 27)

Thus, for Grimaldi, truth and justice *do* exist in the world, and they may be both found and represented by the rhetorical enthymeme. However, in the end, Grimaldi's argument for this epistemological and axiological function for the enthymeme must rest less on the "strength" of truth and justice than on the enthymeme's ability to correspond to both a "natural" reasoning process and an unproblematized reality.

Grimaldi's strong interpretations of rhetoric's epistemological and ethical determinacy are set against Aristotle's many assertions that rhetoric is "not concerned with any special or definite class of subjects" (*Rhet.* 1355b5) and that the subjects of rhetorical deliberation must present us with "alternative possibilities" (*Rhet.* 1357a1–5, 20). Although some of the ambivalence concerning rhetoric's ethical and epistemological status may be attributed to Aristotle, it is clear that Grimaldi must suppress the contingent and indeterminate dimensions of rhetoric in order to endow it with the cultural authority of both philosophy and ethics.

Instituting Productive Knowledge

In the end, what is at stake for Cope and Grimaldi is securing a disciplinary space for rhetoric; but in order to institute rhetoric as a formal discipline, both must transform it. In particular, they must extricate rhetoric from the epistemological model of productive knowledge and refashion it according to the specifications of the foundationalist paradigm. As we have seen, this reconstruction may yield rhetoric as science, philosophy, or ethics. What it does not yield is the model of productive knowledge outlined in the Aristotle corpus. It is clear that the epistemological paradigm of productive knowledge was eclipsed by the foundationalist/philosophical model of knowledge. But the "reinvention" of the productive paradigm may serve two useful functions for those who would either observe or institute rhetoric in our own cultural and historical context.

First, productive knowledge may serve as a heuristic for exploring what was left on the cutting floor of epistemological foundationalism. It is this "use" of productive knowledge as a means of critique that I have appropriated in my discussion of Cope and Grimaldi. Productive knowledge contrasts with virtually every distinguishing feature of the foundationalist paradigm. The productive paradigm does not require a stable object of knowledge. One duty, in particular, that productive knowledge does not assume is that of description, which is foundationalism's highest office. According to the foundationalist paradigm, "knowledge" is the accurate representation of an object or activity, mediated by the interpreter/scholar and secured by theoretical descriptions generally aimed at obscuring the constructed character of those objects or activities.[31] The scholar is thus the hierophant of the border between nature and culture, the arbiter of the boundary between what is and what can be. One way of characterizing the foundationalist paradigm is to describe it as a hermeneutic model of knowledge—one that aims at the description and interpretation of objects of knowledge—without examining how either objects of knowledge or their interpreters are constructed.

If the foundationalist paradigm is a hermeneutic model of knowledge, then we might describe a productive paradigm as an inventional model of knowledge; and herein I would suggest lies a second function for the reinvention of the productive paradigm. Productive knowledge never attempts to overcome the contingencies of time and circumstance, nor does it attempt to effect the breach between objects and value upon which the foundationalist paradigm is precipitously constructed. Indeed, in abnegating the task of defining autonomous objects of knowledge—particularly any task that attempts to make a distinction between object and value—the productive paradigm, as an inventional model of knowledge, would focus attention on the practices by which we invent both exemplary texts and exemplary interpreters. More important, such a model would refuse to base its cultural authority on its ability either to define impenetrable processes of nature or to reflect immutable structures of reality and truth. Instead, such a perspective would foreground the limits and contingency of its cultural authority. Indeed, in a productive paradigm, both interpreters and their objects of interpretation might be viewed not as static entities but rather as temporary victories in contests of competing standards of value. Rather than securing the boundaries of "what is," an inventional model of knowledge would mark the shifting and contestable borders of what is possible.

Notes

1. It would be impossible to mention every scholar who is exploring canon and discipline formation. Thomas Kuhn's *The Structure of Scientific Revolutions* (1970) and Michel Foucault's *The Archaeology of Knowledge* (1972) did much initially to focus attention on the issues that a multitude of scholars now address. Some of the most insightful work has been done by Barbara Herrnstein Smith in *Contingencies of Value* (1988). A particularly provocative and often overlooked examination of the occultation of time in the production of aesthetic exemplars may be found in Jacques Derrida's *The Truth in Painting* (1987); Derrida also confronts related issues in such articles as "The Age of Hegel" (1986) and "The Principle of Reason: The University in the Eyes of Its Pupils" (1983). Though I refer only to Bourdieu's *Outline of a Theory of Practice* (1977), similar arguments are made in *Distinction* (1984) and *Homo Academicus* (1988).

2. The significance of *kairos*, the opportune moment, cannot be underestimated in ancient rhetorical theory. For a discussion of the relationships among *techne*, *metis*, and *kairos*, see Detienne and Vernant 1978. Bourdieu 1977 is, to a great extent, an argument for the reintroduction of "time" into theoretical representation. See especially pp. 6–8, 105–106, 162–163, 180; Bourdieu offers his own discussion of rhetorical *kairos* on p. 20.

3. The "contents" of each domain of knowledge are discussed in *Met.* 1026a19 and *EN* 1139b20–1141b20.

4. The opposition between theoretical and practical rhetorics has virtually governed the history of rhetoric. One of the most familiar expressions of this opposition appears in George Kennedy's division of rhetoric into three categories: technical, sophistic, and philosophical. Though the classifications of rhetoric by Cope and Grimaldi exemplify this conflict, a thorough discussion of the opposition is beyond the scope of this chapter. For a survey of the conflict between theoretical and practical rhetorics, see Sutton 1986.

5. Fish's discussion of foundationalist theory (Fish 1985) is taken from the collection of articles that debate the consequences of foundationalism and antifoundationalism, entitled *Against Theory: Literary Studies and the New Pragmatism*. It should be noted, however, that there are many definitions of foundationalist theory, and generally those who are most concerned with defining it are equally concerned with critiquing it. Richard Rorty's *Philosophy and the Mirror of Nature* is a detailed examination of philosophical foundationalism, which he describes as follows: "Philosophy as a discipline ... sees itself as the attempt to underwrite or debunk claims to knowledge made by science, morality, art, or religion. It purports to do this on the basis of its special understanding of the nature of knowledge and of the mind. Philoso-

phy can be foundational in respect to the rest of culture because culture is the assemblage of claims to knowledge, and philosophy adjudicates such claims. ... Philosophy's central concern is to be a general theory of representation, a theory which will divide up culture into the areas which represent reality well, those which represent it less well, and those which do not represent it at all" (Rorty 1979, 3).

6. Many theorists have attempted to describe the alchemical processes by which culture is transmuted into "nature." A particularly interesting analysis may be found in the chapter entitled "Technique" in Castoriadis 1984. In *Outline of a Theory of Practice*, Bourdieu defines his concept of the *habitus* as "history turned into nature, i.e., denied as such" (Bourdieu 1977, 78).

7. "The practical privilege in which all scientific activity arises never more subtly governs that activity (insofar as science presupposes not only an epistemological break but also a *social* separation) than when, unrecognized as privilege, it leads to an implicit theory of practice which is the corollary of neglect of the social conditions in which science is possible" (Bourdieu 1977, 1).

8. Vernant makes exactly the same argument as Lobkowicz. In *Myth and Thought Among the Greeks*, Vernant contends that the technological achievements of ancient Greece had very little to do with the control and mastery of nature. Their value resided instead in their capacity for provoking wonder, astonishment, and admiration (Vernant 1983, 283).

9. Unless otherwise noted, parenthetical references to the Aristotle are taken from *The Complete Works of Aristotle*, the Revised Oxford Translation, edited by Jonathan Barnes (Barnes 1984). *EN* equals *Nicomachean Ethics*. *Met.* = *Metaphysics*. *Pol.* = *Politics*. *Rhet.* = *Rhetoric*.

10. In the *Nicomachean Ethics*, Aristotle offers his own version of the Pythagorean Doctrine: "To judge from the lives that men lead, most men, and men of the most vulgar type, seem (not without some reason) to identify the good, or happiness, with pleasure; which is the reason why they love the life of enjoyment. For there are, we may say, three prominent types of life—that just mentioned, the political, and thirdly the contemplative life" (*EN* 1095b15).

11. Both Plato and Aristotle make detailed cases for a ruling or guardian class whose life, largely devoted to speculation, is supported by lower classes. This argument involves Plato in the intricate notion of distributive justice and entangles Aristotle in a functionalist view of the state in which he admits that happiness is not likely to be the possession of all classes. See *Pol.* 1264b20.

12. "There are some arts whose products are not judged of solely, or best, by the artists themselves, namely those arts whose products are recognized even by those who do not possess the art; for example, the knowledge of the house is not limited to the builder only; the user, or, in other words, the master, of the house will actually be a better judge than the builder, just as the pilot will judge better of a rudder than the carpenter, and the guest will judge better of a feast than the cook" (*Pol.* 1282a17–23).

13. The passage from the *Metaphysics* is one of the most explicit articulations of the epistemological triad: "All thought is either practical or productive or theoretical" (1025b25). Regarding the triad as "the only true and natural classification," Cope references Bonitz's note on 1025b18. It is interesting to note that Cope does not point to the more extensive discussions of the triad elsewhere in the *Metaphysics*. It is this taxonomy that guides my discussion.

14. Rhetoric further contrasts with certain knowledge in that like dialectic it is "indifferent to the truth of its conclusions, so far as it is considered as an art" (Cope 1867, 9).

15. This focus on material causality is not hard to defend within the corpus. As Cope notes, a frequent refrain throughout the corpus is that any treatment of a subject will "be considered sufficient if its distinctness and exactness be only in proportion to its subject matter (or materials)" (Cope 1867, 11). Indeed, this resonates in Aristotle: "Our discussion will be adequate if it has as much clearness as the subject-matter admits of; for precision is not to be sought for alike in all discussions, any more than in all the products of the crafts" (*EN* 1094b13).

16. Ross's translation is taken from Barnes's *Complete Works* (1984).

17. For discussions of the impact of associationist psychology on rhetorical theory, see William F. Woods, "Nineteenth-Century Psychology and the Teaching of Writing" (1985), and Sharon Crowley, "Invention in Current-Traditional Rhetoric" (1985).

18. For a full discussion, see "Tithenai ta phainomena" in Owen 1986, 239–251. Both Owen and Martha Nussbaum suggest that the boundary between empirical fact and dialectical material in Aristotelian thought, if it existed at all, was indefinite and permeable. See also Nussbaum 1986, 245–251.

19. Indeed, John Stuart Mill would go as far as to argue that such a science could predict human behavior in the same way the physical sciences predicted natural events. See Mill 1875, Bk. 6, Chap. 2.

20. Kuhn explains the notion of exemplars as "concrete puzzle" solutions in his "Postscript—1969" to *The Structure of Scientific Revolutions*, 2d ed. See especially Kuhn 1970, 175, 187–191.

21. In a footnote Grimaldi does refer to Gorgias' use of *poesis* to describe both *logos* and sculpture. Grimaldi uses the passage to define only rhetoric's relationship to poetics and not productive knowledge: "In many ways it is difficult to see how the rhetorician is not, as far as Aristotle is concerned, as much a maker as the poet. The rhetorician is making something according to certain definite rules for a definite purpose. In both instances language is the medium; the goal is different in that the object of the poet is knowledge directed toward contemplation, that of the rhetorician knowledge directed toward action" (Grimaldi 1972a, 8 n. 8).

22. Grimaldi makes an even more forceful case for the importance of enthymematic form in the conclusion: "The scientific syllogism is ... basically ... an instrument for the acquisition of knowledge which takes apparently separate and independent concepts and puts them into a structure which leads to new knowledge. In the same way the enthymeme gives structure to the sources which contribute to belief or conviction. In both instances the scientific syllogism and the rhetorical syllogism, as structural form, stand apart from their sources. ... The only permanent element in 'syllogism' is its structure as a form of inference. Its apodeictic, dialectical, rhetorical character is determined by its content, or the source material it uses" (Grimaldi 1972a, 137).

23. Of *eikos*, Grimaldi writes: "*Eikos* is so substantially and obviously grounded in the real order that the majority of men accept it as a totally acceptable representation of the truth" (Grimaldi 1972a, 110).

24. Grimaldi cites Lukasiewicz 1951, 20: "All Aristotelian syllogisms are implications of the type "if *alpha* and *beta*, then *gamma*."

25. Grimaldi explains, "As a general guide it can be said that enthymemes developed from *eikota* and *semeia anonyma* represent the kind of reasoning which can be found in Aristotelian dialectics, while those from *tekmeria* present more the character of scientific reasoning as found in the *Analytics*" (Grimaldi 1972a, 106).

26. It should be noted that whatever relationship Grimaldi draws between the *Analytics* and the *Rhetoric*, his conception of "probability" contrasts with the sophistic notion of probability argument. For Sophists, such as Protagoras, the probable marked a distinct epistemological domain; it was not simply the attenuation of certain knowledge.

27. Grimaldi is, of course, largely responsible for articulating definitive distinctions between general and specific topics. His discussion may be found in Grimaldi 1972a, 115–135.

28. Using Roemer's numbering of the *koinoi topoi*, Grimaldi gives the following breakdown: (1) antecedent-consequent, or cause-effect: VII, XI, XIII, XIV, XVII, XIX, XXIII, XXIV; (2) more-less: IV, V, VI, XX, XXV, XXVII; (3) some form of relation: I, II, III, VIII, IX, X, XII, XV, XVI, XVIII, XXI, XXII, XXVI, XXVIII (Grimaldi 1972a, 131).

29. Grimaldi admits that this interpretation of the *koinoi topoi* is more indebted to the *Topics* than to the *Rhetoric*. His specific defense of his use of the *Topics* may be found in Grimaldi 1972a, 134–135.

30. Roberts's translation is found in Barnes's edition of the *Complete Works* (Barnes 1984). George Kennedy (1991, 34) translates the passage as follows: "But rhetoric is useful [first] because the true and the just are by nature stronger than their opposites, so that if judgments are not made in the right way [the true and the just] are necessarily defeated [by their opposites]."

31. It is precisely the social and political power of description in demarcating the so-called given world that is the focus of Bourdieu's critique of the theory/practice opposition. Bourdieu explains: "The instruments of knowledge of the social world are ... political instruments which contribute to the reproduction of the social world by producing immediate adherence to the world, seen as self-evident and undisputed" (Bourdieu 1977, 164). The social and political valence of those descriptions is raised even higher when what is described is our very process of knowing: "The theory of knowledge is a dimension of political theory because the specifically symbolic power to impose the principles of the construction of reality—in particular, social reality—is a major dimension of political power" (165).

6 Violence, Apathy, and
the Rhetoric of Philosophy

PAGE DUBOIS

The philosopher of contemporary academic life seems sometimes to model himself on the philosopher of the Platonic and post-Platonic schools. The level of verbal violence, abuse, and contempt is very high in the rhetoric of philosophical exchange, yet the cultivation of a pose of "apathy," of emotionlessness, or of a commitment to the pure pursuit of truth earns admiration and respect. I once witnessed a colloquium in a university philosophy department. The invited guest was a candidate for an academic position in the department, which numbered among its twenty-five faculty members one woman, untenured. The guest gave a lecture about metaphor, using Hjelmslevian categories. In the question period, the resident faculty member in the field of philosophy of language adduced, as an example of the matter of metaphor being discussed, the word "bitch," a word he pronounced repeatedly with great relish, asking the guest to comment on how the word "bitch" functioned in terms of her categories. It was quite clear to all present how that particular example had come to him, and why he was taking such pleasure in uttering the word "bitch" again and again. But there was no way to incorporate a critique of his aggression and veiled violence into the discussion. The "philosophical" intercourse going on in the room focused only on the logical consequences of the candidate's arguments for the professor's example. And although in other such situations, where a candidate is being grilled by a department's resident faculty, it is difficult to metacommunicate about power and abuse, in this case the frame of the "philosophical," the shared communal sense of the task of philosophy, its codes, seemed to prohibit the importation of such matters into the discussion.

Philosophy departments sport few women; often women indoctrinated into the codes of the discipline police most militantly the boundaries of the field. I think of Ruth Marcus's attack on Derrida and other poetic types she saw as interlopers, lowering the standards of the philosophical community. She acted out a present crisis in the discipline of philosophy, expressed in the outraged protests of the analytic philosophers against deconstruction, in the desire of such as Allan Bloom to justify the elite practices of the study of philosophy, in the dogged work of Alan Badiou, in *Manifeste pour la philosophie*, attempting to show that we are now at a world-historical juncture for the renaissance of his beloved field. The discipline seems in crisis, seeking manfully to resuscitate the queen of the humanities, while the feminization of the humanities proceeds apace.

To be philosophical is to be "wise, calm, temperate, frugal." The compliment addressed to someone, that she or he is "philosophical," occurs in the context of some experience: One is always philosophical "about" something, in the face of something, usually something painful—disease, loss. Alexander Pope, in 1717, in a letter to Lady Mary Wortley Montague, writes: "What with ill-health and ill-fortune, I am grown so stupidly philosophical as to have no thought about me that deserves the name of warm or lively" (*Oxford English Dictionary*, hereinafter *OED*). Pope suffers illness and impoverishment and becomes philosophical, purged of emotion, of the "warm and lively." The everyday language sense of "the philosophical" had its correlates in the philosophical tradition. I am curious about the paradigm of philosophical temperance, first about the way in which Western philosophical thought has often required suffering to precede knowing, and also why the privileged attitude of the philosopher toward experience, after suffering, is emotionlessness, the "apathy" of the ancient post-Platonic philosophical schools, an apathy that in its rhetoric proleptically conceals violence.

"Apathy," the vaunted, surgical emotionlessness of philosophers, serves often, as it did in the scene I described, as a mask for aggression, for violence and anger in intellectual exchange. Anyone who has seen John Searle in action, in person or in print, can testify to the level of rage and aggression permitted the great men in the field of philosophy. What is most interesting to me is not that such emotions should play themselves out in the field, because perhaps their leaking forth in other fields is what is most curious, but rather that philosophy should so often have claimed for itself a position above the emotions, a place in a terrain uncontaminated by feeling. The figural dimension of philosophy, its rhetoric, betrays violence even as it argues against violence. The very production of philosophy as a field was premised on the exclusion of emotion from the practice of logic and "philosophical" dialectic; its differentiation from poetry and tragedy served in part also to produce the category of gender. Philosophers were distinguished, through the discourse of emotionlessness, from slaves and women; women in particular, who were once objects, sites of sexual labor, were reinscribed in the rhetoric of philosophical texts as subjects of emotions, in distinction from the philosophical men who remained tranquil, undisturbed by the storms of feeling rampant in lesser beings, invulnerable to the pains of such existential events as torture.

*   *   *

In ancient Greek, emotion is *pathos*, "anything that befalls one" (Liddell, Scott, and Jones, *Greek Lexicon*, hereinafter LSJ). The use of the word for powerful feeling implicitly attributes external or alienated agency to that feeling; one is set upon by lust and is carried away by the emotion. *Apatheia* is the want of sensation, insensibility, derived from the adjective *a-pathes* without passion or feeling. In pre-Platonic texts the word *apathes* denotes inexperience, a lack of visitation by emotion. In the ancient texts, the root *path-* does not mean suffering in the sense of pain; it denotes only experience, the lived encounter with the events of human existence. The Christian notion of *pathos*, the "passion," contaminates our ideas about this semantic nexus. The Christian description of Jesus' experience at the time of his death overlays the word passion with connotations of bodily anguish and affliction. The subsequent evolution of the word passion alters its meaning, making it almost its own contrary. Passion now means active desire, rather than "passive" experience. Passion comes to mean: "An eager outreaching of the mind towards something; an overmastering zeal or enthusiasm for a special object; a vehement predilection" (*OED*). The meaning has changed from suffering, without the connotation of pain, the visitation and experience of feeling, to the contrary of *passio* or passivity, that is, activity.

The ancient Greek word *apatheia*, like the Greek *aletheia*, "truth," "unhiddenness," is what is called an alpha-privative word, formed through the negation of the positive term for feeling. More than other kinds of contraries, the alpha-privative words preserve the presence of the contrary; it is as if instead of hate, we called the contrary of love un-love. So the Greeks make these words—*a-letheia*, unhiddenness, for truth, *a-topia*, placelessness, for eccentricity, *a-ponia*, nonexertion, for laziness, *a-polis*, a cityless person, for an outlaw. The kind of semantic formations that occur in positive terms in English, or those that have a variety of forms of negation, are in Greek endlessly and alliteratively rendered with this privation, this alpha that both preserves and takes away the sense of the word's meaning.

This argument is beginning to sound quite deconstructive; I want rather to make a Hegelian move here, to argue that the Greeks allow for experience by accounting for *pathos*, as an encounter, almost as possession; then they valorize the mastery of experience, and of those feelings that accompany human experience, by cultivating and celebrating an attitude of *apatheia*, "emotionlessness," an attitude that both recognizes the presence of *pathe*, feelings, and negates them at the same time. It is this condensed, imploded, syncopated, proleptic narrative that becomes the model of the philosophical life. The rhetoric of philosophy, if not its explicit discourse, conveys violence even while decrying it.

Michel Foucault has discussed how the occasions of eating, having sex with boys, being married, offered to the civilized ancient male opportunities for self-mastery (Foucault 1986b). I want to consider here *why* such mastery was deemed necessary for the philosophical life, and how the discourse of emotions was implicated in the project of mastery. Foucault seems to ignore the inevitable consequences for *others* of the master's self-mastery—slaves, boys, and women are mastered and subjected, with violence if necessary, by the philosophical man.

Obviously, Plato's argument about poetry, about the expulsion of the poets from the Republic, about the poet's unhealthy stimulation of tears and emotion at tragic performance, stands at the origin of the philosophical rejection of emotion, a rejection of emotion that is literally, etymologically, a rejection of experience itself. For Plato, the simulated representations of tragedy, poetry, and art are reprehensible because they are representations, but in fact for him all experience, all bodily life, has the quality of reflection, a mundane and faded representation of the pure abstraction of the metaphysical realm of the ideas. The visitation of emotions is a sign of our unfortunate corporeality. Yet the emotions of desire and love, bound as they are to the divine residues of the celestial good in the human realm, can prod men toward the beginning of a philosophical quest.

In Plato these matters are always complicated by the contradictory representation of the arguments against art in the artful form of the dialogue, by Plato's own status as a poet. In a dialogue like the *Sophist*, the figures of speech create a persistent, insistent tug against the logic of the speakers' arguments. Although the ostensible narrative of the dialogue, an encounter with and refutation of the work of Parmenides, takes place in a form that can be reduced by contemporary analytic philosophers into those hideous little algebraic formulas that remind one of Lacan's most obscure Borromean excesses and cause catatonia in most readers, the figural language of the dialogue betrays a current of homicidal violence. The narrative mastery of emotion, of the impulse toward violence, takes place in tension with the figural expansion of emotion, of violence.

The argument proceeds as an attempt to hunt down the Sophist by giving a description of him. Although Socrates does not appear in this dialogue, the "Stranger" serves as *arkhon*, or commander; the Stranger's representation of the process in which he and his interlocutor Theaetetus are engaged resembles an account of the chasing down of a criminal, like the hunt for the murderer of Laios in *Oedipus Rex:* "If ... we meet with the Sophist at bay, we should arrest him on the royal warrant of reason, report the capture, and hand him over to the sovereign. But if he should find some lurking place among the subdivisions of this art of imitation, we must follow hard upon him, constantly dividing the part that gives him shelter, until he is caught" (*Sophist* 235c; Plato 1921). The joke has its sinister side; logic and dialectic are police arts. Philosophy becomes a method of arrest and discipline; philosophical argument is a dividing, a splitting, a fracturing of the logical body, in other words, a process that resembles torture. In the following exchanges, the Stranger uses the state's legal power to torture as a metaphor for the pursuit of true definition. He mentions the argument of Parmenides against the position that "the things that are not, are": "So we have the great man's testimony, and the best way to obtain a confession of the truth may be to put the statement itself to a mild degree of torture (*basanistheis*)" (*Sophist* 237b). The legal language of testimony is pursued in the analogy of the *basanos* "torture"; the *logos*, speech or argument, of Parmenides is itself to be subjected to torture.[1]

The violence of the state, performed against the slave in torture for legal evidence, is transferred to the context of the philosophical conversation. The *elegkhos*, "elenchus," the word most often used to describe the process of philosophical dialectic in Plato's early work, was first of all a "cross-examining, testing, for purposes of disproof or refutation" (LSJ); it too thus has legal connotations. Here the testing, the torture, is to be enacted not against a body but against the disembodied arguments of the absent Parmenides, whose *logos* must be made to yield up truth under philosophical interrogation. In this sense, the conversation between the Stranger and Theaetetus, his companion, itself resembles a scene of torture. And perhaps all these dialogues, these occasions for presumed dialectic, are contaminated by the association with torture.

This dialogue abounds in displaced and misrecognized violence; although the argument pretends to be concerned purely with the logic of Parmenidean ontology, the speakers' language betrays parricidal rage. At one point the Stranger explains that Parmenides and others seem to be treating them as children (*Sophist* 242), telling them a story (*muthon*) about what is. He connects the refutation of "father" Parmenides' argument with parricide (*patraloian*) (241d). By refuting Parmenides' philosophical position, and with that the whole Eleatic tradition, the children rebel and commit a symbolic parricide. Later, conflict between philosophical schools is characterized as a *gigantomachia*, a mythical battle between the gods and giants that also had its parricidal aspects, as an attempt to dethrone Zeus, the upstart sovereign who took over power from his elders. The argument rages between those who attribute reality only to the disembodied and those who maintain that there are only realities with bodies. "But the bodies of their opponents, and that which is called truth (*aletheian*) they break into small fragments in their arguments, calling them, not existence, but a kind of generation combined with motion" (246c). Philosophical work is conflict, represented with this imagery of violence, of the smashing of both truth and bodies into bits.

The torture of arguments seems a displacement of torture of the Sophist; in part this description of the argument with the Sophist, who is never present in this dialogue, serves to represent him as slavish, therefore under Athenian law as liable to torture and as vulnerable to the violence of the philosopher, who dwells in the realms of light. The "Stranger," the figure in the dialogue who takes the position of master of the other participant, Theaetetus, continually refers to the Sophist as prey, and his interlocutor shares his view of their absent opponent. "Certainly, sir, what we said at the outset about the Sophist seems true—that he is a hard sort of beast to hunt down. Evidently he possesses a whole armory of problems (*problematon*), and every time that he puts one forward to shield him, we have to fight our way through it before we can get at him" (*Sophist* 261a). The word *problematon*, used punningly here, means both a "barrier, screen, armor, defence, something put forward as an excuse or screen," and "a proposition or a problem in Geometry" (LSJ). The metaphor is of something thrown forward, projecting. The Sophist defends himself physically and argumentatively with his "problems," his armor. Philosophical debate between Sophists and Platonists is represented as a duel, a battle, with arguments serving as metaphorical shields. But the duel is one-sided. The Sophist is hunted down like an animal and turns on his pursuers when cornered, brandishing his problems as defenses. The imagery comes from war and from the hunt, but if the animal's "armor" is his natural defenses, claws, quills, hide, these are inadequate to the assault of the human weapons of iron and irony.

The *Sophist* presents a bizarre spectacle of violence, parricide, man-hunting, torture, and bondage, all conducted alongside a highly sophisticated debate concerning the Eleatic position rejecting the reality of "what is not." In fact, Plato does commit an act of philosophical parricide here, the attempted destruction of the position of his predecessor Parmenides, betraying a desire to wipe out Parmenides' disciples and his sons, along with him. The text exhibits this desire covertly by metaphorizing the emotion of rage, by presenting figures for violence, by playing on language that allows a double reading, figures that pretend to philosophical objectivity but also recognize and affirm what is at stake in argument, the annihilation of one's opponent in the *agon*. Torture, tracking, execution, here become important figures for philosophical labor.

*   *   *

How do the post-Platonic philosophers develop the attitude toward philosophical labor of their philosophical father? How is their attitude, called *apatheia*, lack of feeling, insensibility, related both to this Platonic phenomenon and to what we now call a "philosophical" attitude?

Although Aristotle, in his *Rhetoric*, categorized the emotions, he did so in order to instruct speakers in how to use the emotions in their orations, to produce conviction. The emotions are the *pathe*, defined by Aristotle as "all those affections which cause men to change their opinion in regard to their judgements, and are accompanied by pleasure and pain" (*Rhetoric* 1378a; Aristotle 1982). Aristotle's view is purely instrumental; the issue is persuasion, and the emotions must be harnessed to serve the effort at persuasion:

> It makes a great difference with regard to producing conviction—especially in demonstrative, and, next to this, in forensic oratory—that the speaker should show himself to be possessed of certain qualities and that his hearers should think that he is disposed in a certain way toward them; and further, that they themselves should be disposed in a certain way toward him. (*Rhetoric* 1377b)

Even here, in the fourth century B.C., the attitude of the philosopher is one of "surgical" detachment and description. The philosopher observes emotion without sharing it and proceeds like Socrates in the Platonic dialogues, like the Stranger in the *Sophist*, to hunt down the emotions, to pursue them relentlessly through division until the quarry is driven to earth. At the conclusion of his catalogue of the emotions, Aristotle says briskly: "The means of producing and destroying the various emotions in men, from which the methods of persuasion that concern them are derived, have now been stated." Emotions are to be evoked and visited upon his auditors as part of the orator's performance. The self-control of the orator and philosopher requires that he survey the field of emotions, assess the value of a particular emotional simulacrum, display it for his audience, produce and destroy it in his audience.

Hellenistic philosophy develops the tendencies already implicit in Platonic and Aristotelian thinking about the emotions. The social context of Hellenistic philosophy is not the democratic city of Athens. Rather, in the diaspora following Alexander the Great's conquest of mainland Greece, philosophy was dispersed and disseminated, detached from the struggles of the *polis*. The nomadic philosophers came to Athens, but it had been transformed from an independent city-state to a unit within one of the huge empires of the post-Alexandrian Mediterranean. Many of the philosophers teaching in Athens came from the East, from parts of the world only recently Hellenized by Alexander. And the great city that he founded, Alexandria, became a rival center of philosophical and intellectual life. Hegel, to cite a supposedly discredited "totalitarian" thinker, says that the Stoic cultivation of invulnerability was a response to an unsettled and threatening political world. Michel Foucault repudiates this explanation, seeming to attribute the development of postclassical emotionlessness to some autonomous, inevitable, irreversible internalization of domination (Foucault 1986b, 41–43).

Remaining a Hegelian to this extent, I still believe that the failure of ancient democracy, the collapse of the citizen's role as political subject, established the conditions for a new ideology of subjectivity. In the postdemocratic age, when participation in political life became senseless, the masculine psyche offered itself as the only terrain for the exercise of power. Emperors and foreign powers ruled the state; the individual controlled only the domain of his own subjectivity and the bodies of his women and slaves. The Hellenistic schools all emphasize "passionlessness" as the ideal state of the philosopher. The skeptic Aristocles says: "Neither our sensations nor our opinions tell us truths or falsehoods. Therefore for this reason we should not put our trust in them one bit. ... The outcome for those who actually adopt this attitude, says Timon, will be first speechlessness, and then freedom from disturbance" (Eusebius 14.18.1–5; Long and Sedley 1987, 5).

Diogenes Laertius says that Anaxarchus "was called the 'happiness man'" because of the "impassivity and contentment of his life" (9.60). Thinkers who follow the philosopher Pyrrho praise him for his indifference to sensation. Cicero says in the *Academica*, "Pyrrho ... held that the wise man is not even aware of (the intermediates between virtue and its contrary), (a state) which is called 'impassivity'" (*Academica* 2.130; Long and Sedley 1987, 19). Athenaeus says, "Timon quite splendidly said, 'Desire is absolutely the first of all bad things'" (*Athenaeus* 337A; Long and Sedley 1987, 20). The achievement of an unshakable equilibrium was seen as the most desirable accomplishment for the philosopher; anything that disrupted his tranquility, his freedom from disturbance, his impassivity, was to be shunned.

Epicurus seems to follow Pyrrho in wanting only freedom from disturbance (*ataraxia*), identifying the empty desires originating in empty opinion as dangers to tranquility:

> This is what we aim at in all our action—to be free from pain and anxiety.
>
> ... what produces the pleasant life is not continuous drinking and parties or pederasty or womanizing or the enjoyment of fish and other dishes of an expensive table, but sober reasoning which tracks down the causes of every choice and avoidance, and which banishes the opinions that beset souls with the greatest confusion. (*Letter to Menoeceus*, 127–132; Long and Sedley 1987, 114)

Reason is set against desire; it alone will produce a harmonious, untroubled soul. The Stoic Seneca says: "What is a happy life? Peacefulness and constant tranquility" (*Letters* 92.3; Long and Sedley 1987, 396). The freedom from emotion recurs as a constant in the works of these post-Platonic thinkers. Apathy is preferable even to pleasure because pleasure can become habitual and cause pain when it is absent. The superior life is one of control and renunciation.

Magical papyri from Greek and Roman Egypt, popular texts contemporary with the philosophical works I have cited, reveal cultural preoccupations similar to those of the Hellenistic philosophers. Many of the magical procedures concern anger (although my favorite is an incantation "to make men who have been drinking at a symposium appear to have donkey snouts to outsiders, from afar" [Betz 1986, 151]. Another guarantees to make a woman mad for a man, by prescribing anointment of the phallus with weasel's dung before intercourse). But many of them are "charms to restrain anger"; for example: "Enter the presence of a king or magnate, and while you have your hands inside your garment say the name of the sun disk while tying a knot in your pallium (a philosopher's cloak) or shawl. You will marvel at the results" (Betz 1986, 179). Another charm reads:

> To make a woman mad after a man: You should bring a live shrew-mouse, remove its gall and put it in one place; and remove its heart and put it in another place. You should take its whole body. You should pound it very much while it is dry; you should take a little of what is pounded with a little blood of your second finger and the little finger of your left hand; you should put it in a cup of wine; and you should make the woman drink it. She is mad after you. (Betz 1986, 250)

The emotions of others can be manipulated through the violence enacted against the mouse. The magician will be able, through the use of his charms, to inflict desire, madness, or death on others, to prevent his own expression of anger toward the king or magnate, to protect himself from the great one's anger. Armed with magic if necessary, using violence against sacrificial animals, the Alexandrian must finally, like the philosopher, be able to control his emotions and therefore to control the emotion of others directed against him.

How are social relations figured around the paradigm of the apathetic philosopher? The division of humankind into two orders of beings is in part reinscribed in these centuries through the discourse of the emotions. In the pre-Platonic world women and slaves are the nonhuman, the barely human, sites of production, reproduction, and erotic labor for male citizens. Even the great heroines of Athenian tragedy stand as characters from the distant past, given embodiment on the stage by young male actors. The production of gender as a category dividing human beings into two kinds occurs through a new mapping of subjectivity; subjectivity is given form through a division of consciousness into emotions and reason. Women are objects, receptacles, until they are granted the limited subjectivity of the emotional, as containers of pure emotion without reason.

In the Platonic *Timaeus*, the speaker describes the place of emotions and desires in the body:

> [The creator's offspring] received from him the immortal principle of the soul, and around this they proceeded to fashion a mortal body, and made it to be the vehicle of the soul and constructed within the body a soul of another nature which was mortal, subject to terrible and irresistible affections—first of all, pleasure, the greatest incitement to evil; then, pain, which deters from good; also rashness and fear, two foolish counselors, anger hard to be appeased, and hope easily led astray—these they mingled with irrational sense and with all-daring love according to necessary laws, and so framed man. (*Timaeus* 69c–d)

The mention of hope "easily led astray" recalls the myth of Pandora, the first woman, a machine, an android who opens a jar full of pestilence, which is then visited upon innocent men. All the emotions catalogued by Plato here are represented as destructive and negative forces within a mortal, inferior soul; what is most intriguing is that they are subsequently, in this account, associated with the female:

> Fearing to pollute the divine any more than was absolutely unavoidable, they gave to the mortal nature a separate habitation in another part of the body ... in the breast ... they incased the mortal soul, and as the one part of this was superior and the other inferior they divided the cavity of the thorax into two parts, as the women's and men's apartments are divided in houses, and placed the midriff to be a wall or partition between them. (*Timaeus* 69d–70a)

The head, the site of the immortal soul, of a passionless, emotionless reason, must be protected from this swamp of feeling, the worst of which is analogized to the women's part of the house, by the "isthmus" of the neck.

In other contexts Plato describes the situation of being overcome by emotion as a state of enslavement. Desire, for example, weakens and degrades the lover, unless it is sublimated to philosophical contemplation. The philosopher must be differentiated from both women and slaves; the discourse of passionlessness, the narrative of experience and its overcoming, serves to produce the identity of the philosopher, who remains distinct by virtue of his mastery over womanly and slavish feeling and emotion. The contrast is pointed strongly in Plato's discussion of the expulsion of the poets from the *Republic*:

> The very best of us, when we hear Homer or some other of the makers of tragedy imitating one of the heroes who is in grief, and is delivering a long tirade in his lamentations ... feel pleasure and abandon ourselves. ... But when in our own lives some affliction comes to us, you are also aware that we plumb ourselves upon the opposite, in the belief that this is the conduct of a man, and what we were praising in the theater that of a woman.
>   ... after feeding fat the emotion of pity there, it is not easy to restrain it in our own sufferings. (*Republic* 10: 605c–606b)

Women abandon themselves to feeling, to the pleasures of feeling, while men properly control such impulses, and must reject the presence of theatrical representations among them, since such representations train them in the expression of emotion. "In regard to the emotions of sex and anger, and all the appetites and pains and pleasures of the soul which we say accompany all our actions, the effect of poetic imitation is the same. For it waters and fosters these feelings when what we ought to do is dry them up, and it establishes them as our rules when they ought to be ruled" (*Republic* 10: 606d). Poetry feeds and waters the emotions, which are the animal, slavish, feminine parts of the human being; the immortal, rational soul needs no nourishment of this sort but flourishes through deprivation and sacrifice. The lovers of the *Phaedrus* find a higher happiness in renunciation and asceticism than in indulgence in desire. The true philosopher is etherealized out of the gross matter of human existence.

Simmias says in the *Phaedo* that most people think that philosophers are "half dead already" (*Phaedo* 64b). In the meditation on death in this dialogue, Socrates explains why the philosopher shuns emotion:

> The soul of the true philosopher ... abstains as far as possible from pleasures and desires and griefs. ...
>
> ... every pleasure or pain has a sort of rivet with which it fastens the soul to the body and pins it down and makes it corporeal, accepting as true whatever the body certifies. The result of agreeing with the body and finding pleasure in the same things is, I imagine, that it cannot help becoming like it in character and training, so that it can never get entirely away to the unseen world, but is always saturated with the body when it sets out, and so soon falls back again into another body, where it takes root and grows. Consequently it is excluded from all fellowship with the pure and uniform and divine. (*Phaedo* 83b–e)

The body is the site of female and slave existence, a ponderous burden that inhibits and restricts the access of the aspiring philosopher to the other realm he yearns for. Emotion is dangerous and contrary to the project of the philosophical life. The extremes of emotion represented metaphorically in a dialogue like the *Sophist*, given an aetiology in the *Timaeus*, are theorized in the *Phaedrus*, where the violence of desire is depicted as leading to its own sublimation in the ecstasy of philosophical revelation. The myth of the charioteer allegorizes the soul of the philosopher, reason being the driver, the horse his desires and appetites. Reason must tame the force of the lustful horse. The curbing of desire will work eventually to allow the soul, which grows wings, to approach the greatest good: "The driver, with resentment even stronger than before, like a racer recoiling from the starting rope, jerks back the bit in the mouth of the wanton horse with an even stronger pull, bespatters his railing tongue and his jaws with blood, and forcing him down on legs and haunches delivers him over to anguish. And so it happens time and again, until the evil steed casts off his wantonness" (*Phaedrus* 254e; Hamilton and Cairns 1961).

This is a move repeated again and again in the philosophical tradition—the expression of desire and of the necessity for its control, violence used in its suppression, and then the claim that emotion has been eliminated from the scene, even though the agent of control has used rage and violence against the supposedly emotional delinquent. Here again we see the pattern of the refusal of emotion in the name of some higher goal, but it is emotion itself that fuels that refusal. Anger and violence in the charioteer of the *Phaedrus* dominate and finally tame the lustful, emotional steed that tries to subvert and destroy the tranquility of the philosophical soul; desire for the "pure and uniform and divine" curbs corporeal desire. Throughout the discourse of ancient philosophy concerning the emotions, *apatheia*, apathy, emotionlessness, is celebrated, but the philosophers cannot but use the language of desire, anger, and violence to describe their rejection of desire, anger, and violence.

Jean-François Lyotard points out that adherents of rival philosophical schools insisted on their own corporeality, farting, masturbating publicly. When the logical impossibility of motion was proven to Diogenes, he got up and walked away (Lyotard 1976, 4–12). But Epicurus is cited many times saying that the invulnerable, impassive, imperturbable wise man, the philosopher, that wise man free from emotions, independent of the world, will suffer pain with indifference. Diogenes Laertius says Epicurus claimed that "even if the wise man is tortured on the rack, he is happy" (10.118; Inwood and Gerson 1988, 34). *Theoria* is the separation of mind from body, the yearning to be invulnerable. This fantasy of philosophical invulnerability may finally be what allows for torture; the body is "other," "others" have bodies. The "others" suffer under torture, but the philosopher can imagine a perfect state of theory, of reason, of apathy, in which he would be happy on the rack.

In a symposium recalled in a volume entitled *Torture and Philosophy*, in many ways an admirable attempt to bring philosophy to bear on a crucial social and political problem, a philosopher recounts with relish a little narrative he concocts, a so-called hypothetical: "Suppose that torturer T is seeking to break the will of victim V by pretending to burn with cigarette butts, rape with trained animals, etc., V's daughter when in fact V's daughter is not in custody but securely out of T's clutches, enjoying herself at a party, ignorant of what is being done to V" (Paskins 1978, 174). (This little narrative suggests that, in the philosopher's attenuated yet baroque imagination, it is not only the case that women are physically tortured, if only in the imagination, but also that *they* get to go to parties.)

In this present moment of revived Alexandrianism, when democracy seems to have been rewritten as the freedom to choose at the Seven-Eleven, when the cultivation of the private realm replaces political action, or when we abandon ourselves to the empire of global postmodernism, philosophers and academics of the First World fantasize philosophically about torture. The heirs of Plato, of the philosophical tradition of apathy and invulnerability, persist in their belief in the possibility and desirability of detachment. They can reason about, authorize, even perhaps engage in the metaphorical or literal torture of others because, for them, being resides elsewhere, in a realm inaccessible to emotion.

There is, to be sure, a counternarrative, another story to be told about the rhetoric of violence and apathy. There is a cultural logic, especially before the fourth century B.C. in Greece, and there are rhetorical practices that sustained and acted out such a logic. I have argued elsewhere, for example, that before Plato cultural logic considered gender in terms of difference, that is, according to an A/B logic, in which women were seen as differing from men rather than as being defective men. Metaphors were used by men to describe women's nature; they were seen in analogy to the earth, to vases, to temples, to ovens, to writing tablets. I argued that, with Platonic metaphysics, these analogical figures for women's reproductive powers were appropriated for philosophical discourse, as the philosopher's mind was seen as the site of true reproduction, of fertile intellectual intercourse among men and of the birth of ideas. Thus the metaphorical description of women no longer served the cultural project of sexual discrimination, and, I argued, women began to be seen not as other but as deficient, as to be defined through a metonymic logic. That is, rather than defined through a network of metaphors, women were figured as related to men through their deficiency, as like men, but lesser, as related through contiguity, or metonymically, as the part for their whole. Aristotle says that women are defective men, lacking the essential ingredient of soul. This metonymic description of the woman in relation to the philosopher, and to men in general, defines their place in the metaphysical trajectory of Western philosophy until the Nietzschean turmoil of the nineteenth and twentieth centuries and is reinscribed, I argue, in the work of Lacan, who sees women's bodies as defined by lack (duBois 1988).

The crucial identification of women with lack and insufficiency occurs as the rhetoric of philosophy adopts the language of violence and its concomitant apathy. Posed against rhetorical torture and the scourging of the opponent in philosophical combat lie the practices of the Sophists and the procedures of the radical democracy of fifth-century Athens. Ancient democracy must, of course, be mapped as an absence. We have only hostile, aristocratic representations of it, from thinkers like Plato, appalled by mob rule, resolutely opposed to sophistic teachings; we have only the most pitiful shreds of the words of the Sophists. The *demos*, the people themselves, have no voice in history; they exist only as figured by these others. The democracy is a present absence, something difficult to capture, since our vision of it is presented by the countertradition, the antidemocrats, the anti-Sophists. But democracy was meant to be rule by the people, an ongoing process of dialogue and debate in the city's assembly. Although aristocrats often ruled the ancient city through powers of eloquence and traditional authority, although slaves, women, and foreigners were excluded from the democratic process, although corruption and bribery often tainted the process and its forms of dialectic, there is nonetheless something extraordinary in the practices of the Sophists and in the Athenian assembly. Their history is one of particularity, of rooted historicity and limited, nontheoretical, absolute temporality.

The logic of democracy, of free debate and what might now be called communicative reason, of equality and equal power among members of a community, *can* give rise to an ever-expanding definition of community. The idea of equality has its own dynamic, a pressure toward the consideration of all in view as entitled to participate in rule by the people. The reforms in ancient Athens of Solon and Kleisthenes, of Ephialtes and Perikles, included economic measures as well as increased citizen participation in political decisions. Such practices as payment for jury duty, for attendance at dramatic festivals, for architectural and military projects that benefited citizen workers, all these had the effect of increasing economic justice, of reducing the inequities of wealth among citizens, of pressing further the inherent and unrealized potential in the logic of democracy. For some ancient thinkers, even slavery itself was eventually called into question: Alcidamas, a rhetorician, argued, "The god left all men free; nature made no one a slave." Such a logic draws such Sophists as Antiphon to recognize the shared nature of all human beings, slave and free alike, and brings the tragedian Euripides to a critique of gender relations in his tragedies on women.

The social practice of rhetoric is born from the resistance of the Sophists to tyranny and comes to serve the citizens of Athenian democracy. Feminists today can use rhetoric as a technique of persuasion, as a science for analyzing the mystificatory language that surrounds us, and as an example for democratic social practices, language that resists tyranny, that remains self-conscious about its own coercive power, that works toward extending social and economic justice, even to members of philosophy departments. It may be this last aspect of rhetoric, its ludic and social dimensions, that offers most, as we recognize differences of class, ethnicity, race, sexual choice, as well as gender. Such a rhetoric participates in a logic of difference, perspectivism, relativism, historicity, temporality, multiplicity, a logic not of coercion and interrogation but of democratic production and exchange of different truths.

Notes

1. For further discussion of this dialogue, and of torture in ancient Greece, see duBois 1991. The praiseworthy replacement of actual torture by rhetorical torture is figured in this dialogue, but unfortunately torture itself has not to this day vanished from the earth. See, for example, Peters 1985 and the numerous volumes on human rights abuses throughout the world published by Amnesty International.

7 Revisionary History: The Dialectical Method

JAMES A. BERLIN

The inaugural call for revisionary histories of rhetoric can be located in Douglas Ehninger's "On Systems of Rhetoric," first published in 1968. Here Ehninger protested the impulse to see "the classical rhetoric as a preferred archetype from which all departures are greater or lesser aberrations" (Ehninger 1968, 140). Historical investigations must seek out multiple and disparate rhetorics, rather than any single, universal, and timeless formulation. The guiding principle in analyzing a rhetoric should be a concern for the role it fulfilled for its users at its own historical time and place. This does not mean that rhetorics never share certain properties. All, Ehninger explained, are focused on the communication process, and it is the attention to this process that makes each a rhetoric and not some other sort of system. Thus, despite the historical variability of rhetorics, it is possible to group certain of them together in terms of the systemic principles that they demonstrate, and these common principles are, once again, historical in nature, that is, they appear during certain chronological moments.

In his essay, Ehninger exemplifies this point by a discussion of three periods: the classical, with its concern for the grammar of the speech act; the eighteenth century, with its development of psychological dimensions of the message-mind relation; and the contemporary (after 1930), with its focus on the social and the effects of language in human communication. Rhetorics then arise out of the contingencies of "need and environment" (Ehninger 1968, 141) and so display marked differences over time. It is also the case, however, that the rhetorics of certain historical periods in responding to their common environment tend to share systemic features. As Robert L. Scott indicates in his generally approbative contribution to Ehninger's effort, the objective of this scheme is to give "some sort of unity to the diversity" (Scott 1975, 439).

Ehninger's call for revisionary histories is today itself in need of revision. Given the passage of more than twenty-four years since its appearance, Ehninger's conception of historical variability would itself suggest such a move. After all, this period has witnessed the formidable challenge to modernist rhetorics posed by poststructuralist formulations. In addition, his closing plea for "a possible metasystem of rhetorics" (Ehninger 1968, 143) introduces an irreconcilable contradiction. Rhetorics are finally as "evolutionary" as they are "revolutionary," Ehninger asserts, so that "through the ages, and despite occasional setbacks, rhetorics have constantly become both richer in content and more embracing in scope" (143). His insistence on plurality is undercut by a quest for historical unity in an unabashed narrative of teleological progress. The security of the permanent brilliance of classical rhetoric is exchanged for the cumulative superiority of contemporary formulations.

Scott does not fall into this trap; however, it should also be noted that neither he nor Ehninger discusses the specificities of the contextual construction of rhetorics, particularly in their relation to power and politics. Both remain on the plane of intellectual history, situating rhetorics within a realm of ideas rather than material and social practices. Finally, neither takes into account the role of signification, of language, in the formation of both historical conditions and rhetorical constructs despite their general acknowledgment of its important role in contemporary rhetorics.

Although these proposals were limited, both served as a rich beginning for revising the work of historiography in rhetoric. I would here like to rethink the historiographic suggestions of Ehninger and Scott by reading their call for pluralistic, chronologically constructed rhetorics across recent structuralist and poststructuralist contributions. I wish also to address their reluctance to explore the specific elements of the contextual environment they name as conditioning the formation of rhetorics, examining in particular the economic, social, and political consequences for rhetorics that historians must consider. Finally, I plan to investigate the rhetorical nature of the historical construction, arguing that this work is as historically dependent as the objects of its study.

My strategy will be fairly straightforward. In the first section of this chapter, I will call upon the critique of traditional historiography offered by Michel Foucault; I shall do so with a view to appraising the value of recent histories of rhetoric. Here I will examine both the backward glance of the avowed classicist and the forward view of the progressive position. Both, I argue, remove rhetoric from the concrete conditions of their constructions. I will next consider the economic, social, and political consequences of this critique, arguing that Foucault fails to provide any viable practice for effective historical intervention. The work of recent Marxists will here be invoked, particularly that of Louis Althusser and Goran Therborn. The central role of rhetoric in the dialectical interaction of agents and the conditions of their experience will be explored. Finally, I will call on Theodor Adorno's conception of the negative dialectic in considering the historical limits of all historical accounts. My overall purpose finally is to provide a model for writing history in a poststructuralist milieu.

Previous Histories

Foucault's historical work is especially instructive when one considers the history of rhetoric. It is Foucault more than anyone other than Marx and his commentators who insists on the inherently rhetorical character of all experience. The study of the human sciences for Foucault is the study of discourse, of the ways in which language—discursive formations—form subjects and the material and social conditions of their experience. Knowledge is a social and historical fabrication that is inscribed in our daily practices, practices that are both discursive and nondiscursive. For Foucault, however, the discursive practices are in a certain sense primary, forming rather than reflecting the nondiscursive. Knowledge is thus inevitably allied with power, the enforcement of one set of discursive and nondiscursive practices over all others. Power and knowledge are indistinguishable, the two ineluctably joined in the performance of quotidian activities. In addition to conceiving of all knowledge as rhetorical—as persuasive as well as coercive through physical and nonphysical devices—Foucault specifically addresses the points at which historical writing is itself imbricated in power-knowledge constructions. Here he is concerned with the way the creation of historical accounts has itself been a part of the endless play for power that is involved in all language use, even though, it should be added, the individual historian may not consciously pursue power. It is this discussion of historical writing as presented in "Nietzsche, Genealogy, History" (Foucault 1977, 139–164) that I will call upon in the first part of this chapter.

Historians of rhetoric have until just recently undertaken a search for the common origin of all rhetorical systems, attempting to locate this origin in a realm of essence beyond accident and appearance.[1] Their assumption has been that there are moments of time in which the essential features of the one true rhetoric can be directly observed. For the classicist, this moment is in the past, in the rhetoric of ancient Greece or Rome, the origin resting, in Foucault's terms, "at a place of inevitable loss, the point where the truth of things corresponded to a truthful discourse, the site of a fleeting articulation that discourse has obscured and finally lost" (Foucault 1977, 143). For the modern, however, the essence of rhetoric is to be found in the here and now, at the end of a long succession of historical progress: "Behind the always recent, avaricious, and measured truth it posits the ancient proliferation of errors" (143). Thus, the classicists—Kennedy and Corbett, for example—refer us to the distant past for the fulfillment of rhetoric, seeing more recent manifestations as fragmentary echoes of this past. The moderns—John Michael Wozniak, Knoblauch and Brannon, Howell—see rhetoric as arriving at its fulfillment in the present, with the past providing the stages of trial that inevitably prepared for it.

Behind both kinds of history is the concept of descent, of a ruling temporal development. For the classicist we are at last ready to restore the golden age of the past, and the influence of this position can be seen in the Connors, Ede, and Lunsford introduction to their *Essays on Classical Rhetoric and Modern Discourse* (1984). For the moderns, we are finally arriving at the new golden age, overthrowing the errors of the past even as we grow organically out of it, an impulse most vividly expressed in Knoblauch and Brannon. For both positions, the purpose of the historian of rhetoric is "to go back in time to restore an unbroken continuity that operates beyond the dispersion of forgotten things; its duty is ... to demonstrate that the past actively exists in the present, that it continues secretly to animate the present, having imposed a predetermined form to all vicissitudes" (Foucault 1977, 146). The historian's task is to record "objectively" this unfolding, confident that there are always order, plan, and design in history, and that the historian is the best suited to discover them. Excluded are "accidents, the minute deviations—or conversely, the complete reversals—the errors, the false appraisals and the faulty calculations that give birth to those things that continue to exist and have value for us" (146). The chaos of the historical record is only appearance beneath which is a unifying origin and presence.

The story of the unfolding of the design of history is, furthermore, the story of great individuals, heroic rhetoricians with the courage and wisdom to change the way people of the past have deliberated and represented their experience—an interpretive strategy found in all of the historians earlier mentioned as well as in the work of Donald Stewart and Sharon Crowley. The emergence of new rhetorics is attributable to the

greatness of individuals and the irresistible wisdom of their recommendations. That certain rhetorics become dominant as a result of a play of
forces—of dominations, to use Foucault's term—rather than through the
efforts of individual subjects and that these subjects themselves represent
the working out of these forces are unthinkable. Always there is some one
individual responsible for the rhetorical doctrines that finally prevail. The
economic, social, political, and cultural conditions of a time are unimportant, providing a mere staging area for the great rhetorician to exploit.
Thus, it is the details of these rhetorics we must lovingly undress and ca-
ress, representing as they do the emanations of their great creators. The
material conditions of the creator count for nothing at all. Rhetorical history is the story of these disembodied ideas freely floating in an intellectual
ether.

Our histories of rhetoric have thus sought the great actors and the great
actions: "the noblest periods, the highest forms, the most abstract ideas,
the purest individualities" (Foucault 1977, 155). Central to this transcendent glance is the denial of the historian's own role in shaping the events
presented. We have refused to acknowledge our "systems of injustice," the
perspectival nature of knowledge, the role of the historian in creating as
much as discovering historical meaning. The historical account insists on
seeing everything without difference: "Nothing must escape it and, more
importantly, nothing must be excluded" (157). Our historians have
claimed objectivity, effacing themselves so that others may speak, adopting
"the fiction of a universal geometry, to mimic death in order to enter the
kingdom of the dead, to adopt a faceless anonymity" (158). Behind this
deference is concealed a "belief in Providence, in final causes and teleology" (158), the historian speaking for the eternal force, the ascetic humility
concealing the alliance with the power of powers—the force behind all
forces.

In sum, our present histories of rhetoric assume a neutral space outside
of time from which the objective historian can record a completed history,
a history in which all conflict can be resolved. The historian finds eternal
rhetorics, immortal rhetoricians, and a universal human nature in all times
and places the same. This history demands the permanent, the constant,
the universal—the search for "destiny or regulative mechanism" rather
than "haphazard conflict" (Foucault 1977, 154). Only the systematic and
stable can sponsor change, as history must always "confirm our belief that
the present rests upon profound intentions and immutable necessities"
(155).

The New Histories

There is more in Foucault that might be invoked in analyzing the inadequacies of our histories of rhetoric. But these additional admonitions and recommendations are, like much of the preceding, inextricably joined with the ideological stance of Foucault himself, a stance that he readily admits (even while, as Eagleton points out, he ignores ideology). The flaw in his position is that it also contains contradictory antirhetorical elements. For Foucault the particular power-knowledge relationship that marks a given historical period forms an all-but-seamless web of constraints, enclosing all acts in an invisible and inescapable net. All realities are constructed by these power-knowledge relations and there is virtually no evading them. Change within these formations, furthermore, is not only unpredictable but also cannot be accounted for. It is finally the result of an irrational eruption. This is why Foucault emphasizes the necessity of history assuming "the form of a concerted carnival" (Foucault 1977, 161), a celebration of diversity and deviance, the joy of the unexpected and comic.

Resistance is, to be sure, inevitable and is to be encouraged, even though it may end only in serving the forces resisted. Hubert L. Dreyfus and Paul Rabinow point out the central failure of Foucault's notion of resistance, explaining that it provides no standards on which resistance can be based:

> Genealogy undermines a stance which opposes it on the grounds of natural law or human dignity, both of which presuppose the assumptions of traditional philosophy. Genealogy also undermines opposing carceral society on the basis of subjective preferences and intuitions (or posing certain groups as carriers of human values capable of opposing carceral society). What are the resources which enable us to sustain a critical stance? (Dreyfus and Rabinow 1983, 206)

Dreyfus and Rabinow go on to address in detail the problematic place of rhetoric in Foucault's scheme:

> How is the resistance to bio-power to be strengthened? Dialectical arguments which appeal to the correct theoretical understanding of human beings and society are hardly sufficient to move large numbers of people and, following Foucault's analysis, are part of the current problem. Clearly, the rhetorical dimension is crucial here. Granted that the Platonic conception of truth is "our largest lie," must we be reduced to a Platonic conception of rhetorical and pragmatic discourse as mere ma-

nipulation? Or is there an art of interpretation which draws on other resources and opens up the possibility of using discourse to oppose domination? (Dreyfus and Rabinow 1983, 207)

Finally, Dreyfus and Rabinow ask whether there is a way to positively resist society and move toward a "new economy of bodies and pleasures" (Foucault, as quoted in Dreyfus and Rabinow 1983, 207).

It is contemporary Marxism that offers the best response to Foucault's brilliant analysis of historiography, both profiting from his critique and offering an alternative to its determinism. Here is found the Foucaultian description of power-knowledge formations placed within a Marxian framework, most notably the suggestions from Foucault on the ways in which discursive practices—rhetoric—reproduce these relationships. The Marxian problematic has always addressed the question of power, although admittedly in terms of nondiscursive material determinants and class conflict rather than as a function of discursive formations. The recent work of a number of Marxists in a variety of disciplines has begun, however, to examine the role of discourse in social formations: in literary studies, Raymond Williams, Terry Eagleton, and Catherine Belsey; in philosophy, the work of the Frankfurt school (preceding Foucault yet anticipating some of his most salient observations), of Louis Althusser, and of Alex Callinicos; and in sociology, the work of Goran Therborn, who offers an application of the thought of Althusser and Foucault. I realize that taken together these figures offer more contradictions than harmonies. They agree, however, in placing discourse—rhetoric—at the center of the reproduction of economic, social, and political activities. In offering recommendations for new histories of rhetoric, I will be calling on features of these Marxian analyses, especially on those of Althusser and Therborn, although I intend to make a statement that cannot be strictly attributable to any one of them.

The new histories of rhetoric must begin to view the formal statements of this discipline as a study that is at the center of social activity. Between the realms of the material and social, on the one hand, and the political and cultural, on the other, is situated the mediation of discourse, of rhetoric broadly conceived. It is no surprise that rhetoric has historically served as the center of education in Western societies. The ability to read, write, and speak in accordance with the code sanctioned by a culture's ruling class is the main work of education, and this is true whether we are considering ancient Athens or contemporary Detroit. These rules are of course inscribed in a rhetoric, systematically designating who can speak, when and where they can speak, and how they can and must speak. Educational institutions inculcate these rules, determining who is fit to learn them and who has finally done so, in this way authorizing who will be heard.

A rhetoric codifies these rules for the members of a society. It is therefore never simply a set of disembodied principles that state the way language is used for purposes of persuasion or communication. It is a set of strictures regarding the way language is to be used in the service of power. It designates who may have access to power and who may not, and it does so in a way even more effective than legal sanctions with all their punitive devices. To use Althusser's term, a rhetoric serves as an important ideological state apparatus. It affirms economic, social, political, and cultural arrangements, doing so in the name of passing on to the young the "natural" rules that govern discursive and, equally important, nondiscursive practices. A society rarely, if ever, of course, sees its rules regarding discourse as a social construction designed to serve a particular set of power arrangements, offering these rules instead as normal, inevitable, "in the nature of things."

I have said that rhetoric is an important ideological apparatus in the schools. In defining ideology and its functioning I will be relying on Therborn's formulation: "The operation of ideology in human life basically involves the constitution and patterning of how human beings live their lives as conscious, reflecting initiators of acts in a structured, meaningful world. Ideology operates as discourse, addressing or, as Althusser puts it, interpellating human beings as subjects" (Therborn 1980, 15). Ideology addresses, interprets, and defines subjects in three important ways, prescribing for them what exists, what is good, and what is possible. Therborn explains:

1. *what exists*, and its corollary, what does not exist: that is, who we are, what the world is, what nature, society, men and women are like. In this way we acquire a sense of identity, becoming conscious of what is real and true; the visibility of the world is thereby structured by the distribution of spotlights, shadows, and darkness.

2. *what is good*, right, just, beautiful, attractive, enjoyable, and its opposites. In this way our desires become structured and normalized.

3. *what is possible* and impossible; our sense of the mutability of our being-in-the-world and the consequences of change are hereby patterned, and our hopes, ambitions, and fears given shape. (Therborn 1980, 18)

From this perspective, ideologies are not prima facie mystifications, necessarily false and mistaken, but are instead inevitable formulations of social classes and groups. Their accuracy in describing the actual conditions of the subjects of these groups must then be judged only after the fact: Some ideological representations are preferable to others in addressing the material and social conditions of a particular historical moment.

It is not difficult to see the place of rhetoric in the interpellation of subjects. A given rhetoric, after all, defines the nature of the model speaker (Plato's philosopher, Quintilian's good man speaking, Emerson's democratic dialectician), the nature of the audience (Aristotle's untrained thinkers, Emerson's everyperson), the nature of the real (Aristotle's rational universe, Campbell's sense data), and the nature of language (Gorgias' constructionist conception, Plato's metaphoric formulation). Rhetoric thus explicitly reinforces the subject's notion of what exists, what is good, and what is possible, and does so, as mentioned earlier, through indicating who may engage in discourse, to whom discourse is to be addressed, and what may be the permissible contents of the message.

An example or two at this point will bring home my point. The case of Plato seems fairly obvious (although not enough to dispel disagreement altogether, as seen, for example, in the contrary interpretations of Donald Stewart and Lawrence Rosenfield). Plato recommends a society rigidly stratified into three classes, with the ruling class of philosopher-kings being the only group authorized to speak with conviction and certainty. Aristotle, in contrast, appears to endorse democracy in his conception of the rhetorical situation. He was, to be sure, writing a rhetoric for the heralded democratic Greek city-state of Athens. An examination of the social conditions during Aristotle's life reveals, however, that they formed a state that bears little resemblance to any modern notion of democracy. During this period, for example, the Athenian population consisted of 50,000 citizens and 100,000 slaves (Barker 1959, 463). It was also a time of great class warfare involving the old landed aristocracy, the new rich mercantile class, the peasant farmers, the hoplite warrior class, and the *thetes*, the group of propertyless wage laborers.

Aristotle's rhetoric must be read within the context of this historical moment, and one must realize that his system is inscribed with an ideology representing his position within this social network. His ethical appeal, for example, is based on notions of prudence, virtue, and goodwill reflective of the interests of the ruling social class in fourth-century Athens. The speaker must display these virtues so as not to be confused with the ex-

cluded other, the members of unauthorized classes. Aristotle's preference
for the rational and deductive is similarly intended to restrict the possibilities of encouraging a form of consciousness that would be counter to the
social order he is recommending. In this case, what exists, what is good,
and what is possible are all circumscribed by an intractable deductive logic
based on first principles that are regarded as beyond interrogation. Finally,
Aristotle's conception of the audience also reflects the sense of class division, offering a description of the emotional appeal that disparages the capacities of the lower ranks in a democratic gathering, while valorizing the
rational powers of the "trained thinkers" whose status has afforded them a
formal education.

To say this is not to diminish the importance of Aristotle's rhetoric in
the history of human affairs or the richness of its recommendations. It is,
however, to acknowledge that a rhetoric is a product of a particular historical moment, and that its historical significance can only be seen in considering it within the economic, social, and political context in which it appears, whether that context is ancient or medieval or modern. Attempts to
celebrate its universal value are, furthermore, suspect because, as I have
said, inscribed within it is the enforcement of a particular ideological formulation. To write rhetorical history in a way that valorizes Aristotelian
rhetoric, for example, may be to encourage in the writing classroom an
ideology originating in an agrarian-mercantile economy that relied on
slavery. (The continued endorsement of the validity of this rhetoric for the
present ought to tell us something about contemporary relations among
social classes.)

In writing rhetorical history it is not enough to locate and consider
rhetorics that reproduced the ideology of the established power structure—in other words, the rhetorics that dominated at schools, the courts,
and the law-making bodies (however defined). As Althusser, Gramsci,
Therborn, and Foucault have demonstrated, there are always ideologies
that arise in opposition to the dominant formation. This is obvious in the
case of revolutionary activity. For example, the rhetoric of Ramus—who
was himself a victim of political reaction—was intended to replace the Ar-
istotelian-inspired rhetoric of the Roman church. Ramus was then to provide the codification of a new set of discursive practices that were to encourage the emerging bourgeoisie on the religious front. Similarly, in
America in the eighteenth century the religious rhetoric of Ramus was
challenged by a secular rhetoric inscribed with an ideology that was instrumental in overthrowing English rule (Halloran 1982). Even the rheto-

rics tolerated by the ruling class are, however, never ideologically homogeneous. As I have attempted to demonstrate in my *Rhetoric and Reality* (Berlin 1987), for example, throughout the twentieth century the American college English department has housed rhetorics based on divergent ideologies, each encouraging discursive practices that call into question the social and political formulations of its rivals. There are always competing rhetorics at any historical moment because there are always competing ideologies, and this is demonstrable despite the fact that our rhetorical histories have attempted to ignore this conflict. This leads to a consideration of the way conflict is treated in the writing of rhetorical history.

From the perspective offered here, the rhetorics that emerge as dominant do not represent the triumph or the defeat of a great spirit or the return to some original truth. The rhetorics that dominate in a particular society represent the winners in an economic, social, and political contest in which the individual participants are themselves as much determined by their own historical moment as they are determiners of it. The rhetorics that prevail represent the success of establishing a particular set of rules for discourse, rules that sanction one ideology at the expense of others. These rules are thus themselves the scene of conflict and contesting. The study of rhetorics of the past can then be seen as an examination of both the products of this struggle and the statements of rules that favor the winning party. The historian of rhetoric is of course engaged in an act of interpretation (more of this later), but she must also remember that the rhetorics themselves are interpretations—interpretations not of some obscure, essential meaning but interpretations intended to serve one or another party in an endless play for power and privilege. And this, of course, is often difficult to see because rhetorics commonly conceal their political loyalties by offering their principles in the name of the unencumbered pursuit of truth, justice, and the authentic (Athenian, or English, or American) way.

Seeing rhetorical systems as the scenes of conflict carries important consequences for writing rhetorical history. The past cannot be regarded as existing simply to produce the present or as a prefiguration of it. The new historian must defamiliarize rhetorics of the past, presenting them as something other than those of the present. The social conflicts that give rise to rhetorics during the contemporary period of monopolistic capitalism cannot be identified as identical to the social conflicts of the past, of periods of competitive capitalism or of feudalism. The rhetorics of other times must be grasped in their uniqueness and singularity, not in their rehearsal of the present.

The historian of rhetoric must, furthermore, search for the rhetorics, not for the rhetoric, of a particular historical moment. She must identify the losers as well as the winners in the play for power, the Sophists as well as the Platos and Aristotles. This will mean examining rhetorics from new perspectives, perspectives appearing within the historical moment—the social and political context—that produced the rhetorics. This has been done, for example, in the attempt by Eric Havelock, Richard Enos, and others to rewrite the Sophists, examining their own language—their own rhetorics—rather than the language Plato invoked to discredit them. These new histories of rhetoric will thus celebrate diversity and deviance, the unexpected and the comic. They will emphasize the plurality of rhetoric, the refusal of rhetorical systems to be equated with each other, to be accounted for in terms other than their own. Although regularities and patterns must be located, the new historian must resist the urge to reduce all rhetorics to master templates—whether of the past or present—that is, to a few dominant patterns declared as inevitable for every time and place.

This leads to a consideration of the interpretive function of histories of rhetoric. The new historians must realize that the desire for historical truth is never disinterested. They must acknowledge that they themselves are involved in a rhetorical enterprise, relying on the rules of a specific rhetoric inscribed with a particular ideology—a version of what exists, what is good, and what is possible. The historian is calling on this rhetoric in a play of power with consequences for the present and the future, doing so, moreover, whether or not she chooses to do so. In other words, even the historian who attempts to stand outside the fray, seeking some transcendent truth, will perforce offer an implicit ideological statement. The history of rhetoric is never above the gaming of politics, and the stakes are usually the highest imaginable: a voice in the formation of the very subjects who constitute society.

No one should know better than the student of rhetoric, furthermore, that the right to choose the writing and speaking activities of students in the classroom is always the center of a contest for power in which the losers are all too commonly not heard from again, a permanent silence falling over them. (I cannot resist citing once again the texts of the first Sophists, texts that have survived only in fragments and in the slight reports of people who were most commonly their opponents.) The historian of rhetoric must seek out the vanquished, giving them as well as the victors a hearing. To return to the main consideration here, both the dominant and the dominated will reflect the influence of the play of power in the historian's own time. No historical account is without consequences for the present, and this fact places considerable responsibility in the hands of the historian.

A history of rhetoric is never innocent. As I have said repeatedly, however much the historian insists on presenting a neutral, objective, straightforward, and unbiased record of events, the history produced will inevitably favor one ideological position over others. This has been conceded by both bourgeois historiographers—Karl Popper, Hayden White, Stephen Pepper, R. G. Collingwood, for example—as well as those from the Left—Perry Anderson, E. P. Thompson, and Barry Hindess and Paul Hirst. A number of these commentators have also written histories, each differing from the others. The figures listed above are one, however, in that all write in a self-consciously dialectical manner: Each acknowledges that the account offered is a product of the interaction of the interpretive framework brought to the concrete historical events and the events themselves. The historian must always choose the story she is to tell, and the choice for White as well as Anderson and Thompson is an ideological one. The historian must thus be aware of her own ideological position: There is no neutral space from which to record a historical thing-in-itself. The writer must in addition identify her predisposition, understanding it herself and making it explicit for the reader. Although it is of course impossible to account for all that shapes one's own consciousness, the historian must nevertheless make accessible all that can be articulated of her ideological stance.

A history of rhetoric will thus necessarily be an interpretation. No historian can record everything, and this selection process alone ensures that interpretation will take place. The historian of rhetoric is, again, always engaged in a rhetorical act. She will present her account in the service of an ideology, a statement about what exists, what is good, what is possible, and how power is be wielded in maintaining these conceptions. This means that certain histories—certain versions of the past—will appear to some readers the most "true," that is, the most comprehensive in offering what is obvious, normal, expected, in the nature of things. These are the histories that are pointed to as definitive by this group of readers, particularly when the valorized ideological stance is accompanied by exhaustive scholarship in its support.

A history, however, can be "definitive" only when viewed from this particular stance. Howell's history of eighteenth-century rhetoric, for example, is definitive only if one approves of certain bourgeois notions of historical progress, that is, only if one celebrates with Howell the victory of the new empirical rhetorics of the emerging capitalist class over the neo-classical rhetorics found among both the old aristocracy and certain sectors of the new middle class. In other words, Howell's version of eighteenth-century rhetoric (Howell 1956) can be judged definitive only from a particular point of view—a specific way of emplotting the events of history, to use White's language, that underwrites a particular ideology. Those who wish to defend neoclassical rhetorics and the ideologies that they represented, however, are not disposed to see Howell's reading as the final word on the period. And those of us who wish to argue that the eighteenth century provides a great diversity of rhetorics growing out of a period rich in ideological contesting are even less inclined to embrace the finality of Howell's account.

My argument, it should now be clear, is for plurality—not rhetorical history but rhetorical histories. I am not, however, celebrating diversity for its own sake, hoping thereby to avoid commitment or controversy. I have made every effort to define my own ideological stance in my histories of rhetoric, refusing to adopt the ruse of offering an "objective" account, an account that arises out of the raw historical record without the taint of interpretation. I am instead encouraging plurality because it alone makes possible an understanding of the ideological stances that are competing at any historical moment. A variety of interpretations, particularly if they are candid in their ideological starting points, will enable us to recognize the variety (or lack of variety) in the economic, social, and political arrangements that are being encouraged at our own moment. A diverse range of histories will lead to clarification, forcing us to acknowledge that our historical judgments are indeed ideological, carrying with them important consequences for the present. It is my confidence that the more keen our awareness of these conflicting ideologies, the better will be our judgment in regarding both the past and the present. Out of the competing versions will come enlightenment about the ideological nature of rhetoric and the need for us to choose rather than to be chosen in passivity—to be dialectically engaged subjects rather than simply interpellated subjects. Indeed, it seems to me that the brightest hope for winning assent to my own ideological stance lies in the proliferation of positions, whereas the acceptance of the position found in my historical work lies in a genuine examination of the consequences entailed within each alternative.

This last argument is, of course, a familiar one in bourgeois democracies: Out of the clash of divergent opinion will emerge the best alternative. The limitation of this principle is that it is honored more in the breach than in the observance, and nowhere is this more apparent than in U.S. universities. In both our rhetorics and our poetics, until just recently, the permissible limits of dissent and diversity have been severely restricted—despite the upheavals of the 1960s—and most conspicuously in our exclusion of the Marxist tradition. Unlike their counterparts in virtually every democratic nation in the world, U.S. universities have engaged in tacit ideological warfare in which the most powerful critique of capitalism available is given no hearing. All the while, of course, these same institutions proudly claim a commitment to academic freedom in the unbiased pursuit of truth.

My plea for plurality in rhetorical history is then political. Awareness that rhetoric and ideology are inevitably imbricated and that they are pluralistic in their manifestations carries the potential for encouraging more equitable and more democratic economic, social, and political arrangements. But there is another consideration—one included in the question of ideological practices just considered—and here I will invoke T. W. Adorno's conception of the negative dialectic. I have been arguing for a dialectical conception of rhetorical history, for seeing a given historical account as the product of the interaction of a particular ideological perspective and the evidence that this perspective enables the historian to identify as relevant and worthy of interpretation. The project of these histories will be to see the individual from the perspective of the whole, the concrete through the concept—in other words, to offer a total perspective, an account that attempts to cover everything, leaving nothing unexplained. Adorno, the neo-Marxist, has cautioned us, however, that no version of the total can ever stand unquestioned, that no formulation of the whole—the whole of society, the whole of rhetorical history—can ever be altogether reliable. All such schemes—Kantian, Hegelian, Marxist—are partial, incomplete, limited. They are inherently susceptible to deconstruction, incapable of explaining all of the historical record, as the facts themselves finally undo any system's final adequacy.

Adorno's response to this dilemma is the negative dialectic. For Adorno, the student of Hegel and Marx, dialectical thinking involves, as Fredric Jameson explains, "thought about thought, thought to the second power, concrete thought about an object, which at the same time remains aware of its own intellectual operations in the very act of thinking" (Jameson 1971, 53). Adorno's negative dialectic goes beyond this, being designed, again in Jameson's formulation, "to offer a theory of the untheorizable, to show why dialectical thinking is at one and the same time both indispensable and impossible, to keep the idea of system alive while intransigently dispelling the pretensions of any of the contingent and already realized systems to validity and even to existence" (55). In the negative dialectic, the observer "has no choice but to affirm the notion and value of an ultimate synthesis, while negating its possibility and reality in every concrete case that comes before it" (56). In other terms, no completely accurate and reliable historical account is attainable, but this does not absolve us of the responsibility to attempt such accounts. Although it is impossible to reduce the objects of history to the subjective categories of our dialectical interpretation, we must continue to make the effort. All accounts are partial, but all reveal something about history and about the movement of our thought in coming to terms with it. Just as we cannot know the future but must nonetheless make judgments about it and act on them, we cannot completely know the past, and yet we must work to understand and judge it in order to understand and judge ourselves in our own moment. We are doomed to be partial, incomplete, mistaken, but we cannot for all this abstain from acting.

This stance makes for a radically different historiographic method. As Adorno explains, the "un-naive thinker knows how far he remains from the object of his thinking, and yet he must talk as if he had it entirely. This brings him to the point of clowning. He must not deny his clownish traits, least of all since they alone can give him hope for what is denied him. Philosophy is the most serious of things, but then again it is not all that serious" (Adorno 1973, 14). (Here Adorno echoes Foucault's endorsement of the carnivalesque in approaching the historical record.) But Adorno is also recommending a political program, one that has as its center the opposition to totalitarianism, to any explanation that pretends to be complete, irrevocable, final, the silencing of further discussion. Such explanations represent the imposition of tyranny. Our only hope in not being able to know everything, in not knowing how to account for every concrete event and for any event completely, is to know as many versions of the whole as we can, as many conceptual systems in their concrete application as is possible, thereby striving, "by way of the concept, to transcend the concept" (14). In this, Adorno is profoundly rhetorical, basing his negative dialectic in the inexorability of the probable in all human affairs—political, philosophical, historical—and thus of our need to discuss and debate what we cannot know with certainty. We must, after all, act, but the decisions that determine our action must be made with this awareness of the unreliability of our evidence and our judgments.

The position I have offered in this chapter carries additional implications for writing histories of rhetoric. Those of us engaged in this enterprise must be rhetorical in a sense even beyond that described earlier. We must agree to disagree, revealing to each other the ideological positions inscribed in our systems, in our concepts of the total called upon in interpreting the individual event. I am calling for a mutually illuminating contention without contentiousness, a debate that need not and should result in hostility and hopeless division. Disagreement, after all, says as much about its initiator as about the object of disagreement, and it is this discussion that is needed to further the value of historical study, not only to historians but also to all serious students of rhetoric. One distinguishing feature of rhetoric is that it is always directly tied to practice. The writing of history and the dialogue between writers of history recommended in this chapter will finally, I am convinced, make for better rhetoric classes and a better body politic.

Notes

1. One recent departure is Thomas M. Conley's excellent *Rhetoric in the European Tradition* (1990), a work I have considered in "Postmodernism, Politics, and Histories of Rhetoric" (Berlin 1990).

8 Coming to Terms with Recent Attempts to Write Women into the History of Rhetoric

BARBARA BIESECKER

An increasing number of rhetorical critics and theorists have begun to re-negotiate their relationship to the history of the discipline.[1] Indeed many of us have found it necessary to question some of our discipline's most basic theoretical assumptions, as we have understood that the rhetorical histories that emerge out of and are shaped by those assumptions have consequences both for the practices of our professional everyday lives and for the lives of our students.[2] Here I think two examples will suffice. The first example is taken from Gerard Hauser's *Introduction to Rhetorical Theory*, a book that deserves serious attention for many reasons, not the least of which is that it is currently being used by many teachers for the express purpose of initiating undergraduate and graduate students to the discipline. The second extract is from the first volume of Karlyn Kohrs Campbell's *Man Cannot Speak for Her*. I have chosen to use this source, as I am persuaded that the intent of Campbell's volumes is to supplement, if not to subvert, the received tradition that Hauser's work represents.

> The Greeks developed public deliberation, or the practice of rhetoric as the means to achieving cooperation. ... Every citizen might raise his voice confident that his views would be weighed in the whole process of assembly deliberation. The program of public deliberation did not establish a class of leaders blessed with special authority to make decisions, nor did it single out a special group whose opinions were esteemed as inherently superior in worth. ... In the democratic assembly, many voices were heard. Each spoke as a partisan. (Hauser 1986, 20)

> Men have an ancient and honorable rhetorical history. Their speeches and writings, from antiquity to the present, are studied and analyzed by historians and rhetoricians. ... Women have no parallel rhetorical history. Indeed, for much of their his-

tory women have been prohibited from speaking, a prohibition reinforced by such powerful cultural authorities as Homer, Aristotle, and Scripture. ... As a rhetorical critic I want to restore one segment of the history of women. (K. Campbell 1989, 1–13)

As feminists we cannot not want to be on the side of Campbell's revisionist history. It is a carefully documented narrative that makes all too visible the ideological agenda at work in Hauser's seemingly transparent and natural history of rhetoric. By exposing the manner in which decidedly male experiences have been made to stand in for the history of rhetoric as such, Campbell manages to bring the discipline and our own self-understandings to crisis. Indeed, having read Campbell's book we are compelled to rethink our roles both in and outside the classroom, as Hauser's implicit claim—that the glory of our origins, which is also our end, justifies our contemporary practices–is radically undone.

Of course, Campbell is not alone in her attempt to refigure the history of the discipline. As Carole Spitzack and Kathryn Carter (1987) have pointed out, and as Karen Foss and Sonja Foss, writing before them (1983), would agree, recent critical essays seeking to discredit the myth that "Man" is rhetoric's hero by writing women into its history find precedence in a relatively prodigious past. Yet even as we congratulate these critics for having taken a decisive step toward eradicating decades of cultural misrepresentation, we must also, Spitzack and Carter point out, caution against the potentially debilitating consequence of their work: female tokenism. Adrienne Rich, speaking to the students of Smith College in 1979, framed the problem of female tokenism in the following way:

There's a false power which masculine society offers to a few women who "think like men" on condition that they use it to maintain things as they are. This is the meaning of female tokenism: the power withheld from the vast majority of women is offered to few, so that it may appear that any truly qualified woman can gain access to leadership, recognition, and reward; hence that justice based on merits actually prevails. The token woman is encouraged to see herself as different from most other women, as exceptionally talented and deserving; and to separate herself from the wider female condition; and she is perceived by "ordinary" women as separate also: perhaps even as stronger than themselves. (Rich 1979, 43)

Like Rich, Spitzack and Carter argue that the project of situating "great women speakers" alongside their better-known male counterparts cuts two ways. On the one hand, the inclusion of a few great women "lends richness and balance to research practices" in the discipline; on the other hand, such projects "can easily support the presumption that the *majority* of women cannot rival male accomplishments" (Spitzack and Carter 1987, 405). That is to say, even as they recognize the importance of writing women's contributions into the history of rhetoric, thereby acknowledging the simple fact that women were not mere spectators of, but vital participants in, an oratorical tradition, Spitzack and Carter refuse to cover over what they understand to be the concomitant risk entailed in such an enterprise. While providing a heritage that potentially enables women to "seize and control their own creative resources" (Spender 1989, 32), the inclusion of particular texts spoken by women serves, albeit unwittingly, to perpetuate the damaging fiction that most women simply do not have what it takes to play the public, rhetorical game.

Although I agree with Spitzack and Carter that one must move with caution against female tokenism, I am also compelled to wonder at what point circumspection leads to silence, stagnation, and inactivity. Is it not the case that at a certain cultural-historical juncture one must risk the potentially dangerous side effects of female tokenism so as to reinstate to their rightful place women's rhetorical achievements? Doesn't the mere inclusion of women's texts in the rhetorical canon make a difference—by destabilizing the subject of rhetorical history that up to this point has been exclusively male, by challenging the suggestion that masculinity and subjectivity are coextensive notions? Should we not take our chances, given that, as Teresa de Lauretis put it, a "'room of one's own' may not avail women's intellection if the texts one has in it are written in the languages of male tradition" (de Lauretis 1989, 15)?

To all of these questions I must respond with a yes and no. But I respond with a yes and no neither because I wish to occupy the safe middle ground of a dialectical sublation nor because I am seeking to take refuge in a less than rigorous deconstructionist dodge. I say "yes and no" because I want to underscore yet another effect of attempts to insert "great women speakers" into the official record we call the canon, an effect that utterly escapes our detection as we weigh only the risks of female tokenism.

I think it is important to notice that recent attempts to render the discipline more equitable by supplementing the canon with texts spoken by women have something like a relationship with what only a few decades ago was coined as affirmative action.[3] In the socioeconomic sphere, of course, affirmative action is the institutionally sanctioned and ensured measure through which a history of injustice is to be rectified. Specific structural mechanisms are set in place to provide equal opportunity to members of disadvantaged or marginal groups. Transposed to the cultural sphere and, more particularly, to the classroom, affirmative action translates into a three-pronged imperative: New knowledges must be read, taught, and learned. In quite practical terms this means that course syllabi, reading lists for comprehensive exams, and curriculum requirements must all be revised. Yet when this strategy (useful as it may be in the social sphere) is made to operate in the cultural sphere, the project misfires. Why do I say that the project misfires when, as I noted earlier, thanks to pioneer feminist projects, a gender difference does seem to be challenging the identity of the field and history of rhetoric?

What I find objectionable in the affirmative action approach to the production and distribution of knowledges—an approach not unrelated to but, in fact, one of the conditions of female tokenism—is its underhanded perpetuation of "cultural supremacy." When deployed in the cultural sphere, affirmative action signifies nothing less than the power of the center to affirm certain voices and to discount others.[4] Despite its ostensible purpose—to move toward multiculturalism by adding new items to an ever-expanding list of "great works"—the affirmative action agenda conserves the putative authority of the center by granting it license to continue to produce official explanations in the designation of what is and what is not worthy of inclusion. Thus, even as the list of "great works" expands over time, the criteria for determining that list need not change. Indeed, for the most part the criteria have remained firmly in place.

This line of thinking compels us to raise a question that the strategy of inclusion does not: What are the criteria against which any particular rhetorical discourse is measured in order to grant or deny its place in the canon? One way into this question is to recognize that the rhetorical canon is a system of cultural representation whose present form is predicated on and celebrates the individual. It is a list of proper names signifying the exceptional accomplishments of particular individuals over time: from Gorgias, Isocrates, Cicero, and Augustine to John Winthrop, Jonathan Edwards, Susan B. Anthony, and Martin Luther King, Jr. To each of these proper names corresponds a text or set of texts, and between them is marked a certain kind of originating function that wins the individual membership in a distinguished ensemble of individuals.

But what is the problem with a criterion that applies equally to all, a criterion that purportedly crosses lines of gender, race, and class and asks only that an individual, any individual, "generate rhetorical works of extraordinary power and appeal" (K. Campbell 1989, 189)? Nothing less than the fact that a system of cultural representation that coheres around the individual subject, that is both master of himself and of his discourse, is not politically disinterested. Already entailed in the valorization of the individual is a mechanics of exclusion that fences out a vast array of collective rhetorical practices to which there belongs no proper name. The exaltation of individual rhetorical actions is secured by way of devaluating of collective rhetorical practices that, one cannot fail to note, have been the most common form of women's intervention in the public sphere. In short, the danger in taking an affirmative action approach to the history of rhetoric is that although we may have managed to insert some women into the canon (and, again, this is no small thing), we will have not yet begun to challenge the underlying logic of canon formation and the uses to which it has been put that have written the rhetorical contributions of collective women into oblivion.

Karlyn Campbell's most recent, and I think landmark, attempt is not immune to such a critique. To be sure, like her predecessors, she plots her revisionist history around the model of the individual speaking subject. Effective rhetorical discourse, that is to say, rhetoric worthy of inclusion in the canon, is the outcome of strategic choices made among available techniques of persuasion on the part of an autonomous individual. Indeed, in organizing her book as a series of cameo appearances by extraordinary women who, "on occasion, found symbolic means of responding" so as to "show that the artistry of this rhetoric generated enduring monuments to human thought and creativity" (K. Campbell 1989, 15), Campbell's revisionist history of rhetoric resolidifies rather than undoes the ideology of individualism that is the condition of possibility for the emergence of the received history of rhetoric.

So far I have suggested that we must be vigilant against the desire to interpret all gestures toward inclusion as inherently revolutionary or *necessarily* disruptive of the status quo. More particularly, I have tried to argue that a feminist rewriting of the history of rhetoric that founds itself on the mandate to secure a place in the canon for "great women speakers" is simply not enough. The mere accumulation of texts does not guarantee that our ways of knowing will change when the grounds for their inclusion and, likewise, our way of deciphering them remain the same. But if a decidedly feminist revisionary history of rhetoric hinges at least in part on our articulating an alternative to the ideology of individualism that has up until now enabled the discipline to identify "the great works," what criterion should take its place?

Interestingly enough, if Karlyn Campbell's most recent work from which I draw my representative generalization marks a certain orthodoxy and ultimately disabling cultural politics operative in the field, it is her earliest work in this area that gestures toward an alternative. In 1973 Campbell published her now famous article entitled "The Rhetoric of Women's Liberation: An Oxymoron." One of the most striking features of this early essay is the way in which it begins to challenge the presumed wisdom and general applicability of traditional theoretical models and customary modes of rhetorical understanding. By taking concrete instances of women's liberation discourse (however narrowly conceived) as her point of departure, Campbell attempts to cut loose from the prevailing tendency on the part of critics to posit rhetorical categories on an a priori basis. Campbell's boldest stroke takes the form of an explicit and seemingly uncompromising challenge to Lloyd Bitzer's theorization of the audience. Given the history of the disenfranchisement of women, Campbell argues persuasively, "It is difficult to view them as an audience, i.e., as persons who see themselves as potential agents of change" (K. Campbell 1973, 78); unlike other rhetorics, rhetorics directed toward the liberation of women must take as their point of departure "the radical affirmation of new identities" (82).

A sensitivity to the constraints that the grafting of theoretical models onto specific discourses imposes on rhetorical analysis is what gives Campbell's essay its critical edge. Yet it is an edge that has been blunted by the force of the tradition within which it was produced: Though she identifies the limits of Bitzer's conceptualization of audience by reopening the question of (female) identity and subjectivity, her uncritical mobilization of the concept-metaphor "consciousness-raising" as the paradigmatic expression of the rhetoric of women's liberation marks the essay's complicity with precisely those normative theorizations that it seeks to oppose. Taken quite literally, consciousness-raising signifies the project of bringing to the surface something that is hidden, the task of making manifest something that is concealed or covered over. Campbell's use of the term, which is underpinned or at least burdened by the whole history of psychoanalytic theory, participates in a depth hermeneutics that posits an irreducible essence inhabiting the subject and a tropology of the psyche that writes presence as consciousness, self-presence conceived within the opposition of consciousness to unconsciousness.[5] Out of this tropology comes Campbell's notion of audience and her understanding of the over-riding exigence that the rhetoric of women's liberation must address. The discourse must, as she puts it, "violate the reality structure," "transcend alienation to create 'sisterhood,'" indeed, must produce "a radical form of consubstantiality" that transcends "differences in age, education, income, etc." (Campbell 1973, 79).[6] Here consciousness-raising marks the deliber-ate attempt to recover the potential originary space *before* the sign "wom-an"; in staging the specifically feminist project in recuperative terms, rhet-oric is understood, once again, as a purposive act that shuttles between consummate, sovereign, though perhaps estranged, identities.

Of course Campbell is right to insist that women's access to subjectivity is indispensable to a political program that seeks, above all else, the em-powerment of women. However, following the cues of both Jacques Lacan (who has taught us to be more than a bit skeptical of "the talking cure") and feminists working between the post-Freudian and materialist perspec-tives (who have warned us of the perils of sifting women's problems through pathologizing filters [Lerner 1990, 16]), I must admit that I find less than satisfactory the conceptualization of history and social change implied in Campbell's reformulation of female subjectivity, a conceptual-ization wherein the ideology of individualism and the old patriarchal alignments are reinscribed. In Campbell's work the possibility for social change is thought to be more or less a function of each individual woman's capacity to throw off the mantle of her own self-perpetuated oppression, to recognize her *real* self-interests (interests that are her own *as* a woman and, thus, are shared by all women), and to intervene on behalf of those in-terests. No doubt, Campbell's promotion of a kind of self-help program plays straight into the hands of the old order, which has consistently sought to deflect critical attention away from those structures of oppres-sion larger than individual consciousness and will. In Campbell's formula-tion positivity lines up with activity, whereas passivity and with it feminin-ity are identified as negative.

If feminists working in the history of rhetoric could deconstruct the all-too-easy bipolarization of the active and the passive, we would go a long way toward dismantling the ideology of individualism that monumental-izes some acts and trivializes others. Not only would we realize that any active intervention is constituted by the so-called passive but also we would realize that the passive is inhabited by an active potential because it *is*, to borrow and turn a phrase from Kenneth Burke, the substance of the active. Thus if, as feminists, we want to produce something more than the story of a battle over the right to individualism between men and women, we might begin by taking seriously poststructuralist objections to the model of human subjectivity that has served as the cognitive starting point of our practices and our histories. Indeed, following Campbell's initial impulse to reexamine and expand "the presumptions underlying symbolic approaches to human behavior" (K. Campbell 1970, 106), I want to argue that the poststructuralist interrogation of the subject and its concomitant call for the *radical* contextualization of all rhetorical acts can enable us to forge a new storying of our tradition that circumvents the veiled cultural supremacy operative in mainstream histories of rhetoric. More specifically, I want to suggest that the strategic appropriation of poststructuralism on the part of feminists sets up the conditions for a "new" definition of *techne* that considerably alters our way of reading and writing history by displacing the active/passive opposition altogether.

A Reencounter with Poststructuralism

As R. Radhakrishnan has argued (1989), what is singular about poststructuralism is its interrogation of identity. Unlike structuralism, Marxism, or Freudian psychoanalysis, poststructuralism attacks identity as such and not just particular and isolated forms or versions of identity. For example, in several of his works Derrida challenges explicitly the presumed integrity of the phenomenological subject, the subject of the humanistic tradition that, as I hinted above and have argued elsewhere, underwrites most contemporary rhetorical analysis, feminist or otherwise (B. Biesecker 1989). Derrida launches a deconstruction of the subject by taking seriously the possibility that the human being, like writing and speech, is constituted by *différance*, as "starting from/in relation to time as difference, differing and deferral."[7] By way of an elaborate argument that I will not attempt to represent here, Derrida shows us how the identity of any subject, like the value of any element in a given system, is structured by and is the effect of its place in an economy of differences. In short, against an irreducible humanist essence of subjectivity, Derrida advances a subjectivity that, structured by *différance* and thus always differing from itself, is forever in process, indefinite, controvertible.

To claim that a movement outside the prison house of the essentialist subject is necessary for writing a new history of rhetoric is not to say that there are no subjects. As Gayatri Chakravorty Spivak has pointed out on more than one occasion, it is possible to read in Derridean deconstruction quite another story about the subject. Put succinctly, it runs as follows: "The subject is always centered. The critic is obliged to notice persistently that this centering is an 'effect,' shored up within indeterminate boundaries that can only be understood as determining" (Spivak 1989, 279). By this reckoning, the presence of an "I" (that is not, however, identical to an "I" 's self-presence—and this is why we must not forget the previous story) records something like the provisional stabilization of a temporality and a spacing that always and already exceeds it. Thus, subjectivity in the general sense is to be deciphered as a historical articulation, and particular real-lived identities are to be deciphered as constituted and reconstituted in and by an infinitely pluralized weave of interanimating discourses and events.

I have drawn attention to Derrida's doubled morphology of the subject because I believe it can enable us to begin to write a quite different history of rhetoric. Were we to follow the trajectory of Derrida's interrogation of the subject, keeping one foot firmly anchored in the former account (the subject is never coincident with or identical to itself and, thus, is open to change) and the other foot in the latter account (the subject is always centered, but that centering can only be understood as an effect of its place in a larger economy of discourses), it becomes possible to forge a storying that shifts the focus of historical inquiry from the question "who is speaking," a question that confuses the subjects of history with the agents for history, to the question "what play of forces made it possible for a particular speaking subject to emerge?" Nonetheless, by claiming Derridean deconstruction for a new history of rhetoric that begins by thinking the subject as "historical through and through," I am not suggesting that we can find in Derrida's work anything like a general theory of history or a coherent set of directives for writing one. In fact, if such a project is not to be given up, if we are to broach the question that Derrida enables us to ask— "what play of forces made it possible for a particular speaking subject to emerge?"—we might find it useful to slip from Derridean deconstruction to Foucaultian archaeology. Perhaps it is worth remarking that this turn to Foucault seeks, as did the prior discussion of Derrida, to identify only a few aspects of his work that may help us to write a feminist history of rhetoric that averts the shortcomings of the affirmative action approach.

In a certain sense the definitive characteristic of Foucault's middle project, *The Archaeology of Knowledge*, is its insistence upon relating the radical reconceptualization of the subject, characteristic of post-Sartrean French thought, to forms of social organization that he calls "discursive forma- tions." But what are these "discursive formations"? And what is the sub- ject's relation to them? To be sure, Foucault mobilizes the concept-meta- phor "discursive formation" in order to work against the widespread tendency among social theorists to presume that the socius is operated by a coherent logic that can account for all relations and practices.[8] Indeed, in the chapter on discursive formations, Foucault emphasizes time and again that the socius is a discontinuous space constituted by heterogeneous fields of objects operated by a "body of anonymous historical rules" (Foucault 1972, 117), a nonstatic arena woven of dispersed "I-slots."

Now it is important to note that although these "I-slots," most often re- ferred to as subject-positions, are neither essential nor constant, they do, at the same time, assure a certain kind of being-in-the-world by "deter- mining what position[s] can and must be occupied by any individual if he is to be a subject" (Foucault 1972, 96) at all. Here Foucault emphasizes the discursivity of the "I," as the condition for its making sense is a function of its positioning in the "stated." Thus for Foucault, identity is defined by way of one's relation to or place in a network of social, political, cultural, and economic practices that are provisional (in the sense of historical and not essential), discontinuous (in the sense of nontotalizable), and norma- tive (in the sense of rule governed and governing).

Like Derrida, Foucault conceives subjectivity and identity as made available by, rather than existing outside of or prior to, language and rep- resentation. Of the subject and its relation to structure Foucault writes:

> So the subject of the statement should not be regarded as identical with the author of the formulation. ... He is not in fact the cause, origin or starting-point of the phenomenon of the written or spoken articulation of a sentence; nor is it that meaningful intention which, silently anticipating words, orders them like the visi- ble body of its intuition; it is not the constant, motionless, unchanging focus of a series of operations that are manifested, in turn, on the surface of discourse through the statements. It is a particular, vacant place that may in fact be filled by different individuals. ... If a proposition, a sentence, a group of signs can be called a "statement," it is not therefore because, one day, someone happened to speak them or put them into some concrete form of writing; it is because the position of the subject can be assigned. (Foucault 1972, 95)

If both Foucault and Derrida redefine the speaking subject as a locus of effects, what distinguishes Foucault's thinking on the subject from

Derrida's is the former's refusal to decipher subjectivity and identity as infinitely or indefinitely pluralized:

> The individual is not to be conceived as a sort of elementary nucleus, a primitive
> atom, a multiple and inert material on which power comes to fasten or against
> which it happens to strike. ... In fact, it is already one of the prime effects of power
> that certain bodies, certain gestures, certain discourses, certain desires, come to be
> identified and constituted as individuals. (Foucault 1980, 98)

Where Derrida would speak of the ever-shifting limits that persistently
thwart our desire to make the subject cohere in any final sense, Foucault
would chart the localized rules and mechanisms of disciplinary power that
ensure the production and reproduction of differentially situated subjects
in a nonstatic but hierarchically organized space. Indeed, Foucault himself
seems interested in marking this constitutive difference between his own
work and Derrida's. At the end of the second edition of *Madness and Civilization* he writes:

> Today Derrida is the most decisive representative of a system in its final glory; the
> reduction of discursive practice to textual traces; the elision of the events that are
> produced there in order to retain nothing but marks for a reading; the invention of
> voices behind texts in order not to have to analyse the modes of implication of the
> subject in discourse; assigning the spoken and the unspoken in the text to an
> originary place in order not to have to reinstate the discursive practices in the field
> of transformations where they are effectuated. ... It is not at all necessary to search
> elsewhere, for exactly here, to be sure not in the words, but in the words as erasures,
> in their *grill*, "the meaning of being" speaks itself.[9]

Though Foucault himself may have been written both too much and too
little by Derrida,[10] suffice it to say here that Foucault's commitment to
demonstrating how specific practices not only constitute distinct forms of
selfhood but also normalize them into being is what lends his work its distinctive ethos.

Feminist and nonfeminist historians alike have claimed that Foucault's
decisive contribution to our understanding of social economies and their
conditions of existence and emergence is encapsulated in his theory of subject positions, a theory that resolutely challenges the assumption that ideology can be demystified because "individuals are not only the inert or
consenting target of ideology and power but are always also the elements
of their articulation" (Foucault 1980, 98). But if individuals emerge always

and already *as* particular lived-expressions of the limits and possibilities of a discursive formation, if, that is to say, subject positions are a matter not of choice but of assignation, is there then no possibility for human agency, rhetorical intervention, social change? To be sure, it is on the issue of human agency that Foucault's work has seemed to prove less than palatable to many critics. Nancy Hartsock's commentary may be taken as somewhat paradigmatic of a generalizable disappointment: "Foucault's is a world in which things move, rather than people, a world in which subjects become obliterated or, rather, recreated as passive objects, a world in which passivity or refusal represent the only possible choices" (Hartsock 1990, 167). If, as Foucault suggests, "power is everywhere," then it seems only reasonable to conclude that there is no place out of which anything like an insurrection may gain its foothold.[11] Set over and against the ubiquitous and hegemonizing effects of power, the very notion of resistance seems nothing more than a fragile proposition.

It would be difficult to object to this gloss on Foucault's project; it is quite true, as Frances Bartkowski has convincingly argued, that "even though he acknowledges quite clearly that 'you can't have one without the other,' Foucault never gives us as committed a look at resistance as we most certainly get at power" (Bartkowski 1988, 44). Having said this much, however, it seems unwise to suggest, as Hartsock does, that the pressing demand for real social change obliges us to rule Foucault, indeed all poststructuralist theory, out of court or to presume, as Blair and Cooper do, that we can simply cover over the problem of human agency by refashioning Foucault into a humanist.[12] To preserve one's own emancipatory projects or salvage one's own disciplinary identity by ignoring Foucault's work altogether or repressing those aspects of it that make us uneasy with ourselves is myopic and politically naive.

Even though Foucault does not write at great length about resistance, there is one thing he makes abundantly clear: We must hold against the temptation to construe resistance as a structure that stands over and against power, as an event subsequent to the establishment of power. Resistance is always and already a structure of possibility within power, and, it should be added, power is always and already a structure of possibility within resistance. Power and resistance are two sides of the same coin and, thus, emerge in tandem. But from where? Out of what? Foucault responds, "of something other than itself" (Foucault 1989, 186).

The implicit challenge to fill out or specify the "other" that is the reserve of power and resistance has already been taken up by a handful of theorists and critics who, in contrast to Hartsock and Blair and Cooper, have attempted to articulate a theory of resistance based on Foucault's "antihumanism." These critics productively regraft Foucault's notion of subject-positions along the lines of a conflict of interpretations schemata. Given that subjects emerge at the heterogeneous intersection of *multiple*, and presumably incompatible, interpellations—race, gender, and class— they cannot be made to cohere as Subjects. Hence, by reading the subject itself as a site of multiple and contestatory inscriptions, one can, they argue, locate a reservoir of revolutionary potential in the gaps, fissures, and slippages of the nonidentical "I."[13]

Though I am more than sympathetic to the claim that lived-experience is a trying, oftentimes exasperating, oftentimes failed, exercise in self-negotiation, I do not think such experience can be exploited as the basis for a theory of change. Hence, my objection to the attempt is not that such experience fails to ring true but, rather, that "the theory of pluralized 'subject-effects' gives an illusion of undermining subjective sovereignty while ... providing a cover for this subject of knowledge" (Spivak 1988, 271).[14] Indeed, it seems to me that such a formula can make sense only if the human being is presumed, however unwittingly, to be motivated by an a priori drive for symmetry, a presumption fearfully analogous to Freud's pleasure principle: At the moment wherein the subject's knowledges become out of sync, at the point upon which the wear and tear of unsynchronized knowing congeals into intolerable epistemic violence, the subject's will-to-coherence manifests itself as a precarious sublation whose name is resistance. As Paul Smith put it in a book that cogently argues for this view, "the colligation of subject-positions, far from entailing a fixed or cerned 'subject,' is effected precisely by the principle which stands against unification—negativity, the forgotten fourth term of Hegel's dialectics" (P. Smith 1988, 156).[15] In short, resistance is taken to be the real-lived outcome of a subject who, knowing that she does not know, is moved by an always and already unfulfilled drive to "get it together."

But must the possibilities for resistance and social change be secured by scrupulously resurrecting an ontological guarantee under the guise of an epistemological imperative? I think not. In fact, were we to allow certain aspects of Derrida's doubled morphology of the subject to interrupt Foucault's thinking on individuals-in-power, a more promising direction for theorizing resistance could be developed.[16] That is to say, because I believe Foucault's take on the subject-in-power is both instructive (in arguing that identity is manufactured and sustained through specifiable discursive means) and limited (in failing to adequately theorize the resources of and possibilities for social change), I want to press the issue of resistance to a further limit within the Foucaultian frame, once again using Derridean deconstruction as my lever.

Retooling *Techne*

Earlier in the chapter I argued that what lends Foucault's work its particular ethos is his commitment to demonstrating how specific practices not only constitute distinct forms of selfhood but also normalize them into being. What I should like to emphasize here is that the Foucaultian analyses of the operations of power circulate almost exclusively within, indeed are orchestrated by, a metaphorics of space. In Foucault's work, space is everything. With the precision of the cartographer, Foucault takes his reader from the leprosariums of the High Middle Ages to the Saint Luke Hospital founded in 1751, from the radical reorganization of the *maison de force* to Bentham's panopticon, from the Victorian bedroom to the analyst's couch. With him, we trace the proliferation of disciplines and the internal necessities that open up the frontiers of knowledge and chart the progressive interiorization of madness and sexuality. Indeed, in Foucault's hands the history of the West is brilliantly divided, anatomized, and mapped as a landscape whose configuration is deciphered almost exclusively in terms of the constellation of objects: walls, irons, windows, mirrors, icons, bodies.

But what would happen if the Foucaultian project was deliberately made to incorporate rather than neglect one of Derrida's pivotal insights—namely, that the subject that is always centered is nonetheless outstripped by *a temporality and a spacing* that always already exceeds it? I have implied it repeatedly: Were this excess that never appears as such figured into the Foucaultian calculation, it would become possible for us to recognize the formidable role structure plays in the (re)constitution of subjectivities and the capacity—albeit nonintentional in the strictest sense of the term—of those subjectivities to disrupt the structure within which and through which they are differently inscribed. Indeed, the exorbitant *play of spacing* is, I would argue, the "other" that is the reserve of power and resistance; *spacing* as such "speaks the articulation of space and time, the becoming-space of time and the becoming-time of space" (Derrida 1976,

68). That such a notion cannot be recognized within Foucaultian archaeology should come as no surprise, as it is that very thing which cannot be reduced to the form of *presence.*

Spacing as the name of that which inaugurates the constitution of time and space, subject and object, self and other, can be related to the central problematics of this chapter—power and resistance. Most important, what must be noticed is that Derrida's particular notion of spacing as an excess that is never thoroughly absorbed by and into the present cannot be thought to be an inherent property of the subject, a pure reserve or ideologically uncontaminated pocket, which assures the subversion of power. In fact, a careful reading of Derrida's work will show that the very possibility of resistance is to be found in the articulation of an act and not in the negativity of the actor. That is to say, Derrida's thinking on spacing shifts the site of resistance from the subject proper to the exorbitant possibilities of the act because spacing in this special sense is precisely that which "suspends the accomplishment or fulfillment of 'desire' or 'will'" (Derrida 1982, 8). In the end, then, such a shift enables us to work within the Foucaultian framework: Subjects are effects of their sociopolitical, historical, economic, and cultural contexts. It also, however, makes it possible for us to push the limits of that framework: In claiming with Foucault that individuals are manufactured and sustained through specifiable discursive means, we need not presuppose that their practices are nothing but reflections of such contexts or that their practices are thoroughly disciplined by them.

But already a finer distinction needs to be made. For if what we are trying to indicate is a certain structure of reserve that breaks open a pathway within the hegemonizing effects of power by means of an act whose effluence eludes the mastery of the acting subject, then the word "practice" simply will not do. Indeed, at least since Aristotle, who seems to have been the first to use it as a technical term, "practice" designates a purposeful doing: "I accomplish (e.g., a journey)," "I manage (e.g., state affairs)," "I do or fare (e.g., well or ill)," and, in general, "I act, I perform some activity" (Lobkowicz 1967, 9). Still today practice is the name for an intended doing, a deliberate—often theoretically informed—activity targeted to some end: practical criticism, practical argument and reasoning, the practice of rhetoric. Thus what I am seeking to point to is not practice per se but, instead, a force or structure of breaching in practice that establishes a cleft or fissure out of which an unforeseen and undesigned transgression may ensue.

Might we not then settle upon the word *techne* as the sign for an exorbitant doing that depends upon practice but that does not obey the imperatives of practice? Here I shall state my claim directly and unequivocally: By scrupulously working within and against the grain of the word's historically constituted semantic field, one can use *techne* to refer to a kind of "getting through" or ad hoc "making do" by a subject whose resources are necessarily located in and circumscribed by the field within which she operates, but whose enunciation, in always and already exceeding and falling short of its intending subject, harbors within it the possibility of disrupting, fragmenting, and altering the horizon of human action out of which it emerges. Now without belaboring the obvious, it should be noted that to use *techne* as a word signifying a way or means by which something gets done is not new in the proper sense of the word. As I pointed out above, Aristotle, and even Plato before him, had said this much. What is "new," however, is the attempt to use *techne* differently by bracketing out the ethical/moral sedimentations that have, through the history of its uses, been attributed to the word, thereby making it possible for us to refuse to grasp the agent of history as identical with her intentions.

I should perhaps emphasize that it is precisely in refusing to conflate the always and already intending subject with the potentially heterogeneous and counterhegemonic effects of action that my use of the concept-metaphor *techne* differs from the way in which Michel de Certeau mobilizes the word. In *The Practice of Everyday Life*, de Certeau makes the important distinction between *techne* as "tactic" and *techne* as "strategy." Although de Certeau distinguishes these two modalities of human action "according to whether they bet on place or on time," he takes both as interventions whose implications can be calculated in advance (de Certeau 1984, 39). Like Levi-Strauss's *bricoleur*, de Certeau's practician tinkers with the rules and tools of the established order and in so doing "establishes a degree of plurality and creativity" within "the place where he has no choice but to live" (30). These deliberate modes of use or reuse are simultaneously, for de Certeau, the modes of historical change. He writes, for example:

> Even when they were subjected, indeed even when they accepted their subjection, the Indians often used the laws, practices, and representations that were imposed on them by force or by fascination to ends other than those of their conquerors; they made something else out of them; they subverted them from within—not by rejecting them or by transforming them (though that occurred as well), but by

many different ways of using them in the service of rules, customs or convictions foreign to the colonization which they could not escape. They metaphorized the dominant order: they made it function in another register. They remained other within the system which they assimilated and which assimilated them externally. They diverted it without leaving it. (de Certeau 1984, 31–32)

Contrary to de Certeau, then, my own use of *techne* seeks to mark out a structure of possibility in action that never entered the space and temporality of the intending consciousness upon which its own legibility depends. Contrary to de Certeau, I am suggesting that if we use *techne* as a word signifying a way, manner, or means whereby something is gained, without any sense of art or cunning (*OED*), then *techne* signifies a bringing-about in the doing-of on the part of an agent that does not necessarily take herself to be anything like a subject of historical or, as in the above instance, cultural change. Used in this way, *techne* displaces the active/passive binary that dominates even de Certeau's thinking on power and resistance. *Techne* points to a heterogeneous history of practices performed in the interstice between intention and subjection, choice and necessity, activity and passivity. It is, as Derrida would put, the trace of "the not-seen that opens and limits visibility" (Derrida 1976, 163).

Back to History

As I see it, this chapter could be summarized as a call for a gender-sensitive history of rhetoric that, in working against the ideology of individualism by displacing the active/passive opposition, radically contextualizes speech acts. And although the historiographical approach advocated here does not deny that over time distinguishable and distinguished speaking subjects emerge, it does suggest that the conditions of possibility for their emergence must be located elsewhere. Thus, for the feminist historiographer interested in rewriting the history of rhetoric, the plurality of practices that together constitute the everyday must be conceptualized as a key site of social transformation and, hence, of rhetorical analysis. To be sure, this is no easy task. Were the critic to take up such a project, not only would she be obliged to confront the limits of her own disciplinary expertise (deciphering "great speeches" would not be enough); she would also be forced to come to the sobering realization that little assistance is to be gained from even the most benevolent enclaves of the academy. It is not only the discipline of rhetoric that is written by the ideology of individualism. History, History and Philosophy of Science, Philosophy, Literary Studies, Foreign Language and Literature programs, and even the more recent Women's Studies and Cultural Studies programs share that history and, thus, its burden with us. History and Philosophy of Science may be the most telling example. Although scientific practice is routinely collective, historians of those practices tend to write figural histories that celebrate, indeed monumentalize, individuals.[17]

More important, perhaps, the critic taking up the project of rewriting the history of rhetoric would be required to come to terms with rather than efface the formidable differences between and among women and, thus, address the real fact that different women, due to their various positions in the social structure, have available to them different rhetorical possibilities and, similarly, are constrained by different rhetorical limits. Indeed, the argument I have put forward presses for a feminist intervention into the history of rhetoric that persistently critiques its own practices of inclusion and exclusion by relativizing rather than universalizing what Aristotle identified as "the available means of persuasion." It obliges the feminist historiographer interested in rewriting the history of rhetoric to take on the full burden of the notion of unequal or nonsynchronous development—obliges her not only to write the story of the differences between women's and men's subject (re)formation but also to write into that account the story of the differences between the positionality of different women. Put simply, it is not enough to declare, "Man cannot speak for her." One must also admit that no individual woman or set of women, however extraordinary, can speak for all women.

Does all of this mean, then, that we must abandon our canon, forfeit our masterpieces, renounce our tradition? Absolutely not. Even though the canon and the histories that have propped it up do not represent the way "things really were," we can learn to read them differently and, thus, teach ourselves something about who we are now or, more precisely, how we have become that which we now understand ourselves to be. Likewise, must the feminist project of retrieving texts spoken and written by women be stopped dead in its tracks? Again, I think not. For what is beginning to emerge there under the guise of information retrieval is the cathected story of what it is that we wish to become. For the academic feminist, however, that story may prove to be the most difficult of all to decipher. For in that story we must begin to read ourselves as part and parcel of the history we so desperately seek to disown.

Notes

1. I wish to thank the Pennsylvania State University Press for permission to reprint this chapter, which first appeared in *Philosophy and Rhetoric* 25, no. 2 (1992): 140–161. Copyright 1992 by The Pennsylvania State University. Reproduced by permission of The Pennsylvania State University Press.

2. There is a steadily growing body of work dealing with the historiography of rhetoric. Although a complete bibliography cannot be presented here, it may be useful to identify a few particularly recent and noteworthy contributions. See, for example, a special volume of *PRE/TEXT: A Journal of Rhetorical Theory* 8 (1987), entitled "Historiography and the Histories of Rhetorics I: Revisionary Histories." See also a special section in the *Western Journal of Speech Communication* 54 (1990) on rhetoric and historiography.

3. For this very interesting connection, I am indebted to the work of Gayatri Chakravorty Spivak. See "On Behalf of Cultural Studies" (forthcoming).

4. See ibid. For an earlier elaboration of this issue see, E. D. Hirsch, Jr., et al., 1989.

5. I borrow the deconstruction of the Freudian tropology of the subject from Jacques Derrida, "Freud and the Scene of Writing," 1978.

6. What cannot go unnoticed here is that Campbell writes out the real-lived differences between women in order to establish a hegemonic feminism upon which she can then build her case. Rendering material differences as immaterial does enable her to construct what at least appears to be an elegant argument that explains a whole history of heterogeneous rhetorical practices at one fell swoop and to continue working within a traditional aesthetic axiology against which the value of particular discourses can be judged as worthy or not of canonization. This point will be taken up later in the chapter.

7. Cited in Culler 1982, 95.

8. For a thorough and astute discussion of Foucault's work and its relation to social theory see Mark Cousins and Athar Hussain, 1984.

9. Quoted in Spivak 1976, lxi–lxii.

10. The point here is not to resurrect influence studies in the old way, but rather to note the uncanny play of *différance* within Foucault's own work.

11. As A. Belden Fields has pointed out, even Foucault leaves us with very little to hold on to. He (Foucault) tells us that "power is amorphous, a machine in which everyone is caught up. And he finds that 'against these usurpations by the disciplinary mechanisms ... we find that there is no solid recourse available to us today'" (Fields 1988, 144–145).

12. See Blair and Cooper 1987. Indeed, in counterdistinction to Blair and Cooper, I do not think it necessary to dress Foucault up in the old humanist drag in order to make him useful for rhetoric. For if rhetorical interventions are articulations of their sociohistorical contexts, it does not follow that they are nothing but reflections of such contexts. This point will be taken up more fully in the next part of the chapter.

13. See, for example, the essays collected in Diamond and Quinby 1988; Balbus 1987; and J. Butler 1990.

14. In this essay Spivak brings the critique of Foucault's and Deleuze's theories of pluralized "subject-effects" to bear upon the Western intellectuals' role within contemporary relations of power.

15. Smith's (1988) book may be summarized as a prolegomena to theorizing resistance. He examines a multitude of contemporary perspectives (Derridean, Althusserian, Marxian, psychoanalytic, feminist, semiotic, anthropological) on the issue and identifies their latent deficiencies. Interestingly enough, Smith never offers a sustained analysis of Foucault's thinking on power and resistance. It would not be far from the truth, however, to identify Foucault as the shadow figure that constitutes the margin of this text.

16. For a discussion of the productive notion of interruption as a cut of sorts that allows something to function, see Spivak 1990, 110–111.

17. For a critique of these histories, see, for example, Harding and O'Barr 1987.

9 The Duality of Rhetoric: Theory as Discursive Practice

CHRISTINE ORAVEC
AND MICHAEL SALVADOR

In the twentieth century the word "rhetoric" is used in two ways. First, it is used as a name for discourse itself as a discrete phenomenon; second, it is used to designate discourse that itself describes or explains discourse. The insight that rhetoric can be viewed in two ways often appears in descriptions of the relationship between theory and practice. For example, Donald Bryant made a distinction between rhetoric as discourse and rhetoric as a body of principles in his highly influential "Rhetoric: Its Functions and Its Scope" (Bryant 1953, 408). Douglas Ehninger extended the distinction by introducing the notion of "systems of rhetoric" (Ehninger 1968; 1975). Maurice Natanson described "philosophic rhetoric" and separated it from rhetorical theory and rhetorical practice (Natanson 1955, 138–139). Paolo Valesio opposed "rhetoric" and "rhetorics" (Valesio 1980, 2–3). And Walter Ong infused the distinction with issues of orality in describing the "rhetorical art," which is oral culture referenced in writing (Ong 1982, 108–116). These, and many more rhetorical theorists, have recognized in the rhetorical phenomenon both a referential and a self-referential quality.

According to these theorists, the self-reflexiveness of rhetoric entails the use of words to discover the use of words: what Kenneth Burke once called "barking about barking." Indeed, one might go as far as to say that this dual nature is a unique quality of rhetorical theory among the contemporary sciences. Physicists do not study physics treatises as physical objects; chemists do not analyze the chemical components of a chemistry paper. Social scientists are just beginning to examine their own practices and products as data. Only rhetorical theorists actually do what they say in the very act of saying.

Other disciplines, however, have taken the lead in evaluating the rhetorical nature of their own practices. Only recently have rhetorical scholars begun to emphasize the proposition that rhetorical theories are themselves rhetorical and can be analyzed as discourses as well as theoretical statements. As Carole Blair and Mary L. Kahl (1990) argue, the construction of histories involves choices that "function advocatively, inviting the reader of this historical text to view the past of rhetorical theory as the historian presents it." The disciplines of science, philosophy, political science, sociology, literary studies, and history have already engaged in lengthy self-examinations (R. H. Brown 1987; Connolly 1987; Dallmayr 1984; de Man 1983; Nelson, Megill, and McCloskey 1987; Ziman 1976). Some of those self-examinations have yielded remarkable insights about the way disciplinary discourse works.

This chapter takes seriously the proposition that rhetorical theory itself comprises a duality of discourse; one side being its discursive quality, the other its self-referential quality. It is an earnest attempt to answer the call "for historians of rhetorical theory to concern themselves with their own choices" (Blair and Kahl 1990). We first examine two approaches by which the tradition of rhetorical theory has been constructed, the philosophical idealist and the historical realist, and show that these approaches have systematically excluded or ignored one or the other of rhetorical theory's two sides. We offer an alternative view of method in rhetorical theory, discursive dialectics, which attempts to address the interrelationship between the two sides of rhetoric as inherent to rhetorical theorizing, if not rhetorical discourse itself. This alternative method is intended, not to replace the other two approaches with a better, more "objective" approach, but to demonstrate how rhetorical theories are, as advocative texts, inevitably positioned relative to each other and to their subject matter.

To illustrate this dialectic approach, we describe three existing theoretical orientations, the functional, symbolic construction, and ideological critical, to expose the advocative nature of rhetorical theories. In particular, we focus both upon the theories' underlying or implicit assumptions *about* rhetoric and their practical functioning *as* rhetoric. This examination shows how rhetorical theories can function as intellectual practices—as kinds of discourses—with assumptions, purposes, motives, and values consistent with those of the interests, organizations, or institutions of which they are a part. In the course of this discussion, we shall argue that the third approach, the ideological critical, fully affirms the nature of rhetorical theory as discourse as well as self-reference.

Two Traditional Methods:
Philosophical Idealism and Historical Realism

In a review article entitled "The Present State of the Study of Ancient Rhetoric," George Kennedy identified two approaches toward the study of rhetoric: "as a historical phenomenon or as a systematic discipline" (Kennedy 1975, 278). The historical orientation investigates the differences in different rhetorical theories in their artistic, literary, political, and legal contexts. The systematic view focuses on the commonalities of rhetorics and the problem of "whether universal, positive statements can be made about what 'rhetoric' is." This investigation will follow Kennedy's distinction in examining two theoretical approaches toward rhetorical theory: what we call philosophical idealism (the "systematic" view) and historical realism (or rhetoric as a "historical phenomenon").

The two approaches can be distinguished in several ways. The philosophical-idealist approach articulates a synchronic, or vertical, view of rhetoric, whereas the historical-realist approach takes a diachronic, or horizontal, view. The propensity of the systematic approach is to "lump" discrete rhetorics together, and the tendency of the historical approach is to "split" related rhetorics apart. Perhaps most significant, the systematic view aims toward the unification of rhetorical theory into one overarching conception of rhetoric; the historical view sees rhetorics as unique, even atomized entities.

Philosophical Idealism: The Vertical View

The vertical, or synchronic, designation refers to histories of rhetorical theory as an evolution of theoretical or discursive refinement—the continuous working out of fundamental issues or structural patterns. Such constructions emphasize the progression of rhetorical theory through time. Of the two dimensions, the vertical view is the more self-referential. This approach privileges the multilevel nature of discourse even as it explains discourse as a phenomenon. Within the philosophical-idealist view, there are two major directions toward the verticality of rhetoric: the scientific and the structural. The aim for both directions is to see rhetoric as a unified structure subtending any particular manifestation—hence, a "vertical" view of rhetorical theory.

Scientific rhetoric views rhetoric as a systematic discipline. It concerns rhetorical studies as they address universal problems in epistemology, ontology, and the philosophy of language. It assumes that rhetoric is a constant phenomenon linked to some unchanging reality—an object or a procedure, a function or a definition. Scientific rhetoric assumes that historical, cultural, and political differences cannot change what is essentially rhetorical. Hence this approach seeks to discover an underlying theme or concept of rhetoric that unites all theories under one basic problem or set of problems. Sometimes the aim is to produce a covering metarhetoric, and history serves to characterize past rhetorical theories as a series of more or less successful attempts toward describing that metarhetoric (Bormann 1980; Harper 1979; Simons 1978; Simons and Aghazarian 1986). Sometimes the aim is to revive current rhetoric in terms of timeless truths or persistent problems or questions (Corbett 1971; Lunsford and Ede 1984; Murphy 1982a). The purpose of the approach is to create a model that "mirrors" rhetoric as it exists (Rorty 1979, 37–49).

This category includes approaches that reduce rhetoric to an essence—a list of essential questions or a definition of rhetoric as essentially epistemic. As Wayne Brockriede recognized, this approach seeks a "monistic" approach to rhetorical theory (Brockriede 1966, 38). Similarly, Michael Halloran, though using the discussion to support another point, unified classical rhetoric under the cultural ideal of "a good man speaking well" (Halloran 1976, 235). Like Brockriede, he argued that a similar unifying theme is not evident, indeed is not compatible, with contemporary theorizing.

A significant problem with the scientific approach is that it obscures historical and political diversity in two ways. By seeing the "rhetorical tradition" as an evolution of "discoveries" toward a definitive "rhetorical theory," this approach obscures how discrete discoveries stemmed from different purposes and guiding assumptions. Further, the scientific approach does not recognize that the scholar who appropriates the past may have an agenda. For example, the classical tradition has frequently been called forth to justify a liberal-pragmatic view of rhetoric (Fisher 1987; Hudson 1932; Perelman 1979). Opponents of that view, however, have used the classical inheritance to justify quite different interpretations, ranging from romantic expressivism to radical materialism (Knoblauch and Brannon 1984; Olian 1968). This range of possible interpretations of the classical tradition suggests that, contrary to the assumptions of the scientific view, the representation of rhetoric is always influenced by a historical/political context that constrains how theory is constructed.

The structural model, alternatively, views rhetorical theory as structured like a language. For the structural model the purpose of history is to provide a set of performances from which basic competencies can be adduced. The ground of discourse is not discourse itself but a set of determining base structures of various sorts—linguistic, cultural, social, or political. Structuralism attempts to satisfy the sense that not everything discourse says is expressed. Like philosophical approaches, structuralist rhetorics often seek to uncover a definitive structure for rhetoric regardless of time and context, as in Roland Barthes's conflation of ancient and contemporary rhetorical theory into one underlying structure. Other remarkable structuralist rhetorics, such as that of Valesio, avoid these problems, but their approaches either can produce an obsession with the trivia of superstructural forms or may see the base structures as so determinative that they overlook idiosyncratic variations in a text (J. Dubois et al. 1981).[1]

Philosophical-idealist theories, then, may run the risk of valorizing the theoretical dimension over the practical and replacing local historical and political concerns with structural ones. These problems may be traced to the explicit assumption that discourse is multilayered and the implicit assumption that the self-referential layer is the most interesting, theoretically speaking. In these respects philosophical idealism is relatively blind to historical and conditional factors impinging upon rhetorical theories.[2]

Historical Realism: The Horizontal View

The horizontal, or diachronic, designation refers to histories of rhetorical theory as an assortment of distinct attempts to answer questions unique to a particular era or group. Such constructions emphasize the local concerns that emerged in a specific cross section or segment of history. Historical realism has been the prevailing practice of rhetorical theorizing for decades. Out of this tradition come the great synoptic histories: those of Baldwin, Howell, and Kennedy, for example. This approach attempts to capture the "natural" history of rhetoric, focusing upon what the ancients said about it "in their own words." Such textbooks as James L. Golden, Goodwin F. Berquist and William E. Coleman's *Rhetoric of Western Thought* demonstrate this approach, focusing on various periods of history and offering an account of what key figures said of relevance to rhetorical theory. This approach assumes that rhetorics are inherently different, possibly in incommensurable ways. Historical realism constitutes an "archaeology" (not in Foucault's but in Valesio's sense), in that it considers rhetorics almost as preliterate, as documents or traces to be recorded, examined, and explained through historical, linguistic, and anthropological means.

At first glance, the historical-realist approach would seem to be the very opposite of the philosophical or scientific. For example, the approach is referential, not cumulative—one theorist can cite another, but the discipline itself does not "progress." Paradoxically, however, historical realism conforms quite nicely with the scientific mode of philosophical idealism, as both marshal "objective" facts, if not into a coherent whole, then at least into a systematic arrangement. As in the scientific mode, the very text of theoretical discourse can be ignored or addressed only for its content, and rhetorical theories can be seen as mere documents of their contextual events. Often, historians offer little reflection as to why certain treatises or passages of texts have been selected as relevant and others overlooked, and the historian does not acknowledge taking a rhetorical stance. The purpose of the historical search is to collect material for eventual processing by the scientist into generalizable truths or laws.

As we have suggested, the historical-realist approach employs a horizontal view of discourse that is one-dimensional, a diachrony embellished with sequential variations that neither refer nor relate in particular to any other phenomenon or discourse. But this horizontal assumption provides the theorist with a significant advantage: It avoids assuming a transcendental "foundation" or "base" to serve as the grounding of the discourse somewhere outside the discourse itself. Rhetorical discourse then is nothing but rhetoric, pure and simple; there are no "assumptive theories" or "essential rhetorics" existing on another plane. In the nontranscendent view, rhetorical theory collapses of its own weight. As a result, a historical approach might aid in liberating discourse from whatever overarching concepts bind it to a preconceived order.

Recently, deconstructionism has laid claim to producing the particularist and nontranscendental view most conducive to liberating theoretical thinking. Derrida and Foucault have presented approaches designed to shatter preconceptions about rhetorical theory as part of a "tradition." But this version of the horizontal model also has its disadvantages. Strictly taken, the conventional structural components of rhetoric, that is, purpose, strategy, intention, audience, and situation, themselves become textualized. Thus text can be valorized over and above any alternative conceptual frame. There is no place for the matrix of ever-shifting signifiers to stop or center. Such an approach flattens the self-referentiality of rhetorical theory, devaluing its important multilayered side.

Further, while in the act of accounting for the existence of differences in discourse, the horizontal view may find itself reconstituting the very hierarchy it tried to resolve. Even as the horizontal view argues against continuity, it puts in its place an alternative explanation for the existence of a particular text; often that explanation is a political one. An entirely horizontal approach cannot avoid establishing some transcendent grounding for discourse. It simply establishes a different *kind* of grounding.[3]

A Third Method: Discursive Dialects

Before describing the third method or approach to rhetorical theory, we wish to digress and survey one of its important antecedents—historical materialism. In its mechanical (or vulgar) form, materialism posited a highly vertical relationship between discourse and its determining conditions. These conditions always included material forces and power relationships but seldom took into account discourse itself acting self-reflexively on other discourse. Hence, the base-superstructure relationship of materialism established a hierarchy in regard to discourse, but one in which the course of history was the determinative factor. Rhetorical theory was reduced to discourse, and discourse was related to material process. Thus to interpret or explain discourse, the theorist did not go to discourse itself but to the determining contexts or situations in which the discourse was embedded. Each of these contexts was particular in its manifestations, even though it was subject to universal principles.[4]

Like the materialist approach, our third approach to rhetorical theory (the discursive-dialectical) assumes that the horizontal interrelates with the vertical. In this view, rhetoric is located in the historical matrix, that set of political, social, and economic influences that makes different any particular instance of theory or discourse. It argues that no single theoretical or cultural ideal can be constructed to unify such diverse theoreticians as Edward Corbett and Michel Foucault. Moreover, to argue for such a view obscures the important political and conceptual diversity central to a vibrant theoretical enterprise.

The discursive-dialectical approach does not merely see rhetoric as a reflection of its historical context, nor does it see rhetoric as independent of structural regularities. Instead, it sees the context itself as constituted both by material and by discursive forces. That is, discursive dialectics is the study of how the structure of discourse depends upon historical variability and how particular historical contexts in turn are generated by associated discursive and political structures. This reflexive turning, often designated by the term "reproduction," is characteristic of rhetoric itself. Thus discursive dialectics views rhetorical theory simultaneously as primary discourse and as self-reflexive discourse without subordinating one dimension to the other. Perhaps the concept of a discursive-dialectical approach to rhetorical theory can be clarified by considering two factors in its construction: how rhetorics are constituted by society as part of the historical matrix and how rhetoric constitutes society as part of that same matrix.

Rhetorics Are Constituted by Society. The argument here is that rhetorics are products of social realities, social content, and social value. Not only does the definition of rhetoric change over time, but so do the ground rules of rhetorical theorizing itself. The very possibility of a unified theory of rhetoric is displaced. Despite the employing of historical assumptions and methods in the writing of rhetorical theory, scholars have yet to recognize the fully historicized nature of theory. Further, our hermeneutical limits make problematic all efforts at understanding past rhetorical theories. We may not be able to understand historical rhetorical theories "on their own terms" at all.

Edwin Black, in his discussion of the revolutionary effect of Christianity upon the concept of rhetoric, hinted at such an outcome by suggesting that equally radical alterations may have occurred during the scientific revolution or with the advent of industrial capitalism (Black 1980, 83). Likewise, the spate of theorizing in speech communication about confrontational and coercive rhetorical tactics during the late 1960s and early 1970s reflected wide reconceptualization of what was considered "legitimate" rhetorical influence in the public realm (Hancock 1972; Scott and Smith 1969). Yet this historicizing of rhetorical theory does not reduce it to a mere reflection of more fundamental social causes. Rhetorical theory itself exerts a constitutive influence upon its environment.

Rhetorics Constitute Societies. Rhetorical theories are prescriptive in nature—they can create agreement about action associated with what is "appropriate" discursive behavior. These cultural expectations can be enabling or constraining and can produce consensus or division. Pedagogy, or the teaching of rhetorical theories in the schools, provides this acculturation in what is appropriate. In addition, implicit rhetorical theories embedded in criticism, art, political platforms, and popular culture also affect action and the further use of discourse (Oravec 1986). Indeed, consciousness of the very tension produced by discrepancies between explicit or implicit theory and rhetorical practice can be a factor that leads to change.

Moreover, rhetorical theories compose part of the discursive context, the intertextual matrix, that constitutes culture. Rhetorics not only shape society directly but also contend with other rhetorical theories and discourses for the existing cultural space. One of the strategies for constituting rhetorical theories as authoritative and therefore deserving of space is to construct histories for them, lines of tradition that lend coherency to discrete events. Rhetorical theories can help shape history and society through their own weight—the conscious accumulation of past pronouncements that justify and prescribe future actions.

But, as suggested by the concept of dialectics, affiliation with these past rhetorical pronouncements can have a two-way influence. Rhetorical theories of the past were shaped by distinct historical contexts that made certain issues problematic and others nonexistent. In our appropriation of certain theories of the past, contemporary issues that were nonproblematic to past theoreticians may remain overlooked. Thus, as the field of speech has experienced, the appropriation of Aristotle might hinder as well as help in the development of such projects as contemporary composition theory. This is because of the nature of *The Rhetoric*'s unique address to its contemporary and future audiences.

In sum, the discursive-dialectical view of rhetorical theory aims to provide an alternative to more strictly vertical and horizontal approaches. Though historical, and hence horizontally based, it attempts to avoid reducing rhetorical theory to a surface manifestation of its historical or deep structural determinants. It sees rhetorics as both products of and productive of their historical, cultural, material, and discursive contexts. It persistently blurs the distinction between rhetoric and rhetorics and shifts ground easily from one to the other. It functions as a criticism of philosophies and rhetorics because it identifies their assumptive bases as rhetorical. And it is motivated, or aligned, with respect to the philosophical, scientific, structural, and historical-realist traditions.

In the illustration that follows, we examine how rhetorical theory manifests its relationship to its social and cultural context through its constitution as a specific kind of discourse. In the twentieth century, traditional rhetorical theories function as intellectual practices, operating within the confines of academic institutions and having a practical impact on how its members, students, and patrons conceive of the world. Consequently, rhetorical theorists call upon past theory or "tradition" to legitimate and authorize contemporary views of rhetoric. In Edward Said's terms, contemporary rhetorical theory "affiliates" with past texts to support its currency in the intellectual community, which decides how theory changes, or if it changes at all (Said 1983, 16–24). Thus to understand fully our rhetorical history, we must attend to the interweaving of theoretical, contextual, and political issues, with rhetorical theories viewed as discursive phenomena directed ultimately to ourselves.

Rhetorical Theories as Institutional Practices: The Functional, Symbolic Construction, and Ideological-Critical Perspectives

This part of our analysis looks at rhetorical studies as an intellectual practice that utilizes theory for both conceptual evolution (the vertical dimension) and political authorization in an institutional context (the horizontal dimension). On the one hand, rhetorical theories provide the underlying assumptions that ground knowledge claims, that is, those premises that guide the kinds of questions raised and how answers are constructed. But just as important, rhetorical theories provide legitimacy to particular scholarly orientations by securing affiliations with authoritative concepts. Therefore, to understand a particular theoretical orientation we must make explicit both its underlying conceptual assumptions and the relation of those assumptions to the affiliative concepts providing institutional authority.

This approach further emphasizes how contemporary practitioners link various theories together to create scholarly orientations, or "perspectives." Perspectives can be identified by noting the common assumptions distinguishing various theories as well as examining the sociopolitical contexts in which the theories and their affiliative concepts arose. Our goal is not to advance a framework to understand all theory but to make explicit the guiding assumptions and political alliances that inform theoretical inquiry in the domain of what has been called American Rhetorical Studies, exemplified by scholars in speech communication (McGee 1983). The framework itself exists only as a foundation for critical dialogue.

Although there are several distinguishable perspectives in American Rhetorical Studies, we concentrate on three prominent ones: The functional perspective, the symbolic-construction perspective, and the ideological-critical perspective. We construct these perspectives around a nexus of affiliations, or a tradition of theory, that authorizes and guides knowledge claims about rhetoric. Moreover, we conceive of these different views as competing for authority within intellectual institutions and as often explicitly responding to and challenging the others. Finally, these three perspectives demonstrate how changing boundaries of theoretical inquiry have influenced American Rhetorical Studies and suggest a possible place for rhetorical study in relation to other domains of inquiry.

To access the dual nature of theory as discursive practice, we focus upon a set of three issues that respond to the diachronic/synchronic tension in rhetorical inquiry. These issues include: What are the motives of inquiry, or to what intellectual and political issues is a theory responding? What is the view of reality in each perspective? What are the key conceptual components of the perspective? This focus emphasizes the interrelationship among these issues in what they reveal about rhetorical study as an intellectual practice.

Motives of Inquiry

The functional perspective refers to the generally accepted starting point and core of American Rhetorical Studies. As outlined by Michael Leff and Margaret Procario, the initial needs of the field were to establish a domain of inquiry for rhetorical theory and to distinguish it from other areas of study. In response to these needs, Herbert Wichelns advocated privileging the persuasive function of public address as the distinguishing content of the field and identified Aristotelian theory as the authoritative basis of research. The functional perspective, then, focused upon how speakers influenced audiences through the intentional use of speech (Smilowitz and Sillars 1982).

Early theorists could thus claim a unified tradition (adopting a synchronic view) by noting those questions common to rhetoric from the ancients to the present day, while simultaneously responding to the contemporary contextual need (a diachronic concern) to delineate a domain of study sanctioned by institutional authority. This interrelationship between a rhetorical "tradition" and its contextual exigence reveals the duality of rhetorical theorizing: theory functioning as discourse about rhetorical phenomena as well as discourse that strives for legitimacy within an intellectual community. Moreover, the functional perspective provided a domain of inquiry and established an area of pedagogy that was of service to mainstream American culture (McGee 1983). However, the tradition claimed by the functional perspective carried with it theoretical blind spots that would prove problematic to later theorizing (Wander 1983).

The symbolic-construction approach developed in step with a move to expand the application of rhetorical theory beyond public address and functional notions of persuasion. Although not analogous with a "Burkean" perspective, symbolic construction drew upon Kenneth Burke's notions of symbolic action, language, and human cooperation, as in Ernest Bormann's fantasy theme analysis or Walter Fisher's earlier notions of "rhetorical fiction" (Bormann 1985; Fisher 1980). Dissatisfied with the limitations of functional theory, those scholars who adopted symbolic construction found in such writers as Burke alternative theoretical traditions from which to draw institutional authority, even as they rejected the tradition of the older perspective (Brock 1980; Griffin 1964; Hochmuth [Nichols] 1952).

Because Burke provided a good degree of legitimacy to the symbolic constructionists, it is important to recognize the motives underlying his efforts. Unlike the proponents of the functional perspective, Burke was not interested in delineating a discipline identified with speech communication. His project involved legitimating the study and analysis of literary works against the dominance of scientific inquiry on the one hand, and materialist philosophy on the other (Burke 1968). That is, Burke attempted to reassert an understanding of symbolic activity into the domains of both academic and political activity. He emphasized the significance of symbolic experience, arguing that "symbolic action" was the analogue for human activity in general (Burke 1973; 1969b). Though functional writers note that in the *Rhetoric* Burke referred to the tradition of Aristotle (Day 1960; L. V. Holland 1955), they ignore the fact that he paid a great deal of attention to rhetorical form and to the tradition of belles lettres, largely sidestepped by functional theory.

Again, the incorporation of Burke in response to a dissatisfaction internal to American Rhetorical Studies reveals the dual functioning of theory as discursive practice. Through theoretical affiliations with Burkean concepts, rhetorical scholars developed formulations of rhetoric and rhetorical discourse that competed with functional assumptions. Simultaneously, the motives of inquiry that informed Burke's thinking in turn impacted the nature of rhetorical inquiry. A new theoretical "tradition" altered the nature of American Rhetorical Studies by opening up the discourses of literature and philosophy to the discipline of speech.

More recent in development, the ideological-critical perspective grew out of response to European social theory, an open rejection of functional assumptions, and a move to extend symbolic construction. Motivated by the notion that earlier perspectives on rhetorical theory emphasized the construction of symbolic realities through collective visions, myths, or narratives, while avoiding fundamental issues of social power, theorists such as McGee (1990), McKerrow (1989), and Mumby (1989) noted the inherent conservatism of such approaches. Faced with continental attacks on modernist conceptions of rationality, human behavior, communication, and material conditions, these writers sought to rehabilitate the role of the critic in the construction of rhetoric, a role that challenged symbolic forces of domination. This shift was most directly illustrated in a turn away from theories of "rhetorical criticism" toward the idea of "critical rhetoric" (McKerrow 1989; McGee 1990). As McGee argues, an emphasis on "rhetorical criticism" accentuates the process of interpretation, of doing criticism, whereas an emphasis on "critical rhetoric" accentuates the production of discourse. The former perspective "is too easily submerged in philosophical or literary thinking (McGee 1990, 275). Thus, with the introduction of continental theorists such as Jürgen Habermas and Michel Foucault, a "fresh" tradition of rhetorical theory was called forth to serve contemporary motives of inquiry.

As we have seen in this overview of the functional, symbolic-construction, and ideological-critical perspectives, successive "traditions" of theorizing have altered the boundaries of rhetorical thought. This comparison illustrates how different motives of inquiry intertwine with theoretical efforts and how particular "traditions" are brought to relevancy. Each perspective called forth particular assumptions and alternate theoretical traditions that directed inquiry in certain directions and not others. Moreover, the perspectives often took shape in competition with one another, justifying themselves by noting the weaknesses of others. The next task before us is to uncover how the theoretical assumptions underlying these perspectives and traditions both enable and constrain rhetorical theory.

Views of Reality

The functional perspective carried with it a "commonsense" view of reality (Belsey 1980) as experienced and then interpreted internally, with those internal thoughts transmitted to others through communication. Seeing the individual subject as generative of rhetorical discourse, the functional view held that internal subjectivity guided action. The commonsense view of the subject was further entrenched by the theories of Campbell and Whately, which emphasized a relationship between rhetoric and the internal faculties of the mind, or the subjective nature of human thought, with the emphasis first upon the rational and secondarily the emotional (Ehninger 1968). This synthesis provided a grounding for the study of argumentative and intentionally persuasive discourses of all kinds, from debate to political speech making. Thus the theoretical affiliations of functionalism reproduced an implicit view of reality which maintained commonsense assumptions about the subjective world.

The symbolic-construction perspective, in affiliating with the theory of Kenneth Burke, implicitly turned on different notions of reality. For Burke, human action was "symbolic action," experience constituted in the forms and structures of language, which always prescribed strategies for dealing with a given situation. Reality, then, was a symbolic reality, appre-hended only through symbolic systems simultaneously forming meaning and prescribing attitudes toward the world. Such an emphasis on the sym-bolic nature of the human world fit squarely with Burke's desire to em-power the study of literary works in the intellectual community, and to recognize the rhetorical significance of such nonargumentative, tacitly persuasive, genres as advertising, propaganda, and cultural entertainments (Burke 1969b). Rhetorical theorists implicitly reproduced similar notions of reality in their affiliated works and thus transformed the boundaries of rhetorical inquiry.

The ideological-critical perspective emphasized the political "positionedness" of reality. As McGee argued, all consciousness is social consciousness, which always carries with it the "brute force of 'power'" (McGee 1980, 4; McGee 1982). Thus, from the ideological-critical per-spective, reality exists only in social consciousness—constituted in dis-course—in which are embedded social relationships of power (Foucault 1972). This view presumed that not only conventional discourse but also institutional structures themselves are discursive and subjects for rhetori-cal study. Note that ideological-critical assumptions competed with both functional and symbolic-construction views of reality. Ideological-critical scholarship demonstrated the influence of alternative domains of inquiry in shaping contemporary rhetorical theory. As European social theory was imported into American Rhetorical Studies, new conceptualizations within the field contended for acceptance.

Key Conceptual Components

In the creation of key conceptual components is where the "dirty work" of theoretical affiliation gets done. The issue here centers upon how competing rhetorical perspectives conceptualize the important components of rhetoric and what theories are called upon to authorize those conceptualizations. As noted above, the earlier functional perspective relied heavily on Aristotelian and nineteenth-century rhetorical concepts, which reproduced a commonsense view of reality. Thus the speaker generated rhetorical discourse that transported subjective thought to an audience. Moreover, the functional view held humans to have a rational nature guiding decision making. This commonsense view of rhetoric provided a limited scope of analysis, however. Modern scholars complained that the world demanded a broader view of the rhetorical enterprise (Bitzer and Black 1971; Black 1978). Also, a linear model of rhetoric empowered positivistic scientific methods in order to claim the road to truth in rhetorical matters; indeed, some theorists called for greater scientific inquiry (Bowers 1972). To a larger extent, however, theorists reacted against the encroachment of positivist science. Several theoretical adjustments were fostered.

First, dominant notions of "rationality" were replaced with notions of "good reasons" or "reasonableness" (Fisher 1987). Here, Stephen Toulmin proved useful to functional views. He replaced limited Aristotelian notions of enthymematic arguments with a variety of argumentative forms (Toulmin, Rieke, and Janik 1979). Further, Perelman's notions of cultural values were incorporated to expand the functional concept of human rationality. Thus, the turn to both Toulmin and Perelman represented a continuing "tradition" of rhetorical theory, that is, from a functional perspective. These affiliations influenced new conceptualizations of rationality to include a variety of forms and values, yet both also maintained a faith in the rational nature of humankind and a commonsense view of reality. Similarly, critics questioned functional concepts of intent, effects, and audience. Lloyd Bitzer offered a more detailed and sophisticated description of the rhetorical situation. Notions of persuasive strategies manifest in rhetorical discourse replaced notions of psychological intent (Bitzer 1968). Moreover, sophisticated notions of fields of argument, again stemming from Toulmin, were advanced to clarify the scope of rhetorical theory.[5] These theoretical modifications altered how rhetorical components were conceptualized but held intact many commonsense notions of rhetoric.

The key conceptual components in the symbolic-construction perspective differed dramatically from those of the functional. Because reality is constituted symbolically, the key rhetorical components under study included symbolic motives, identification, and the structures and forms of language. Critics, for example, no longer held the speaker as solely gener-

ative of rhetorical materials but rather sought to uncover the symbolic reality of the speaker's situation as revealed through the materials of language. The entire ground of rhetorical inquiry shifted significantly from
the functional perspective. The "tradition" claimed by functionalism lost
much force for symbolic construction. Rather than discovering how individuals use language, much symbolic analysis focused upon how "language
uses humans"; that is, how symbol systems constitute social reality. An example of this approach, fantasy theme analysis, sought with varying degrees of sophistication to reveal the symbolic structures guiding human
understanding and action. The point is that a theoretical perspective,
grounded on the "traditions" of dramatism and symbolic action, competed
with and challenged functional notions of rhetoric.

With the ideological-critical perspective, we see another significant
shift in both theoretical conceptualization and tradition. This perspective
concerned itself with power relationships endemic to discursive practices.
That is, while agreeing that human reality was intertwined with symbol
systems, this perspective held that those systems themselves did not provide the key components of rhetoric and emphasized that specific discursive practices situate individuals in the matrix of power. For example,
Burleson and Kline (1979), using the work of Habermas, noted that
speech acts constrain who gets to speak and in what manner. Thus the
speech act structure determined power relationships in the practice of everyday conversation. Beyond identifying discursive structures that reinforced hierarchies of control, the ideological-critical perspective embraced fully the dialectic nature of critical practice. Critics were viewed as
active agents of rhetorical construction, "proposing" original texts out of
the raw materials of critical analysis (Brummett 1990).

McGee (1980; 1990), McKerrow (1989), and Mumby (1989) explicitly
challenged the functional and the symbolic construction views of rhetoric,
arguing that both overlook fundamental issues of power. By operating
from divergent theoretical assumptions with an alternate "tradition" of
theoretical inquiry, the ideological-critical view also challenged functional
assumptions. For example, the ideological-critical perspective challenged
functional views of the subject through the incorporation of contemporary
critical theory. Whereas the functional view held that the subject constituted discourse, the ideological view held that the subject is constituted in
discourse. Borrowing from such writers as Foucault, the theorists who
held the ideological-critical view argued that a given discourse provides a
space for an "authorial" subject (or speaker) and a receiving subject (audi-

ence) and situated both in relations of power (Blair and Cooper 1987). In sum, the key conceptual components of the functional perspective are represented by the term "argument"; for symbolic construction the terms "fantasy theme," "narrative," or "myth" suffice; for those who espouse the ideological-critical approach the terms "discursive practices" or "discourse" will do.

Rhetorical Traditions and the Practice of Theorizing

The three perspectives proposed above illustrate a dialectic reading/construction of rhetorical theory and rhetorical traditions. That reading emphasizes the horizontal issues, or historically situated concerns, which motivated theory development within a particular historical milieu. It also attends to the vertical, or synchronic, "borrowing" of institutional authority from one era to another. By maintaining this dual focus we are able to delineate the currents of intellectual inquiry and institutional competition informing our scholarly practices. Such a focus highlights both how "traditions" of inquiry are constructed in service to contemporary concerns and how the assumptions and limitations embedded in previous theorizing may be reproduced in current efforts. Thus the dialectic approach provides a vehicle for historians to examine the choices, both expressed and hidden, animated by their constructions of "the rhetorical tradition."

A contemporary debate provides one final illustration. Recent theorists have argued extensively over the concept of "public knowledge" (Bitzer 1978; Farrell 1976, 1978; Carleton 1978; McGee and Martin 1983; McGee and Nelson 1985). Struggling with the increasingly diverse nature of modern society and growing complexity of rhetorical exchange, rhetoricians have construed "public knowledge" in line with functional, symbolic interpretive, and ideological-critical motives and assumptions. Functional definitions have posited public knowledge as a kind of repository of collective human experience. Bitzer (1978), for example, appeals to a public knowledge that "affirms all mankind," while Perelman (1979) writes of a "universal audience" that transcends the values and concerns of the immediate auditors of public discourse. Symbolic constructionists, in contrast, are apt to locate public knowledge within distinct forms of discourse, as in Fisher's (1987) view of the essential role of narrative form in human understanding, or Rushing's (1989) emphasis on mythic archetype. Ideological-critical writers like McGee (1980), however, advance public knowledge as symbolic structures called forth through discourse but rooted in material power relations.

From a dialectic view, each of these theories of public knowledge reveals a duality of rhetoric. Each advocates a position toward contemporary institutional concerns while standing on top of a theoretical tradition (constructed by the theorist) that both confirms and constrains the alternative perspectives. Functional approaches, rooted in a tradition that places ultimate judgment in the hands of a distinct audience that grants or denies acceptance of deliberate propositions, are faced with the need to account for the enigmatic nature of mass-mediated and multicultured auditors of contemporary rhetoric. Symbolic constructionists, confronted by the ever more evident realities of technological and material influences on modern society, are challenged to reassert the role of symbolic structures in a world where people have less and less access to public dialogue. Ideological-critical writers, faced with theoretical attacks on notions of unitary and coherent texts, struggle to reassert a role for the critic in making meaning out of a fragmented and turbulent postmodern world.

To enter into rhetorical "theory building" is to choose a series of presuppositions about rhetoric, a foundation of institutional authority, and an agenda for inquiry. With our histories of the rhetorical tradition thus understood, we may begin to focus more directly and more constructively on the differences between alternative views. Rather than arguing with a theory because it does not meet the agenda of an alternative perspective, assaults that we are often disposed to initiate, we may be better able to push our own constructions toward better questions and worthier answers.

Conclusion

In constructing a history or tradition of inquiry, we argue that rhetorical theorists should become aware of the implications of philosophical-idealist or historical-realist approaches. Theorists should consider adopting a more discursive-dialectical viewpoint that articulates the complex interrelationship between discursive structures and historical, social, and political realities. In so arguing, we recognize that even rhetorical theories themselves, being discourses, have affiliations grounded in the context of their place and time. Multiple perspectives upon rhetoric emerge in divergent contexts and develop in line with different motives of research and views of reality.

Thus scholars can construct different rhetorical perspectives to make explicit underlying assumptions and affiliations guiding various claims to knowledge. By focusing upon the central issues of theoretical inquiry (that is, the nature of reality, issues of value, and so forth) rather than on "great men" or "common questions," we are better able to see why some consider the great men not so great or why common questions may not be common. Such a discussion may help identify when theoretical works found knowledge claims on differing or even contradictory premises and might foster a greater understanding of what particular theories have to offer.

The dialectic approach also allows for contemporary rhetorical theory to be seen as an increasingly important field of inquiry. The study of rhetoric provides a location for collision and synthesis of competing conceptual frameworks. Until now, the theoretical dialogue in many fields of inquiry has not taken into account fully the divergent assumptions of competing perspectives. When we are able to see the implications of underlying assumptions, and the rhetorical power of theoretical discourse within institutions, we will be in a position to reassert rhetorical analysis as a major force in the synthesis of a variety of conceptual domains.

Even so, the particular realm of rhetorical inquiry as a distinct discipline must become less and less clear, as it becomes more and more central to the project of investigating the discursive nature of intellectual practices in general. The core of rhetorical studies will become an acceptance of rhetoric itself as a duality capable not only of discursive statement but also of self-reflexive inquiry. It is this pluralist, dialectical approach that will secure the crucial significance of rhetorical theory to all of the intellectual disciplines that express their purposes in language.

Notes

1. Arnoldo Momigliano (1981) makes a similar criticism of Hayden White's version of structuralism.

2. One approach within philosophical idealism that attempts to avoid some of its rigidities is the "history of consciousness" view employed by Hayden White (1973), Walter Ong (1982), Douglas Ehninger (1968), and John Campbell (1981; 1982; 1984). This view employs the grouping or bunching of rhetorics into epistemologies, eras of consciousness, or even cognitive metaphors. In Ehninger's view, for example, various periods of history operate under divergent contexts of political and social experience. Thus to reach a fuller understanding of past rhetorical theory we must seek to understand the problems and experiences relevant to its time. The approach can swing toward the idealist or the historicist pole. In White's view, for example, rhetorics are forms inherent in the modes of consciousness that produce rhetorical practice, much like constitutive rules. Similarly, Richard Enos has called

for cognitive approaches to research in the history of rhetoric, though with a historicist edge (Enos 1985, 38).

Yet even the "history of consciousness" approach has its problems. Its assumptions are grounded in philosophical idealism of a Kantian or even Hegelian stripe. Its issues tend to revolve around the origin of the structures, whether they be in the mind, in culture, or in language itself. Without a determination of these origins, any particular argument for a given set of historical structures or cognitive frameworks has a quality of arbitrariness. Often, the history of consciousness approach assumes an expanding consciousness or even a spiritual ascent. What seems to be missing is the grounding of idealist methods in examples of the discourse or particular rhetorical theories, a deficiency one might expect to be remedied by historical realism. But when this orientation is examined, the results are as disappointing as with the history of consciousness approach.

3. Paul de Man (1979) argues a similar point.

4. Modern examples of vulgar reflectionism are hard to find. Terry Eagleton (1976) and Fredric Jameson (1982) come close. But see Eagleton's later description of rhetoric as political power (1983a).

5. An example of the work being done in this area is the section on "Argumentation in Special Fields" in Zarefsky, Sillars, and Rhodes 1983, 170–284.

10 Some Rudiments of Histories of Rhetorics and Rhetorics of Histories

VICTOR J. VITANZA

If you venture to think in America, you also feel an obligation to provide a historical sketch to go with it, to authenticate or legitimize your thoughts. So it's one moment of flashing insight and then a quarter of an hour of pedantry and tiresome elaboration—academic gabble. ... One has to feel sorry for people in such an explanatory bind. Or else (a better alternative) one can develop an eye for the comical side of this.

—Saul Bellow

... history is not a fair copy but a palimpsest, whose deleted layers must be thrust to light, written together in their eposodic rhythms rather than repressed to unruptured narrative.

—Terry Eagleton

In order to look for beginnings one must become a crab. The historian looks backwards; at last he also believes backwards.

—Nietzsche

Praefatio I; or, a Pre/amble

In what follows, I have sketched out what I will call "rudiments" of both actual and possible historiographies of rhetorics. In my discussion of these historiographies, I have included such disciplines, metadisciplines, or fields as rhetoric and composition (aka written communication, as variously practiced in Departments of English) and rhetoric communication (aka oral communication, as practiced in Departments of Speech), and, in a few cases, I have also included classical studies (philology). I have included and combined the three under the general rubric *rhetoric* and have selected what I consider to be representative historians *only* to illustrate several, selected aspects of each model of historiography.

Now, this is a simple statement of purpose, but my use of the adverb "only" should not signal to the reader that I am innocent, or am feigning innocence. I am well aware that what I am *only illustrating* has, nonetheless, wide disciplinary implications across the three academic departments that I have attempted here to recombine (perhaps by way of an interdepartmental missive) while pointing to their differences, implications not only across the three but also within each of them. When "Speech people" walked out of English departments at the beginning of this century—and I believe that they had to—a gap (an abyss) was created, across which it is now extremely difficult to speak or write. We communicate at cross-purposes; we engage in a dialogue of the deaf (see Burke 1976; Howell 1976; Ried 1987; Berlin 1985). But, to be sure, the rift between Speech and English—either as oral versus written discourses or as rhetorical (political) versus rhetorical (poetic) discourses—is an ancient one, and it need not be rehearsed here (Ong 1982; Kennedy 1980, 108–119). The important point is that the rift, the gap (an abyss) was ... is always already ... there. To this point, I will eventually return, for it is this rift that I wish to address ultimately.

*   *   *

Hegel remarks somewhere that all facts and personages of great importance in world history occur, as it were, twice. He forgot to add: the first time as tragedy, the second as farce.

—Karl Marx

It is necessary to understand, for now however, that the history of the troubles between English and Speech is threatening to repeat itself (as the fiction goes), within Departments of English—this time, with written communication teachers attempting to walk away from "literary (formalist, modernist) types" in order to start their own departments or units within the university. But the issue is even more complicated and certainly different from the Speech walkout, for there is, in this secessionist movement, no consensus among written communication teachers, or "rhetoricians," in English. While they talk and write of breaking away, they simultaneously are showing signs of breaking away even from themselves. A subgroup wants to drop the word "rhetoric" itself from the set phrase "rhetoric and composition," maintaining that "composition" (writing instruction) was born in the nineteenth century in American colleges, and that it broke off at that point from the history of rhetoric. This tendency to break apart is further exemplified by the positivist/cognitivists who often will have nothing to do with the critical theorists and vice versa. (At a 1991 College Composition and Communication Conference, a positivist/empiricist announced in a research network meeting that for the health of "the discipline" it would be necessary *to exclude* anyone who included Michel Foucault in his or her bibliography!)

I could continue with politically sublime and ridiculous examples, many of which have to do with the theory-practice split, but, recently, Robert Connors illustrated my point about what some people, including himself, take to be happening to "rhetoricians" and "compositionists" in Departments of English: "Our discipline ... is spinning centrifugally to pieces" (Connors 1989, 232). With a similar metaphor he writes: "We are already pursuing research paths so disparate that many thoughtful people have feared that the discipline may fly apart like a dollar watch. ... It is for this reason, I submit, that part of the intellectual task of composition studies today is to understand and unify itself as a discipline" (235; cf. Raymond 1982). Unification is to be achieved, Connors maintains, through "rhetorical history." If Connors is right, the act of writing rhetorical history carries with it the burden of building a new disciplinary community. Yet historians of rhetoric and composition in English departments seem to be at odds with each other (see Berlin et al. 1988). And yet far from such a utopian wish, I (among those who are at odds) write under the conviction that both Speech people and now the English rhetoric people should pull up stakes and just keep on walking, much like the early Sophists did. If rhetoric is to have any future, or (better put) if rhetorics are to have any future-anterior histories—I am going to insist (or is it to incite)—they will have had to be nomadic (cf. Deleuze 1977).

*   *   *

The abyss is the foundation of the possible.

—Georges Bataille

My purpose, then (as I stated in the opening paragraph), is not to reconcile this disciplinary problem but to sketch out "rudiments" of both actual and possible historiographies of rhetorics; it is not to encourage unification but to represent the impulse toward fragmentation. My hope is two-fold: First, as *paradoxa* (dispute), I hope that my sketch might help to identify how and why historians of rhetoric differ; and, second, as *doxa* (opinion) cum *paralogia* (disconnectedness), I hope that my sketch—my paradoxological sketch—might allow us, some more of us, to come to an understanding of the perverse necessity to work *against* any attempt to realize a so-called unified theory, or synthesis, of various protocols for writing "rhetorical history." And why would I work paradoxically against, that is, both alongside and contra to?

Because, as I suggest intermittently throughout this chapter, any unified theory of historiography is always purchased at the expense of excluding the Other, or specifically at the expense of what Michel Foucault (1977) has called a "counter-memory," or what Michel Serres (1982) has called "excluded thirds," or "noise," or what I have previously called "antibody rhetorics" (Vitanza 1987). And yet, as I also suggest throughout the chapter, what is excluded always has a way of returning, on its own fantastic, hegemonic terms, when repressed, suppressed, oppressed. Such is the way of "counter-memory." History *does*—no matter how we might resist—repeat itself, at least, as farce.

*   *   *

… excess reveal[s] itself as truth.

—Friedrich Nietzsche

Therefore, unlike Connors and virtually all of my colleagues, but definitely like Roland Barthes in *The Pleasure of the Text*, my own act of writing histories of rhetoric is driven by the desire to have a *Society of the Friends of the Text (or Hysteries of Rhetorics)*:

> Its members would have nothing in common (for there is no necessary agreement on the texts of pleasure) but their enemies: fools of all kinds, who decree foreclosure of the text and of its pleasure, either by cultural conformism or by intransigent rationalism … or by political moralism or by criticism of the signifier or by stupid pragmatism or by snide vacuity or by destruction of the discourse, loss of verbal desire. Such a society [of rhetoric] would have no site, could function only in total atopia; yet it would be a kind of phalanstery, for in it contradictions would be acknowledged, … difference would be observed, and conflict rendered insignificant (being unproductive of pleasure). (Barthes 1975, 14–15)

Yet, desiring *some more*, just as Barthes himself ever desires *still more*, I would accept the "fools" and the jokers as I accept myself (and hope that my [good] readers, in turn, will have accepted me). For how else, as Barthes says, could I be "the writer [who] is always on the blind spot of systems, adrift; ... be the joker in the pack ... [or] the dummy in the bridge game; necessary to the meaning (the battle), but deprived of fixed meaning; [my] place, [my] (exchange) *value* ... varies [as floating signifier] according to the movements of history, the tactical blows of the struggle" (Barthes 1975, 35; Barthes's emphasis).

*   *   *

A wild practice ... , one that does not provide the theoretical credentials for its operations and which raises screams from the philosophy of "interpretation" of the world.

—Louis Althusser

If possible, however, I would desire to be even a wilder card than a joker (a wilder jester at court than ever previously tolerated. My "I" would be a floating, drifting signifier). And to that end (or beginning) I would have us move on, perpetually, to a *third place* outside this dispute (*paradoxa, dissoi logoi*), to that of a sub/versive paralogy (*dissoi paralogoi*). We will have eventually been there. (We will have perpetually returned to, ventured there to that wild place, that-which-has-been-repressed place, because of discipline, metadiscipline.) Let's cut and paste, blast and uproot. Let's hereafter dis/engage in anacoluthons and asyndetons. Our motto: *Tmesis.*

*   *   *

It is equally deadly for a mind to have a system or to have none. Therefore, it will have to decide to combine both.

—Frederich Schlegel

Praefatio II; or, Another Pre/amble

With this all initially said and undone, it is still necessary, before discussing specific historiographies of rhetorics, once again to mention several additional presuppositions of mine:

My procedure is simple enough; I have chosen the following categories:

I.   Traditional Historiography
     A.   Traditional history that has time (narrative) as a major category
     B.   Traditional history that does not emphasize time or "Man" as a major category

II. Revisionary Historiography
     A.   Revisionary history as full disclosure
     B.   Revisionary histories as self-conscious critical practices

III. "Sub/Versive" *Hysteriography*
     A.   Anti-Platonic
     B.   Anti-Aristotelian

But let's not be misled by this, my apparently simple choice of terms. When I use them, I express less some fixed scheme and less some automatic belonging of historians of rhetoric to each one of them, but more the way that I (for my own personal tactical reasons) identify historians and myself with each category. As we proceed, my tactic—which is a tactic without a strategy (Barthes 1977, 172)—will become more obvious; I am, after all, from time to time, a "sub/versive." Moreover, the three major historiographical categories that I identify are only one set, to be sure, among other actual and possible sets of categories. When I say "actual" I do not mean this word in any positivistic sense. We historians do talk, though loosely, in terms of "traditional" and "revisionary" histories, and, therefore, I wish to call on this, for the most part, shared predisposition, even though we might quibble about these two terms and might even equivocate when using them. So as to diminish quibbling, I am *not* suggesting that "revision" is going on only within that category, nor am I suggesting that any one historian of rhetoric is necessarily stuck in any one category. I assume throughout, instead, that "revision" is going on all the time (revision is all there is) and that it is possible for, say, a traditional historian momentarily to step out of his/her most frequented category. So as to acknowledge the value of equivocation, however, I also assume here a multiview of "revision" as being enacted quite differently across the various three categories and their subsets. Thucydides, no doubt, thought of himself as a "revisionary historian." And Augustine similarly, no doubt, viewed himself as a "revisionary 'rhetorician.'" But why stop here with the value of equivocating about the "revisionary" when, to be sure, some future youngster in historiographies of rhetorics will have to conceive of, even less or more equivocally, the "sub/versive" as terribly "traditional" and, therefore, in dire need of yet still further "revisions." It should be, after all is said and undone and redone, that way with rhetorics.

These, then, are some of what I mean by "actual" categories of history. When I say "possible" categories, however, I mean that the very idea and practice of categorizing itself not only greatly excludes the Other, or the "counter-memory" (as I suggested earlier), but also creates the very conditions of the possibilities for "sub/versively" including what has been, heretofore, systematically excluded. As a case in point, when Ferdinand de Saussure conceived of language as *la langue* (system, grammar) and *le parole* (individual speech act), he also created the conditions of the possibilities for what Jacques Lacan calls *lalangue* (babble/Babel, babylonianisms). As Jean-Jacques Lecercle says: "*Lalangue*," for Lacan, "is the absence, in any given text, of coherent structure, or rather the proliferation of structures," which for the logician and the linguist must be rejected because the "absence" and the "over-proliferation" cannot fit into the calculus of the overall desired logical linguistic system that each is attempting to describe, and that by contrast the psychoanalyst must *take up with* (Lecercle 1985, 80–82). Analogically, I am saying, then, that both "traditionalists" and "revisionists" individually and together dialectically create the conditions of the possibilities for "sub/versives."

*   *   *

> *In many languages of the world counting has never been developed. In some languages of New Guinea … people … count: one thing, two things, many things, and then must stop; one man translated his counting system into Pidgen English for me as one fellow, two fellow, plenty fellow.*
>
> —Kenneth Pike

If, therefore, out of the "actual" comes the "possible," and if out of the "possible" comes the "sub/versive," what, in addition, might the "sub/versive" be? As I have said elsewhere, an answer to this question can be found simply but perversely by counting "one," "two," and "some more" (Vitanza 1991a) and no more. Or as I suggested earlier, it is as simple as thinking of what can come out of the dispute (*paradoxa, dissoi logoi*) between "traditional" and "revisionary" so that we—that is, "some more" of us—can reach for a third (*paralogos*, *dissoi paralogoi*) paracategory. I have (and will have) categorized and finally paracategorized in dis/order to establish a third element (language, *lalangue*) of a para/category that would destroy the categorizing (one, two, and some more), that would unname the naming, that would finally make the activity of categorizing and constructing "covering laws" ironic. This third countercategory or paracategory is what I call and will have eventually discussed as "sub/versive hysteriography" (based on a quasi-Lacanian, feminist neologism, history/hysteria).[1]

More specifically: Instead of a dialectics of history between "traditional" and "revisionary," "sub/version" favors a nonsynthesized baroque allegorizing of hysterias and (schizo) pastiches. Instead of a dialectic between the one of homogenization and the many of heterogeneity systematized, sub/version favors radical, performative heterogeneities leading to dispersion. (It constantly searches for third/some-more subject and object positions.) Instead of a dialectical arborescence (the branching logic of trees), it favors the middleness, between/ness of rhizomes (see Deleuze and Guattari 1987, 3–25; Deleuze and Parnet 1987, 1–35). Instead of a stable but progressive academic discourse, it favors a hybrid based on dissimilar, if not competing, antistyles. Hence, the dispersive, performative style(s) of this discourse—an olio of notes and clippings, reviews of books or articles, heuristic meditations, pugilistic arguments, parenthetical digressions, redactions, conflations, asides, postponements, misrepresentative antidotes, and brief explanatory or argumentative academic articles. I stand with Barthes when he says:

> I am increasingly convinced ... that the fundamental operation of [a] loosening method is ... fragmentation, and ... digression, or ... *excursion*. I should therefore like the speaking and the listening that will be interwoven here to resemble the comings and goings of a child playing beside his [sic] mother, leaving her, returning to bring her a pebble, a piece of string, and thereby tracing around a calm center a whole locus of play within which the pebble, the string come to matter less than the enthusiastic giving of them. (Barthes 1983, 476–477)

Traditional Historiography

What I am labeling as "traditional historiography" has in discussions of history proper such labels as "the documentary model of historical understanding," "the archival model," or "the objectivist model of knowledge."

The disciplinary protocol of traditional historiography is generally an activity of gathering documents (e.g., wills, diaries, testimonies, newspapers, bureaucratic reports, archaeological artifacts) and then combining these documents together or inserting them into an already existing, but incomplete, historical account. This activity is guided by principles of hypothesis formation, testing, and explanation. I will be blunt and say that the style of this activity can be terribly naive: The practitioners of traditional historiography write *as if* the data are representations of manifest reality. They write *as if* from an omniscient point of view. They think of history *as if* it is relatively value neutral and without any rhetorical or ideological dimensions. And they delimit the function of historical imagination, if ever, to the task of "filling in the lacunae" (*mise en abyme*) between and among known facts.

Cause/Effect and Serial

What I have labeled as traditional historiography falls into two broad categories. The first has as its major locus *time* and, therefore, emphasizes narrative events, periodization, and clearly demarcated beginnings, middles, and endings, whether they be informed by linear, cyclical, or *causal* logics. The second kind, predominantly *serial* rather than *causal*, has little or no relation to time, that is, to time as experienced by human beings. In their extreme forms, accounts of this type evolve independently of human beings without upholding the notion of man as the agent of history. Let's discuss them separately, but perversely. (In the midst of the traditional, I become a sub/versive!)

Serial. Schools of historiography that are associated exclusively with the second category of serial—or seemingly nonnarrative histories—are "quantitative history" (or "cliometrics"), which is influenced by econometrics and is concerned with collecting a series of economic facts (such as the history of prices) that can be—and often are—sifted through and processed in a computer; such schools are "social history of ideas, or of *mentalité*," which is influenced by the sociology of ideologies and is concerned with a series of facts (such as demographic attitudes toward sex, death, religion) that can also be processed in a computer. (This category, among others, can be counter to what is called "Kings and Battles Histories" in that *mentalité* history often sets aside so-called great men and high culture in order to focus on low or popular culture.) And more specifically, there is "The *Annales* School of History," which allows some of its practitioners to be less interested in the idea that the individual "makes history" (history is anonymous), and which substitutes quite systematically the *longue durée*, or "long time span," for brief narrative events. An example of "The *Annales* School" is Fernand Braudel's (1972) classic two-volume work *The Mediterranean and the Mediterranean World in the Age of Philip II*, in which Braudel gives us a history of tides, rock formations, and flora and fauna, with man reserved for the closing pages of the second volume of the history and no more important than the previous items catalogued.[2]

   Cause/Effect (Sort of). An exception to what I referred to earlier as the naïveté of "traditional historiography"—which is composed of and by "the documentary model of historical understanding," "the archival model," or "the objectivist model of knowledge"—is yet another traditional model generally referred to as "the covering-law model." (It is this very exception, as an un-covering, that I take as my opportunity to intervene again into this exposition on traditional historiography. Cause/effect can be and in many cases is thought of in tropological terms as a set of metonymic relationships [Burke 1969a; H. White 1978].) It is this possible shift from cause/effect as a topological relationship to a tropological one that I will be concerned with. Therefore, in what follows, be forewarned that I will not discuss this covering-law (cause/effect) model as it might be expected (cf. Mandelbaum 1974; Murphey 1980).

   Though, to be sure, primarily applicable to the first category of historiography (cause/effect, historicity) and only infrequently pertaining to the second (serial, which I sketched out above, as ahistoricity), the covering-law model, unlike the other models, can and does and will, as I will insist and incite, yield histories that approach being self-conscious, self-reflective, and therefore potentially more sub/versive (ahistorical) in their inclusion of (the possibilities of) poetic discourse. (I would go so far as to say that when the covering law is uncovered, when cause/effect becomes unraveled, becomes radically contiguous, there can be a return of the serial, but the radically serial [see Barthes 1976].) I am not saying that this model per se is sub/versive, but I am saying that a few practitioners of the model who have set aside the dominant discourse of history writing (i.e., discursive, topological discourse) in order to take up with the discourse that for the most part has been excluded (appositional, tropological discourse) have recreated, wittingly or unwittingly, the conditions for the possibilities of a subversive way of thinking about the discourses of history.[3] I have in mind Giovanni B. Vico (1968, his four stages) and Oswald Spengler (1934, his Faustian, rise and fall principle), or Stephen Pepper

(1966b, his "root metaphors") and Hayden White (1973, 1978, his tropology of discourse). Vico, Pepper, and White capture discourses and construct a *grammar* of history, just as Kenneth Burke (1984) constructs attitudes toward history. Theirs is a calculus of variations. Therefore, though potentially sub/versive, "the covering-law model" is, nonetheless, akin to the positivistic side of history writing.

Let us get more serpentine and labyrinthine: I would, like Penelope, not only weave and unweave (during the day, and then the night) but also perform both activities simultaneously (turning day into night, night into day). I would reach for, as the tropes will allow us, the absurdist moment. I, therefore, cannot discuss a traditional historiography without simultaneously discussing a sub/versive; a discursive without an appositional; the political without a poetic (*letteraturizzazione* [Kennedy 1980]). I cannot discuss the suits separately; I must shuffle them and I must include plenty, if not some more, jokers. And so: I want to continue this discussion of the covering-law model, then, by further interrogating this model in relation to Hayden White (whom Hans Kellner likens to Odysseus, "the man of many turns" [Kellner 1989, 193]) and to Michel Foucault (whom I would liken to my Penelope).

Although White encourages us to associate his view of historiography with a poetic root metaphor covering-law model, his view, as I have suggested, also provides for the possibility of an analytical procedure that can globally account for (give a *logos* of) disciplinary protocols of history writing and their correspondence to four specific tropes/modes (with their possible combinations and permutations). Indeed, beyond history writing, White's historiographical poetics identifies with and absorbs (or "covers") altogether other disciplines such as psychology and economics. It is possible, in other words, that White could be taken as working in the structuralist or "The Grand Theory" tradition (Skinner 1985), and consequently that his four tropes/modes would be perceived as onto-genetic principles and, therefore, to a high degree, de*term*inistic of human action and, therefore, antihumanistic.[4]

But, to be sure, White is hard to place but easy to in/appropriate. (And this is what makes him so sub/versively valuable.) In my own preliminary classification on its way to declassification, I locate White as overlapping with a traditional covering-law model of historiography, which his own argument favors, and with my second form of revisionary historiography, which I will later discuss under the rubric of "revisionary histories as self-conscious critical practice." (White would have to be placed in this second form of historiography, if we wish to put a premium on his theses of "the historical text as literary artifact" and "the fictions of factual representation" [White 1978, see chaps. 3 and 5 respectively]). White similarly in his own scheming locates Foucault as overlapping, that is, as both included in "decoding Foucault" (chap. 11) and as excluded in the "absurdist moment" in literary theory (chap. 12). This overlapping, these inevitable double theses/binds—included and excluded, integration and dispersion, rational and absurd—make it easy, in turn, for me to include Foucault securely within my third paracategory, within what I call "sub/versive" histories, or what White might call my absurdist moment in rhetorical history. As I will disclose later, it is "the absurdist moment" and a third language (the complete liberation of the jokers/jesters in the deck) that subverts the law, that dehistoricizes any grand temporal narrative, and that even frees a previously tightly woven serialization. (Hence, both cause/effect and serial narratives are cut loose, freed, and dispersed to become little, but nonhomogenized, narratives.)

The very association of White and Foucault wonderfully complicates any attempt (mine or anyone else's) at understanding and systematizing the general model of the covering law. The classifier of historiographies is constantly confronted with such conflicting, contradictory associations. Logic, grammar, and even a philosophical rhetoric carry within themselves the seeds of their own (affirmative) deconstruction. The realization of this perverse tendency in language, however, gets us all a step closer to a counterideology, to rhizomes, and finally to "sub/versions." It is a step I am taking myself, so that even as I classify I may end up also as a paraclassifier or declassifier; I may end up (begin again?) not as a classifier, not as an engager in *topos* or *eutopos*, but as a dis/engager in *atopos* (see Barthes 1977, 49).

Histories of Rhetoric as Traditional

Thus far, I have examined and then complicated some of the basic principles of traditional historiography; now I want to turn to exemplary histories of rhetorics, first, identifying their specific characteristics, then, citing some examples, and, finally in more detail, describing some ideological clashes between traditionalists and nontraditionalists. Predominately all the histories of rhetoric—of which, to be sure, there are very few, though a growing number—fit into this first general category of the traditional: in particular, under the label of the "documentary model of historical understanding" or the "archival model." None of the so-called traditional historians, however, thinks in terms of a strict analytical or poetic "covering-law model," though each does think in terms of a simple grand narrative, namely, *The* History of Rhetoric. They, in orientation, are more philosophical in their rhetoric, albeit Aristotelian, than rhetorical in their rhetorics, or sophistics. I make these judgments with great hesitancy, for a few of these historians know better but, nonetheless, do not practice, a *sophisti*cated historiography.

*   *   *

For the most part, the histories of classical (Greco-Roman) rhetoric are beginning attempts at working within the research protocol of the "archival model." These histories suffer for the most part, as ancient history based on this model most often does, from a lack of sources; after all, two or more thousand years has a way of depleting the archives; and then what is available, as M. I. Finley (1987a, chaps. 1–3) argues about classical archives in general, might possibly be fraudulent (cf. Murphy 1983a, 3).

If rhetorician-archivalists have their dreams of newly discovering ancient or modern sources, they also have their commonsensical, traditional assumptions of what it is *to do history* with these sources. They assume, for the most part, however, that texts and artifacts are "manifest." They assume the Croce-Veyne doctrine of "simple description without method" (Finley 1987a, 1). They write of Aristotle, "The evidence of the canon is so clear" (Kinneavy 1987b, 185).

Furthermore, these historians talk much about the necessity of knowing the past so that we will not repeat its mistakes (Connors 1984; Murphy 1982b). This is a rather naive Santayanian notion that assumes we, in the first place, can manifestly or hermeneutically agree on what the "mistakes" are, and that if we do agree, we will then not perversely—in the face of reason—duplicate the "mistakes." To be sure, there are all kinds of relations between the past and the present, but for the most part they are undisclosed because of a naive approach to historiography; or all kinds of relations, for that matter, between the past and the future, as in the narrative possibilities of the "future anterior" (Clément 1983, 123; Derrida 1981a, 3, 8). If traditional historians want to discover in the past a lesson for the present, they might as well announce their desires as historians and admit the bias that informs their history writing. In my partial agreement with Marx (1984), I believe that history must repeat itself, but *as farce* (cf. N. O.

Brown 1974, 55–57). As long as there is a preponderance of traditional historians of rhetoric, I am forced/farced, therefore, to write hysteries.

And finally, in respect to rhetoric and politics, these traditional historians place great faith variously in the Greek *paideia* (Jaeger 1970; cf. Momigliano 1982), in "the logic [*logos*] of good reasons" (Booth 1974; Fisher 1978), and in bourgeois humanism (Soper 1986). They do not question what is "good" about such "reasons," when such reasons keep over 50 percent of the population, in the (so-called free) West alone, in a state of perpetual exclusion or oppression. Behind the *paideia* and its "good reasons" (*logos*), there is the notion of "humanism"—specifically, the notion that human beings are free, or empowered, to deliberate on any issue and to arrive at consensus (*homologia, pathos*). To be sure, though this logic of the *polis* served "free men" well in the fifth and fourth centuries B.C., such a logic/discourse misserved women and other slaves—namely, the nonelite majority. Today, history repeats itself through perhaps a more subtle oppression of the population. But even the so-called ruling class is subjected. What traditional historians are not aware of—or can/will not admit to or question—is that the speaking/thinking subject (*ethos*) of humanism is not free but caught in both the modes of production of "good reasons" and even worse in their accompanying modes of cooperation. It would do these traditional historians well to read Finley's account of "The Heritage of Isocrates" (Finley 1987b) and the heritage's elitist impact on education up to the present and, I would add, consequently, on canon formation and historiography; and it would also do these traditionalists well to become concerned with how the humanist speaking-subject (*ethos*) has become not only logically untenable in a post-Cartesian world but also politically suspect (J. Butler 1987; B. H. Smith 1988; Vitanza 1993).

As I have sketched out in the above discussion, these traditional historians fetishize history, and it is this very fetishization that, in turn, contributes to these historians' naive readings of history as manifest and as humanistic (men make history) and as liberating (men are free). This fetishistic relation with the material of history can only lead them, therefore, to think of rhetoric as having a unified tradition. Hence, *The* History of Rhetoric.

*   *   *

Let us now turn to some of these representative historians. I shy away from listing their names (a reader of this manuscript suggested that I put them in an endnote), for the charges I have leveled against them are, indeed, strong charges. I include them here in the text, nonetheless, for finally I must be about my business, as they are about theirs. As we so fondly say, "History will judge." The historians that I have in mind are, specifically, G. Kennedy[5] (1963, 1988), J. Murphy (1974, 1982b), C. S. Baldwin ([1924] 1959), W. S. Howell (1956, 1971), H. I. Marrou ([1956] 1964), W. Jaeger (1970), E. M. Cope (1970), W. Grimaldi (1958, 1972b), B. Vickers (1988), A. Scaglione (1972), E.P.J. Corbett (1989), F. D'Angelo (1975), and W. R. Winterowd (1983); and, most recently, R. Connors (1981, 1984, 1986), W. Horner (1982), J. T. Gage (1984), M. Leff (1983, 1988), J. Raymond (1982), J. Kinneavy (1982, 1984, 1987a, 1987b), R. Barilli (1989), N. Johnson (1991), T. Conley (1990), and T. Cole (1991). There are others aplenty.

*   *   *

Some illustrations: To quickly illustrate this category of traditional historiography, I will in passing discuss a few additional aspects of these historians, by giving two examples—really representative anecdotes—initially in respect to Robert Connors/James Berlin, who are in English; then in respect to George Kennedy, Robert Scott, and Michael Leff, on the one hand, and Victor Vitanza, on the other, who are in Speech, Classics, and English. Each anecdote is a demonstration of ideological clashes—among traditional historians (Connors, Kennedy, and Leff) and a revisionist (Berlin) and a sub/versive (Vitanza)—that are for the most part written at cross purposes and that allow us, wonderfully, to see our differences.

In a review of James Berlin's *Writing Instruction in Nineteenth-Century American Colleges*, Robert Connors himself returns to the eternally repressed. He writes: "As popular history this book has much to recommend it; it is well-organized, interesting, readable. Readers need, however, to be forewarned: this is not an objective book. [Berlin] has an axe to grind" (Connors 1986, 247, 249; cf. Berlin 1987, 17–18). What Connors says in theory and then what he says in practice are in conflict; let's take a closer look. First of all, Connors favors in this statement the commonsense ideology of "clarity." Then, Connors dives deeply into the archives (Connors 1986, 248–249) and thereby catalogs the numerous authors and books that Berlin, as a scholar, neglects to even mention. (At this point, in particular, Connors can sound like a revisionary historian advocating full disclosure, with his emphasis on including texts that Berlin has, blindly and ideologically[?], excluded.)

Connors nowhere cites, however, that Berlin intends completeness (who could ever pretend to completeness in any history?), nor does Connors indicate that he himself in digging into the archives is motivated

by wanting to set an ideological distortion straight (unless we are to assume that Connors is intellectually offended by the particular ideology
that Berlin employs quite consciously and openly [see Berlin 1984, 11–12]
and, therefore, would rather have Berlin employ no ideology at all or, better put, have him feign the ideology of being without an ideology). What
does motivate Connors, instead, is a traditional concern for scholarly objective completeness; supposedly, the (apparent) negligence on Berlin's
part is what makes the book a "popular history" and not a more favored,
scholarly (and I must add, mythical) *Total and Monolithic History.* (The bias
in favoring this one genre over others is traditional in academia.)

The second anecdote of an ideological clash is between, on the right
hand, Leff (1988), Kennedy (1988), and Scott (1988) separately, and, on
the left, Vitanza (1987). It would take far too much space to identify, for
example, how Vitanza's three critics (he refers to them as "the gang of
three") speak at cross purposes with his various positions. In a nutshell,
however, each of the critic-traditional-historians attacks Vitanza for not
knowing *The* History of Rhetoric, or some aspect of it (the supreme [ad
hominem] disgrace!), whereas Vitanza never attempts to write such a history in the first place but engages in *farce* (as the eternal return of the oppressed) and suggests ways of revising the grand narrative (of *The* History)
and its characters by way of establishing what he calls sub/versive Third
Sophistic histories/hysteries (the love of contradiction) in lieu of philosophical history (the fear of contradiction). He further states that he desires the recognition not only of the negating/exclusionary concepts of
"disciplinarity" or "metadisciplinarity" but also the possibilities of "non-
disciplinarity"; furthermore, in parallel fashion, he states that he desires
for histories of rhetorics not only a recognition of classical rhetoric as engaging in persuasion (Aristotle) and modern rhetoric as engaging in identification and intersubjectivity (Burke) but also the inclusion of a third (sophistic) notion of rhetorics as dis/engaging in intertextuality. Finally, he
speaks of rhetorics as not "factual" but "performative" (he has been influenced by ethnographers of performance theory such as Clifford Geertz
and Victor Turner).

Kennedy attacks Vitanza's particular use of Ovid; Scott, Vitanza's use of
Cicero; and Leff (and at much greater length), Vitanza's "revision" (or
"spectacular reduction") of the full, grand narrative of history and of every
canonized figure in it, especially Aristotle, Isocrates, and Ramus. Whereas
Kennedy and especially Scott (with his Yiddish joke) join in on "the fun,"
Leff does not leave his, more often than not, serious Olympian status.

Kennedy attacks Vitanza's call for histories based on intertextuality by suggesting that they would be socially irresponsible and dangerous; he argues: "A fundamental psychological fact of human life is that most people cannot cope with a universe in which there is no absolute truth and they are left on their own. Of the various efforts to give some sense of psychological security, the Aristotelian tradition of logocentrism seems to me among the least objectionable" (Kennedy 1988, 230).

Vitanza, in his counterresponse (1988), points out, among other things, that what his critics attempted was a deconstruction of his deconstruction. He admits that their turnabout is fair play, but whereas their use of this tactic has a strategy motivating it (a goal, which is the compulsory, permanent return to the grand-fetishistic narrative of *The* History of Rhetoric), Vitanza's perpetual use of the tactic is without the strategy of returning and then maintaining a single favored, tragic point of stasis (neo/Aristotelian or otherwise); Vitanza's tactic is to move out of "negative deconstruction" to "affirmative deconstruction," in other words, to a third, nonsynthesizing position. Or it can be said that whereas Vitanza's critics wish to favor tragedy (a boundary situation, synecdoche), Vitanza favors a comical, farcical position. In response to Kennedy's charge of irresponsibility, Vitanza countercharges that Kennedy is speaking out of a master/slave morality (see Nietzsche 1969, 58–60). Vitanza states, like the aesthetic Bohemian Kenneth Burke (1968), that his desire "is concerned with such intellectual vagabondage, such aspects of 'irresponsibility,'" that would "constitute a grave interference with the cultural code behind" Kennedy and company's enterprise to write *The* History of Rhetoric (Burke 1968, 121).

As we proceeded through these examples of disputes between traditionalists and revisionists and a sub/versive, what should have become evident inductively is that each dispute is a result of the favoring of different/heterogeneous research protocols, or genres, or disciplinary matrices, with one more generally acceptable over the other. One of the most famous disputes, and suitable as a paradigm here, is to be found in Ulrich Wilamowitz-Moellendorff's response(s) to Friedrich Nietzsche's *The Birth of Tragedy* (see Kaufmann 1967; also, Arrowsmith 1990; Nietzsche 1990). For Wilamowitz, Nietzsche had "perverted" philology. Not unlike Wilamowitz, traditional historians and critics make the same charge. Traditional historians and revisionaries and sub/versives view language (and their relationships to it) very differently. What must be kept in mind when engaging in and reviewing these disputes is that they are sites/loci of what

Jean-François Lyotard (1988) would call "differends," which "would be a case of conflict, between (at least) two parties, that cannot be equitably resolved for lack of a rule of judgment applicable to both arguments. One side's legitimacy does not imply the other's lack of legitimacy. However, applying a single rule of judgment to both in order to settle their differend as though it were merely a litigation would wrong (at least) one of them" (xi). As Lyotard says, "A universal rule of judgment between heterogeneous genres is lacking in general" (xi). Judiciary/forensic discourse, which can deal only with a *litigation*, cannot deal with a *differend*, which is composed of (at least) two genres, phrases in dispute—except to silence or rule out of court all (let us say again) jesters, jokers, fools. A deck (a systematic gathering) of cards, composed of king, queen, jack, et cetera, and a wild card, a joker, must be played not just syntactically, hypotactically, hierarchically (i.e., without the perpetual challenge of the jester-joker) but, I have to insist and incite, must always be played paratactically (at times, anarchically), with the floating-drifting signifier. (This difference/differend will be pursued as I develop this discussion, especially in the light of a sub/versive hysteriography.)

Revisionary Historiography

Like the traditional, there are two forms of revisionary historiographies: I call the first "revisionary history as full disclosure" and the second "revisionary histories as self-conscious critical practices." This category of the revisionary is more problematic than the traditional one, primarily because the first of the two forms of revisionary histories overlaps with both the traditional and the second form of the revisionary. The first form of the revisionary functions here either as an extension of traditional historiography or as a break from it, depending on whether it is informed by the historian's desire to produce actual or possible histories. The more that the first form is tied to the actual, the more it differs *in kind* from the second form, and therefore the easier it is for some traditionalists to accept; conversely, the more that the first form breaks from the actual, the more it differs only *in degree* from the second, and therefore the more difficult it becomes to distinguish it from the second.

As I discuss the most important assumptions made by revisionary historians, I also want to keep an eye on the degree of self-consciousness exercised, which is tantamount to the degree of suspicion exercised. I seek to delineate distinct stages of self-consciousness and suspicion not in the hope of producing a more precise classification but in the hope of demonstrating a general point: Namely, that the more self-consciousness, and consequently the greater suspicion, the closer we move to the third category, "sub/versive hysteriography." More important, I want to show that there is a point beyond which self-consciousness and suspicion necessarily move historiography beyond the domain of revision and inevitably take historiographical practice onto the realm of the sub/versive. My discussion about the various degrees of self-consciousness and suspicion, then, seeks not only to illustrate diversity among revisionary practices but also to identify the point of no return, the irrevocable divide that spins self-consciousness and suspicion beyond the revisionary impulse to the sub/versive.

The first revisionary form of historiography is informed by a hermeneutical principle that activates an attitude toward the past that ranges from a quasi-traditional view of history to an ideological self-awareness of history writing. As quasi-traditional, an historian's attitude toward the past is guided by the impulse to address a "wrong" interpretation of the facts or to accommodate previously undisclosed facts. What is regarded as a wrong interpretation is some other, earlier historian's fallacious use or "inaccurate perception" of the manifest "reality." And since reality here is still addressed in terms of what are still conceived of as objective archival facts, revision in this instance is thought of as "correction." The notion of "accommodating previously undisclosed facts" may refer to a historian's will to supplement or to correct the historical record by incorporating new, significant archival facts that have been "discovered." But it can also refer to the historian's desire to include facts that have been in varying degrees present in the consciousness of the time but deflected in earlier histories because of some prevailing ideology. Depending on whether writers of existing histories are viewed as having unwittingly omitted or misperceived facts or wittingly excluded or distorted facts, revision here can be thought of either as "correction/addition" or as "recollection/reconception." Accordingly, revision can be directed either toward correcting a "wrong" interpretation or toward setting straight a "social wrong."

The hermeneutical principle in the second form, by contrast, begins with an understanding that *all* writing (thinking) is a form of self-deception, which for the most part is unwittingly achieved across sets of deeply rooted, unself-conscious predispositions or ideologies and consequently approaches all facts as always already interpretations in themselves. There is here not only a distrust in surface or manifest reality but also a distrust in naive, conscious explanation and understanding. Such a hermeneutics is what Paul Ricoeur (1978) calls "the hermeneutics of suspicion" to which I will return shortly.

Revisionary History as Full Disclosure

Like traditional historiography, revisionary history of the first kind is still very much committed to archival facts, though there is at times a conscious understanding that texts are interpreted (deflected) across ideologies, and that archival facts themselves on occasion are subject to not only physical corruption but also ideological distortion. Therefore, revisionary history emphasizes the rewriting of history with the primary purpose of the full disclosure of the facts, making what was wrong "right"; making what was a partial picture a complete one. Its primary conceptual starting place is that of inserting in the record what was not previously available or what was systematically (implicitly or explicitly) excluded.

The best example that I know of, say, in the seventeenth century is Gilles Menage's *Historia Mulierum Philosopharum* (1984), which is addressed to a woman of high wit and which is a history of ancient women philosophers, about sixty-five of them, each of whom is treated in brief biographical form and identified with the relevant philosophical school. Even though no new facts are added (since the book merely collects in a single volume what was already available in scattered form in ancient sources), the writer obviously is revising, in that he/she (?) brings to light, contrary to common opinion, that there, indeed, were women engaged in the philosophical enterprise. (A similar modern-day examination of the displacement of women can be found in Finley 1977; Fauré 1981; Waithe 1987; Kelly-Gadol 1984.)

Another example, this time in the nineteenth century, is that of "romantic" historiography (such as the kind employed by Jules Michelet in *Roman History* or *Life of Luther*), which attempts to acknowledge what previous histories had repressed such as the violence done to human beings that was not seen as violence by the historians of the day but only as the conditions of the development of civilization. (This "romantic" historiography is greatly more self-conscious than the previous example; it is also attacked by traditional historians as being excessively irresponsible in its interpretations, its imaginary excesses [see Gossman 1986; cf., however, Barthes 1987]).

More recently, revisionary historians, as they have actually been called, have focused on how, for example, blacks or women or other minorities have played an important role in history, though they have been ideologically excluded in historical accounts. What readily comes to mind are such early popular works by Tillie Olsen (1983) and Joanna Russ (1983). Another example is Frances Fitzgerald's *America Revised: History Schoolbooks in the Twentieth Century* (1980). Ideological deflection is accounted for in this book as a quite conscious activity practiced not only by authors of textbooks but also by publishers who try to design a book for a given market. More recently, there is the work of Martin Bernal, who challenges the entire Europocentric view of Greek Athenian culture (as the so-called cradle of civilization) with a counterview of what he calls "Black Athena" (Bernal 1987). Moreover, there is the work of Stephanie H. Jed, which reveals how specifically the rape of Lucretia, or how in general "a narrative sequence of chastity, rape, corruption, and self-castigation" (Jed 1989, 7), is used historiographically as a means of liberating Rome from the Tarquins and the founding of Republican Rome (9–10) and later as the means of founding any state or movement such as humanism itself (8, 14). (I would insist, in this light, that we must be not only highly suspicious of humanism, as I suggested earlier, but also suspicious of our use of Helen and Hellenism itself! Which means, for example, that we are going to have to be suspicious of Isocrates himself.)

Along with these particular revisionary historians, however, is a group of so-called revisionary historians involved in the recent German *Historikerstreit*, or specifically with the controversy over the Holocaust—namely, whether it occurred, and if it did occur, whether it has the significance many historians wish to find in it (Nolan 1988; cf. Lyotard 1988). Revisionary history, like any form of history, can be used to silence what cannot not, must not not, be told.

As these examples suggest, the historiography becomes less focused on the simple adding of facts (about minorities in general) and more focused on how interpretations of various facts (about the Holocaust, humanism) get deflected/reflected across ideologies. Moreover, the historiography begins to challenge our basic sense of identity and what we hold to be sacrosanct. But in none of the cases (except for Jed) has there been a disclosed (explicit) desire to account hermeneutically for ideological distortion at the level of language or the unconscious. When I come across a hermeneutical sophistication of this sort—as in the works of Helene Cixous and Catherine Clément (1986), Luce Irigaray (1985), Julia Kristeva (1986),

Gayatri Spivak (1987), and so many others—I place these historians and feminists in the next category even though they may have also had full disclosure as one of their aims.

Histories of Rhetoric as Full Disclosure

There is a small, but important, emerging group of historians of rhetoric (and philosophy) whose primary or intermittent purpose in revising history is to correct misinformed or misunderstood views. They accomplish philological studies of particular concepts or key words, such as "rhetoric" itself. Or they are interested in pointing out how much of the history of rhetoric is depicted in a methodology and vocabulary that is inappropriate because it is "philosophical," and that, therefore, distorts or mispresents rhetoricians and their histories or—worse—excludes what desires to be variously said in relation to writing histories of rhetorics.

In this group I would among others include E. Havelock (1982, 1983), W. Ong (1958, 1982), C. J. Swearingen (1982, 1991), for their work on literacy; D. Stewart (1978, 1979), on Fred Newton Scott; W.K.C. Guthrie (1971), G. B. Kerferd (1981a, 1981b), B. E. Gronbeck (1972), R. L. Enos (1976, 1987), C. Segal (1962), M. Untersteiner+ (1954), S. Jarratt+ (1991), J. Poulakos+ (1984), S. Rosen (1983), S. Whitson+ (1991), R. Moss+ (1982), E. Schiappa (1990a, 1991), their work on the Sophists; T. Poulakos+ (1988) and N. Loraux (1986), on epideictic; T. Perkins (1984) and Welch (1990), on Isocrates; G. Kustas (1970), on Byzantine rhetoric; R. McKeon (1987), C. Perelman and L. Olbrechts-Tyteca (1958), W. Grimaldi (1972b), and P. Valesio (1980), their work on Aristotle; V. Florescu (1970), "rehabilitation" of rhetoric, culminating in the work of Perelman; J. de Romilly+ (1985), the first three lectures of *Magic and Rhetoric*; M. Halloran (1975, 1982), S. Crowley+ (1984, 1990), and J. Berlin+ (1984, 1987), nineteenth through twentieth centuries; S. North (1987), on writing instruction as a field; D. Ehninger (1968, 1975) and R. Scott (1975), on the categories of the history of rhetoric; J. Lyne (1985), H. Simons (1985, 1990), J. Nelson, A. Megill, and D. McCloskey (1987), "the rhetoric of inquiry" group and its various metadisciplinary functions. (I have used a plus sign (+) to designate that the work of the individual historian, on occasion, overlaps also with the second category of revisionary history.)

Some significant work by these revisionary historians is being done on the Sophists, whose legendary ideological suppression makes nearly anything written on them some sort of disclosure. It was seldom the case, however, that the Sophists went undisclosed. They were, along with the pre-Socratics, in fact, accounted for in *The* History of Philosophy, but accounted for in primarily philosophical terms (Kofman 1987). Moreover and more important, the strategy of traditional historians of rhetoric has been to perpetuate this prejudice of philosophy and to tell much of *The* History of Rhetoric in either Platonic or mostly Aristotelian terms, with their accompanying different epistemologies and ontologies and with the philosophers (namely, Aristotle) as "good guys" and the Sophists (pick any) as "bad—or at least highly questionable—guys" (see Kennedy 1980; Vickers 1988; Cole 1991).

As a number of nineteenth-century and early twentieth-century historians have disclosed (e.g., Grote 1868; Gomperz 1955; Zeller 1955), the Sophists need to be discussed separately from philosophy and depicted in respect to their own terms. More recently, historians of philosophy and of rhetoric (e.g., Guthrie 1971, Kerferd 1981a, 1981b, Segal 1962, Untersteiner 1954, and J. Poulakos 1984) have built on their predecessors by either distinguishing between philosophical and rhetorical discourses or distinguishing among Platonic, Aristotelian, and sophistic discourses, with their various epistemologies. They have pointed out how traditional philosophers and Sophists differed in respect to such key terms or concepts as dialectic and *dissoi logoi*, or *physis* (nature) and *nomos* (law, custom); or have differed on *areté* (excellence, political virtue) as either ideal or material/ practical. Whereas traditional philosophical discourses have testified to and have been steadily concerned with absolute over relative, or *physis* over *nomos*, or with a *logos* without both *mythos* and *doxa*, sophistic discourses, by contrast, have generally demonstrated a penchant for relativisms over the absolute, *nomos* (local *nomoi*) over *physis*, and a penchant for a mixture of *logos* and *mythos* and *doxa*.[6]

The influence of traditional philosophy on rhetoric, as in a "philosophical rhetoric" (Kennedy 1980; Mason 1989), must be seen for what it is— namely, and I put it mildly here, a disrespect for the rhetorical dimensions of "facts" and, consequently, a narrowing and denying of possibilities. No doubt, Plato viewed philosophy (dialectic) as the copingstone of the sciences (*Republic* 534e). Such a copingstone (like Occam's Razor), when used to tell *The* History of Rhetoric instead of histories of rhetorics, however, accomplishes three things: It, for the most part unconsciously, reads all key terms and ideas according to its own predispositions; it flattens differences (or turns them into melodrama); and it creates the illusion of a grand narrative and thereby excludes, deflects, represses, and eventually politically oppresses, by cutting away, all that does not fit.

*   *   *

... I learned first from de Man and then from Derrida the importance of reading absolutely literally. And of course the word "literally" is like the word "history." Like any master word, it is a catachretical word.

—G. C. Spivak

While there is much work going on in the area of the Sophists, there is also the beginning of a valuable series of disputes. Similar to the Kennedy/Scott/Leff attacks on Vitanza, Edward Schiappa has recently taken on, in general, how some revisionist historians have been representing the Sophists, but in particular how the historian John Poulakos in a sequence of essays has rendered them. So as to minimize unproductive misunderstandings, I would say that my sense of Schiappa's critical attitude in this dispute is that he is not practicing what I have called here a traditional historiography; I see him perversely as a revisionary historian of the first kind, i.e., as a historian concerned with a full disclosure of the facts, but with the aim of revising the revisers and their revisions; moreover, Schiappa, as a revisionary historian, announces his predispositions as those based on Richard Rorty's (1984) view of historiography. (I am very leery of Schiappa's use of Rorty's historiographies of philosophy and not rhetoric.) I must admit at the same time, therefore (I have mixed feelings about all of this), that when reading Schiappa, I think that I hear a traditionalist (in sheep's clothing) attempting to outmaneuver a revisionist. (If so, then fine. Let the games begin.) What is especially interesting about Schiappa's writings is that his attempt at full disclosure runs counter to that of Poulakos's attempts at full disclosure.

To understand this controversy, we must recount that Schiappa initially argued that there is no evidence in authentic texts that the word *rhetorike* was used in the fifth century B.C., though it can be found in early fourth-century texts; he suggests that Plato coined the word (Schiappa 1990a). This on the surface is an interesting point, for it suggests that the disclosure of a single philological fact comes with the demand to see all histories of rhetoric that have not taken this fact into account as blatant misperceptions, as incorrect, and as anachronistic!

Extending this argument elsewhere, this time, however, by questioning the resurgence of interest in the Sophists (a "steady stream" about to become a "tidal wave" [Schiappa 1990c, 193]), Schiappa employs Rorty to distinguish between two kinds of historiography, or hermeneutical principles: The first is "rational reconstruction," which exhibits "creativity and modern utility"; the second, "historical reconstruction," which favors the "historical fact," "historical grounding," "how the author and his or her contemporaries understood the text" (193–194). (This distinction may parallel the distinction that J. Poulakos [1984] finds between the Sophists, as the "possible," and Aristotle, as "the actual.") Schiappa favors the latter, and he sees Poulakos, whose work he interrogates, as favoring the former and, therefore, as greatly contributing to recent historians' looking into the mirror of the Sophists (cf. Rorty 1979) only to see themselves and not the Sophists, whoever they were. Schiappa states in his argument that he is not suggesting that "historical reconstruction" should not be done, but, agreeing with Rorty, "done 'differently'" (Schiappa 1990c, 196). Schiappa thereby continues by saying that Poulakos blurs the distinction, thinking that he is actually and accurately representing the Sophists as they perceived themselves.

J. Poulakos (1990) responds to Schiappa by arguing that knowing the so-called philological facts is not enough and, besides, such a narrow notion of facts, to begin with, is "false" thinking (cf. Arrowsmith 1990). Referring to Nietzsche (1968a, 481, 556), Poulakos argues that facts are interpretations. Moving from Nietzsche, whom many readers might not want to assent to, Poulakos then refers to R. F. Holland, Eric Havelock, and Charles Segal, having said what Nietzsche has said. Poulakos concludes that Schiappa is "unaware of the rhetorical character of facts" (J. Poulakos 1990, 221). Then, Poulakos argues that Schiappa's approach to philological interpretations is one that is basically a romantic hermeneutic (see Gadamer 1975), which assumes that we as readers can understand texts the way their authors or contemporaries of the authors might have understood them (J. Poulakos 1990, 220–221).

Having found fault with Schiappa's philological approach ("his narrow factualism" and "naive view of reading" [J. Poulakos 1990, 220]), Poulakos then engages in and tests the very language game of classical philology that Schiappa himself employs in his attempt to prove that the word *rhetorike* is not to be found until the fourth century B.C. Poulakos immediately finds fault with Schiappa's procedure as a philologist (222); he says that using Dave Packard's IBYCUS and the *Thesaurus Linguae Graecae* compact disc, he "found matches in Aeschylus, Aesop, Antiphon, Democritus, Isocrates, Lysias, and Thrasymachus" (222). Though *rhetorike* is not found in the nominative case (singular), it is found in other cases. Poulakos says that all that Schiappa's argument proves, when verified, is that "Plato was the first to use the term rhetoric in the nominative case (singular)" (223). Poulakos's additional argument is that even if the word *rhetorike* was never used and if it did not exist at all, this would be no argument for the claim that rhetoric was not practiced or theorized on, or specifically that the Sophists were not rhetoricians (223). Absence of proof is not proof of absence.

This discussion between Schiappa and Poulakos continues, and as I said, it is too long and complicated to report here. Schiappa (1990b) counterresponded to Poulakos and has continued his attempt to problematize the construct "sophistic rhetoric" (Schiappa 1991). What I find especially amusing about this extended exchange is that the alleged two sides are not really that fixed (except in a chiasmus), nor should they be, nor do the two historians, especially Poulakos, really think that they should be. Going back to Schiappa's use of Rorty's distinction between the two historiographical approaches of "rational" and "historical reconstruction," we can see that Poulakos himself is well aware that the construct "sophistic rhetoric" can be stretched analogically too far. In his unpublished article with Steve Whitson (Poulakos and Whitson 1990), Poulakos argues against the feminist revisionists Susan Jarratt and Nedra Grogan (forthcoming) and Jarratt (1990, 1991), who attempt "to forge an alliance between the Greek Sophists of antiquity and the feminists of postmodernity." Those readers of Schiappa may be inclined to see Poulakos's argument here as standing in contradiction to his response to Schiappa. I think not, for what Poulakos is against is not "historical reconstruction" or the "actual" per se but against what he would see (as he, in fact, sees it) as less than adequate *performance* of the language games of either "rational" or "historical reconstruction," which he finds in both Schiappa (a rational reconstructionist) and in Jarratt (a historical reconstructionist). No doubt, this discussion will continue, as it must, and especially along performative lines.

Revisionary Histories as Self-Conscious Critical Practices

Unlike "revisionary history as full disclosure," revisionary history of the second kind is not at all a part of the disciplinary protocol of traditional history writing, for it is greatly more self-conscious in relation to not only ideological distortion but also attempts to account for such distortion. It is a form of historiography, in my particular view, that is deeply influenced by post-Enlightenment, self-conscious critical, hermeneutical practices of such thinkers as Marx, Nietzsche, and Freud; it is a historiography that grows consciously out of what Paul Ricoeur and Richard Palmer call "the hermeneutics of suspicion" (Ricoeur 1978, 32–36; Palmer 1969, 43–45; cf. Bruns 1982, esp. chap. 4, 88–107; Vitanza 1992). With the appearance of these three hermeneuts, the concepts of "fact," "reality," "subject/*ethos*," "reason/*logos*," and "history" take on much less stable meanings than heretofore realized.

*   *   *

> *Reader, I think proper, before we proceed any farther together, to acquaint thee that I intend to digress, through this whole history, as often as I see occasion, of which I am myself a better judge than any pitiful critic whatever; and where I must desire, all those critics to mind their own business, and not to intermeddle with affairs or works which no ways concern them; for till they produce the authority by which they are constituted judges, I shall not plead to their jurisdiction.*

—H. Fielding

Palmer speaks of "the hermeneutics of suspicion" as having a goal of the destruction of "a false reality," or, as the Marxists say, "a false consciousness." (This hermeneutic is suspicious of surface reality and of conscious understanding.) One source of this "false consciousness" is Descartes; though he doubted everything, he did not doubt himself (his *ethos*) as a speaking-subject; or more generally, he did not doubt his own consciousness, which was for him a starting point back to the world. The new hermeneutics, however, doubts/problematizes even this Cartesian speaking-subject, or consciousness. Such a hermeneutics has as its goal the "destr[uction of] masks and illusions in a relentless rational effort at 'demystification.'" For Marx, Nietzsche, and Freud, "true thinking was an exercise in 'suspicion' and doubt" (Palmer 1969, 44). True thinking, in dis/respect to the speaking-subject, to *ethos*, is "iconoclastic" (see Vitanza 1993).

But as a sub/versive hysteriography will disclose, this characterization of suspicion by Palmer and especially by Ricoeur must be held in suspicion itself. Let us take a closer look and turn to perhaps the most notable of the modern-day hermeneuts of suspicion, Fredric Jameson, in his advocacy of

Marxism. Like Ricoeur, Jameson's thinking begins and ends with a *double thinking* of hermeneutics—the one positive, the other negative. In *The Political Unconscious*, Jameson quotes the following, by now much-celebrated, passage from Ricoeur: "According to one pole, hermeneutics is understood as the manifestation and restoration of a meaning. ... [A]ccording to the other pole, it is understood as a demystification, as a reduction of illusion" (Ricoeur 1978, 27; Jameson 1981, 284). (There is something of an analogous relationship here between my two categories for revisionary history and Ricoeur's and Jameson's for hermeneutics.) Jameson continues, in his quoting of Ricoeur, in regard to

> this double solicitation and urgency: on the one hand, purify discourse of its excrescences, liquidate the idols, go from drunkenness to sobriety, realize our state of poverty once and for all; on the other hand, use the most "nihilistic," destructive, iconoclastic movement so as to *let speak* what once, what each time, was *said*, when meaning appeared anew, when meaning was at its fullest. Hermeneutics seems to me to be animated by this double motivation: willingness to suspect, willingness to listen; vow of rigor, vow of obedience. (Ricoeur 1978, 27 [Ricoeur's emphasis]; Jameson 1981, 284)

For Jameson, this double (or dialectical) thinking allows for a demystification of the modes of production, while it simultaneously allows for a utopian vision of the world—namely, it allows "that a Marxist negative hermeneutic, a Marxist practice of ideological analysis proper, must in the practical work of reading and interpretation be exercised simultaneously with a Marxist positive hermeneutic, or a decipherment of the Utopian impulses of these same still ideological cultural texts" (Jameson 1981, 296).

Jameson's work is quite impressive, but I do have problems with Ricoeur's and Jameson's *uses* of hermeneutics; for like any "demystifiers" or revisionists who attempt to provide us with a "demythologized" view of the world (or history), the practicing demystifiers of the institutions that survive Marx and Freud—I purposefully exclude Nietzsche and his interpreters for the sub/versive—have in turn only given us surrogate icons, only given us other forms of mystification and, therefore, other mythologies that are ideologically encrusted with a scientistic or a utopian point of view and that are designed, quite ironically, to suppress and to repress all other points of view. (These hermeneutic-demystifiers, these revisionists, were/are never "suspicious" enough!) Specifically, then, what I critique Jameson for attempting, in the words of Gilles Deleuze and Félix Guattari

(1983), is a deterritorialization and then a *"re*territorialization"—that is, a *re*coding as a *re*turn, though more subtly, to the (dreaded) status quo of mystification, political oppression. What is wanted, instead, is a sub/versive "*de*territorialization," or *de*coding, or multiple "lines of flight," or perpetual suspicions.

Jameson's stated revisionary intentions (and those of his Marxist colleagues) are, indeed, noble. From my nomadic-"sub/versive" perspective, however, their intentions are highly problematic. I agree with Jameson when he says "that everything is 'in the last analysis' political" (Jameson 1981, 20); but I also agree with Kenneth Burke when he says that the aesthetic subsumes the political (Burke 1968, 113) and agree with him again that human beings are "rotten with perfection" (Burke 1966, 16), but I would add, however, they/we are also *blessed with perversity*. For me, as I think for Burke, this aesthetic that informs the political is not situated in the unconscious, unless it be planted/coded there by some colonizer such as a Freud or a Jameson. My general impression, which is postcolonial, is that Jameson's totalizing tendency (Jameson 1981, 19–20) must exclude far too many of us. Even though he accepts Deleuze and Guattari, he does not accept them on their own terms (22). Jameson works hard at trying to create a phalanstery, but his political vision (of the unconscious) thwarts his attempt. Jameson's system unfortunately necessitates a gulag, which means that the jokers, or a particular joker, would have to be excluded from the deck, so as to maintain the so-called integrity of the whole.

*   *   *

To be sure, Marx demanded that the world not be interpreted, *but changed*, but in order to know what was wanted (if we read Marx as a humanist), we had, nonetheless, to interpret it. (Hence, Jameson's hermeneutics.) Marx said that the State had been ill and consequently had made us all ill, but that the new State would cure all of us. Such was his (hoped for) newer covenant! As one of three major hermeneuts of suspicion, Marx, however, was not suspicious enough (nor today are Marxists or readers of Marx) about himself (or about themselves) and about us all. His/their guile was not met by double guile and then triple guile, and so on (see Ricoeur 1978, 34). The world (humankind's history), after all, *did not change*! The temporary humanism of Marx's (at times, wonderfully) contradictory and paradoxical and almost pararhetorical thinking was mixed with and then finally betrayed by the worst form of totalitarianism. (Some historians needed to make Marx's texts consistent and, therefore, their referents consistent.) I believe such betrayal was and will ever be inevitable, especially for those involved, directly or indirectly, in "the modes of production" of specifically what Milan Kundera calls "The Grand [utopian] March" (Kundera 1986, part 6). (The mode of literary, political production that I am referring to here is e/utopianism. I would rather engage in an "atopianism.")

Another cause (if we can speak of "a cause," and whichever of Althusser's three conceptions of cause that we may choose [see Jameson 1981, chap. 1]) is not economics or poor communication, which can, therefore, be fixed (recoded, reterritorialized) in yet another newer covenant. (I do not, as a case in point, have faith in Habermasian neo-Enlightenment thought as a cure based on efficient and honest [!] communication. Such thought is horribly Europocentric and totalitarian; such thought slouches toward *homologia*, just as does any talk about the logic of good reasons [see Habermas 1979, 1987].) The cause, instead, is masculine hegemony, which is, as I alluded to earlier, disciplined and rotten with perfection. And the cause is in our failure to think of any successful alternatives to capitalism. And most of all, the cause is in language (*logos*) itself. What remains, then, is a postmodern "sub/versive" pastiche of capitalism and socialism, of their various linguistic hegemonies.

But then, in respect to the revisionaries, let us not forget the Freudians, who are no better off, nor for that matter are we because of them. Along with the Marxists, the Freudians are confronted with the charge that instead of demythologizing or demystifying or revising the world of the human psyche—the world of suppression and repression—they have only domesticated such forms of terror in the business of psychoanalysis. Freudians, too, have universalized the unconscious in such themes as the signifier-as-phallus, castration, *eros* and *thanatos*. They, too, have the vexing problem of answering the question, What went wrong? They have their Doras and Wolfmen. As Deleuze and Guattari (1983, 55) say, "Psychoanalysis is like the Russian [Marxist] Revolution; we don't know when it started going bad." (Psychoanalysis, indeed, never lets go! Let us, therefore, sub/vert Freudianism even beyond Herbert Marcuse [1962] and N. O. Brown's [1959] revisions.)

Consequently, Marxist and Freudian self-conscious critical practices have had to be and must continue to be further "demystified," as they have been tentatively, but not nearly enough, by Jameson and Jacques Lacan, by Gayatri Spivak and Juliet Mitchell; or they have to be (to use a more relevant Nietzschean concept now) "destructed" (with the demystification of every destruction becoming a further construction to be, in turn, de[con]structed). And then on to Deleuze and Guattari's third position of agent as "schizo" and agency as "schizo-analysis."

*   *   *

(What I most need to do is to record experiences, not in the order in which they took place—for that is history—but in the order in which they first became significant for me.)

—Lawrence Durrell

Such talk (in this my digression), however, gets us apparently beyond a discussion of our present category, but then again a uncertain imbrication and confusion of categories is inevitable because of the association of the three hermeneuts of suspicion. Given my bias of counterbalancing (cutting up, jestering, juggling, drifting), I will reserve the ultimate demystifiers, Nietzsche and his followers (such as Foucault and Lyotard and Deleuze and Guattari and their parapolitical, radical nongoals), for what I call "sub/versive hysteriography" (or perhaps schizography), whose beginningless and endless nongoal is perpetual demystification, sustained through the attitude of what I also call sophistic undecidability. Such a deconstructive or sub/versive activity is often, however, perceived as "degenerat[ing] into the simple exercise of doubt" (Palmer 1969, 44–45), into skepticism and nihilism. Or this sub/versive activity is perceived by Marxists as a dangerous poststructuralist hedonism that is ahistorical, favoring the paradigmatic/synchronic axis of language over the syntagmatic/diachronic axis (Lentricchia 1980, 145; Lentricchia 1983; Eagleton 1983b, 150; and Eagleton 1981, 101–113). Such a criticism, however, is warranted by a nostalgia for Platonic/Kantian/Hegelian (e)utopic-epistemic knowledge and logic, which reign supreme over and within philosophical rhetoric. If some Marxists believe that their goal someday is not to have to be a Marxist, their implied goal is also someday not to have to be a rhetor(ian), not to have to be an advocate for their (totalizing, self-evident) views (see Eagleton 1983b, 161). Once the linguistic modes of production have been properly changed (recoded, reterritorialized, revised), so then will humankind be properly changed. (Do not interpret, only change!) There will be no need, then, for linguistically/rhetorically turning things over. It will be merely a matter of managing (engineering) discourse. But then, I think that (the perversity of) discourse (*logos*) cannot finally be managed (cf. Foucault 1977; Kofman 1987).

*   *   *

It is the inattentive reader who loses my subject, not I. Some word about it will always be found off in a corner, which will not fail to be sufficient, although it may be concise. I seek out change indiscriminately and tumultuously. My style and my mind alike go wandering.

—Montaigne

A self-conscious critical practice and language ... rhetoric ... philology ... linguistics: I intimated earlier and in passing that revisionary historians—actually all historians—differ over their attitudes toward language (*logos*), whether commonsensical, momentarily suspicious, or forever suspicious. As Gerald Bruns (1982) points out, rhetoric (language, discourse), for a Nietzsche,

> is another name for deception, artifice, fabrication, illusion, unnatural utterance, the lie, figuration (the worst sort of contraband [*lumpenproletarian?*] discourse), and so on. To this traditional characterization of rhetoric, however, Nietzsche adds [in an extramoral and in, as I would think, a Third Sophistic rhetorical sense] a crucial note: "Language [discourse] is rhetoric"—whence no utterance ... can be above suspicion. [Nietzsche] plays a purposefully skeptical variation upon a basic Enlightenment theme, as when, in the seventeenth century, defects in the natural languages of men were regularly diagnosed as a way of authorizing the construction (or imagination) of philosophical languages, whence we obtain our concept of language as such, that is, our conception of language as a system (*langue*). Nietzsche's terrible truth ... is that these "defects" of native utterance are not able to be removed or corrected—are not accessible to rational or philosophical reform: they have not crept into language from a nearby garden of rhetorical abuses, nor are they the accidental corruptions of this or that tongue; rather, they are part of the essence of language. They are descriptive of its basic operations, its grammar, or what language must do in order to be what it is. (Bruns 1982, 90; see Nietzsche 1989, 246–257)

This view of language as being unreliable, of course, does not just begin in the seventeenth century, as Bruns historically locates it; if we can speak of mythical origins, it is Parmenidian. Parmenides and his "sons"— Cratylus, Plato, and then Aristotle—were very much aware of the unreliability of language (*logos*) and, therefore, did what they could, through a will-to-authority, to make language (rhetoric) behave itself, to make it "philosophical" (that is, "decidable" and nonsophistic), to make speakers of language sound as if they could speak with control, with "critical authority," over the magical elements within language itself. The attempt here, of course, is to make language a function of the speaking-subject, who says what s/he means, and means what s/he says. As Wittgenstein (1968, 47e) has said: "Philosophy is a battle against the bewitchment of our intelligence by means of language" (cf. Rosenmeyer 1955).

"Sub/version" unlike revision nurtures itself on such verbal magic or "bewitchment." It attempts to tap into the potentially sub/versive side of language, while perpetually being suspicious of the incipient reactionary (either fascistic or e/utopian) side. It perpetually demystifies *ethos* (the speaking-subject) and *logos* (epistemic or probabilistic knowledge) and *pathos* (the polis, community, or consensus). It is a paracategory of comedic/farcical hysteriography that properly is an extension of Nietzsche— that sophistic hermeneut of a quite different suspicion. He recognizes (unmasks) the will-to-knowledge as, in its degenerate form, the will-to-power. Such a recognition (or demystification) of knowledge denies its own author/ity (as the speaking-subject), and in denying its own authority, it denies the possibility of any stable (homological) position from which a dominant ideology (such as a moral or political one) could be announced as privileged, be it either a position based on *logos* (i.e., the logic of good reasons) or on *pathos* (i.e., interpretative communities).

My sense, a sub/versive's sense, is that *history is not human*.[7] We, in other words, are more so the function of language than the opposite. My sense is that we are along for the ride with histories. And therefore, it will be asked, who/what is to protect us all? (Oh, how we desire a Master!) And, of course, there is every reason for us to be afraid. In reading Slavoj Zizek, I discovered his remembrance of what Ernesto Laclau in a private conversation told him about language. Zizek recalls, "It is not only Stalinism which is a linguistic phenomenon, but language itself which is a Stalinist phenomenon" (Zizek 1989, 174). I believe this assessment is, indeed, the case. But language is not only a Stalinist phenomenon, for I take solace in what Foucault says as well about "counter-memory" and "transgression" in language:

> The philosopher [for me, a Stalinist personification of one condition of the possibility of language] is aware that "we are not everything"; he learns as well that even the philosopher does not inhabit the whole of his language like a secret and perfectly fluent god. Next to himself, he discovers the existence of another language [the "counter-memory"] that also speaks and that he is unable to dominate, one

that strives, fails, and falls silent and that he cannot manipulate, the language he spoke at one time and that has now separated itself from him, now gravitating in a space increasingly silent. (Foucault 1977, 41–42)

It is this "counter-memory" that I would tap into for sub/versive ends and for perpetually new beginnings (demystifications).

I will end this section with a quote from Lyotard, who speaks of the problem of language and the problem of humanism and suggests a similar reconception of doing history along the lines that I (will) have been variously suggesting. Lyotard says:

It is not the people that is fickle, but "language." ... Maybe prose is impossible. It is tempted on one side by despotism [hypotaxis] and on the other by anarchy [parataxis]. It succumbs to the seduction of the former by turning itself into the genre of all genres (the prose of the Popular Empire) and to the seduction of the latter by trying to be no more than an unregulated assemblage of all phrases (the vagabond's prose). ... But the unity of genres is impossible, as is their zero degree. Prose can only be their multitude and the multitude of their differends [i.e., their phrases in dispute across incommensurable genres]. (Lyotard 1988, 158)

*   *   *

As I began this section devoted to revisionary history, I will end it: Each and every historiography, at least, implies a hermeneutic. The hermeneutic that I have taken (and, for my purposes, modified, by separating Nietzsche from Marx and Freud) is the most radical of "six modern definitions" that Palmer (1969, chap. 3) has given us. Though this is the most radical of the definitions, it is still, nonetheless, very conservative where it leaves off: Palmer stops with H.-G. Gadamer, after which hermeneutics really begins to become its most radical, self-conscious self and subsequently develops, quite ironically, into a posthermeneutics. (Instead of demystifying a meaning in a text with the idea of returning to some pristine, natural state of meaning, that is, a state without mystification, a posthermeneutic creates meaning after meaning, perpetual demystification and demystification, never privileging one over the others, and creates meanings with the sole purpose of resisting and disrupting any nostalgic pull toward a natural state of meaning or oneness/wholeness. A posthermeneutic would see anything less than perpetual demystification as only remystification.)

What I am putting forth as "the historiography of self-conscious critical practices" pretty much ends, then, with the possibilities of Palmer's sixth definition. Another way of saying this is that as long as "self-conscious critical practices" are informed by and limited to Palmer's and Ricoeur's notion of a hermeneutic of suspicion, the historiography produced— whether drawing directly or indirectly on the texts of Marx, Freud, or Nietzsche—falls securely within the second category of revision. It is, however, an engagement (or disengagement) in a posthermeneutic (as I described it above) on the texts of Marx and Freud, but especially the texts of Nietzsche, that gives us a "sub/versive hysteriography," which I will elaborate on more fully later.

There are numerous critics and historians who, I would claim, are working within the guidelines issued by Palmer and Ricoeur and, therefore, who are performing "self-conscious critical practices." Their efforts have centered on the political nature of history, and though many of them are Marxists (or post-Marxists), they have been willing in varying degrees to embrace some aspects of poststructuralism so as to further their critiques. Besides Jameson, Eagleton, and Lentricchia, I have in mind Ernesto Laclau and Chantal Mouffe (1985), Gayatri Spivak (1987), Michael Ryan (1982), and Stanley Aronowitz (1990), who successfully combine Marxism and deconstruction. In embracing poststructuralist practices, they have given up some of the more orthodox themes present in Marx's texts (such as economic determinism and proletarian revolution) and therefore have become (in the Levi-Straussian and Derridian sense) "*bricoleurs*" practicing, on occasion, "mythomorphic discourse" (see Derrida 1972). In addition to these contemporary practitioners of Marxist (or post-Marxist) historiography, there are other historians today who do not see themselves strictly as Marxists or Freudians but who are better described in more general terms as products of The Age of Marx, Nietzsche, and Freud. They are such historians as Hayden White (whom I have previously discussed), Dominick LaCapra (1983, 1985a, 1987), and Hans Kellner (1989). They are, indeed, rare creatures in the profession of history itself, which is predominantly conservative and orthodox (see LaCapra 1985b). These same critics and historians, for some time now, along with their precursors, have been influencing a group of revisionary historians of rhetoric.

Histories of Rhetoric as Self-Conscious Critical Practices

Almost exclusively, the form of revisionary history of rhetoric focusing on self-conscious critical practices is achieved by way of direct or indirect references to the hermeneuts of suspicion. (Though these three hermeneuts may not be even mentioned, often their influence is through such other suspicious hermeneuts as Foucault or Martin Heidegger.) Marx has influenced James Berlin (1984, 1987, 1988) and Takis Poulakos (1989, 1990). The only historian that I know of who has attempted to write a brief history of rhetoric across the Marxist ideology is Terry Eagleton (1981). Nietzsche has to a small degree influenced Nancy Streuver (1970); and to a greater degree, Susan Jarratt (1991); John Poulakos (1993). Nietzsche, through Foucault, has negatively, but also positively, influenced James Berlin (see Chapter 7 herein). Freud himself, or Freud as revised through Jacques Lacan, has not influenced to a great degree any revisionary historian of rhetoric, although some work is being done by Samuel Jaffe. The only historian who actually mentions and develops all three hermeneuts— Marx, Nietzsche, and Freud—into the overall framework of a history of rhetoric is Samuel Ijsseling (1976).

Other examples of historians of this kind of revisionary history are very few and by no means have they in every case completely embraced and enacted the "self-conscious critical practices" of the three hermeneuts of suspicion; they are C. H. Knoblauch and L. Brannon (1984, their failed attempt to use Foucault); W. Covino (1983, 1988); N. Partner (1985, 1986); P. Kameen (1980) and L. Worsham (1987) (their use of Heidegger, in composition theory); J. A. Campbell (1982, 1984, his use of E. Voegelin); J. Neel (1988, his use of Derrida and the Sophists); M. McGuire (1980, his use of Nietzsche on *ethos* and values); R. Lanham (1976, chaps. 1–2); V. Farenga (1979, on the "origin" of rhetoric); E. C. White (1987, on *kairos*, invention, and the Sophists); E. Grassi (1976), J. Sutton (1986), C. Schrag (1985), and M. Heim (1981) (the relationship between rhetoric and philosophy); R. Barthes (1988, lecture notes on history of rhetoric); J. Schilb (1987, critiques of recent histories); R. Moss (1982, on sophistry), J. de Romilly (1975, the fourth lecture); J-F. Lyotard (1988, his use of Nietzsche and the Sophists); J. Atwill (1990, 1992, her deconstruction of Aristotle and her examination of the contingencies of historical representation); and B. Miller (1987) and J. Poulakos (1984) (their use of Heidegger, on the Sophists).

*   *   *

I will end this section with a brief discussion of Ijsseling's history, which is by far the richest example of everything that I have thus far discussed from the first paragraph to this very point. Ijsseling's history is an olio of traditional and revisionary histories: More specifically, Ijsseling's history-cum-histories perversely (and I think for productive ends) combines the approaches used by Corbett (1989, 114–176), Eagleton (1981), and Barthes (1988). It combines the commonsensical, matter of fact, traditional approach of Corbett with the self-conscious, Marxist-revisionary approach of Eagleton as well as the poststructuralist approach of Barthes. My reading of Ijsseling's history (histories), therefore, is that it-cum-they are an embodiment of Mineapean satire on (or an anatomy of) writing histories.

The subtitle of Ijsseling's book is "An Historical Survey," and indeed it is. However, upon closer inspection, it is not a "survey" in any conventional sense. The opening chapter, "The Rehabilitation of Rhetoric," starts out, to be sure, in a traditional manner, almost similarly to V. Florescu's "Rhetoric and Its Rehabilitation in Contemporary Philosophy" (1970). But the similarity between these two authors' starting points ends quickly: For whereas Florescu has rhetoric "rehabilitated" across a neo-Aristotelian rhetoric, as put forth by Perelman, Ijsseling has rhetoric "rehabilitated" across Marx, Freud, and Nietzsche, the "hermeneuts of suspicion," whose names become the title heading for Ijsseling's Chapter 13. One other very important distinction is that whereas Florescu has rhetoric historically "rehabilitated" in philosophy, Ijsseling, like Grassi (1976; cf. 1987), has philosophy "rehabilitated" in rhetoric. Philosophy becomes self-conscious when philosophers begin to ask the (rhetorical) question, Who is actually speaking whenever something is said?—the question that ends the first chapter of Ijsseling's history and that becomes the title of the last chapter. Such a question comes not only from the three hermeneuts of suspicion but also from their successor Martin Heidegger. Such a question dispels any trust in manifest reality and in consciousness and consequently destroys the possibility of traditional hermeneutics and historiography.

I have said that Ijsseling's history is an embodiment of Mineapean satire on (or an anatomy of) writing histories. Let's take a closer look: Ijsseling's history has sixteen chapters, ten of which could be already found in any traditional history of rhetoric; they are, like Corbett's history, flat and matter-of-fact. What is especially curious is that these ten chapters (2 and 4 through 12) in no way follow from the discussion in the first chapter, which ends with a series of questions informed by self-conscious critical practices. What is even more curious is that Chapter 3, "Isocrates and the Power of Logos," breaks the flow of traditional historiography by giving a radical, Heideggerian interpretation of Isocrates. It is *not* again until the closing chapters, 13 through 16, that such a critical practice is ever either referred to or allowed to shape the narrative or argument. The final chapters, then, return to and take up the closing questions of the initial chapter. At this point, it becomes self-evident that the rest of the book is going to be written across self-conscious critical practices (like Eagleton's and Barthes's) developed by the three hermeneuts of suspicion and then especially Heidegger. Not only is this history Mineapean, but it is also a history of the Question of Being in relation to rhetorics. (Ijsseling's doctoral thesis was on Heidegger. The influence is unmistakable.)

Sub/Versive Hysteriography

Nietzsche—even while "speaking" through Heidegger—saw a necessity to rewrite history, to subvert traditional views of history. To refine this point, I want to quote at length a single passage from *Beyond Good and Evil*:

> The hybrid European—all in all, a tolerably ugly plebeian—simply needs a costume: he requires history as a storage room for costumes. To be sure, he soon notices that not one fits him very well; so he keeps changing. Let anyone look at the nineteenth century with an eye for these quick preferences and changes of the style masquerade; also for the moments of despair over the fact that "nothing is becoming." It is no use to parade as romantic or classical, Christian or Florentine, baroque or "national," *in moribus et artibus:* it "does not look good." But the "spirit," especially the "historical spirit," finds its advantage even in this despair: again and again a new piece of prehistory or a foreign country is tried on, put on, taken off, packed away, and above all *studied:* we are the first age that has truly studied "costumes"—I mean those of moralities, articles of faith, tastes in the arts and religions—prepared like no previous age for a carnival in the grand style, for the laughter and high spirits of the most spiritual revelry, for the transcendental heights of the highest nonsense and Aristophanean derision of the world. Perhaps this is where we shall still discover the realm of our *invention*, that realm in which we, too, can still be original, say, as parodists of world history and God's buffoons—perhaps, even if nothing else today has any future, our *laughter* may yet have a future. (Nietzsche 1966, 150)

I take this passage to be a seed plot for what I call a "sub/versive hysteriography of rhetoric."[8] Nietzsche's view of (performative) history would be concerned with costumes, carnivals, and laughter. But, to be sure, we are thinking here about more than mere costumes, which do suggest a time not just for fun but for tolerated, controlled rebellion, institutionalized, domesticated subversion (as in Mikhail Bakhtin's medieval and Rabelaisian world [1984] and, I must add, Bakhtin's Stalinist world). Such words as "rebellion" and "subversion," however, can be disconcerting, for they strongly suggest an attack on and overthrow of the status quo. They connote two parties in dispute about *power* or, in other terms, about what is to be—that is, how history is to be interpreted; both parties (one for the status quo; the other, revolution) claim that a vision for a better society (one that is usually founded on some onto-theological or materialist-economic principle) informs their rights either to maintain the present or to reconceive it altogether. Such revolutions may be total or seemingly partial, may be solely intellectual without a praxis or with a devastating praxis (witness the result of Marx's eleventh thesis on Feuerbach).

*   *   *

This great ear ... an inverse cripple.

—Friedrich Nietzsche

The ... understanding of a text is not determined by the size of the ear. ... It is to Ariadne's small ears that Dionysus speaks. ... Women's small ear is this third ear mentioned by Nietzsche, the artistic ear which, position[ed] itself beyond metaphysical oppositions such as truth and falsehood, good and evil, depth and surface, clarity and obscurity ...

—Sarah Kofman

Sub/version—as it is depicted, politically (and always historiographically) in this discussion, however—situates itself with neither of these two parties in dispute (the one for the status quo, the other for revolution). Sub/version understands that the overthrow of a political position (or, as far as that goes, any position or ideology) for the sake of redemption is only a capitulation to eventual recapitulation (such ricorsos, or revolutions, will not stop, as a Christian Vico or a scientistic reading of Marx would maintain). Grand revolutions against fascism or totalitarianism only end up being new (political, critical, cultural, historiographical) fascisms or totalitarianisms. Reactivist e/utopianism, when blood has been spilled and when not successful (how can it ever be?), only demands greater reactivist e/utopianisms. (This apparently is part and parcel of its principle mode of production.) I would rather take my chances with Foucault's kind of resistance, his brand of neoanarchism (see Merquior 1985, chap. 10), or, even more, take my chances with Deleuze and Guattari's form of disruption (1983). But most of all I would rather trek with Nietzsche's tactic to avoid being reactionary. Nietzsche, in *Thus Spoke Zarathustra*, best describes—and suggests in the strongest terms—what would and has happened when history is conceived as a redemption of the past:

> To redeem those who lived in the past and to recreate all "it was" into a "thus I willed it"—that alone should I call redemption. ... But now learn this too: the will itself is still a prisoner. Willing liberates; but what is it that puts even the liberator himself in fetters? "It was"—that is the name of the will's gnashing of teeth and most secret melancholy. Powerless against what has been done, he is an angry spectator of all that is past. The will cannot will backwards; and that he cannot break time and time's covetousness, that *is* the will's loneliest melancholy.
>
> ... And so ... he wreaks revenge on whatever does not feel wrath and displeasure as he does. Thus the will, the liberator, took to hurting; and on all who can suffer he wreaks revenge for his inability to go backwards. This, indeed this alone, is what *revenge* is: the will's ill will against time and its "it was."
>
> ... *The spirit of revenge* ... has so far been the subject of man's best reflection; and where there was suffering, one always wanted punishment too.
>
> For "punishment" is what revenge calls itself; with a hypocritical lie it creates a good conscience for itself. ... "Things are ordered morally according to justice and punishment." (Nietzsche 1968a, 251–252; Nietzsche's emphasis)

*   *   *

If hysteriography implies a nonfascistic, nontotalitarian hermeneutic, as I discussed earlier, in respect to "suspicion," it also implies, as I have been suggesting now, an aesthetic/academic/ethical/pragmatic nonfascistic, nontotalitarian "politics" (parapolitics), which needs to be described if only briefly and incompletely. The fascism and totalitarianism that are being discussed here are not merely the politics of a Hitler or a Mussolini, or of a Stalin or a Mao, or of a Reagan or a Bush. As Foucault says, it is a "fascism in us all, in our heads and everyday behavior, the fascism that causes us to love power, to desire the very thing that dominates and exploits us" (Foucault 1983, xiii; cf. Holland 1987).

Sub/versive politics is especially concerned with pedagogical politics, or rather a postpedagogical politics. Sub/version sees teaching (of all kinds) as the teaching of history. (It reasons, teaching is to pedagogy *as* history is to historiography.) In the classroom, teaching is by definition limited to genus-species analytics, or dialectics. That is, it is limited to what is unique, codifiable, and then teachable (see Vitanza 1991b). Teaching is what Socratic-Platonic-Aristotelian dialectics (though differently in some ways) engage in. What is finally not teachable is seen as noncodifiable and, therefore, irrational or nonrational. If, as Aristotle says, "all men by nature desire to know" (1941, 980a), this "desire to know" by philosophical decree must be made rational (cf. J. Butler 1987; Rajchman 1991). It, therefore, must be a desire (appetite) to know that undergoes the negation inherent in species-genus analytics.

Teaching, however, is not limited to the traditional *genus*(class)room; for it especially includes in the larger classroom such other fascistic/totalitarian teachers as social workers, legislators, clerics, psychoanalysts, lobbyists, and plumbers—all those who attempt to stop the free flow of (libidinalized) desire. Once again, they wish to code, or recode, reterritorialize this desire—potentially free-flowing desire—across the negative (what I have been calling species-genus analytics) instead of allowing this desire to remain in its affirmative nature. For the points of view of sub/version, the ego-imaginary as individual (as fascism and as an effect of *kapital*) and the superego-symbolic as state (as totalitarianism) repress this libidinalized desire. Deleuze and Guattari say it quite well:

> If desire is repressed, it is because every position of desire, no matter how small, is capable of calling into question the established order of a society: not that desire is asocial, on the contrary. But it is explosive; there is no desiring-machine capable of being assembled without demolishing entire social sectors. Despite what some revolutionaries think about this, desire is revolutionary in its essence—desire, not left-wing holidays!—and no society can tolerate a position of real desire without its structures of exploitation, servitude, and hierarchy being compromised. ... It is therefore of vital importance for a society to repress desire, and even to find something more efficient than repression, so that repression, hierarchy, exploitation, and servitude are themselves desired. It is quite troublesome to have to say such rudimentary things: desire does not threaten a society because it is a desire to sleep with the mother, but because it is revolutionary. ... Desire [however] does not "want" revolution, it is revolutionary in its own right, as though involuntarily, by wanting what it wants. (Deleuze and Guattari 1983, 116)

How, then, is the weakening and dispersing of fascism and totalitarianism to be accomplished so that libidinalized desire might freely flow? In answering this question, I will be concerned only with the writing of *The History of Rhetoric*, which *is* the history of supression, repression, and oppression. What follows, as a possible answer, is a witch's brew.

Sub/Version and Hysteriography

I will briefly describe, thus, what I see are six pararudimentary ingredients for the sub/versive in respect to historiographies (but here, specifically, hysteriographies) of rhetorics. The six characteristics are in two parasets—one that I take from Foucault (1977, 139–164), who in turn has adapted them from a Dionysian (Sophist) Zarathustra, Christ, Nietzsche; and a second of my own that I offer to complement Foucault's (see Vitanza 1987). The first set is composed of three anti-Platonic purposes of history; the second, three anti-Aristotelian purposes of hystery.

The Anti-Platonic Purposes of History. The first is "parodic," "farcical," and hyperbolic, "directed against reality, and opposes the theme of history as reminiscence or recognition," pushing views of history that are considered "received" or "sacred" to the limits of the "carnivalesque" (Foucault 1977, 160). The aim here is to disperse any single, official view of reality or covering law that would warrant such a view.

The second is "the systematic dissociation of identity," or of a single or stable self, say, in terms of gender or sex (Foucault 1977, 161). This reference to the dissociation of a single or stable self is of the utmost importance for sub/versive history cum hystery and is to be found in Nietzsche, who in *The Genealogy of Morals* writes of his rejection of the metaphysics of substance: "There ... is no such substratum; there is no 'being' behind doing, effecting, becoming; 'the doer' is merely a fiction added to the deed—the deed is everything" (Nietzsche 1969, 45). Along the same lines, Deleuze and Guattari write: "The schizoanalytic slogan of the desiring-revolution will be first of all: to each its own sexes" (Deleuze and Guattari 1983, 296). Likewise, Judith Butler writes: "Gender ought not to be construed as a stable identity or locus of agency from which various acts follow; rather, gender is an identity tenuously constituted in time, instituted in an exterior space through a stylized repetition of acts" (J. Butler 1990, 140). The aim here is to disperse the two primary political categories of *male* and *female* to a radical (nonsynthesized third) number of genders.

And the third is "sacrificial, directed against truth, and opposes history as knowledge." This final purpose "reveals that all knowledge [i.e., the will-to-knowledge] rests upon injustice [and] that the instinct for knowledge is malicious [fascistic, arborescent]" (Foucault 1977, 162–163). The aim here is to disperse a negative, dialectic form of the will-to-knowledge.

Foucault best sums up these three characteristics in the name of what he calls "effective" history. He writes:

"Effective" history differs from traditional history in being without constants. Nothing in man—not even his body—is sufficiently stable to serve as the basis for self-recognition or for understanding other men [sic]. The traditional devices for constructing a comprehensive view of history and for retracing the past as a patient and continuous development must be systematically dismantled. ... History becomes "effective" to the degree that it introduces discontinuity into our very being—as it divides our emotions, dramatizes our instincts, multiplies our body and sets it against itself. "Effective" history deprives the self of the reassuring stability of life and nature, and it will not permit itself to be transported by a voiceless obstinacy toward a millennial ending. It will uproot its traditional foundations and relentlessly disrupt its pretended continuity. This is because knowledge is not made for understanding; it is made for cutting. (Foucault 1977, 153–154)

The Anti-Aristotelian Purposes of Hystery (Womb-laughter). The first is to dispel—stylistically to sub/vert—Perelman's "new [philosophic] rhetoric": Perelman writes, "there is nothing of philosophical interest in a rhetoric that is understood as an art of expression, whether literary or verbal" (Perelman 1973, 808; cf. Vickers 1988). We agree (with the underside of this statement); therefore, as opponents of Perelman's arborescent "new rhetoric," sub/versive hyster(y)ians of rhetoric must (re)establish the (rhizomic) groundworks for rewriting histories in the form of "an expressive, literary rhetoric" that will expel the influence of philosophy. They must write a hyster(y)ia of the libidinalized desire-of-the-other, what Jacques Lacan sees as *lalangue* (babel/babble) and the Unconscious; ... sub/versive hysterians must indulge in the literary expressive or in what I have labeled "selph-expressive negative polylectic," not a schoolboy self-expressive use of language (and must stop saying "use" of language, implying a "philosophical authority of a speaker" [see Vitanza 1993]); for a sub/versive rhetoric says that language uses ... speaks ... man and woman and on to unidentifiable thirds (e.g., hermaphrodites) in unlimited rhetoricity and historicity; language—*lalangue* and the Unconscious—therefore, is always already speaking, ... is spoken by the perversity of the psycho-pathology of everyday history, by libidinalized desire-in-language, by "the antibody rhetoric"; ... sub/versive hysterians must come to write, therefore, as if they are returning to the locus of hysteria, must give themselves to speaking and writing as hysterics, to speak with their bodies (i.e., pantomime language) instead of their minds (cf. Vico 1968; Farenga 1979), to put themselves in the position of the analysand instead of analyst, to return to a heterological mode of being, to speak and to write the way Dora, ... the way Judge Schreber, ... the way Lacan (in his seminars) "spoke" and "wrote"; sub/versive hysterians must engage in a savoir faire (unsavory affair) with the unconscious, a locus for ethical paratheory and praxis; and then contra/dictorially, must act on the assumption that "the unconscious does not mean anything. ... The unconscious does not speak, it engineers. It is not expressive or representative, but productive" (Deleuze and Guattari 1983, 180).

So much of rhetorics, from Plato and Aristotle to the present, are spoken (seemingly ... given the illusion of their-cum-its commonsense ideology) in the vocabulary of philosophy and the *paideia*—such vocabulary with its concepts and genres is inevitably self-sub/verted, just as Nietzsche, Heidegger, Derrida, and Kristeva have demonstrated how texts (themselves) self-sub/vert (through desire-in-language) the vocabulary of philosophy in dis/order to take a step beyond philosophy-as-"a-mirror-of-nature" to philosophy-as-"therapy" or as-"edification" (see Rorty 1979). ... We need therapy (especially those of us who see ourselves as analysts) because of our sickness unto critical-authority-over-language (Death) ... though we can never be cured of this sickness. ... And why not? A cure is a form of domesticated violence; it would be the end of *dissoi paralogoi*, of difference, of juggling! The cure would be total philosophy/*paideia*/paranoia. ... Death (of another sort) itself.

The second (imbricated with the first) is that the sub/versive hyster(y)ians of rhetoric must actually come to write us out of this philosophical, fascistic-paranoid, arborescent vocabulary and its conceptual framework of philosophical rhetoric into another competing, contrary framework that I call a "postmodern; or, Third Sophistic hyster(y)ia of the antibody rhetoric" (see Vitanza 1991a). The antibody rhetoric battles the diseased tradition of "philosophical rhetoric." Kenneth Burke has told us in his *Grammar of Motives:* "What we want is not terms that avoid ambiguity, but terms that clearly reveal the strategic spots at which ambiguities necessarily arise" (Burke 1969a, xviii).

In contrast, however, beyond Burke, what we need and desire, in a postmodern hyster(y)ia of the antibody rhetoric, is not just terms that reveal, account for, the strategic spots at which ambiguities necessarily arise, but terms that create, detonate, and exploit these ambiguities (libidinalized desire-in-language [Kristeva 1980]). Like the original Sophists who practiced *dissoi logoi*, the Third Sophistic practitioners, then, in writing their new hyster(y)ias of the antibody rhetoric, will practice what I call *dissoi paralogoi* (see Vitanza 1987; 1991a). "Paralogy"—an antimethodology discussed by Jean-François Lyotard (1984)—will replace *logoi*, the death-bed-rock of the *polis* and *paideia*. But this *dissoi paralogoi* is not binary: Whereas the deconstructive reading of a binary revalorizes the excluded second (the supplement), the "para-" here introduces the nonsynthesized "excluded third" (Serres 1982) and allows for and embraces infinite regress (Vitanza 1993). Hence, the breakup of the binary and a reaching for radical multi-plicities/heterogeneities. The Third Sophistic hyster(y)ians will espouse the various stylistic, critical practices of composing called lateral writing or split writing or op writing, will espouse allegories of hyster(y)ias. Heterologies, the natural/unnatural desire-in-discourse, will flourish ... like rhizomes over the rhetorical *lalangue*scape.

The third (imbricated with the first and second) is that the writers of these new sub/versive hyster(y)ias, unlike Burke, will construct not "rep-resentative anecdotes" but "mis/representative an*ti*dotes" (vertiginous, rhizomic allegories-of-libidinalized-desire). Remember: Always allego-rize, Always hystericize! (contrary to what Jameson says!). The purpose, this time—as it is for Burke—is curative. But the hyster(y)ias of the anti-body rhetoric will be paradoxically (*pharmakonically*) "curative fictions" that sustain life, without ever a cure. (Remember: There can be no cure! There can be no overthrow of fascism/totalitarianism. For cure itself is a kind of death. Therefore: Better misprison than the prison of death.) In words inspired by Mikhail Bakhtin (1984), the fictions will take the form of the Hippocratic novel, informed by Hippocrates' teachings of the thera-peutic power of laughter. (As Nietzsche says, "Even laughter may yet have a future" [Nietzsche 1974, 74].) Or they will be fictions that are carnivalesque, bringing about liberation from the hierarchically arranged prevailing tragic truth; or they will be fictions that will, in the words of Foucault this time, "free [us] from all unitary and totalizing paranoia [fas-cism]" (Foucault 1983, xiii). (This kind of anticomposing process and antigenre will be a postmodernist extension of Greek declamations based on *Plasmata* [see Russell 1983].) What the Third Sophistic hyster(y)ias of the antibody rhetoric are, then, are *plasma* transfusions/transumptions into the diseased body of the history (suppressed/repressed hysteria) of philosophical rhetoric.

*   *   *

... All this and still some more, then, will have given us a *Society of the Friends of the Text (or Hysteries of Rhetorics)*.

Notes

1. The spelling of subversion as "sub/version" is to distinguish it from its normal, every-day usage. The slash allows for the visual recognition of a secondary, supplementary "ver-sion" of *The* History of Rhetoric. The effort, in part, throughout is to deconstruct the con-cept of the grand narrative for a supplementary (sub/valued) one. But this is no mere negative deconstruction, for in "version" is also implied the favoring of verse, poetry, literary dis-course, *letteraturizzaziones*, as a sub/versive, third force in language, a force that can be called upon as a means of reaching for an affirmative deconstruction of any dominant, hegemonic discourse. For a fuller discussion of the concept of hysteria and hysteriography, see Vitanza 1990.

2. For *Mentalités* history, see LaCapra 1985a, chap. 3. For the *"Annales* School," see Ricoeur 1983; Stoianovich 1976; Aymand 1972; Skinner 1985. For a discussion of Braudel, see Kellner 1979. See, especially, Fauré 1981, who focuses on how the *Annales* School has ne-glected the subject of "witchcraft." For narrative logic, see Ankersmit 1983 (cf. 1989); Hall 1990; Cebek 1986. For econometrics, see Lorwin and Price 1972; Fogel 1970. For history and the social sciences, see Krug 1967. For psychohistory, see Gay 1985; LaCapra 1987.

3. For the poetic view of history, see LaCapra on Gay (LaCapra 1985a, 26, n. 19) and on White (LaCapra 1985a, 34; LaCapra 1983). See Momigliano's (1981) attack on White. About the poetic view, Collingwood writes: "The imagination is *a priori:* we cannot but imagine what cannot but be there. The historical imagination [has] as its special task to imag-ine the past: not an object of possible perception, since it does not now exist, but able through this activity to become an object of our thought" (Collingwood 1956, 242); "the his-torian's picture of the past is thus in every detail an imaginary picture, and its necessity is at every point the necessity of the *a priori* imagination" (245). Collingwood is careful, however, to make a distinction between history and fiction; see his three rules (246). Also, see Carrard 1992.

4. White in his introduction (1978) says, however, that he does not view the tropes as "onto-genetic": "If it [the pattern of tropological prefiguration] appeared universally as an analytical or representational model for discourse, we might seek to credit it as a genuine 'law' of discourse. But, of course, I do not claim for it the status of a law of discourse, even of the discourse about consciousness (since there are plenty of discourses in which the pattern does not fully appear in the form suggested), but only the status of a model which recurs per-sistently in modern discourses about human consciousness. I claim for it only the force of a convention in discourse itself, in the modern Western cultural tradition" (H. White 1978, 12–13). These few sentences do not negate the overall sense present in White's works—at least, for me—that the Burkean tropes and Fryean modes (or radicals of presentation) are a "covering law." For a similar assessment of White, see LaCapra 1985a, 34. For a comparison of White and LaCapra, see De Bolla 1986. There is the additional problem of deciding whether or not White is working within the humanist or antihumanist traditions; see Kellner 1980, for White as a humanist.

5. *Without whom* (along with Murphy and others), *nothing*. I am specifically beginning to suspect, however, that Kennedy is in the process of slowly deconstructing himself. His move-ment from *The Art of Persuasion in Ancient Greece* (1963) to his article in response to me (1988) is a giant step. Specifically, he recants: 'When I wrote my first book, I put on the title page a quotation from the Chicago Platonist Paul Shorey: 'We are freed from rhetoric only by

knowledge of its history.' I no longer believe that is possible or even desirable" (Kennedy 1988, 232). His most recent introduction to and rendition of Aristotle's *Rhetoric* (Kennedy 1991) similarly make me think that yet another major change might be about to occur. He has me presently asking: What will have Professor Kennedy, or his *logos*, wrought? If he becomes even more radical, he will have forced me, and others, to become even more far left than humanly possible!

6. An exception to this general statement, of course, would be a Gorgias who favors *physis*, not as some thing but as no thing. It has been suggested, however, that Gorgias is parodying Parmenides (see Guthrie 1971, 193–194).

7. This position of mine can be confused with Walter Benjamin's or Louis Althusser's, but it should not be. Nor should my position be confused with a structuralist position or any possible onto-theological position. Similarly, it should not be confused with a vulgar form of determinism.

8. Nietzsche commented a great deal on history; see, e.g., his "On the Uses and Disadvantages of History for Life" (Nietzsche 1988). I could have taken other passages from other writers, e.g., from Walter Benjamin, his "Theses on the Philosophy of History" (1968), which, though it has a metaphorical-baroque, Marxist slant, is equally "sub/versive." See Bahti 1979; Eagleton 1981, chaps. 1–2; or still other passages from Lyotard, in his "The Sign of History" (1988), which is "sub/versive" in its attempts to bear witness to what has been silenced by finding new idioms for "history writing" or yet again from a satirical Marx himself, in the *18th Brumaire* (1984), the opening page. I have been impish enough to have embraced, nonetheless, this movement from tragedy to farce that Marx alludes to in his opening pages, and I will continue to embrace it, but I would make it a farce beyond good and evil. Cf. N. O. Brown 1974.

Afterword: Reading Rhetorical Redescriptions

HANS KELLNER

The one thing clear about the authors who have contributed to *Rethinking the History of Rhetoric* is that they wish to change that history rather than merely to add to it or correct it. What they wish to change is a paradigm thousands of years old, cast in the mythos of romance. In this tale, good confronts evil in the developing and modulating forms of reason and emotion, the interchangeably higher and lower aspects of human understanding. The duality of the human individual, divided and torn in both the classical and the Christian traditions between the forces of soul and body, provides a marvelous field for displacements. This old romance is marked at its inception (if we may ever meaningfully speak of an inception) by the identification of reason and truth with philosophy (of a certain kind), and of emotional irrationalism and deception with rhetoric (of a certain kind). Thereafter, the substitutions and permutations are processed algorithmically to produce that broad view of Western cultural history in which the history of rhetoric resides.

Philosophy wants to admit and explicate the emotions, however reluctantly, and thus embody the *entire* human soul, becoming a home for rhetoric. Rhetoric wants to incorporate logic, thus making the same imperialistic claim and becoming a mode of philosophy. Male and female, free and slave, light and darkness, seriousness and frivolity—all may be plugged into the system to produce discourse. The terms are theoretically reversible. For example, to "identify" and celebrate women's ways of knowing or the rhetorical styles of the oppressed, to counterpose the rhetoric of night and darkness against enlightenment and its coruscating demystifications, or personal authenticity against social formalism, is still to live and think within the romance. The plot reigns secure because it really doesn't care much who is on top at the moment, or how the players are identified in any particular instance, or who wins any given conflict. Romance, the struggle of good and evil, knight and dragon, cowboy and Indian, self and other, insists only that one or the other side be encoded as the "good guy" for the time being, so that even the dragon (that ultimate "other," embodying like the Indian in the social code the untamed part of our Western selves) may easily serve as hero (and when that happens we call it Romanticism).

If I am correct in identifying the mythos of rhetorical history as romance, I must also note the great structural difficulty of escaping it. The one thing romance needs is a next episode, so that the series (to use the language of television, once the greatest purveyor of romance) never be canceled. As long as an opposition can be developed, and as long as we can be persuaded to identify with one or another of the protagonists, romance goes on. Tragedy and comedy become only powerful moments in the romantic saga, each neutralizing the other sooner or later. At any moment, however, the power of fantasy must turn the history into a daydream that must have a hero. Freud's suggestion in "Creative Writers and Day-Dreaming" that "we can never give anything up; we only exchange one thing for another" (Freud 1959, 145) implies the tenacity of our forms of experience. Many of the chapters in this volume assume the structure of the story they want to replace.

It is not surprising that this should be so. The difficulty of effecting change, rather than noting it, in our representations of the past is considerable because of the rather strict genre constraints on what a persuasive historical account may be. Traditionally, the question of genre belongs to poetics, the question of persuasion to rhetoric. There is, however, a rhetoric of poetics, and genre is its locus. Let us consider a few questions about persuasive change in historiography. To begin, I shall stipulate what is almost a given among the contributors to this collection, that historical accounts are primarily—I should prefer to say, among other things—interested, motivated, actions undertaken to *do* something in the social world. That something, Nietzsche and Foucault remind us, has to do with power. And that power, Kant maintained, was the power to fashion a future by fashioning a version of the past. This, I presume, explains the otherwise peculiar passion shown here for the historiography of rhetoric. The passion comes from the confidence, however tenuous, that the ability to speak entails the ability to move things toward the heart's desire.

The problem is how to fashion a version of the past and make it stick, make it *do* something. Where is its authority to come from? It is hard to avoid the three sources of persuasive (that is, nonviolent) authority known to the old tradition—logos, pathos, ethos—in looking at this question. The general tension between logos and pathos as centers of authority, thinly disguised exchanges that they are for the dual human essence, tends to slight ethos, which is the *social* arena of persuasion. Stanley Fish relates the story of a graduate student who countered Fish's ideas about "interpretive communities" and their importance in directing interpretation by stating that although he, the student, was convinced of this view and had rejected his earlier opinions about persuasion, he could not account for the change of opinion under the new doctrine because nothing about his situation in the world had changed. Fish asked the graduate student whether he would have been persuaded if the ideas in question had come from an undergraduate student in the graduate student's own freshman composition class. The answer was, probably not (Fish 1989, 145). In effect, the ethos of professorial authority embedded in the academic and social system made the decision possible, if hardly necessary. There is, Fish tells us, a "nesting" of authoritative powers; ethos wears many disguises.

There is a clearly implied desire to persuade in these chapters, all of which resort to the Aristotelian modes in various ways. None of the authors expresses the credo of "every group its own historian," described by Peter Novick in his study of recent American historiography. Ethos in historiography has many sources, of course, but genre is the primary one because it adjudicates culturally acceptable and morally coded forms. Decorum reinscribes the goodness and social responsibility of the orderly binary beauty of romance and brands as irresponsible or at best frivolous and sterile any hint at an absurdist or chaotic view of the past. These last are not ethical because they disrupt the genre, hence not persuasive, hence hardly rhetorical at all.

The decorum of revisionist rhetorical historiography involves reevaluating the Sophists, those archetypes of the "usual suspects" who are periodically rounded up to make things happen. A century ago Nietzsche pointed out this historiographical regularity: "Every advance in epistemological and moral knowledge has reinstated the Sophists" (Nietzsche 1968b, 428). Their reinstatement is never really that, but rather a change of roles. It becomes their turn to play the underdog hero; and role reversal itself becomes the plot. A return to the Sophists reminds us that the arguments that have gone on for so long, and will not go away, are not what they seem to be. They seem to be about the way things *are*, and as such hold out tantalizing promises of resolution, promises never fulfilled. Reflection upon sophistics and the history of rhetoric calls to mind the possibility that it is the *names* of things that we have, not the things, that the disputes are about how names are to be distributed in the world, what will come to be and cease to be in any renaming operation. Where does the authority to rename come from? It is up for grabs, on a playing field that is fortunately never level, given the weight of "expectation," but still more open to human creativity and will than any other.

The desire to redefine the world that characterized the sayings of Heraclitus (or at least a hefty 34 percent of them, according to Eric Havelock) is taken up again today. As Richard Rorty, the contemporary philosopher of redefinition, put it: "We shall, in short, be where the Sophists were before Plato brought his principle to bear and invented 'philosophical thinking': we shall be looking for an airtight case rather than an unshakable foundation. We shall be in what Sellars calls 'the logical space of reasons' rather than that of causal relations to objects" (Rorty 1979, 156–157). Reality is quite indifferent to our descriptions of it, so we may redescribe and define the world, the past, and ourselves as we see fit for our purposes. Imagination, rather than reason, Rorty maintains, is the central human faculty; the chief instrument of change is the talent for speaking differently (Rorty 1989, 7). No one will mistake that the authority of the victim is invoked in a number of these essays and awarded to the Sophists. The Sophists are said to have been silenced, repressed, even tortured. Misrepresented, the Sophists are outcasts from the tradition, although they provided much of the work that was unjustly appropriated by their oppressors. The victimized Sophists can lead us into a better world. The last shall be first. This "family romance" of rhetoric insists that our true parents are other than those somewhat tedious disciplinarians who made us eat broccoli and argue in enthymemes. We, the progeny of the Sophists, suffer from the internalization of their repression and must learn to throw off the ways of knowing (and hence, the expectations) of the dominant tradition. So we are told.

*   *   *

The chapters in this book begin with a classic confrontation: Cicero's famous denunciations of Catiline before the Senate of Rome. David Konstan brings to the fore in Chapter 1 the basic circularity of Cicero's argument, a circularity that Konstan attributes to all appeals to legitimacy. Cicero aimed at Catiline the charge of violating the old ways, the Roman traditions and values. This charge, however, and the enthymemes in which it was couched, inevitably bent and redefined the old ways in the interests of its case. Arguments, Konstan suggests, cannot legitimately appeal to values but must only seem to be appealing to what is in actuality being defined by the appeal itself. To call on history in the form of tradition is to hide the force of the current needs that motivate that call. With this historical discussion, Konstan inaugurates the central argument of this book, that appeals to the rhetorical tradition configure a version of that tradition in the act of calling it forth. Like Cicero in Konstan's account, one cannot claim the legitimacy of the rhetorical tradition "as it really was" because, as Huizinga once remarked about the past, there is no "it" there, only a string of texts.

The image of Isocrates presented by Andrew Ford (Chapter 2) emphasizes his role as the source of a classical tradition that locates the power and beauty and essence of rhetoric in the speech artifact, the written *text*. The aesthetic formalism derived from associating rhetoric with the arts and crafts does indeed place in the background any political and social motivations for assuming the universal, that is, philosophical, status of one's own discourse. A story of the past stretching from Isocrates to structuralist poetics can well be imagined from Ford's perspective. Ford is quite right to note that all formalisms are reductive (as what is not?), and that such reductions can be of great value. His emphasis on the price of any formal understanding is crucial. It poses the questions that must be asked of any act of historical or rhetorical redefinition: What does it cost? What is gained? By whom? What is lost? Is it worth it? These considerations of discursive economics are questions that Isocrates (at least Ford's Isocrates) was well equipped to undertake because he knew that although every statement must take a particular form, which exacts a considerable discursive cost in the guise of reduction or ideological bias, it is also the only game in town. One may be aware of the dangers of passively contemplating verbal icons, but the text, post-Isocrates, will not go away.

John Poulakos in Chapter 3 faces these problems in his attempt to find a useful narrative form for the story of the Sophists. Their scattered texts lead to a scattered rhetoric and narrative frustration, but a full-bodied account of such a fragmentary record will not be credited. His helpful solution is to create a model, reductive and imperfect like all models, based upon the notions of opportunism, playfulness, and possibilism. The test of a historical model is what it can *do*, and this one accomplishes quite a bit, both by relating the elements of the Sophist image to the traditional topics of Greek culture, especially their renowned competitiveness and exhibitionism, and by producing effective readings of appropriate texts. This Sophist model is a windup doll, "ultimately disposable" in Poulakos's words, but ready (and well equipped) to take on the Sophist models crafted by other hands. In a sense, this is a compelling figure for any historical vision. It is a picture, a suggestion, a hypothesis, a metaphor, to be put into circulation and competition with other versions, other suggestions. Some will prevail for a while, others will win few adherents, but it is against each other, not against "the past," that the contest will take place.

Aristotle's version of the sources of rhetoric, the most successful one we have, competed with and subjected other models by isolating the sophistic origins of rhetorical discourse as a lesser, marginal form. Jane Sutton suggests in Chapter 4 that, like the barley drink that Heraclitus insists must be stirred lest it separate, Aristotelian rhetoric worked by sitting and sedimenting. In this figure, the Sophists became the devalued dregs, like the barley that gave the drink its kick. We see that any analytic discourse must elevate logos and devalue the rest of the soul because of its genre constraints. Aristotle, I suspect, was doomed to demote the Sophists because his global (chosen, to be sure) task was to *un*stir the world. We could say that from Socrates on, the goal of philosophy was to remove completely the traces of primeval chaos that began the universe, to separate tragedies from comedies once and for all. Another form of philosophy (Heraclitean, for example) might have imagined its job to be stirring the barley drink, but not the one that prevailed. Stirring the drink in order to mix up sedimented hierarchies seems an apt image for the new history of rhetoric.

In Chapter 5 Janet Atwill explicates Aristotle's three forms of knowledge in order to find a more comfortable chamber for rhetoric within the ancestral home. The *practical*, long rejected by classical anti-artisanal snobbism, is too limiting; the *theoretical*, linked with leisure and thus rejected by modern (reverse) snobbism, suffers from an unfashionable taint of foundationalism. What remains, Atwill contends, is *productive* knowledge, which is situated, contingent, and focused on possibility. Thus, Aristotle himself authorizes the currently redefined rhetoric, inventive rather than interpretive, primary rather than reactive, substantive rather than formal. Indeed, Nancy Streuver has recently made similar claims for historical knowledge, which she likens to the "low sciences," impure in method, problem-solving in aim. Perhaps "productive" knowledge is the Aristotelian version of the "new fuzziness" espoused by Rorty, who sees the proper task of philosophy (small "p") as simply coping rather than doing or explaining.

Although Plato is its principal target, Page duBois's Chapter 6 on violence and apathy begins the discussions of the Sophists because her princi-

pal tactic strikes me as precisely the gesture of imaginative, interested redefinition that is the essence of modern sophism. The figural violence of
Platonic rhetoric contra the Sophist reveals a sublimated desire to annihi-
late the other side. Thus, the apathy, the detachment and unemotionality
of the philosopher who wants to destroy a given emotion in his audience
by demonstrating through argument that such emotions do not cloud his
own judgment, permits actual torture by making "other" both the body of
the philosopher and the bodies of others, as duBois sees it. The "heirs of
Plato" known to duBois thus authorize torture because reality is for them
in a different realm, somewhere else than the bodies they inhabit and are.

It is the example, the hypothetical, the allegorical, that is duBois's target; her task of redefinition is to reverse literality and figurality, so that apathy becomes the cardinal act of philosophical aggression. The goal is to
instill a policing mechanism or consciousness-raising in the heads of the
heirs of Plato that will impede any future dismemberment of an argument,
or lead toward any victory in reasoned debate. Using the resources of language and analogy against analogical language itself, duBois's redefinition
leaves the "heirs of Plato" with little room for maneuver. Her redefinition
of the disinterested dialectician as sadist echoes directly the disgust of
Goethe and Blake with the scientists for putting Nature "on the rack."

In a discussion that could also be read next to duBois's, Barbara
Biesecker confronts the dilemma of escaping from romance in Chapter 8,
on the marginalization of women's voices in the history of rhetoric. The
gender imbalance of available sources makes a simple shifting of values ineffective; women may be given the white hats, so to speak, but Aristotle's
shadow still looms, however incorrect he is made to seem. To admit the
texts of women into the rhetorical canon is necessary, but such tokenism
perpetuates an emphasis on individual consciousness while suppressing
the inchoate, difficult to define, realm of rhetorical practices, codes, and
representations for which we have no name. And here, with the hitherto
nameless, is where Biesecker sets her standard. The individual, and its fantasy image, the hero, is the essence of romance. By challenging the genre
of the history of rhetoric at its core, Biesecker faces a difficult task: to give
names to a field of collective experience in such a way that this newly defined area will *work* in its assigned socio-rhetorical task, but will not fall
back into the older genres and vocabularies, which are still broadly dominant.

At issue is a new "way of knowing." Biesecker recommends a
poststructural approach to the identity of the rhetorical subject, an ap-

proach that will take note of the situatedness of any subjects, and of the fissures of race, class, and gender that make any concept of the subject suspect. Naturally, Derrida and Foucault play large roles in her account. What strikes me, however, is Biesecker's recognition of the contradictions of her position, which requires her to abjure the cult of individuals while using the language of the subject ("Derrida challenges ... ," "Derrida launches ... ," "Derrida shows ... ," "Derrida advances ... "). In proposing a renewed concept of *techne* as a process of purposeful positionality, which dissolves the active/passive binary entailed by notions of purpose and position, she acknowledges what is to me the crucial force, desire. Whatever its source in individual purpose or situational givens, we want things. Above all, perhaps, we want to *be* things. Here, the power of romance reassumes its sway, and I find a splendid statement of Kant's notion of history in Biesecker's words, "the cathected story of what it is we wish to become."

Like Biesecker, James Berlin (Chapter 7) wants to escape the "great individual" mode of rhetorical history and its "loving" attention of old treatises; his method is to *historicize*, which he defines as attending to the "economic, social, political, and cultural conditions of a time." Yet if a principal part of any interest in the history of rhetoric is to decide what a properly rhetorical stance and method might be, it is ironic that Berlin notices no similar problem for history. If one were to say "Rhetoricize!" Berlin would appropriately respond: "What do you mean by that?" "For whose interest?" "Describe your motives and situation." The command to "Historicize!" however, entails precisely the same ambiguities because, just as there is no given rhetorical method by which discourse can be made more universally persuasive, so there is no given way of historicizing anything. To apply a certain way of historicizing to a certain selection of authors and texts for a certain purpose is quite valid, even inescapable, but to claim that the method can illuminate the debatable meaning of the rhetorical tradition by an appeal to the bedrock of historical context is open to question.

In my view, Berlin's historicizing of, say, Aristotle's *Rhetoric* doesn't help much. To be sure, Aristotle's social world differed radically from ours, just as Greek democracy differed from "ours"—and I sense that "our worlds" also differ mightily. Yet there were many competing rhetorics in that world, and many set in the same social context (or possible social contexts). Berlin's quick intuition that Aristotle's ethical values (prudence, virtue, and good are mentioned) correspond to the doctrines of a particular class ("the ruling social class"—the sort of phrase that gives historians the pip) demonstrates his confidence that ruling classes always counsel such virtues.

Were these the characteristics of that "ruling social class"? Were other classes coached in rashness, vice, and evil by other rhetors? Berlin criticizes Foucault for lacking a theory of change, rather as the student mentioned above questioned Stanley Fish; and he approvingly cites Dreyfus's and Rabinow's statement that rhetoric is what is missing from Foucault, a way of getting people to see and act differently. In the end, Berlin's pluralist prescription is to provide "as many versions of the whole as we can" for the purpose of approximating truth. If his purpose were basically aesthetic and his goal to test the powers of humanistic creativity in fashioning stories about the past, I would see no problem. But this is not the case.

This is my contention: that it is the power of story, so undone by many chapters in this volume, that can make people change, and that such stories will be single authored and feature heroes (which may be classes, races, genders, or individuals). The only way to overcome an existing narrative is to fashion a new one, "better" because it is better suited to immediate needs and widely perceived to be so. In so doing, one encounters a host of theoretical difficulties. At the risk of being misunderstood, I question the obligation of the historian to "make accessible all that can be articulated of her ideological stance." On the one hand, I grant that the sincerity effect is a powerful rhetorical device; the illusion of disinterest that accompanies confessions of one's interestedness cannot be dismissed. If, on the other hand, a historian (or a poet—the advice seems to be widely applicable) is the best judge of his position, if the historian (or the statesman) knows best what lies in her soul (as the Greeks would have understood it), then what need for the caveat? To repeat to a reader in a "subject-position" that the writer is also in a "subject-position" implies a theory of readership akin to Gorgias' pathetic depiction of Helen as an enslaved creature possessed of no powers of resistance to any physical or discursive challenge whatever. Criticisms of any prevailing historical paradigm will fail to dislodge it unless another, more powerful and compelling vision is proposed and articulated. Plural visions may be characteristic of a "crisis" in a field; but crises are rarely long-lived. Rhetoric always presupposes a marketplace, an arena of persuasion in which descriptions can compete; it is just the same with historical narratives. But you must have one, and it will probably be the work of one hand and loaded with the flaws that come from representation itself. Self-consciousness doesn't lessen the cost at all.

Christine Oravec and Michael Salvador (Chapter 9) seem to herald the end of rhetorical inquiry proper in joining Berlin in a call for a dialectical pluralism of self-aware, self-examining concepts. Their useful review of recent work on rhetorical theory demonstrates the splendors and miseries of diversity. Mediating the vertical and the horizontal models of the relation of rhetorical thought and practice to the world, the synchronic and the diachronic, the systemic and the historical, the structural and the social, is certainly a useful task. James Berlin, however, could not quite convince me that his hope for a total picture of things could be approached by a plurality of visions regulated by an Adornian awareness that all models of totality harbor totalitarianism, and Oravec and Salvador similarly make me wonder what all this will look like.

It does not seem farfetched to note the resemblance of this approach to another neo-Hegelian vision of an end, namely the "end of history" recently proposed by Francis Fukuyama. The very victory of rhetorical self-awareness envisioned by many of the contributors in this volume will so overcome discursive boundaries and so complicate the position of the theoretician, audience, and situation that rhetoric will itself lose its definition. Just as the theoretical victory of one ideology signals the end of ideology for Fukuyama, so the ascendancy of a postmodern rhetorical self-consciousness will make functionally obsolete the tale of the combat of rhetoric and philosophy, both of which will dissolve comfortably into an as-yet-unnamed something that looks rather like that current entity, discourse. This appears to be happening already in the work of rhetorical postphilosophers like Richard Rorty. Ironically, in this story, philosophy has taken on the burden of concealment and deception, while rhetoric is to be the instrument of the "unconcealed" (*aletheia*), which had been the "truth" of the philosopher from Plato to Heidegger. The moralism of the traditional romance has switched sides again. Once unscrupulous rascals, the rhetoricians have donned the pious weeds of the sages. With such claims to uprightness on both sides, the possible plots look sober indeed.

Well, perhaps not quite so sober. Victor Vitanza begins Chapter 10 with a recognition that the "rift," which I have identified as the source of the romance of rhetorical history, is at the heart of the current situation, in which an ideology of difference threatens to fragment all identities. Yet another institutional cleavage instigated by a walkout of the rhetors may be in the offing; it is not clear whether it was the split of speech communication or the impending split of the compositionists that is to be viewed as tragic. Must this happen at the end of every century? Vitanza hopes not and advises the parties to the disputes in the nomadic mode of "keep on walking." In fact, he sees both events as farce. "Keep on walking" reminds me of the 1960s slogan "Keep on trucking," and Vitanza of the nomadic "Mr. Natural," anti-guru of R. Crumb's *Zap* comics. When Vitanza senses that "history is not human," not the product of human intentions or the producer of real meanings, he seems to repeat the wisdom passed on by "Mr. Natural" to his foil, "Flakey Foont," who inquired, while skateboarding past the bearded, sandaled sage, "What does it all mean, Mr. Natural?" To which "Mr. Natural" replied, "Don't mean shit, boy."

Yet the comparison must be tempered. Vitanza's statement about history is modified by a note insisting that his position should not be confused with those of Benjamin, Althusser, structuralism, or any onto-theology. Perhaps, after all, Mr. Natural falls into the last category. Vitanza's "hysteriography" is always in motion, always saying what it is not (including denials that it is a mode of negation), always dodging the bullets of identity, which it fears are inevitably shot by fascist systems of rational power. So the nomad "hysterian" is always already not there, or rather is somewhere else, so to speak, practicing a postmodern sort of what Barthes called *la critique Ni-Ni*, "neither-norism" (but without a middle), which will upset the binaries of any possible future romance of the history of rhetoric. In essence, Vitanza wants "to expel the influence of philosophy" because like duBois he sees it as a danger. Unlike duBois, however, he eschews metaphor policing, and unlike Berlin or Oravec and Salvador, he feels no obligation to tell "the whole truth" or anything at all. His nomadism, "keep on walking," is a perpetual stirring of the barley drink, which seems an inevitable response to a current impasse, as consistent as it is impossible.

*   *   *

The power of the three modes of persuasion, logos, pathos, and ethos, to determine the plot of the Aristotelian history of rhetoric, the history Aristotle indicated long before the events had transpired, is striking. This tripartite distinction, however, as the Romantics (not to mention earlier figures like Pascal) realized, makes obscure much that is most palpably real in human experience. It is one naming system that maps out the human soul (to employ a term from another such system), but the history of Western thought has developed many others, which it is useful to compare with the Aristotelian threesome. Is not the reason for Aristotle's power his amazing skill in choosing the "right" names for things, names so useful that they assure us that the things they name actually exist? The story about Adam's replying, when naming the animals, that he had called the "tiger" by that name "because it looked like a tiger," surely applies even better to Aristotle. His names seem to have been there all along.

Yet, the passion for reason that informs the prose of Voltaire, the authenticity claimed by a man of unbounded feelings like Rousseau, the logic of the passions that marks the dazzling Freudian rhetoric, can hardly be sorted neatly into the modes of persuasion. In these discourses, what is solid resides not at the points of the triangle but rather in regions of the field so remote as to involve an entire task of remapping. We have no proper terms for these things, only discourses (Enlightenment, Romanticism, Psychoanalysis, and these terms are themselves leaky vessels) built upon the instability and ambiguities of logos, pathos, ethos. What I am suggesting is that Aristotle's naming of the three modes is already a victory of logos; his demotion of pathos and ethos as nonrational appeals writes a history of rhetoric on the spot, and a powerful history it has proven to be. One is forced to use its forms to play almost any game at all. Can one defend the nonlogical modes of persuasion without rewriting Aristotle's history? Or is writing itself in thrall to that story?

The terms John Poulakos proposes are eminently suitable for counterhistorical reflection because they focus indirectly on the single term that is too seldom addressed. That term is *expectation*. It is in expectation, always present, that the social and the individual, the formal and the contextual, genre and audience response, find their intersection. We smile at the story of Adam and the tiger because it contrasts an unimaginable world without expectation, the world of primal naming, with our inescapable world in which naming systems are in place, in which everything must remind us of *something*. The question, consequently, that must be addressed each time a new attempt to retell, rename, the story fails and is reabsorbed by an old plot, and old romance, is, What did you expect? Many of the essays here rely on a fear of totalitarianism, torture, fascism. One would not expect this, given the collapse of communism and the immense recent improvements in the regimes of what was once the Third World. Most of the dread here, however, is figural, of metaphoric torture, fascisms of thought, interpretive totalitarianisms. With the dissolution of the distinction between literal and figurative language comes a surprising distrust of images and a corresponding fencing in of an area for play, for combat that does not kill and maim. If every word is a fighting word, a lot of fighting will result; I interpret this as the victory for literalism.

The mood often called postmodern can be represented (however imperfectly) as another pendular swing toward the sophistic stance that I believe to be most salubrious when it is most amoral. Figural understanding not only asserts its rights as a central form of human knowledge, it imperialistically aims at annihilating its *ennemi frère*, literality, claiming it as only another figure in guilty disguise. Tropologies flourish. Syllogisms become the products of molecular metonymies as the poetic imagination casts its sway. Radical nominalisms demolish the authority of not only essentialized notions (identity, race, and gender are the sitting ducks of our time, as virtue or justice were in other times) but also the particularized terms of rhetoric and philosophy. Nothing is perceived, everything is read, and reading is impossible. "At least in the life of the mind, ventures should be carried through to the end," as N. O. Brown once wrote. Here, perhaps, we find another rift, a rift between those who see the nonrhetorical, the nonconstructed, and who dare to envision some form of history that tries to characterize it and those who will not. Here I feel closest to James Berlin, whose Marxism reminds him that there are things that are somehow real, that nature is more (how much more!) than a social vocabulary, and that our nervous systems feel pain that is not constructed and that will ultimately end. There is a hefty irony in the fact that the amoral rhetorical art that seeks to make the best case for any position whatever is the disinterested side, even as it insists that all of its products will be quite interested. The philosophical rhetoric of truth has an insistent interest in revealing and enkindling truth in the souls of an audience; hence its interest is in the disinterestedness of any of its products, as truth is not properly speaking an interest at all.

Is there not a conflict in these essays between the general mood of antifoundationalism, and the very foundational position regarding the contamination that flows from metaphors? Rather than a linguistic, undetermined, channel for shifting situational, historical interests, rhetoric becomes a dangerous mode of activity full of the infection present at its creation. This virus, whether the image of torture or the existence of slavery in ancient Athens, is to be isolated and branded not merely because of its regrettable historical trace but also because it lives on and threatens future generations. Such reminders of a world beyond the rhetorical are disarming; they bespeak a level of things that are difficult, if not impossible, to accommodate as socially constructed. Pain, the product of torture, brings to the fore the individuality of the nervous system, which is both our human center and what we share with the higher animals. To my knowledge, however, the preference of anyone offered the option of physical pain or verbal abuse is unanimous, at least in societies like ours that lack a warrior ethic.

The cost of such a reminder is the backgrounding of our social selves, which have devised swaps in languages. Apathy, the philosopher's happiness, is resistance to pain, which is seen as an absolute. The pain of age, of war, of argument and disagreement with friend and enemy must be borne. There is another pain, not to be overlooked, articulated by Richard Rorty.

> Ironism, as I have defined it, results from awareness of the power of redescription. But most people do not want to be redescribed. They want to be taken on their own terms—taken seriously just as they are and just as they talk. The ironist tells them that the language they speak is up for grabs by her and her kind. There is something potentially very cruel about that claim. For the best way to cause people long-lasting pain is to humiliate them by making the things that seemed most important to them look futile, obsolete, and powerless. (Rorty 1989, 89)

What did we expect?

The crucial historical situation defining all modes of challenging the social status quo has been the loss of faith in any particular social group as the agent of change. Indeed, this has been the major ideological fact of the century. Faith in the proletariat necessitated a highly traditional rhetorical practice that brought the truth of things to light, rousing the emotions as it raised the consciousness of a waiting audience. This essentially Jacobin rhetoric, now a dusty museum display hauled out occasionally by labor unions and liberation theologians, emphasizes material oppression and direct action against the oppressor or at least eternal commemoration of such action. At the same time it holds forth a very clear and distinct image of the goal, a certain kind of state, a certain kind of society, a certain kind of humanity. This rhetoric was based upon a modernist, scientific way of knowing the historical world to its bottommost foundational processes and its totality.

That is all gone. It was already passing when Gramsci, sitting in a prison cell, decided that what had gone wrong was that the oppressed had become the agents of their own oppression. His notion of cultural hegemony, so different from and more subtle than the Jacobin-Marxist conspiratorial theory of ruling class domination, inevitably led to the Pogo version of class conflict: "We have met the enemy, and they is us!" The rhetoric of struggle changed dramatically. Slogans and targets remained as the vestiges of the Jacobin modernist vision, but the real game was being played on the field of self-examination, endlessly seeking, endlessly finding the traces of otherness in oneself, or more likely in one's comrade. The traditional rhetoric of struggle was the telescope that had helped to spy the far-off shore and to steer the bark toward haven.

The newer language, however, and the concepts it offers, is not telescopic, but kaleidoscopic. This entails some costs. In unmasking the rhetorical stratagems of various historical approaches and requiring a strict adherence to new, more stringent, rules of historical behavior, the new historians of rhetoric may have thrown away all their best cards. The "great person" theory of history may well repress the conditions of possibility and situationality, the economic, social, and political conditions that enable a discourse to emerge. To miss the overwhelming power of fantasy and identification with the hero of a story, however, is to overlook the central tenet of both psychoanalysis and narratology. What rhetoric must confront is the reality of desire. We live and create ourselves in stories, about which we may know nothing beyond what we like. Our stories are rhetorical in part, carrying messages about the world and rules for decoding it. Behind these stories, in the unstoried locus of "things as they are," may reside the beauty of eternal Platonic forms or the sublime terror of authentic chaos. I don't know and cannot imagine how to find out. Both are, in a sense, dream material, mythic. But a new, a rethought history of rhetoric, must surely pay attention to desire, story, genre, if it wants to produce more than a set of infinitely varied aesthetic objects.

*   *   *

In Umberto Eco's *The Name of the Rose*, a monastery (and, perhaps, a cultural tradition) is destroyed because of a maniacal effort to suppress the "lost" half of Aristotle's *Poetics*, which deals with comedy. The seriousness of the monastery and of the vision of life it affirms is at stake. The religious question—did Christ ever laugh?—is merged with the social question of carnival, sneering mirth, perennial *in*correctness, the challenges to social decency, propriety, what nice people say and think. And the authority for all of this marginalized social levity and leavening is presumed to lie with the philosopher, apparently by all parties to the case. The force of the vision of a lost answer, a lost permission slip that will validate deep urges and absolve the guilt that their expression brings forth, is, as the saying goes, "with us." Searching for the lost text, the purloined letter, the true founders of the royal line, or the villain who killed the father-king goes on and on. For historians uncannily repeat the rediscovery of a new past, an awakening that properly identifies the true ancestor, the one who most closely resembles what we "actually" are, or wish to be (Orr 1986, 1–2). It seems that the meaning of living "afterward" is to write over and over "After-words" like this one.

The Afterword is a genre that tests the power of rhetorical description. It must be apart from the body of the text in space (at the end, almost a part of the end apparatus), and in time (having been written after the other essays were complete), and voiced by a different speaker, even if that speaker bears the same name as the author of the text (as in the "Afterword" to one's own book). The "afterness" of the "Afterword" is of the sort the French call arrière pensée, or afterthought; it is a version of *l'esprit d'escalier*, "staircase wit," the brilliant conversational response that one thinks of on the staircase, after one has departed from the occasion and the moment when it might have made an effect. What is interesting about *l'esprit d'escalier*, of course, is how often we tell others, and convince ourselves, that we actually uttered the words that came to us too late. In other words, the afterness is repudiated as shameful, weak; tempo (not ripeness) is all in a conversation. The "Afterword" is therefore a genre for the *slow*, or, worse, the late arrival.

Whatever authority a latecomer may claim, and it is slight indeed, must derive from the lateness itself, that is, from the distance between his own perspective and those of the conversation he encounters. Not daring, as a matter of etiquette, to ask for a recounting of each point in debate, he finds himself guessing a lot, imagining what must lie behind the odd array of ideas that seem, at that stage of events, quite natural to the other parties, however strongly they disagree. He may be surprised to find old acquaintances in unexpected and troubling positions, pleased to find utter strangers whose views accord so perfectly with his own, and relieved that his "afterness" exempts him from having to take a stance on each issue, like a presidential candidate. This relief is the safe distance of irony, with its license to understand differently, to redescribe what has gone before.

One might object that this description of the late arrival does not specify anything, because it is also the condition of any participant in discourse. As Kenneth Burke remarked somewhere (a phrase that could begin a vast number of sentences), we all enter "the conversation" when it is well under way and leave it in what always seems to be the middle; lateness is an existential state, however much Nietzsche would wish us to forget it and act as though everything is a beginning.

References

Achard, Guy. 1981. *Pratique rhetorique et ideologie politique dans le discourse "optimates" de Ciceron.* Leiden: E. J. Brill.

Adorno, Theodor W. 1973. *Negative Dialectics.* Trans. E. B. Ashton. New York: Continuum.

Althusser, Louis. 1971. *Lenin and Philosophy and Other Essays.* Trans. Ben Brewster. London: New Left Books.

Anderson, Perry. 1974a. *Lineages of the Absolutist State.* London: New Left Books.

———. 1974b. *Passages from Antiquity to Feudalism.* London: New Left Books.

———. 1980. *Arguments Within English Marxism.* London: Verso.

Ankersmit, F. R. 1983. *Narrative Logic: A Semantic Analysis of the Historian's Language.* The Hague: Martinus Nijhoff.

———. 1989. "Historiography and Postmodernism." *History and Theory* 28: 137–153.

Aristophanes. 1982. *The Clouds.* Trans. B. B. Rogers. London: William Heinemann Ltd.

Aristotle. 1941. *Metaphysics.* In *The Basic Works of Aristotle*, ed. Richard McKeon, 689–934. New York: Random.

———. 1954. *The Rhetoric and the Poetics.* Trans. W. Rhys Roberts. New York: Modern Library.

———. 1962. *The Nichomachean Ethics.* Trans. Martin Ostwald. Indianapolis: Bobbs-Merrill Company.

———. 1982. *The "Art" of Rhetoric.* Trans. J. H. Freese. London: William Heinemann Ltd.

———. 1984a. *The Nichomachean Ethics.* Trans. W. D. Ross, revised by J. O. Urmson. In *The Complete Works of Aristotle.* 2 vols., ed. Jonathan Barnes, 1,729–1,868. Princeton: Princeton University Press.

———. 1984b. *Sophistical Refutations.* Trans. W. A. Pickard-Cambridge. In *The Complete Works of Aristotle.* 2 vols., ed. Jonathan Barnes, 278–315. Princeton: Princeton University Press.

Aronowitz, Stanley. 1990. *The Crisis in Historical Materialism: Class, Politics, and Culture in Marxist Theory.* Minneapolis: University of Minnesota Press.

Arrowsmith, William. 1990. Introduction to Friedrich Nietzsche, "We Classicists." In *Unmodern Observations*, 307–320. New Haven: Yale University Press.

Attridge, Derek. 1987. "Language as History/History as Language: Sassure and the Romance of Etymology." In *Post-structuralism and the Question of History*, ed. Derek Attridge et al., 183–221. Cambridge: Cambridge University Press.

Atwill, Janet M. 1990. "Refiguring Rhetoric as Art: Aristotle's Concept of *Techne* and the Humanist Paradigm." Diss., Purdue University, West Lafayette, Indiana.

———. 1992. "Contingencies of Historical Representation." Unpublished manuscript.

Aymand, Maurice. 1972. "The Annales and French Historiography." *Journal of European Economic History* 1: 491–511.

Bahti, Timothy. 1979. "History as Rhetorical Enactment: Walter Benjamin's Theses 'On the Concept of History.'" *Diacritics* 9: 2–17.

Bakhtin, Mikhail. 1984. *Rabelais and His World.* Trans. Helene Iswolsky. Bloomington: Indiana University Press.

98 *References*

Balbus, Isaac D. 1987. "Disciplining Women: Michel Foucault and the Power of Feminist Discourse." In *Feminism as Critique: On the Politics of Gender*, ed. Seyla Benhabib and Drucilla Cornelly, 110–127. Minneapolis: University of Minnesota Press.

Baldwin, Charles S. [1924] 1959. *Ancient Rhetoric and Poetic Interpreted from Representative Works*. Gloucester: Peter Smith.

———. [1928] 1959. *Medieval Rhetoric and Poetic (to 1400) Interpreted from Representative Works*. Gloucester: Peter Smith.

Barilli, Renato. 1989. *Rhetoric*. Minneapolis: University of Minnesota Press.

Barker, Ernest. 1959. *The Political Thought of Plato and Aristotle*. New York: Dover.

Barnes, Jonathan, ed. 1984. *The Complete Works of Aristotle*. 2 vols. Princeton: Princeton University Press.

Barthes, Roland. 1972. *Mythologies*. Trans. Annette Leavers. New York: Hill and Wang.

———. 1975. *The Pleasure of the Text*. Trans. Richard Miller. New York: Hill and Wang.

———. 1976. *Sade/Fourier/Loyola*. Trans. Richard Howard. New York: Hill and Wang.

———. 1977. *Roland Barthes by Roland Barthes*. Trans. Richard Howard. New York: Hill and Wang.

———. 1981. "The Discourse of History." Trans. Stephen Bann. In *Comparative Criticism: A Yearbook*, ed. E. S. Shaffer, 3–20. Cambridge: Cambridge University Press.

———. 1983. "Inaugural Lecture, College de France." In *A Barthes Reader*, ed. Susan Sontag, 457-478. New York: Hill and Wang.

———. 1987. *Michelet*. Trans. Richard Howard. New York: Hill and Wang.

———. 1988. "The Old Rhetoric: An Aide-memoire." In *The Semiotic Challenge*, 11–94. Trans. Richard Howard. New York: Hill and Wang.

Bartkowski, Frances. 1988. "Epistemic Drift in Foucault." In *Feminism and Foucault: Reflections on Resistance*, ed. Irene Diamond and Lee Quinby, 43–58. Boston: Northeastern University Press.

Belsey, Catherine. 1980. *Critical Practice*. London: Methuen.

Benjamin, Walter. 1968. *Illuminations*. New York: Harcourt, Brace and World.

Bennington, Geoff. 1987. "Demanding History." In *Post-structuralism and the Question of History*, ed. Derek Attridge et al., 15–29. Cambridge: Cambridge University Press.

Bennington, Geoff, and Robert Young. 1987. "Introduction: Posing the Question." In *Post-structuralism and the Question of History*, ed. Derek Attridge et al., 1–11. Cambridge: Cambridge University Press.

Benoit, W. 1990. "Isocrates and Aristotle on Rhetoric." *Rhetoric Society Quarterly* 20: 251–260.

———. 1991. "Isocrates and Plato on Rhetoric and Rhetoricians." *Rhetoric Society Quarterly* 21: 60–72.

Berlin, James A. 1984. *Writing Instruction in Nineteenth-Century American Colleges*. Carbondale: Southern Illinois University Press.

———. 1985. "Rhetoric and Poetics in the English Department: Our Nineteenth-Century Inheritance." *College English* 47: 521–533.

———. 1987. *Rhetoric and Reality: Writing Instruction in American Colleges 1900–1985*. Carbondale: Southern Illinois University Press.

———. 1988. "Rhetoric and Ideology in the Writing Class." *College English* 50: 477–494.

_____. 1990. "Postmodernism, Politics, and Histories of Rhetoric." *PRE/TEXT* 11: 169–187.

Berlin, James A., et al. 1988. "The Politics of Historiography." *Rhetoric Review* 7: 5–49.

Bernadini, P. A., and A. Veneri. 1981. "Il *Gorgia* di Platone nel guidizion di Gorgia e l' 'areo' Gorgia nel guidizio di Platone (Athen. 11, 505d–e)." *Quaderni Urbinati di Cultura Classica* 36: 149–160.

Bernal, Martin. 1987. *Black Athena: The Afroasiatic Roots of Classical Civilization.* Vol. 1: *The Fabrication of Ancient Greece, 1785–1985.* New Brunswick, N.J.: Rutgers University Press.

Betz, Hans Dieter, ed. 1986. *The Greek Magical Papyri in Translation Including the Demotic Spells.* Chicago: University of Chicago Press.

Biesecker, Barbara. 1989. "Rethinking the Rhetorical Situation from Within the Thematic of Differance." *Philosophy and Rhetoric* 22: 110–130.

Biesecker, Susan. 1991. "Rhetorical Discourse and the Constitution of the Subject." *Argumentation* 5: 155–169.

Bitzer, Lloyd F. 1968. "The Rhetorical Situation." *Philosophy and Rhetoric* 1: 1–14.

_____. 1978. "Rhetoric and Public Knowledge." In *Rhetoric, Philosophy and Literature: An Exploration,* ed. Don. M. Burks, 75–93. West Lafayette, Ind.: Purdue University Press.

Bitzer, Lloyd, and Edwin Black, eds. 1971. *The Prospect of Rhetoric: Report of the National Development Project.* Englewood Cliffs: Prentice-Hall.

Black, Edwin. 1978. *Rhetorical Criticism: A Study in Method.* Madison: University of Wisconsin Press.

_____. 1980. "The Mutability of Rhetoric." In *Rhetoric in Transition: Studies in the Nature and Uses of Rhetoric,* ed. Eugene E. White, 71–85. University Park: Pennsylvania State University Press.

Blair, Carole, and Martha Cooper. 1987. "The Humanist Turn in Foucault's Rhetoric of Inquiry." *Quarterly Journal of Speech* 73: 151–171.

Blair, Carole, and Mary L. Kahl. 1990. "Introduction: Revising the History of Rhetorical Theory." *Western Journal of Speech Communication* 54: 148–159.

Blank, D. 1988. "Socratics vs Sophists on Payment for Teaching." *Classical Antiquity* 4: 1–49.

Blass, Frederick. 1879. *Isocratis Orationes.* Leipzig: Teubner.

_____. 1892. *Antiphontis Orationes et Fragmenta.* Leipzig: Aedibus B. G. Teubneri.

_____. 1962. *Die Attische Beredsamkeit.* 2 vols. Repr. of 1892 2d ed. Hildesheim: Olms.

Bledstein, Burton J. 1976. *The Culture of Professionalism: The Middle Class and the Development of Higher Education in America.* New York: W. W. Norton.

Bonnefond, Marianne. 1983. "Espace, temps et ideologie: le sénat dans la cité romaine républicaine." *Dialoghi di archeologia,* ser. 3: 37–44.

Bonner, Robert J. 1927. *Lawyers and Litigants in Ancient Athens.* Chicago: University of Chicago Press.

Booth, Wayne. 1974. *Modern Dogma and the Rhetoric of Assent.* Chicago: University of Chicago Press.

Bormann, Ernest G. 1980. *Communication Theory.* New York: Holt, Rinehart.

_____. 1985. *The Force of Fantasy: Restory the American Dream.* Carbondale: Southern Illinois University Press.

Bourdieu, Pierre. 1977. *An Outline of a Theory of Practice.* Trans. Richard Nice. Cambridge: Cambridge University Press.

_____. 1984. *Distinction.* Trans. Richard Nice. Cambridge: Harvard University Press.

_____. 1988. *Homo Academicus.* Trans. Peter Collier. Stanford: Stanford University Press.

Bowers, John Waite. 1972. "The Pre-Scientific Function of Rhetorical Criticism." In *Contemporary Rhetoric: A Readers' Coursebook,* ed. Douglas Ehninger, 163–172. Glenview, Ill.: Scott, Foresman.

Braudel, Fernand. 1972. *The Mediterranean and the Mediterranean World in the Age of Phillip II.* 2 vols. Trans. Sian Reynolds. New York: Harper and Row.

Brock, Bernard. 1980. "Rhetorical Criticism: A Burkeian Approach." In *Methods of Rhetorical Criticism: A Twentieth-Century Perspective,* ed. Bernard L. Brock and Robert L. Scott, 348–388. Detroit: Wayne State University Press.

Brockriede, Wayne. 1966. "Toward Contemporary Aristotelian Theory of Rhetoric." *Quarterly Journal of Speech* 52: 33–40.

Brown, Norman O. 1959. *Life Against Death.* Middletown, Conn.: Wesleyan University Press.

_____. 1974. *Closing Time.* New York: Vintage.

Brown, Richard Harvey. 1987. *Society as Text: Essays on Rhetoric, Reason, and Reality.* Chicago: University of Chicago Press.

Brummett, Barry. 1990. "How to Propose a Discourse." *Communication Studies* 41: 128–135.

Bruns, Gerald L. 1982. *Inventions: Writing, Textuality, and Understanding in Literary History.* New Haven: Yale University Press.

Bryant, Donald C. 1953. "Rhetoric: Its Functions and Its Scope." *Quarterly Journal of Speech* 39: 401–424.

Burke, Kenneth. 1966. *Language as Symbolic Action.* Berkeley: University of California Press.

_____. 1968. *Counter-Statement.* Berkeley: University of California Press.

_____. 1969a. *A Grammar of Motives.* Berkeley: University of California Press.

_____. 1969b. *A Rhetoric of Motives.* Berkeley: University of California Press.

_____. 1973. *The Philosophy of Literary Form.* 3d ed. Berkeley: University of California Press.

_____. 1976. "The Party Line." *Quarterly Journal of Speech* 62: 72–68.

_____. 1984. *Attitudes Towards History.* 3d ed. Berkeley: University of California Press.

Burleson, Brant, and Susan L. Kline. 1979. "Habermas' Theory of Communication: A Critical Explication." *Quarterly Journal of Speech* 65: 412–428.

Burnet, John. 1964. *Greek Philosophy: Thales to Plato.* New York: St. Martin's Press.

Butler, H. E., trans. 1921. *The Institutio Oratorio of Quintilian.* Vol. 2. Loeb Classical Library. Cambridge: Harvard University Press.

Butler, Judith. 1987. *Subjects of Desire.* New York: Columbia University Press.

_____. 1990. *Gender Trouble: Feminism and the Subversion of Identity.* New York: Routledge.

Cahn, M. 1987. "Der Ort des rhetorischen Wissens: Kunst und Nature bei Isokrates." *Berichte zur Wissenshaftsgeschichte* 10: 217–228.

_____. 1989. "Reading Rhetoric Rhetorically: Isocrates and the Marketing of Insight." *Rhetorica* 7: 121–144.

Campbell, John Angus. 1981. "Historical Reason: Field as Consciousness." In *Dimensions of Argument: Proceedings of the Second Summer Conference on Argumentation,* ed. George Ziegelmueller and Jack Rhodes, 101–113. Annandale, Va.: Speech Communication Association.

_____. 1982. "Eric Voegelin's Order in History: A Review." *Quarterly Journal of Speech* 68: 80–91.

_____. 1984. "A Rhetorical Interpretation of History." *Rhetorica* 2: 227–266.

Campbell, Karlyn Kohrs. 1970. "Ontological Foundations of Rhetorical Theory." *Philosophy and Rhetoric* 3: 97–108.

_____. 1973. "The Rhetoric of Women's Liberation: An Oxymoron." *Quarterly Journal of Speech* 59: 74–86.

_____. 1989. *Man Cannot Speak for Her: A Critical Study of Early Feminist Rhetoric.* Vol. 1. New York: Greenwood Press.

Carleton, Walter M. 1978. "What Is Rhetorical Knowledge? A Response to Farrell and More." *Quarterly Journal of Speech* 64: 313–328.

Carrard, Phillippe. 1992. *Poetics of the New History: French Historical Discourse from Braudel to Chartier.* Baltimore: Johns Hopkins University Press.

Carse, James P. 1986. *Finite and Infinite Games: A Vision of Life as Play and Possibility.* New York: Baltimore Books

Carter, J. M. 1972. "Cicero: Politics and Philosophy." In *Cicero and Virgil: Studies in Honour of Harold Hunt,* ed. John R.C. Martyn, 15–36. Amsterdam: A. M. Hakkert.

Castoriadis, Cornelius. 1984. *Crossroads in the Labyrinth.* Trans. Kate Soper and Martin H. Ryle. Cambridge: MIT Press.

Cebek, L. B. 1986. "Understanding Narrative Theory." *History and Theory* 25: 58–81.

Chomsky, Noam. 1965. *Aspects of Theory and Syntax.* Cambridge: MIT Press.

Cixous, Helene, and Catherine Clément. 1986. *The Newly Born Woman.* Trans. Betsy Wing. Minneapolis: University of Minnesota Press.

Clark, Donald Leman. 1957. *Rhetoric in Graeco-Roman Education.* New York: Columbia University Press.

Classen, C. Joachim. 1981. "Aristotle's Picture of the Sophists." In *The Sophists and Their Legacy,* ed. G. B. Kerferd, 7–24. Wiesbaden: Franz Steiner.

Clément, Catherine. 1983. *The Lives and Legends of Jacques Lacan.* Trans. Arthur Goldhammer. New York: Columbia University Press.

Cole, Thomas. 1991. *The Origins of Rhetoric in Ancient Greece.* Baltimore: Johns Hopkins University Press.

Collingwood, R. G. 1946. *The Idea of History.* Oxford: Oxford University Press.

_____. 1956. *The Idea of History.* New York: Oxford University Press.

Conley, Thomas M. 1990. *Rhetoric in the European Tradition.* New York: Longman.

Connolly, William E. 1987. *Politics and Ambiguity.* Madison: University of Wisconsin Press.

Connor, W. R. 1971. *New Politicians of Fifth-Century Athens.* Princeton: Princeton University Press.

Connors, Robert J. 1981. "The Rise and Fall of the Modes of Discourse." *College Composition and Communication* 32: 444–455.

_____. 1984. "Historical Inquiry in Composition Studies." *The Writing Instructor* 4: 157–167.

_____. 1985. "Mechanical Correctness as a Focus in Composition Instruction." *College Composition and Communication* 36: 61–72.

_____. 1986. Review of *Writing Instruction in Nineteenth-Century American Colleges,* by James Berlin. *College Composition and Communication* 37: 247–249.

_____. 1987. "Personal Writing Assignments." *College Composition and Communication* 38: 166–183.

_____. 1989. "Rhetorical History as a Component of Composition Studies." *Rhetoric Review* 7: 230–240.

Connors, Robert J., Lisa S. Ede, and Andrea Lunsford. 1984. "The Revival of Rhetoric in America." In *Essays on Classical Rhetoric and Modern Discourse*, ed. Robert J. Connors, Lisa S. Ede, and Andrea Lunsford. Carbondale: Southern Illinois University Press.

Cooper, Lane. 1932. *The Rhetoric of Aristotle*. New York: D. Appleton and Company.

_____. 1935. "The *Rhetoric* of Aristotle." *Quarterly Journal of Speech* 21: 10–19.

Cope, Edward M. 1867. *An Introduction to Aristotle's Rhetoric*. Cambridge: Macmillan.

_____. 1877. *The Rhetoric of Aristotle with a Commentary*, ed. John Sandys. 3 vols. Cambridge: Cambridge University Press.

_____. 1970. *The Rhetoric of Aristotle with a Commentary*, ed. and rev. J. E. Sandys. 3 vols. Hildesheim: Olms.

Corbett, Edward P.J. 1965. *Classical Rhetoric for the Modern Student*. Oxford: Oxford University Press.

_____. 1971. *Classical Rhetoric for the Modern Student*. New York: Oxford University Press.

_____. 1989. *Selected Essays*, ed. Robert J. Connors. Dallas: Southern Methodist University Press.

Cousins, Mark, and Athar Hussain. 1984. *Michel Foucault*. New York: St. Martin's Press.

Covino, William. 1983. "Thomas De Quincy in a Revisionist History of Rhetoric." *PRE/TEXT* 4: 121–136.

_____. 1988. *The Art of Wondering: Revisions in the History of Rhetoric*. Montclair, N.J.: Boynton/Cook.

Crawford, Michael. 1978. *The Roman Republic*. London: Fontana.

Crowley, Sharon. 1979. "Of Gorgias and Grammatology." *College Composition and Communication* 30: 279–283.

_____. 1984. "New-Romanticism and the History of Rhetoric." *PRE/TEXT* 5: 19–37.

_____. 1985. "Invention in Current-Traditional Rhetoric." *College Composition and Communication* 36: 51–60.

_____. 1990. *The Methodical Memory: Invention in Current-Traditional Rhetoric*. Carbondale: Southern Illinois University Press.

Culler, Jonathan. 1982. *On Deconstruction: Theory and Criticism After Structuralism*. Ithaca: Cornell University Press.

D'Angelo, Frank J. 1975. *A Conceptual Theory of Rhetoric*. Cambridge: Winthrop.

Dallmayr, Fred. 1984. *Language and Politics*. Notre Dame: University of Notre Dame Press.

Davies, J. K. 1971. *Athenian Propertied Families*. Oxford: Oxford University Press.

Day, Dennis G. 1960. "Persuasion and the Concept of Identification." *Quarterly Journal of Speech* 46: 270–273.

De Bolla, Peter. 1986. "Disfiguring History." *Diacritics* 16: 49–58.

de Certeau, Michel. 1984. *The Practice of Everyday Life*. Trans. Steven Rendall. Berkeley: University of California Press.

de Lauretis, Teresa. 1989. "The Essence of the Triangle or, Taking the Risk of Essentialism Seriously: Feminist Theory in Italy, the U.S., and Britain." *Differences: A Journal of Feminist Cultural Studies* 1: 3–37.

Deleuze, Gilles. 1977. "Nomad Thought." In *The New Nietzsche*, ed. David B. Allison, 142–149. New York: Dell.

Deleuze, Gilles, and Felix Guattari. 1983. *Anti-Oedipus: Capitalism and Schizophrenia*. Minneapolis: University of Minnesota Press.

———. 1987. *A Thousand Plateaus: Capitalism and Schizophrenia*. Minneapolis: University of Minnesota Press.

Deleuze, Gilles, and Claire Parnet. 1987. *Dialogues*. Trans. Hugh Tomlinson and Barbara Habberjam. New York: Columbia University Press.

de Man, Paul. 1979. "Semiology and Rhetoric." In *Allegories of Reading*, 3–20. New Haven: Yale University Press.

———. 1983. *Blindness and Insight: Essays in the Rhetoric of Contemporary Criticism*. 2d rev. ed. Minneapolis: University of Minnesota Press.

de Romilly, J. 1973. "Gorgias et le pouvoir de la poésie." *Journal of Hellenic Studies* 93: 155–162.

———. 1975. *Magic and Rhetoric in Ancient Greece*. Cambridge: Harvard University Press.

———. 1985. *A Short History of Greek Literature*. Trans. Lillian Doherty. Chicago: University of Chicago Press.

Derrida, Jacques. 1972. "La pharmacie de Platon." In *La dissémination*. Paris: Seuil.

———. 1976. *Of Grammatology*. Trans. Gayatri Chakravorty Spivak. Baltimore: Johns Hopkins University Press.

———. 1978. "Freud and the Scene of Writing." In *Writing and Difference*. Trans. Alan Bass, 196–231. Chicago: University of Chicago Press.

———. 1980. "The Law of Genre." In *On Narrative*, ed. W.J.T. Mitchell, 51–78. Chicago: University of Chicago Press.

———. 1981a. *Dissemination*. Trans. Barbara Johnson. Chicago: University of Chicago Press.

———. 1981b. "Plato's Pharmacy." In *Dissemination*. Trans. Barbara Johnson, 67–171. Chicago: University of Chicago Press.

———. 1982. "Differance." In *Margins of Philosophy*. Trans. Alan Bass. Chicago: University of Chicago Press.

———. 1983. "The Principle of Reason: The University in the Eyes of Its Pupils." *Diacritics* 13: 1–20.

———. 1986. "The Age of Hegel." In *Demarcating the Disciplines*, ed. Samuel Weber, 3–34. Minneapolis: University of Minnesota Press.

———. 1987. *The Truth in Painting*. Trans. Geoff Bennington and Ian McLeod. Chicago: University of Chicago Press.

Detienne, Marcel, and Jean-Pierre Vernant. 1978. *Cunning Intelligence in Greek Culture and Society*. Trans. Janet Lloyd. New York: Humanities Press.

Diamond, Irene, and Lee Quinby, eds. 1988. *Feminism and Foucault: Reflections on Resistance*. Boston: Northeastern University Press.

Diels, Hermann, and Walter Kranz, eds. 1952. *Die Fragmente der Vorsokratiker*. 3 vols. Berlin: Weidmann.

Diogenes Laertius. 1925. *Lives*. Trans. R. D. Hicks. London: William Heinemann Ltd.

Dionysius of Halicarnassus. 1974. "Life of Isocrates." In *Dionysius of Halicarnassus. The Critical Essays*. Vol. 1. Trans. S. Usher. Cambridge: Harvard University Press.

Dodds, E. R. 1959. *Plato: Gorgias.* Oxford: Oxford University Press.

———. 1973. *The Ancient Concept of Progress and Other Essays on Greek Literature and Belief.* Oxford: Clarendon.

Dreyfus, Hubert L., and Paul Rabinow. 1983. *Michel Foucault: Beyond Structuralism and Hermeneutics.* Chicago: University of Chicago Press.

Dubois, J., et al. 1981. *A General Rhetoric, by Group Mu.* Baltimore: Johns Hopkins University Press.

duBois, Page. 1988. *Sowing the Body: Psychoanalysis and Ancient Representations of Women.* Chicago: University of Chicago Press.

———. 1991. *Torture and Truth.* New York: Routledge.

Duprell, Eugene. 1948. *Les Sophistes.* Neuchâtel: Editions du Griffon.

Eagleton, Terry. 1976. *Criticism and Ideology.* London: Verso.

———. 1981. "A Small History of Rhetoric." In *Walter Benjamin or Towards a Revolutionary Criticism,* 101–113. London: Verso and NLB.

———. 1983a. "Conclusion: Political Criticism." In *Literary Theory: An Introduction,* 194–217. Oxford: Blackwell.

———. 1983b. *Literary Theory: An Introduction.* Oxford: Blackwell.

———. 1986. *Against the Grain: Essays 1975–1985.* London: Verso.

Edel, Abraham. 1982. *Aristotle and His Philosophy.* Chapel Hill: University of North Carolina Press.

Ehninger, Douglas. 1968. "On Systems of Rhetoric." *Philosophy and Rhetoric* 1: 131–144.

———. 1975. "Coloquy II. A Synoptic View of Systems of Western Rhetoric." *Quarterly Journal of Speech* 61: 448–453.

Enos, Richard Leo. 1976. "The Epistemology of Gorgias' Rhetoric: A Re-examination." *The Southern Speech Communication Journal* 42: 35–51.

———. 1985. "The History of Rhetoric: The Reconstruction of Progress." In *Speech Communication in the Twentieth Century,* ed. Thomas W. Benson, 28–40. Carbondale: Southern Illinois University Press.

———. 1987. "Aristotle, Empedocles, and the Notion of Rhetoric." In *In Search of Justice: The Indiana Tradition in Speech Communication,* ed. Richard J. Jensen and John C. Hammerback, 5–21. Amsterdam: Rodopi.

———. 1988. *The Literate Mode of Cicero's Legal Rhetoric.* Carbondale: Southern Illinois University Press.

Farenga, Vincent. 1979. "Periphrasis on the Origin of Rhetoric." *Modern Language Notes* 94: 1,033–1,055.

Farrell, Thomas B. 1976. "Knowledge, Consensus and Rhetorical Theory." *Quarterly Journal of Speech* 62: 1–14.

———. 1978. "Social Knowledge II." *Quarterly Journal of Speech* 64: 329–334.

Fauré, Christine. 1981. "Absent History." *Signs* 7: 71–80.

Favory, F. 1975. "Classes dangereuses et crise de l'état." In *Texte, politique, idéologie: Cicéron.* Actes de la table ronde—Annales littéraires de l'université de Besanon: Centre de recherches d'histoire ancienne, 20: 109–234.

Feyerabend, Paul. 1978. *Against Method.* London: Verso.

Fields, A. Belden. 1988. "In Defense of Political Economy and Systemic Analysis: A Critique of Prevailing Theoretical Approaches to the New Social Movements." In *Marxism and the*

Interpretation of Culture, ed. Cary Nelson and Lawrence Grossberg, 141–156. Urbana: University of Illinois Press.

Finley, M. I. 1977. *Aspects of Antiquity.* 2d ed. New York: Penguin.

———. 1987a. *Ancient History.* New York: Penguin.

———. 1987b. *The Use and Abuse of History.* New York: Penguin.

Fish, Stanley. 1985. "Consequences." In *Against Theory: Literary Studies and the New Pragmatism,* ed. W.J.T. Mitchell, 106–131. Chicago: University of Chicago Press.

———. 1989. *Doing What Comes Naturally: Change, Rhetoric, and the Practice of Theory in Literary and Legal Studies.* Durham and London: Duke University Press.

Fisher, Walter. 1978. "Toward a Logic of Good Reasons." *Quarterly Journal of Speech* 64: 376–384.

———. 1980. "Rhetorical Fiction and the Presidency." *Quarterly Journal of Speech* 66: 119–126.

———. 1987. *Human Communication as Narration: Toward a Philosophy of Reason, Value and Action.* Columbia: University of South Carolina Press.

Fitzgerald, Frances. 1980. *America Revised: History Schoolbooks in the Twentieth Century.* New York: Vintage.

Florescu, V. 1970. "Rhetoric and Its Rehabilitation in Contemporary Philosophy." *Philosophy and Rhetoric* 3: 193–224.

Fogel, Robert William. 1970. "Historiography and Retrospective Econometrics." *History and Theory* 9: 245–264.

Fornara, Charles William. 1983. *The Nature of History in Ancient Greece and Rome.* Berkeley: University of California Press.

Foss, Karen A., and Sonja K. Foss. 1983. "The Status of Research on Women and Communication." *Communication Quarterly* 31: 195–204.

Foucault, Michel. 1972. *The Archaeology of Knowledge and the Discourse on Language.* Trans. A.M. Sheridan Smith. New York: Pantheon Books.

———. 1977. *Language, Counter-Memory, Practice.* Trans. D. F. Bouchard and Sherry Simon. Ithaca: Cornell University Press.

———. 1978. *The History of Sexuality.* Vol. 1: *An Introduction.* Trans. Robert Hurley. New York: Pantheon.

———. 1980. *Power/Knowledge: Selected Interviews and Other Writings,* ed. Colin Gordon. Trans. Colin Gordon, Leo Marshall, John Mepham, and Kate Soper. New York: Pantheon.

———. 1983. Preface. In *Anti-Oedipus,* by Gilles Deleuze and Felix Guattari, xi–xxiv. Minneapolis: University of Minnesota Press.

———. 1986a. *History of Sexuality.* Vol. 3: *The Care of the Self.* Trans. Robert Hurley. New York: Random House.

———. 1986b. *History of Sexuality.* Vol. 2: *The Use of Pleasure.* Trans. Robert Hurley. Harmondsworth: Penguin.

———. 1989. "Clarifications on the Question of Power." In *Foucault Live,* ed. Sylvere Lotinger. Trans. John Johnston, 179–192. New York: Semiotext(e).

Freeman, Kathleen. 1966. *The Murder of Heroes and Other Trials from the Athenian Laycourts.* London: MacDonald and Company.

Freud, Sigmund. 1959. *The Standard Edition of the Complete Psychological Works.* Vol. 9. Trans. James Strachey. London: Hogarth Press.

Gadamer, Hans-Georg. 1975. *Truth and Method.* New York: Crossroads.

Gage, John T. 1984. Review of *Rhetorical Traditions and the Teaching of Writing,* by C. H. Knoblauch and Lil Brannon. *Rhetoric Review* 3: 100–105.

Gardiner, Patrick, ed. 1974. *The Philosophy of History.* London: Oxford University Press.

Garner, Richard. 1987. *Law and Society in Classical Athens.* London: Croom Helm.

Gay, Peter. 1974. *Style in History.* New York: Oxford University Press.

———. 1985. *Freud for Historians.* New York: Oxford University Press.

Golden, James L., Goodwin F. Berquist, and William E. Coleman. 1989. *The Rhetoric of Western Thought.* 4th ed. Dubuque, Iowa: Kendall/Hunt.

Gomperz, Theodor. 1955. *Greek Thinkers: A History of Ancient Philosophy.* Vol. 1. London: John Murray.

Gossman, Leonel. 1986. "History as Decipherment: Romantic Historiography and the Discovery of the Other." *New Literary History* 18: 23–58.

Gramsci, Antonio. 1979. *Letters from Prison.* Trans. Lyne Lawner. London: Quartet Books.

Grant, Michael. 1973. *Selected Political Speeches of Cicero.* Rev. reprint. Harmondsworth: Penguin.

Grassi, Ernesto. 1976. "Rhetoric and Philosophy." *Philosophy and Rhetoric* 9: 200–216.

———. 1980. *Rhetoric as Philosophy: The Humanist Tradition.* University Park: Pennsylvania State University Press.

———. 1987. "Why Rhetoric Is Philosophy." *Philosophy and Rhetoric* 20: 68–78.

Griffin, Leland M. 1964. "The Rhetorical Structure of the 'New Left' Movement: Part 1." *Quarterly Journal of Speech* 50: 113–135.

Grimaldi, William. 1958. "Rhetoric and the Philosophy of Aristotle." *Classical Journal* 53: 371–375.

———. 1972a. *Studies in the Philosophy of Aristotle's Rhetoric.* Wiesbaden: Franz Steiner Verlag.

———. 1972b. "Studies in the Philosophy of Aristotle's Rhetoric." *Hermes* 25: 1–151.

———. 1980. *Aristotle, Rhetoric I: A Commentary.* New York: Fordham University Press.

Gronbeck, Bruce E. 1972. "Gorgias on Rhetoric and Poetic: A Rehabilitation." *The Southern Speech Communication Journal* 38: 27–38.

Grote, George. 1868. *A History of Greece.* Vol. 8. London: John Murray.

Grube, G.M.A. 1965. *The Greek and Roman Critics.* London: Methuen and Co.

Guthrie, W.K.C. 1971. *The Sophists.* New York: Cambridge University Press.

———. 1975. *Plato, The Man and His Dialogues. A History of Greek Philosophy,* vol. 4. Cambridge: Cambridge University Press.

Habermas, Jürgen. 1975. *Legitimation Crisis.* Trans. Thomas McCarthy. Boston: Beacon Press.

———. 1979. *Communication and the Evolution of Society.* Trans. Thomas McCarthy. Boston: Beacon Press.

———. 1987. *The Philosophical Discourse of Modernity: Twelve Lectures.* Trans. Frederick Lawrence. Cambridge: MIT Press.

Hall, John R. 1990. "The Time of History." *History and Theory* 19: 113–131.

Halloran, Michael. 1975. "On the End of Rhetoric, Classical and Modern." *College English* 36: 621–631.

———. 1976. "Tradition and Theory in Rhetoric." *Quarterly Journal of Speech* 62: 234–241.

———. 1982. "Aristotle's Concept of Ethos, or If Not His Somebody Else's." *Rhetoric Review* 1: 58–63.

———. 1983. "Rhetoric in the American College Curriculum: The Decline of Public Discourse." *PRE/TEXT* 3: 245–269.

Hamilton, Edith, and Huntington Cairns, eds. 1961. *The Collected Dialogues of Plato.* Princeton: Princeton University Press.

Hancock, Brenda Robinson. 1972. "Affirmation of Negation in the Women's Liberation Movement." *Quarterly Journal of Speech* 58: 264–271.

Harding, Sandra, and Jean F. O'Barr, eds. 1987. *Sex and Scientific Inquiry.* Chicago: University of Chicago Press.

Harper, Nancy L. 1979. *Human Communication Theory: The History of a Paradigm.* Rochelle Park, N.J.: Hayden.

Hartsock, Nancy L. 1990. "Foucault on Power: A Theory for Women?" In *Feminism/Postmodernism*, ed. Linda J. Nicholson, 157–175. New York: Routledge.

Hauser, Gerard. 1986. *Introduction to Rhetorical Theory.* New York: Harper and Row.

Havelock, Eric A. 1957. *The Liberal Temper in Greek Politics.* New Haven: Yale University Press.

———. 1982. *The Literate Revolution in Greece and Its Cultural Consequences.* Princeton: Princeton University Press.

———. 1983. "The Linguistic Task of the Presocratics." In *Language and Thought in Early Greek Philosophy*, ed. Kevin Robb, 7–82. LaSalle, Ill.: Hegeler Institute.

Hegel, G.W.F. 1974. *Hegel's Lectures on the History of Philosophy.* Trans. E. S. Haldane and Frances H. Simson. 3 vols. New York: Humanities Press.

Heim, Michael R. 1981. "Philosophy as Ultimate Rhetoric." *Southern Journal of Philosophy* 19: 181–195.

Herodotus. 1966. *Works.* Trans. A.D. Godley Harvard. London: William Heinemann Ltd.

Hill, Forbes. 1972. "The *Rhetoric* of Aristotle." In *A Synoptic History of Classical Rhetoric*, ed. James J. Murphy, 19–77. New York: Random House.

Hindess, Barry, and Paul Hirst. 1975. *Pre-Capitalist Modes of Production.* London: Routledge and Kegan Paul.

———. 1977. *Mode of Production and Social Formation.* London: Macmillan.

Hinks, D.A.G. 1940. "Tisias and Corzx and the Invention of Rhetoric." *Classical Quarterly* 34: 61–69.

Hirsch, E. D., Jr., Gayatri Spivak, Roger Shattuck, Jon Pareles, and John Kaliski. 1989. "Who Needs the Great Works: A Debate on the Canon, Core Curricula, and Culture." *Harper's*, September: 43–53.

Hochmuth [Nichols], Marie. 1952. "Kenneth Burke and the 'New Rhetoric.'" *Quarterly Journal of Speech* 38: 133–144.

Holland, Eugene W. 1987. "Introduction to the Non-Fascist Life: Deleuze and Guattari's 'Revolutionary' Semiotics." *L'Esprit Créateur* 27: 19–29.

Holland, L. Virginia. 1955. "Kenneth Burke's Dramatistic Approach in Speech Criticism." *Quarterly Journal of Speech* 41: 352–358.

Holland, R. F. 1953. "On Making Sense of a Philosophical Fragment." *Classical Quarterly* 6: 215–220.

Horner, Winifred Bryan. 1982. "Rhetoric in the Liberal Arts: Nineteenth-Century Scottish Universities." In *The Rhetorical Tradition and Modern Writing*, ed. Jerry Murphy, 85–94. New York: Modern Language Association.

Howell, Wilbur Samuel. 1956. *Logic and Rhetoric in England, 1500–1700*. Princeton: Princeton University Press.

———. 1971. *Eighteenth-Century British Logic and Rhetoric*. Princeton: Princeton University Press.

———. 1976. "Two-Party Line: A Reply to Kenneth Burke." *American Journal of Speech* 62: 69–77.

Hudson, Hoyt H. 1932. "The Field of Rhetoric." *Quarterly Journal of Speech* 9: 167–180.

Hudson-Williams, H. LL. 1951. "Political Speeches in Athens." *Classical Quarterly* 65: 68–73.

Hunt, Everett Lee. 1962. "Plato and Aristotle on Rhetoric and Rhetoricians." In *Studies in Rhetoric and Public Speaking in Honor of James Albert Winans*, ed. A. M. Drummond, 3–60. New York: Russell & Russell.

Hussey, Edward. 1972. *The Presocratics*. New York: Charles Scribner's Sons.

Iggers, Georg G. 1984. *New Directions in European Historiography*. Rev. ed. Middletown, Conn.: Wesleyan University Press.

Ijsseling, Samuel. 1976. *Rhetoric and Philosophy in Conflict*. The Hague: Martinus Nijhoff.

Inwood, B., and L. P. Gerson. 1988. *Hellenistic Philosophy: Introductory Readings*. Indianapolis: Indiana University Press.

Ioppolo, Anna Maria. 1986. *Opinione e scienza: Il dibattito tra Stoici e Accademici nel III e nel II secolo a. C.* Rome: Elenchos Colana di testi e studi sul pensiero antico 12.

Irigaray, Luce. 1985. *Speculum of the Other Woman*. Trans. Gillian C. Gill. Ithaca: Cornell University Press.

Irwin, T. 1979. *Plato: Gorgias*. Oxford: Clarendon Press.

Isocrates. 1928, 1929, 1945. *Isocrates*. 3 vols. Trans. George Norlin and LaRue Van Hook. London: William Heinemann Ltd.

Jackson, Gabriele Bernhard. 1968. *Vision and Judgement in Ben Jonson's Drama*. New Haven: Yale University Press.

Jaeger, Werner. 1970. *Paideia: The Ideals of Greek Culture*. 3 vols. Trans. Gilbert Highet. New York: Oxford University Press.

Jameson, Fredric. 1971. *Marxism and Form*. Princeton: Princeton University Press.

———. 1981. *The Political Unconscious*. Ithaca: Cornell University Press.

———. 1982. "The Symbolic Inference; or, Kenneth Burke and Ideological Analysis." *Critical Inquiry* 4: 507–524.

———. 1988. "Criticism and History." In *The Ideologies of Theory, Essays 1971–1986*. Vol. 1, 119–136. Minneapolis: University of Minnesota Press.

Jarratt, Susan C. 1985. "A Victorian Sophistic: The Rhetoric of Knowledge in Darwin, Newman, and Pater." Diss., University of Texas, at Austin.

———. 1987a. "The First Sophists and the Uses of History." *Rhetoric Review* 6: 67–78.

———. 1987b. "Toward a Sophistic Historiography." *PRE/TEXT* 8.1–2: 9–27.

————. 1990. "The First Sophists and Feminism: Discourses of the 'Other.'" *Hypatia* 5: 27–41.

————. 1991. *Rereading the Sophists: Classical Rhetoric Refigured.* Carbondale: Southern Illinois University Press.

Jarratt, Susan C., and Nedra Grogan. Forthcoming. "The Splitting Image: Postmodern Feminism and the Ethics of Ethos." In *Ethos: New Essays in Rhetorical and Critical Theory.* Dallas: Southern Methodist University Press.

Jebb, R. C. 1893. *The Attic Orators from Antiphon to Isaeus.* 2d. ed. 2 vols. London: Macmillan.

————. 1962. *The Attic Orators from Antiphon to Isaeus.* 2 vols. New York: Russell & Russell.

Jed, Stephanie H. 1989. *Chaste Thinking: The Rape of Lucretia and the Birth of Humanism.* Bloomington: Indiana University Press.

Johnson, Nan. 1991. *Nineteenth-Century Rhetoric in North America.* Carbondale: Southern Illinois University Press.

Johnson, R. 1957. "A Note on the Number of Isocrates' Pupils." *American Journal of Philology* 78: 297–300.

Johnston, Harold Whetstone, and Hugh MacMaster Kingery. 1910. *Selected Orations and Letters of Cicero.* Chicago: Scott, Foresman and Co.

Johnstone, Christopher Lyle. 1980. "An Aristotelian Trilogy: Ethics, Rhetoric, Politics, and the Search for Moral Truth." *Philosophy and Rhetoric* 13: 1–24.

Johnstone, Henry W., Jr. 1978. *Validity and Rhetoric in Philosophical Argument: An Outlook in Transition.* University Park, Pa.: Dialogue.

Jones, W.H.S., trans. 1923. *Hippocrates.* Vol. 1. Loeb Classical Library. Cambridge: Harvard University Press.

Kameen, Paul. 1980. "Rewording the Rhetoric of Composition." *PRE/TEXT* 1.1–2: 79–93.

————. 1985. "Composition: Inscribing the Field." *Boundary 2* 13: 213–231.

Kaufmann, Walter. 1967. "Translator's Introduction." In Friedrich Nietzsche. *The Birth of Tragedy and the Case of Wagner,* 3–13. New York: Vintage.

Kellner, Hans. 1979. "Disorderly Conduct: Braudel's Mediterranean Satire." *History and Theory* 18: 197–222.

————. 1980. "A Bedrock of Order: Hayden White's Linguistic Humanism." *History and Theory* 19: 1–29.

————. 1988. "The Deepest Respect for Reality: Rhetoric and History." *Groniek* 100: 107–120.

————. 1989. *Language and Historical Representation: Getting the Story Crooked.* Madison: University of Wisconsin Press.

Kelly-Gadol, Joan. 1984. "Did Women Have a Renaissance?" In *Women, History and Theory: The Essays of Joan Kelly,* 19–50. Chicago: University of Chicago Press.

Kennedy, George. 1963. *The Art of Persuasion in Greece.* Princeton: Princeton University Press.

————. 1972. *The Art of Rhetoric in the Roman World, 300 B.C.–A.D. 300.* Princeton: Princeton University Press.

————. 1975. "The Present State of the Study of Ancient Rhetoric." *Classical Philology* 70: 278–282.

————. 1980. *Classical Rhetoric and Its Christian and Secular Tradition from Ancient to Modern Times.* Chapel Hill: University of North Carolina Press.

_____. 1983. *Greek Rhetoric Under Christian Emperors.* Princeton: Princeton University Press.

_____. 1984. *New Testament Interpretation Through Rhetorical Criticism.* Chapel Hill: University of North Carolina Press.

_____. 1988. "Some Reflections on Neomodernism [a response to Vitanza]." *Rhetoric Review* 6: 230–233.

_____. 1991. *On Rhetoric: A Theory of Civic Discourse.* Oxford: Oxford University Press.

Kerferd, G. B. 1981a. "The Future Direction of Sophistic Studies." In *The Sophists and Their Legacy,* ed. G. B. Kerferd. Wiesbaden: Franz Steiner.

_____. 1981b. *The Sophistic Movement.* Cambridge: Cambridge University Press.

Kinneavy, James L. 1982. "Restoring the Humanities: The Return of Rhetoric from Exile." In *The Rhetorical Tradition and Modern Writing,* 19–28. New York: Modern Language Association.

_____. 1984. "Translating Theory into Practice in Teaching Composition: A Historical View and a Contemporary View." In *Essays on Classical Rhetoric and Modern Discourse,* ed. Robert J. Connors, Lisa S. Ede, and Andrea A. Lunsford, 69–81. Carbondale: Southern Illinois University Press.

_____. 1985. "Deconstructing the Rhetoric/Poetic Distinction: The Platonizing of Rhetoric and Literature." *Dieciocho* 8: 70–77.

_____. 1987a. *Greek Rhetorical Origins of Christian Faith.* New York: Oxford University Press.

_____. 1987b. "William Grimaldi—Reinterpreting Aristotle." *Philosophy and Rhetoric* 20: 183–200.

Knoblauch, C. H., and Lil Brannon. 1984. *Rhetorical Traditions and the Teaching of Writing.* Montclair, N.J.: Boynton/Cook.

Kofman, Sarah. 1987. "Nietzsche and the Obscurity of Heraclitus." *Diacritics* 17: 39–55.

Konstan, David. 1986. "Ideology and Narrative in Livy, Book I." *Classical Antiquity* 5: 197–215.

Kristeva, Julia. 1980. *Desire in Language: A Semiotic Approach to Literature and Art.* Trans. Thomas Gora et al. New York: Columbia University Press.

_____. 1986. "Woman's Time." in *The Kristeva Reader,* ed. Toril Moi, 188–213. New York: Columbia University Press.

Krug, Mark M. 1967. *History and the Social Sciences.* Waltman, Mass.: Blaisdell.

Kuhn, Thomas S. 1970. *The Structure of Scientific Revolutions.* 2d ed. Chicago: University of Chicago Press.

Kundera, Milan. 1986. *The Unbearable Lightness of Being.* New York: Harper and Row.

Kustas, George L. 1970. "The Function and Evolution of Byzantine Rhetoric." *Viator* 1: 55–73.

LaCapra, Dominick. 1983. *Rethinking Intellectual History.* Ithaca: Cornell University Press.

_____. 1985a. *History and Criticism.* Ithaca: Cornell University Press.

_____. 1985b. "On Grubbing in My Personal Archives: An Historiographical Expose of Sorts (or How I learned to Stop Worrying and Love Transference)." *Boundary 2* 13.2–3: 43–67.

_____. 1985c. "Rhetoric and History." In *History and Criticism,* 15–44. Ithaca: Cornell University Press.

_____. 1987. "History and Psychoanalysis." *Critical Inquiry* 13: 222–251.

LaCapra, Dominick, and Steven L. Kaplan, eds. 1982. *Modern European Intellectual History*. Ithaca: Cornell University Press.

Laclau, Ernesto, and Chantal Mouffe. 1985. *Hegemony and Socialist Strategy: Towards a Radical Democratic Politics*. New York: Verso.

Lanham, Richard. 1976. *The Motives of Eloquence*. New Haven: Yale University Press.

_____. 1988. "The 'Q' Question." *SAQ* 87: 653–700.

Larson, Magali Sarfatti. 1977. *The Rise of Professionalism: A Sociological Analysis*. Berkeley: University of California Press.

Last, Hugh. 1943. Review of H. J. Haskell, *This Was Cicero: Modern Politics in a Roman Toga*. *Journal of Roman Studies* 33: 93–97.

Lecercle, Jean-Jacques. 1985. *Philosophy Through the Looking-Glass*. La Salle, Ill.: Open Court.

Leff, Michael C. 1973. "Redemptive Identification: Cicero's Catilinarian Orations." In *Explorations in Rhetorical Criticism*, ed. G. P. Mohrmann, Charles J. Stewart, and Donovan J. Ochs, 158–177. University Park: Pennsylvania State University Press.

_____. 1983. "The Topics of Argumentative Invention in Latin Rhetorical Theory from Cicero to Boethius." *Rhetorica* 1: 23–44.

_____. 1988. "Serious Comedy: The Strange Case History of Dr. Vitanza." *Rhetoric Review* 6: 237–245.

Leff, Michael, and Margaret Organ Procario. 1985. "Rhetorical Theory in Speech Communication." In *Speech Communication in the Twentieth Century*, ed. Thomas W. Benson, 3–27. Carbondale: Southern Illinois University Press.

Leggatt, Alexander. 1981. *Ben Jonson: His Vision and His Art*. New York: Methuen.

Lentricchia, Frank. 1980. *After the New Criticism*. Chicago: University of Chicago Press.

_____. 1983. *Criticism and Social Change*. Chicago: University of Chicago Press.

Lentz, T. M. 1989. *Orality and Literacy in Hellenic Greece*. Carbondale: Southern Illinois University Press.

Lerner, Harriet Goldhor. 1990. "Problems for Profit?" *The Women's Review of Books* 8: 16.

Lidov, J. B. 1983. "The Meaning of Idea in Isocrates." *La Parola del passato* 38: 273–287.

Lobkowicz, Nicholas. 1967. *Theory and Practice: History of a Concept from Aristotle to Marx*. Notre Dame: University of Notre Dame Press.

Long, A. A., and D. N. Sedley. 1987. *The Hellenistic Philosophers*. Vol. 1. Cambridge: Cambridge University Press.

Loraux, Nicole. 1986. *The Invention of Athens: The Funeral Oration in the Classical City*. Trans. Alan Sheridan. Cambridge: Harvard University Press.

Lord, C. 1981. "The Intention of Aristotle's *Rhetoric*." *Hermes* 109: 326–339.

Lorwin, Val R., and Jacob M. Price, eds. 1972. *The Dimensions of the Past: Materials, Problems, and Opportunities for Quantitative Work in History*. New Haven: Yale University Press.

Lukasiewicz, J. 1951. *Aristotle's Syllogistic: From the Standpoint of Modern Formal Logic*. Oxford: Clarendon.

Lunsford, Andrea. 1981. "Essay Writing in Teachers' Responses in Nineteenth-Century Scottish Universities." *College Composition and Communication* 32: 434–443.

Lunsford, Andrea, and Lisa S. Ede. 1984. "On Distinctions Between Classical and Modern Rhetoric." In *Essays on Classical Rhetoric and Modern Discourse*, ed. Robert J. Connors, Lisa S. Ede, and Andrea Lunsford. Carbondale: Southern Illinois University Press.

Lyne, John. 1985. "Rhetorics of Inquiry." *Quarterly Journal of Speech* 71: 65–73.

Lyotard, Jean-François. 1976. "Sur la force des faibles." *L'Arc* 64: 4–12.

———. 1984. *The Postmodern Condition: A Report on Knowledge*. Trans. Geoff Bennington and Brian Massumi. Minneapolis: University of Minnesota Press.

———. 1988. *The Differend*. Trans. George Van Den Abbeele. Minneapolis: University of Minnesota Press.

Mandelbaum, Maurice. 1974. "The Problem of 'Covering Laws.'" In *The Philosophy of History*, ed. Patrick Gardiner, 51–65. London: Oxford University Press.

Marcuse, Herbert. 1962. *Eros and Civilization*. New York: Vintage.

Marrou, Henri I. [1956] 1964. *A History of Education in Antiquity*. Trans. George Lamb. New York: Sheed and Ward; reprint, Mentor.

Marx, Karl. 1984. *The 18th Brumaire of Louis Bonaparte*. New York: International Publishers.

Masaracchia, A. 1983. "Isocrates e le scienza." In *Saggi di storia del Pensiero scientifico dedicati a Valerio Tonini*, ed. V. Cappelletti et al., 23–46. Rome: Jouvence.

Mason, Jeff. 1989. *Philosophical Rhetoric*. London: Routledge.

McGee, Michael C. 1980. "'The Ideograph': A Link Between Rhetoric and Ideology." *Quarterly Journal of Speech* 66: 1–16.

———. 1982. "A Materialist's Conception of Rhetoric." In *Explorations in Rhetoric: Studies in Honor of Douglas Ehninger*, ed. Ray McKerrow, 23–48. Glenview, Ill.: Scott, Foresman.

———. 1983. "American Rhetorical Studies as an Intellectual Practice." Lecture delivered at Pennsylvania State University, November 8, 1983.

———. 1990. "Text, Context, and the Fragmentation of Contemporary Culture." *Western Journal of Speech Communication* 54: 274–289.

McGee, Michael C., and Martha A. Martin. 1983. "Public Knowledge and Ideological Argumentation." *Communication Monographs* 50: 47–56.

McGee, Michael C., and John S. Nelson. 1985. "Narrative Reason in Public Argument." *Journal of Communication* 35: 139–155.

McGuire, Michael. 1980. "The Ethics of Rhetoric: The Morality of Knowledge." *Southern Speech Communication Journal* 45: 133–148.

McKeon, Richard. 1942. "Rhetoric in the Middle Ages." *Speculum* 17.1: 1–32.

———. 1971. "Uses of Rhetoric in a Technological Age: Architectonic Productive Arts." In *The Prospect of Rhetoric*, ed. Lloyd F. Bitzer and Edwin Black, 44–63. Englewood Cliffs: Prentice-Hall.

———. 1987. *Rhetoric: Essays in Invention and Discovery*, ed. Mark Backman. Woodridge, Conn.: Ox Bow Press.

McKerrow, Raymie E. 1989. "Critical Rhetoric: Theory and Practice." *Communication Monographs* 56: 91–111.

Menage, Gilles. 1984. *The History of Women Philosophers*. Trans. Beatrice H. Zedler. [*Historia Mulierum Philosopharum*. 1690] Lanham, Md.: University Press of America.

Merquior, J. G. 1985. *Foucault*. Berkeley: University of California Press.

Mill, John Stuart. 1875. *System of Logic*. London: Longmans.

Miller, Bernard A. 1987. "Heidegger and the Gorgian *Kairos.*" In *Visions of Rhetoric: History, Theory and Criticism*, ed. Charles Kneupper, 169–184. Arlington: Rhetoric Society of America.

Mitchell, Juliet. 1984. *Women: The Longest Revolution.* New York: Pantheon.

Mitchell, Thomas N. 1979. *Cicero: The Ascending Years.* New Haven: Yale University Press.

Momigliano, Arnaldo. 1981. "The Rhetoric of History and the History of Rhetoric: On Hayden White's Tropes." *Comparative Criticism: A Yearbook*, ed. E. S. Shaffer. 3: 259–268.

———. 1982. *Essays in Ancient and Modern Historiography.* Middletown, Conn.: Wesleyan University Press.

Moss, Roger. 1982. "The Case for Sophistry." In *Rhetoric Revealed*, ed. Brian Vickers, 207–224. Binghamton, N.Y.: Center for Medieval and Early Renaissance Studies.

Mumby, Dennis K. 1989. "Ideology and the Social Construction of Meaning: A Communication Perspective." *Communication Quarterly* 37: 291–304.

Murphey, Murray G. 1980. "Explanation, Causes, and Covering Laws." *History and Theory* 25: 43–57.

Murphy, James J. 1974. *Rhetoric in the Middle Ages.* Berkeley: University of California Press.

———, ed. 1978. *Medieval Eloquence.* Berkeley: University of California Press.

———. 1979. "The A-Historian's Guide: Or, Ten Negative Commandments for the Historian of Rhetoric." In *H Texnh: Proceedings of the Speech Communication Association 1979 Doctoral Honors Seminar*, ed. Richard Leo Enos and William E. Wiethoff, 1–8, n. p.

———. 1982a. "Rhetorical History as a Guide to the Salvation of American Reading and Writing: A Plan for Curricular Courage." In *The Rhetorical Tradition and Modern Writing*, ed. James J. Murphy, 3–12. New York: Modern Language Association.

———, ed. 1982b. *The Rhetorical Tradition and Modern Writing.* New York: Modern Language Association.

———. 1983a. "The Historiography of Rhetoric: Challenges and Opportunities." *Rhetorica* 1: 1–8.

———, ed. 1983b. *Renaissance Eloquence.* Berkeley: University of California Press.

Natanson, Maurice. 1955. "The Limits of Rhetoric." *Quarterly Journal of Speech* 41: 133–139.

Neel, Jasper. 1988. *Plato, Derrida, and Writing.* Carbondale: Southern Illinois University Press.

Nelson, John S. 1983. "Political Theory as Political Rhetoric." In *What Should Political Theory Be Now?* ed. J. S. Nelson, 176–193. Albany: State University of New York Press.

Nelson, John S., Allan Megill, and Donald N. McCloskey, eds. 1987. *The Rhetoric of the Human Sciences.* Madison: University of Wisconsin Press.

Nietzsche, Friedrich. 1966. *Beyond Good and Evil.* Trans. Walter Kaufmann. New York: Vintage.

———. 1968a. *Thus Spoke Zarathustra.* In *The Portable Nietzsche*, ed. and trans. Walter Kaufmann, 103–439. New York: Vintage.

———. 1968b. *The Will to Power.* Trans. Walter Kaufmann and R. J. Hollingdale. New York: Vintage.

———. 1969. *On the Genealogy of Morals and Ecce Homo.* Trans. Walter Kaufmann. New York: Vintage.

———. 1974. *The Gay Science.* Trans. Walter Kaufmann. New York: Vintage.

_____. 1988. "On the Uses and Disadvantages of History for Life." In *Untimely Meditations*, trans. R. J. Hollingdale, 57–124. Cambridge: Cambridge University Press.

_____. 1989. "Truth and Lying in an Extra-Moral Sense." In *Friedrich Nietzsche on Rhetoric and Language*, ed. and trans. Sander L. Gilman, Carole Blair, and David J. Parent, 246–257. New York: Oxford University Press.

_____. 1990. "We Classicists." In *Unmodern Observations*. Trans. William Arrowsmith, 321–387. New Haven: Yale University Press.

Nolan, Mary. 1988. "*The Historikerstreit* and Social History." *New German Critique* 44: 51–80.

North, Stephen M. 1987. *The Making of Knowledge in Composition: Portrait of an Emerging Field*. Montclair, N.J.: Boynton/Cook.

Novick, Peter. 1988. *The Noble Dream: The "Objectivity Question" and the American Historical Profession*. Cambridge: Cambridge University Press.

Nussbaum, Martha C. 1986. *The Fragility of Goodness*. New York: Cambridge University Press.

Olian, J. Robert. 1968. "The Intended Uses of Aristotle's Rhetoric." *Speech Monographs* 54: 137–148.

Olsen, Tillie. 1983. *Silences*. New York: Laurel.

Ong, Walter J. 1958. *Ramus, Method, and the Decay of Dialogue*. Cambridge: Harvard University Press.

_____. 1982. *Orality and Literacy*. London: Methuen.

Oravec, Christine. 1986. "The Democratic Critics: An Alternative American Rhetorical Tradition in the Nineteenth Century." *Rhetorica* 4: 395–421.

Orr, Linda. 1986. "The Revenge of Literature: A History of History." *New Literary History* 18: 1–22.

Osborn, Michael. 1967. "Archetypal Metaphor in Rhetoric: The Light-Dark Family." *Quarterly Journal of Speech* 53: 115–126.

Owen, G.E.L. 1986. *Logic, Science and Dialectic: Collected Papers in Greek Philosophy*, ed. Martha Nussbaum. London: Gerald Duckworth & Co.

Palmer, Richard E. 1969. *Heremeneutics: Interpretation Theory in Schleiermacher, Dilthey, Heidegger, and Gadamer*. Evanston: Northwestern University Press.

Partner, Nancy F. 1977. *Serious Entertainments: The Writing of History in Twelfth-Century England*. Chicago: University of Chicago Press.

_____. 1985. "The New Cornifucius: Medieval History and the Artifice of Words." In *Classical Rhetoric and Medieval Historiography*, 5–60. Kalamazoo: Western Michigan University Press.

_____. 1986. "Making Up Lost Time: Writing on the Writing of History." *Speculum* 61: 90–117.

Paskins, Barrie. 1978. "Torture and Philosophy." *Aristotelian Society* 52: 169–194.

Pepper, Stephen Coburn. 1966a. *Concept and Quality: A World Hypothesis*. La Salle, Ill.: Open Court.

_____. 1966b. *World Hypotheses*. Berkeley: University of California Press.

Perelman, Chaim. 1973. "Rhetoric." *Encyclopedia Britannica*.

_____. 1979. *The New Rhetoric and the Humanities: Essays on Rhetoric and Its Applications*. Dordrecht, Holland: D. Reidel.

Perelman, Chaim, and L. Olbrechts-Tyteca. 1958. *The New Rhetoric: A Treatise on Argumentation*. Trans. John Wilkinson and Purcell Weaver. Notre Dame: Notre Dame University Press.

Perkins, Terry M. 1984. "Isocrates and Plato: Relativism vs. Idealism." *Southern Speech Communication Journal* 50: 49–66.

Peters, Edward. 1985. *Torture*. Oxford: Basil Blackwell.

Picard, Charles. 1951. "Représentations Antiques de l'Apologue dit de Prodicos." In *Comptes Rendues de l'Academie des Inscriptions et Belles Lettres*, 310–322. Paris: Librairie C. Klincksieck.

――――. 1953. "Nouvelles Remarques sur l'Apologue dit de Prodicos: Heracles entre le Vice et la Virtue." *Revue Archéologique* 42: 10–41.

Plato. 1921. *Sophist*. Trans. Harold North Fowler. Cambridge: Harvard University Press.

――――. 1926. *Lesser Hippias*. Trans. H. N. Fowler. London: William Heinemann.

――――. 1977. *Protagoras*. Trans. W.R.M. Lamb. London: William Heinemann.

Plutarch. 1960. "Life of Isocrates." In *Moralia*. Vol. 10. Trans. H. N. Fowler. Cambridge: Harvard University Press.

Pollitt, J. J. 1974. *The Ancient View of Greek Art*. New Haven: Yale University Press.

Popper, Karl Raimund. 1966. *The Open Society and Its Enemies*. Princeton: Princeton University Press.

Poulakos, John. 1983a. "Aristotle's Indebtedness to the Sophists." In *Argument in Transition: Proceedings of the Third Summer Conference on Argumentation*, ed. D. Zarefsky, M. O. Sillars, and J. Rhodes, 27–42. Annandale, Va.: Speech Communication Association.

――――. 1983b. "Gorgias' *Encomium on Helen* and the Defense of Rhetoric." *Rhetorica* 1: 1–19.

――――. 1983c. "Toward a Sophistic Definition of Rhetoric." *Philosophy and Rhetoric* 16: 35–48.

――――. 1984. "Rhetoric, the Sophists, and the Possible." *Communication Monographs* 51: 215–226.

――――. 1986. "Gorgias' and Isocrates' Use of the Encomium." *Southern Speech Communication Journal* 51: 215–226.

――――. 1989. "Early Changes in Rhetorical Practice and Understanding: From the Sophists to Isocrates." *Texte* 8: 307–324.

――――. 1990. "Interpreting Sophistical Rhetoric: A Response to Schiappa." *Philosophy and Rhetoric* 23: 218–228.

Poulakos, John, and Steve Whitson. 1990. "The Search for an Alliance Between the Greek Sophists and Postmodern Feminists: A Response to Jarratt and Grogan." Paper presented at the 11th Annual Temple University Conference on Discourse Analysis.

Poulakos, Takis. 1987. "Isocrates' Use of Narrative in the *Evagoras*: Epideictic Rhetoric and Moral Action." *Quarterly Journal of Speech* 73: 317–328.

――――. 1988. "Toward a Cultural Interpretation of Classical Epideictic Oratory." *PRE/TEXT* 9: 147–166.

――――. 1989. "Epideictic Rhetoric as Social Hegemony: Isocrates' *Helen*." In *Rhetoric and Ideology*, ed. Charles Kneupper, 156–166. Arlington: Rhetoric Society of America.

――――. 1990. "Historiographies of the Tradition of Rhetoric: A Brief History of Classical Funeral Orations." *Western Journal of Speech Communication* 54: 172–188.

Radermacher, L. 1951. *Artium Scriptores. Reste der voraristotelischen Rhetorik*. Vienna: Rohrer.

Radhakrishnan, R. 1989. "Feminist Historiography and Post-Structuralist Thought: Intersections and Departures." In *The Difference Within: Feminism and Critical Theory*, ed. Elizabeth Meese and Alice Parker, 189–206. Amsterdam: John Benjamins Pub.

Rajchman, John. 1991. *Truth and Eros*. New York: Routledge.

Raymond, James. 1982. "Rhetoric: The Methodology of the Humanities." *College English* 44: 778–783.

Rich, Adrienne. 1979. "Privilege, Power, and Tokenism." *Ms*, September: 42–44.

Ricoeur, Paul. 1977. *The Rule of Metaphor*. Trans. Robert Czerny with Kathleen McLaughlin and John Costello, S. J. Toronto: University of Toronto Press.

———. 1978. *Freud and Philosophy*. Trans. Denis Savage. New Haven: Yale University Press.

———. 1983. *Time and Narrative*. Vol. 1. Trans. Kathleen McLaughlin and David Pellauer. Chicago: University of Chicago Press.

Ried, Paul E. 1987. "The Bylston Professor in the Twentieth Century." *Quarterly Journal of Speech* 73: 474–481.

Rorty, Richard. 1979. *Philosophy and the Mirror of Nature*. Princeton: Princeton University Press.

———. 1984. "The Historiography of Philosophy: Four Genres." In *Philosophy in History: Essays on the Historiography of Philosophy*, ed. Richard Rorty et al., 49–75. Cambridge: Cambridge University Press.

———. 1987. "Pragmatism and Philosophy." In *After Philosophy: End or Transformation?* ed. Kenneth Baynes, James Bohman, and Thomas McCarthy. Cambridge: MIT Press.

———. 1989. *Contingency, Irony, and Solidarity*. Cambridge: Cambridge University Press.

Rosen, Stanley. 1983. *Plato's Sophist: The Drama of Original and Image*. New Haven: Yale University Press.

Rosenfield, Lawrence W. 1971. "An Autopsy of the Rhetorical Tradition." In *The Prospect of Rhetoric*, ed. Lloyd Bitzer and Edwin Black. Englewood Cliffs: Prentice-Hall.

Rosenmeyer, Thomas G. 1955. "Gorgias, Aeschylus, and *Apate*." *American Journal of Philology* 76: 225–260.

Ross, W. D. 1959. *Aristotle: A Complete Exposition of His Works and Thought*. Cleveland: World Publishing Company.

Rummel, R. 1979. "Isocrates' Ideal of Rhetoric: Criteria of Evaluation." *Classical Journal* 75: 25–35.

Rushing, Janice Hocker. 1989. "Evolution of 'The New Frontier' in Alien and Aliens: Patriarchal Co-Optation of the Feminine Archetype." *Quarterly Journal of Speech* 75: 1–24.

Russ, Joanna. 1983. *How to Suppress Women's Writing*. Austin: University of Texas Press.

Russell, D. A. 1983. *Greek Declamation*. Cambridge: Cambridge University Press.

Ryan, Michael. 1982. *Marxism and Deconstruction*. Baltimore: Johns Hopkins University Press.

Said, Edward. 1983. *The World, the Text, and the Critic*. Cambridge: Harvard University Press.

Scaglione, A. 1972. *The Classical Theory of Composition. From Its Origins to the Present. A Historical Survey*. Chapel Hill: University of North Carolina Press.

Scanlon, Thomas F. 1986. "*Historia Quasi Fabula:* The Catiline Theme in Sallust and Jonson." *Themes in Drama* 8: 17–29.

Schiappa, Edward. 1988. "The Historiography of Rhetoric: Conflicts and Their Implications." *The Writing Instructor* 8: 15–22.

———. 1990a. "Did Plato Coin *Rhêtorikê?*" *American Journal of Philology* 111: 457–470.

———. 1990b. "History and Neo-Sophistic Criticism: A Reply to Poulakos." *Philosophy and Rhetoric* 23: 307–315.

———. 1990c. "Neo-Sophistic Rhetorical Criticism or the Historical Reconstruction of Sophistic Doctrines?" *Philosophy and Rhetoric* 23: 192–217.

———. 1991. "Sophistic Rhetoric: Oasis or Mirage?" *Rhetoric Review* 10: 5–19.

Schilb, John. 1986. "The History of Rhetoric and the Rhetoric of History." *PRE/TEXT* 7: 11–34.

———. 1987. "Differences, Displacements, and Disruptions: Toward Revisionary Histories of Rhetoric." *PRE/TEXT* 8: 29–45.

Schlegel, Fredrich. 1968. *Dialogue on Poetry and Literary Aphorisms.* Trans. Ernst Behler and Roman Struc. University Park: Pennsylvania State University Press.

Schrag, Calvin. 1985. "Rhetoric Resituated at the End of Philosophy." *Quarterly Journal of Speech* 71: 164–174.

Scott, Robert. 1975. "A Synoptic View of Systems of Western Rhetoric." *Quarterly Journal of Speech* 61: 439–447.

———. 1988. "Non-Discipline as a Remedy for Rhetoric? A Reply to Victor Vitanza." *Rhetoric Review* 6: 233–237.

Scott, Robert L., and Donald K. Smith. 1969. "The Rhetoric of Confrontation." *Quarterly Journal of Speech* 55: 1–8.

Segal, Charles P. 1962. "Gorgias and the Psychology of the Logos." *Harvard Studies in Classical Philology* 66: 99–155.

Serres, Michel. 1982. *Hermes: Literature, Science, Philosophy.* Baltimore: Johns Hopkins University Press.

Shackleton Bailey, D. R. 1965. *Cicero's Letters to Atticus. Vol. 1 (Books 1–2).* Cambridge: Cambridge University Press.

Shorey, P. 1909. "Physis, Melete, Episteme." *Transactions and Proceedings of the American Philological Association* 40: 185–201.

Silverman, Kaua. 1983. *The Subject of Semiotics.* New York: Oxford University Press.

Simons, Herbert W. 1978. "Genre-alizing About Rhetoric: A Scientific Approach." In *Form and Genre: Shaping Rhetorical Action,* ed. Karlyn Kohrs Campbell and Kathleen Hall Jamieson, 33–50. Falls Church: Speech Communication Association.

———. 1985. "Chronicle and Critique of a Conference." *Quarterly Journal of Speech* 71: 52–64.

———, ed. 1990. *The Rhetorical Turn: Invention and Persuasion in the Conduct of Inquiry.* Chicago: University of Chicago Press.

Simons, Herbert, and Aram A. Aghazarian. 1986. "Genres, Rules, and Political Rhetoric: Toward a Sociology of Rhetorical Choice." In *Form, Genre, and the Study of Political Discourse,* ed. Herbert Simons and Aram Aghazarian, 45–58. Columbia: University of South Carolina Press.

Skinner, Quentin, ed. 1985. *The Return of Grand Theory in the Human Sciences.* Cambridge: Cambridge University Press.

Smilowitz, Michael, and Malcolm Sillars. 1982. "The Research Orientation of the Early Twentieth Century Speech Profession." Paper delivered at the Speech Communication Association Convention, November, Louisville.

Smith, Barbara Herrnstein. 1988. *Contingencies of Value*. Cambridge: Harvard University Press.

Smith, Bromley. 1920. "Prodicus of Ceos: The Sire of Synonymy." *Quarterly Journal of Speech Education* 6: 51–68.

————. 1921. "Corax and Probability." *Quarterly Journal of Speech* 7: 13–42.

Smith, Paul. 1988. *Discerning the Subject*. Minneapolis: University of Minnesota Press.

Snell, B. 1953. *The Discovery of the Mind*. Trans. T. G. Rosenmeyer, from the second edition. Cambridge: Harvard University Press.

Solmsen, F. 1929. *Die Entwicklung der Aristotelischen Logik und Rhetorik*. Berlin: Weidmann.

Soper, Kate. 1986. *Humanism and Anti-Humanism*. La Salle, Ill.: Open Court.

Spender, Dale. 1989. "Women and Literary History." In *The Feminist Reader: Essays in Gender and the Politics of Literary Criticism*, ed. Catherine Belsey and Jane Moore, 21–33. New York: Basil Blackwell.

Spengler, Oswald. 1934. *The Decline of the West*. Trans. C. F. Atkinson. New York: Knopf.

Spitzack, Carole, and Kathryn Carter. 1987. "Women in Communication Studies: A Typology for Revision." *Quarterly Journal of Speech* 73: 401–423.

Spivak, Gayatri Chakravorty. 1976. "Translator's Introduction." In Jacques Derrida, *Of Grammatology*. Baltimore: Johns Hopkins University Press.

————. 1987. "Subaltern Studies: Deconstruction Historiography." In *In Other Worlds: Essays in Cultural Politics*, 197–221. New York: Methuen.

————. 1988. "Can the Subaltern Speak?" In *Marxism and the Interpretation of Culture*, ed. Cary Nelson and Lawrence Grossberg, 271–313. Urbana: University of Illinois Press.

————. 1989. "The New Historicism: Political Commitment and the Postmodern Critic." In *The New Historicism*, ed. H. Aram Veeser, 277–292. New York: Routledge.

————. 1990. "Practical Politics of the Open End." In *The Post-Colonial Critic: Interviews, Strategies, Dialogues*, ed. Sarah Harasym, 95–112. New York: Routledge.

————. Forthcoming. "On Behalf of Cultural Studies." *Social Text*.

Sprague, Rosamond Kent, ed. 1972. *The Older Sophists*. Columbia: University of South Carolina Press.

Ste. Croix, G.E.M. de. 1981. *The Class Struggle in the Ancient Greek World: From the Archaic Age to the Arab Conquests*. Ithaca: Cornell University Press.

Stewart, Donald. 1978. "The Barnyard Goose, History, and Fred Newton Scott." *English Journal* 67: 4–17.

————. 1979. "Rediscovering Fred Newton Scott." *College English* 40: 539–547.

————. 1983. "The Nineteenth Century." In *The Present State of Scholarship in Historical and Contemporary Rhetoric*, ed. Winifred Bryan Horner, 151–185. Columbia: University of Missouri Press.

————. 1984. "The Continuous Relevance of Plato's *Phaedrus*." In *Essays on Classical Rhetoric and Modern Discourse*, ed. Robert J. Connors, Lisa S. Ede, and Andrea A. Lunsford. Carbondale: Southern Illinois University Press.

Stockton, D. L. 1971. *Cicero: A Political Biography*. London: Oxford University Press.

Stoianovich, Traian. 1976. *French Historical Method: The Annales Paradigm.* Ithaca: Cornell University Press.

Streuver, Nancy S. 1970. *The Language of History in the Renaissance.* Princeton: Princeton University Press.

_____. 1974. "The Study of Language and the Study of History." *Journal of Interdisciplinary History* 4: 401–415.

Stuart, D. R. 1928. *Epics of Greek and Roman Biography.* Berkeley: University of California Press.

Sutton, Jane. 1986. "The Death of Rhetoric and Its Rebirth in Philosophy." *Rhetorica* 4: 203–226.

_____. 1987. "Rhetorikens dod—och dess panyttfodelse inom filosofin." Trans. Stina Hansson. *Tidskrift för litteraturvetenskap* 3: 8–19.

_____. 1991. "Rereading Sophistical Arguments: A Political Intervention." *Argumentation* 5: 141–157.

Swearingen, C. Jan. 1982. "The Rhetor as Eiron: Plato's Defense of Dialogue." *PRE/TEXT* 3: 289–336.

_____. 1991. *Rhetoric and Irony: Western Literacy and Western Lies.* New York: Oxford University Press.

Therborn, Goran. 1980. *The Ideology of Power and the Power of Ideology.* London: New Left Books.

Thompson, E. P. 1962. *The Making of the English Working Class.* London: V. Gollancz.

Thucydides. 1960. *The Peloponnesian War.* Trans. Benjamin Jowett. New York: Bantam Books.

Todorov, T. 1982. *Theories of the Symbol.* Trans. Catherine Porter. Ithaca: Cornell University Press.

Toulmin, Stephen. 1958. *The Uses of Argument.* Cambridge: Cambridge University Press.

Toulmin, Stephen, Richard Rieke, and Alan Janik. 1979. *An Introduction to Reasoning.* New York: Macmillan.

Tyan, Michael. 1982. *Marxism and Deconstruction.* Baltimore: Johns Hopkins University Press.

Tyrrell, William Blake. 1978. *A Legal and Historical Commentary to Cicero's Oratio pro C. Rabirio perduellionis reo.* Amsterdam: Adolf M. Hakker.

Untersteiner, Mario. 1954. *The Sophists.* Trans. Kathleen Freeman. New York: Philosophical Library.

Valesio, Paolo. 1980. *Novantiqua: Rhetorics as a Contemporary Theory.* Bloomington: Indiana University Press.

Vallozza, M. 1985. "*Kairos* nella teoria retorica de Alcidamante e di Isocrate, ovvero nel' oratoria orale e scritta." *Quaderni Urbinati di Cultura Classica* 21: 119–123.

Vasaly, Ann. 1985. "The Masks of Rhetoric: Cicero's *Pro Roscio Amerino.*" *Rhetorica* 3: 1–20.

Vernant, Jean-Pierre. 1983. *Myth and Thought Among the Greeks.* London: Routledge & Kegan Paul.

Vickers, Brian. 1982. "Territorial Disputes: Philosophy *versus* Rhetoric." In *Rhetoric Revealed,* ed. Brian Vickers, 247–266. Binghamton, N.Y.: Center for Medieval and Early Renaissance Studies.

_____. 1988. *In Defense of Rhetoric.* Oxford: Clarendon.

Vico, Giambattista. 1968. *The New Science*. Trans. Thomas Goddard Bergin and Max Harold Fisch. Ithaca: Cornell University Press.

Vitanza, Victor. 1987. "Critical Sub/Versions of the History of Philosophical Rhetoric." *Rhetoric Review* 6: 41–66.

———. 1988. "Cackling with Tears in My Eyes; or, Some Responses to 'The Gang of Three': Scott-Leff-Kennedy." *Rhetoric Review* 7: 214–218.

———. 1990. "An Open Letter to My 'Colligs': On 'Counter'-Ethics, Para/Rhetorics, and the Histerical Turn." *PRE/TEXT* 11: 237–287.

———. 1991a. "Some More Notes, Towards a Third Sophistic." *Argumentation* 5: 117–139.

———. 1991b. "Three Countertheses: A Critical In(ter)vention into Composition Theories and Pedagogies." In *Contending With Words*, ed. Patricia Harkin and John Schilb, 139–172. New York: Modern Language Association.

———. 1992. "Two Propositions: On the Hermeneutics of Suspicion and on Writing the History of Rhetoric." In *Discourse Studies in Honor of James Kinneavy*, ed. Rosalind Gabin. Potomac, Md.: Studia Humanitatis.

———. Forthcoming. "Concerning a Post-Classical Ethos, as Para/Rhetorical Ethics, the 'Selphs,' and The Excluded Third." In *Ethos: New Essays in Rhetorical and Critical Theory*. Dallas: Southern Methodist University Press.

Voegelin, Eric. 1966. *Plato*. In *Order and History*, 5 vols. Baton Rouge: Louisiana State University Press.

Waithe, Mary Ellen, ed. 1987. *History of Ancient Women Philosophers: 600 B.C. to 500 A.D.* Vol. 1: *History of Women Philosophers*. Dordrecht, Netherlands: Martinus Nijhoff.

Wander, Philip K. 1983. "The Ideological Turn in Modern Criticism." *Central States Speech Journal* 34: 1–18.

Wander, Philip K., and Steven Jenkins. 1972. "Rhetoric, Society and the Critical Response." *Quarterly Journal of Speech* 58: 441–450.

Weaver, Richard M. 1953. *The Ethics of Rhetoric*. Chicago: Henry Regnery.

Weber, Samuel. 1987. *Institution and Interpretation. Theory and History of Literature*. Vol. 31. Minneapolis: University of Minnesota Press.

Welch, Kathleen. 1990. *The Contemporary Reception of Classical Rhetoric: Appropriations of Ancient Discourse*. Hillsdale: Lawrence Erlbaum.

White, Eric C. 1987. *Kaironomia: On the Will-to-Invent*. Ithaca: Cornell University Press.

White, Hayden. 1973. *Metahistory: The Historical Imagination in Nineteenth-Century Europe*. Baltimore: Johns Hopkins University Press.

———. 1978. *Tropics of Discourse*. Baltimore: Johns Hopkins University Press.

———. 1981. "The Value of Narrativity in the Representation of Reality." In *On Narrative*, ed. W.J.T. Mitchell, 1–24. Chicago: Univeristy of Chicago Press.

———. 1982. "Getting Out of History." *Diacritics* 12: 3–13.

———. 1984. "The Question of Narrative in Contemporary Historical Theory." *History and Theory* 23: 2–33.

———. 1987. *The Content of the Form: Narrative Discourse and Historical Representation*. Baltimore: Johns Hopkins University Press.

Whitson, Steve. 1991. "On the Misadventures of the Sophists: Hegel's Tropological Appropriation of Rhetoric." *Argumentation* 5: 187–200.

Wichelns, Herbert A. 1958. "The Literary Criticism of Oratory." In *The Rhetorical Idiom: Essays in Rhetoric, Oratory, Language and Drama*, ed. Donald C. Bryant, 5–42. Ithaca: Cornell University Press.

Wilcox, Stanley. 1942. "The Scope of Early Rhetorical Instruction." *Harvard Studies in Classical Philology* 53: 121–155.

_____. 1943. "Corax and the Prolegomena." *American Journal of Philology* 64: 1–23.

Williams, Raymond. 1976. *Keywords: A Vocabulary of Culture and Society*. New York: Oxford University Press.

_____. 1977. *Marxism and Literature*. New York: Oxford University Press.

Winterowd, W. Ross. 1983. "Post-Structuralism and Composition." *PRE/TEXT* 4: 79–92.

Wittgenstein, Ludwig. 1968. *Philosophical Investigations*. 3d ed. Trans. G.E.M. Anscombe. New York: Macmillan.

Wood, Neal. 1988. *Cicero's Social and Political Thought*. Berkeley: University of California Press.

Woods, William F. 1985. "Nineteenth-Century Psychology and the Teaching of Writing." *College Composition and Communication* 35: 20–41.

Wooten, Cecil W. 1983. *Cicero's Philippics and their Demosthenic Model: The Rhetoric of Crisis*. Chapel Hill: University of North Carolina Press.

Worsham, Lynn. 1987. "The Question Concerning Invention: Hermeneutics and the Genesis of Writing. *PRE/TEXT* 8: 197–245.

Wozniak, John Michael. 1978. *English Composition in Eastern Colleges, 1850–1940*. Washington, D.C.: University Press of America.

Xenophon. 1923. *Memorabilia*. Trans. E. C. Marchant. New York: G. P. Putnam's Sons.

Zarefsky, David, Malcolm Sillars, and Jack Rhodes, eds. 1983. *Argument in Transition: Proceedings of the Third Summer Conference on Argumentation*. Annandale: Speech Communication Association.

Zeller, Eduard. 1955. *Outlines of the History of Greek Philosophy*. 13th ed. Trans. J. R. Palmer, rev. by Wilhelm Nestle. New York: Humanities Press.

Ziman, John. 1976. *The Force of Knowledge: The Scientific Dimension of Society*. Cambridge: Cambridge University Press.

Zizek, Slavoj. 1989. *The Sublime Object of Ideology*. New York: Verso.

About the Book and Editor

Rethinking the History of Rhetoric is an interdisciplinary collection that reexamines major aspects of the rhetorical tradition. Taking the stance that certain classical rhetorics contain social significance not only for their times but also for present society, the contributors approach rhetorical theory as social advocacy.

Thus, this volume joins in the current resurgence of anti-scholastic and anti-postmodern versions of rhetoric. It makes a case against both the conventional understanding of rhetoric as mere style and the contemporary postmodern understanding of rhetoric as mere linguistic figuration of no social import.

The contributors provide a unique reflexivity as they reveal their own backgrounds as scholars and historicans of rhetoric—their own ideological and institutional embeddedness. These revelations inevitably result in historical accounts that themselves become rhetorical constructs—constructs shaped by social commitments at present. Whether these commitments are articulated in the form of social critique or of cultural possibility, the contributors are united in approaching history writing as a socially situated practice.

As a whole, this collection brings to the forefront and attempts to negotiate the doubly social character of rhetorical theory—both at the moment of its production and at the moment of its narration.

Takis Poulakos is assistant professor of rhetoric at the University of Iowa and author of *Rhetoric for the Polis: Isocrates* (forthcoming).

About the Contributors

Janet M. Atwill has published articles on classical rhetoric and postmodern theory and is presently completing a book on ancient rhetoric and humanism. She is assistant professor at the University of Tennessee, where she teaches courses in the history and theory of rhetoric.

James A. Berlin is professor of English at Purdue University and author of *Writing Instruction in Nineteenth-Century American Colleges* (1984) and *Rhetoric and Reality* (1987).

Barbara Biesecker, assistant professor of rhetoric at the University of Iowa, has written several articles on rhetorical theory, feminist theory, and poststructuralism. Her book on Kenneth Burke's theory of rhetoric is nearing completion.

Page duBois is professor of classics and comparative literature in the Literature Department at the University of California at San Diego. She is the author of articles on gender, rhetoric, and classical and Renaissance literature, and of *History, Rhetorical Description and the Epic* (1982), *Centaurs and Amazons: Women and the Prehistory of the Great Chain of Being* (1982), *Sowing the Body: Psychoanalysis and Ancient Representations of Women* (1988), and *Torture and Truth* (1991).

Andrew Ford has taught classics at Cornell University, Princeton University, and Smith College. He is the author of a book on oral poetics, *Homer: The Poetry of the Past* (1992), and of articles on ancient criticism and rhetoric in such journals as *Arion* and *Common Knowledge*. He is currently at work on a study of the origins of literary criticism in classical Greece.

Hans Kellner is professor of English and director of the Graduate Rhetoric Program at the University of Texas at Arlington. A historian by training, Kellner has written extensively on the rhetoric of historical discourse and theories of literature. Besides *Language and Historical Representation: Getting the Story Crooked* (1989), Kellner has published a number of essays, including: "Beautifying the Nightmare: The Aesthetics of Postmodern History," (*Strategies: A Journal of Theory, Culture, and Politics*, 1991); and "Hayden White and the Kantian Discourse: Tropology, Narrative, Freedom," in *The Philosophy of Discourse: The Rhetorical Turn in Twentieth-Century Thought*, ed. C. Sills and G. H. Jensen (1992). "After the Fall: Reflections on Histories of Rhetoric," in *Writing Histories of Rhetoric*, ed. V. J. Vitanza, is forthcoming.

David Konstan is the John Rowe Workman Distinguished Professor of Classics at Brown University. He has published *Roman Comedy*, a translation of Simplicius' commentary on the sixth book of Aristotle's *Physics*, and studies of Catullus, Epicurean philosophy, and Marxist historiography of antiquity. *Sexual Symmetry*, on the representation of love in the ancient novel, is forthcoming. He is currently working on friendship in the classical world.

Christine Oravec is associate professor of communication at the University of Utah. She has written on the theory of epideictic speaking for the journal *Philosophy and Rhetoric* and has contributed a chapter on the concept of identification to the volume *The Legacy of*

Kenneth Burke. Her other scholarly interests include environmental discourse, nineteenth-century rhetorical theory, and rhetorical criticism.

John Poulakos is associate professor of rhetoric at the University of Pittsburgh and author of *The Sophists* (forthcoming).

Michael Salvador is assistant professor of speech communication in the Edward R. Murrow School of Communication at Washington State University. His scholarly interests center on rhetorical theory as it relates to the practice of criticism. Most of his published research focuses on the public discourse of activist organizations, particularly consumer and environmental groups.

Jane Sutton is associate professor in the Department of Speech Communication at Pennsylvania State University, York. She has presented scholarly papers at conferences including the International Society for the History of Rhetoric and has published articles in the history of rhetoric on such themes as the conflict between rhetoric and philosophy and the presence/absence of woman in rhetorical theory. Sutton is currently working on a book on the birth and death of rhetoric from the origins of democracy in the fifth century B.C. to its demise in late nineteenth-century culture.

Victor J. Vitanza is associate professor of English at the University of Texas, Arlington, where he teaches courses in composition and rhetorical and critical theory. He is the founding editor of *PRE/TEXT: A Journal of Rhetorical Theory* and is the director of the Center for Rhetorical and Critical Theory. He has two edited volumes forthcoming: *PRE/TEXT: The First Decade* and *Writing Histories of Rhetoric*. He is presently completing a book on historiographies of rhetoric.

Index

Active–passive polarity, 159–160, 169
Actuality–ideality opposition, 69–71, 73
Adorno, Theodor, 137, 149, 150
Affirmative action, 155–156, 157
Afterwords, 256
Alcidamas, 64–65, 74(n4), 88
Alexander the Great, 126
Althusser, Louis, 137, 141, 142, 144, 197
Ambiguity, 26, 236, 248, 252
American Rhetorical Studies, 182–189
America Revisited: History Schoolbooks in the Twentieth Century (Fitzgerald), 213
Anaxarchus, 126
Anaximenes, 88
Anderson, Perry, 147
Anger, 127, 128
Annales School of History, 201–202
Antiphon, 76, 87, 88, 133
Apathy, 119, 120, 127, 131, 132, 247, 254
Aristocles, 126
Aristocracy, 20, 23, 27, 44, 45, 51, 56, 133, 143
Aristophanes, 52(n6), 57, 88
Aristotle, 6, 32, 33, 36, 85(fig.), 88, 126, 132, 143–144, 154, 167, 168, 183, 187, 205, 208, 209, 224, 233, 246, 247, 248, 251, 252
    Metaphysics, 96, 97, 115(n13)
    Nicomachean Ethics, 96, 97, 98, 99, 101–102, 108, 115(n10)
    Politics, 98–99
    Rhetoric, 6, 41, 58, 75–76, 77–89, 91–114, 125, 181
Aristotle and His Philosophy (Edel), 93
Art, 35, 99, 102, 115(n12), 122
    practical, 100–105
    See also under Rhetoric
Associationist psychology, 103–104, 105
Athenaeus, 127
Audiences, 158, 159, 183, 187, 189, 190, 253
Authority, 4, 12, 20, 27, 156, 182, 184, 189, 225, 242, 244

Bacon, Francis, 103–104

Badiou, Alan, 120
Bailey, Shackleton, 27
Bakhtin, Mikhail, 213, 237
Baldwin, Charles S., 177, 207
Barthes, Roland, 29(n1), 177, 196–197, 200, 229
Bartkowski, Frances, 164
Bellow, Saul, 193
Belsey, Catherine, 141
Berlin, James, 207–208, 228
Bernal, Martin, 213
Biesecker, S., 61
Binaries. *See* Oppositions
Bitzer, Lloyd, 158, 187, 189
Black, Edwin, 180
Blair, Carole, 164, 174
Blank, David, 37
Blass, Frederick, 42
Bledstein, Burton, 91
Bloom, Allan, 120
Bormann, Ernest, 184
Bourdieu, Pierre, 91, 92, 95, 114(nn 1, 2), 115(n7), 117(n31)
Brannon, Lil, 138
Braudel, Fernand, 202
Brockriede, Wayne, 176
Brown, N. O., 253
Bruns, Gerald, 224
Bryant, Donald, 173
Burke, Kenneth, 159, 173, 184, 186, 203, 208, 209, 221, 236, 237, 256
Burleson, Brant, 188
Burnet, John, 95–96
Butler, Judith, 234

Caesar, Julius, 17, 20, 23, 28, 29
Cahn, Michael, 32, 42
Callinicos, Alex, 141
Campbell, John Angus, 143, 185, 191(n2)
Campbell, Karlyn Kohrs, 153–154, 157, 158–159, 171(n6)
Canonicity, 91, 93, 114(n1), 155, 156, 157, 170, 206
Capitalism, 149, 180, 222